G000070176

Dublin
City and District Street Guide

General Travel Information	Route Planner	I
	Index and Legend to Map pages	II
	Travel Services and Local Radio Stations	III
	Motoring Information	IV
	Dart and Suburban Rail Lines	V
	Dublin Bus Route Network	VI
Dublin City and District Maps		1
City Centre Maps		59
Tourist Information	The Story of Dublin	64
	Places to Visit	65
	Churches and Cathedrals	72
	Libraries	74
	Art Galleries	75
	Museums	76
	Some Famous Dublin People	77
	Dublin's Parks and Gardens	79
	Dublin as a Sporting Centre	81
	Dublin Alive Alive Oh!	82
	Embassies	83
	Dublin Bus Information	84
Industrial Estates and Business Parks		88
Index to Hospitals		89
Index to Street Names		90

Map data compiled from OSi 1:1000 Database and updated from October 1999 aerial photography.

SPECIAL THANKS TO BORD FÁILTE AND DÚCHAS THE HERITAGE SERVICE.

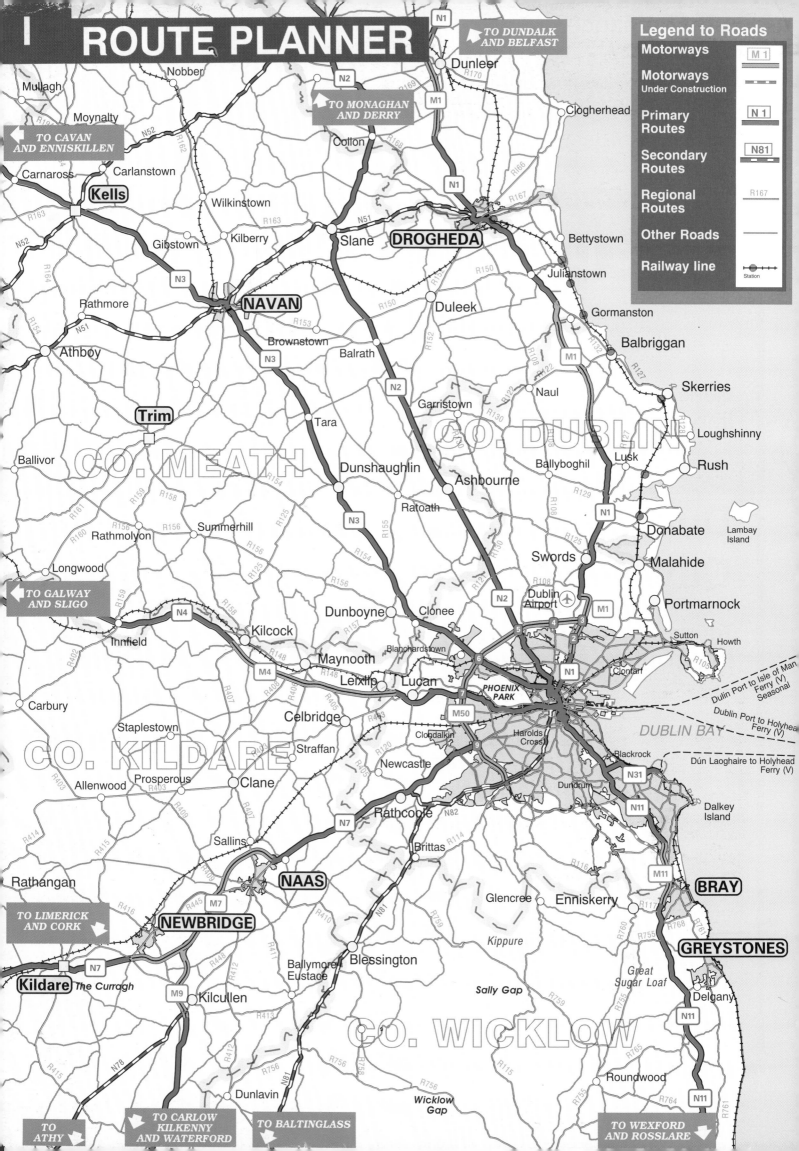

INDEX TO MAP PAGES

Please note that the yellow areas will appear
on more than one page e.g.
Sutton appears on both pages 24 and 25.
Ringsend appears on both pages 37 and 61.

CITY CENTRE MAP IS AVAILABLE
ON PAGES 59 TO 62 AT
A SCALE OF 1:10 000
SEE INDEX BELOW.

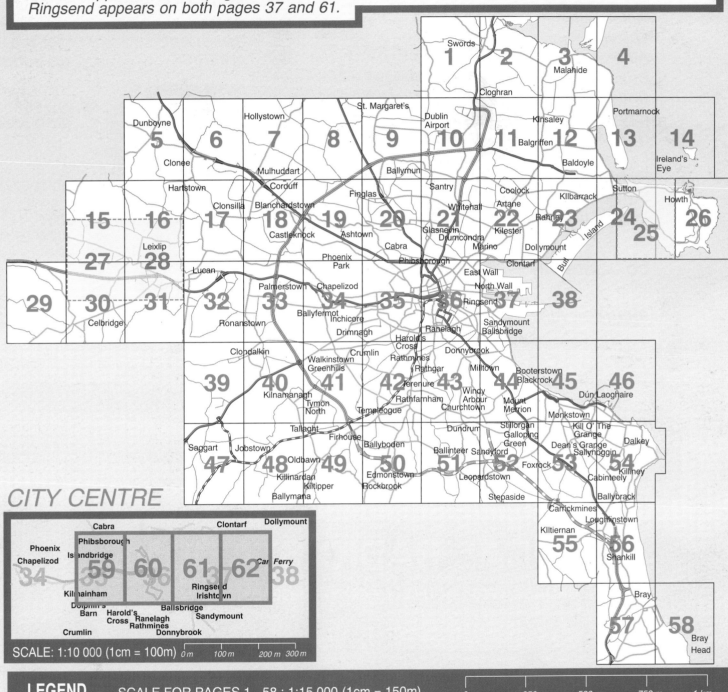

CITY CENTRE

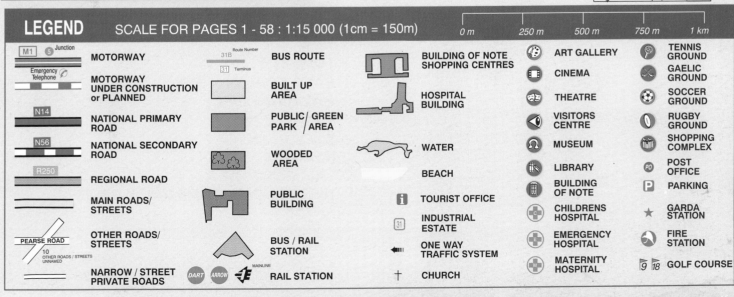

SCALE: 1:10 000 (1cm = 100m)   0m   100m   200m   300m

LEGEND   SCALE FOR PAGES 1 - 58 : 1:15 000 (1cm = 150m)   0m   250m   500m   750m   1 km

M1 5 Junction	MOTORWAY	31B Route Number	BUS ROUTE	
Emergency Telephone	MOTORWAY UNDER CONSTRUCTION or PLANNED	31 Terminus	BUILT UP AREA	
N14	NATIONAL PRIMARY ROAD		PUBLIC/ GREEN PARK / AREA	
N56	NATIONAL SECONDARY ROAD		WOODED AREA	
R250	REGIONAL ROAD		PUBLIC BUILDING	
	MAIN ROADS/ STREETS		WATER	
PEARSE ROAD	OTHER ROADS/ STREETS		BEACH	
	NARROW / STREET PRIVATE ROADS		TOURIST OFFICE	

	BUILDING OF NOTE SHOPPING CENTRES		ART GALLERY	TENNIS GROUND
	HOSPITAL BUILDING		CINEMA	GAELIC GROUND
			THEATRE	SOCCER GROUND
	WATER		VISITORS CENTRE	RUGBY GROUND
	BEACH		MUSEUM	SHOPPING COMPLEX
i	TOURIST OFFICE		LIBRARY	PO POST OFFICE
31	INDUSTRIAL ESTATE		BUILDING OF NOTE	P PARKING
	ONE WAY TRAFFIC SYSTEM		CHILDRENS HOSPITAL	GARDA STATION
DART ARROW MAINLINE	BUS / RAIL STATION / RAIL STATION		EMERGENCY HOSPITAL	FIRE STATION
†	CHURCH		MATERNITY HOSPITAL	9 18 GOLF COURSE

AIR

DUBLIN AIRPORT	814 1111
Aer Lingus	
Information	886 6705
Reservations	886 8888
Air France	844 5633
British Airways	1 800 626 747
British Midlands	283 8833
City Jet	844 5566
Delta Airlines	676 8080
Lufthansa	844 5544
Ryanair	609 7800
Swissair	677 8173
Virgin Atlantic	873 3388

CORK AIRPORT	(021) 313131
(10a.m. - 11p.m.)	

SHANNON AIRPORT	
	(061) 471666

SEA

STENA SEALINK	
DUBLIN PORT	855 3277
DÚN LAOGHAIRE	204 7700
CORK	(021) 272965
ROSSLARE	(053) 33115
LIMERICK	(061) 316259
IRISH FERRIES	1890 313131
DUBLIN	661 0715
CORK	(021) 551995
ROSSLARE	(053) 33158
BRITTANY FERRIES	
CORK	(021) 277801
SWANSEA / CORK FERRIES	
CORK	(021) 271166

RAIL

IARNRÓD ÉIREANN IRISH RAIL	
INCLUDING DART SUBURBAN RAIL	836 6222

BUS

BUS ÁTHA CLIATH DUBLIN BUS	873 4222
BUS ÉIREANN IRISH BUS	836 6111

ROAD

A.A. RESCUE FREEPHONE	677 9481
R.A.C. RESCUE FREEPHONE	676 0113

LOCAL RADIO STATIONS

NATIONAL AND LOCAL WEATHER AND ROAD INFORMATION
ARE BROADCAST FERQUENTLY ON THE FOLLOWING WAVELENGTHS.

RTE

RADIO 1	FM 88.2 90 MHz
2FM	FM 90.4 92.2MHz
	MW 1278 kHz
RAIDIO NA GAELTACHTA	FM 92.6 102.7MHz
	MW 828 kHz
LYRIC FM	FM 96 99MHz

INDEPENDENT RADIO

ANNA LIVIA	103.2FM
ATLANTIC 252	252khz
98FM	98FM
TODAY FM	100-102FM
EAST COAST RADIO	94.9FM/102.9FM
RAIDIÓ NA LIFE	106.4FM
PHOENIX FM	105.2FM
D.S.C.R. FM	104.9FM
NEAR FM	101.6FM
TALLAGHT FM	107.2FM
WEST DUBLIN COMMUNITY RADIO	96FM
FM104	104.4FM

RTE HAS IMPLEMENTED AN AUTOMATIC TUNING SYSTEM (RDS) ON ITS THREE NATIONAL FM NETWORKS. AN RDS RECEIVER CONTINUALLY SCANS FOR THE BEST SIGNAL, GIVING OPTIMUM RECEPTION AT ALL TIMES.

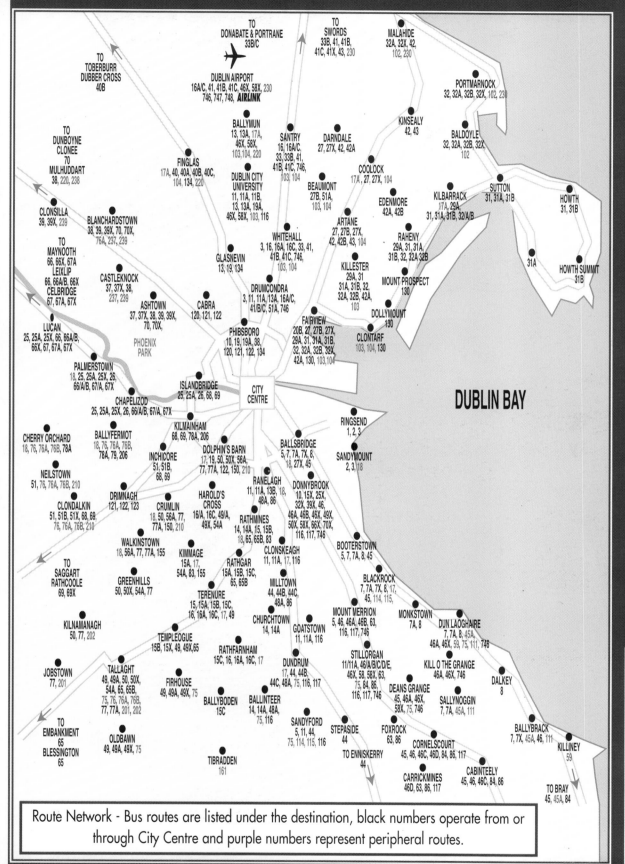

Dublin Bus operates the bus network in the greater Dublin area. This network extends from Balbriggan in North County Dublin to Kilcoole in County Wicklow and westwards as far as Kilcock, County Kildare.

Route Network - Bus routes are listed under the destination, black numbers operate from or through City Centre and purple numbers represent peripheral routes.

INFORMATION BUREAU AND CUSTOMER SERVICE

Tel. (01) 873 4222   9am to 7pm (Mon - Sat)

Dublin Bus, 59 Upr. O'Connell Street, Dublin 1.

Website: www.dublinbus.ie
e-mail: info@dublinbus.ie

Sept. 2000

Dublin Bus

D   E   F

1

Corbalis Golf Links

18

Strand

IRISH   SEA

2

Biscayne

COAST

Castle
Robbswall

Sports
Ground

ROAD

R106

32A

102

230

3

MONKS
MEADOW

32

32B

LIMETREE   ELMS COURT

AVENUE

CONVENT LANE

ASHLEY RISE

HEATHER
GARDENS

WHEATFIELD
GROVE

WALK

HARRIS

BRACKEN DRIVE

KELVIN CLOSE

WALK

HEATHER

Martello
Tower

4

WENDELL AVENUE

230 102 32X

NICHOLLS
CLOSE

BLACKTON
CLOSE

DEWBERRY
PARK

1

MARTELLO COURT

WENDELL
AVE

CARRICKHILL

PORTMARNOCK

CARRICKHILL
PARK

RISE

COPE

AVE

STRAND

GREEN
CRESCENT

ROAD

32B

CARRICKHILL
CLOSE

WALK

CARRICKHILL
HEIGHTS

BEACH

PINE
CT

DRIVE

BROOK CT

102
230

Hotel

D   E   F

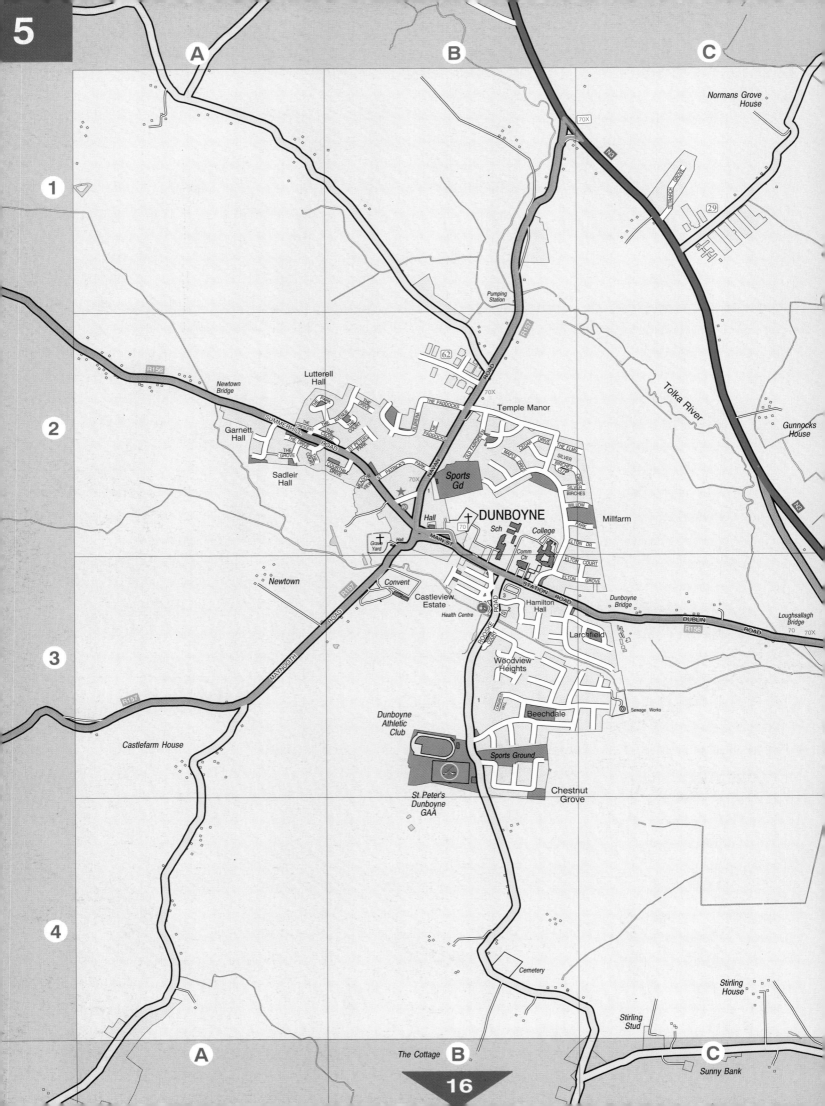

A B C

1

2

DUNBOYNE

3

4

Normans Grove House

Gunnocks House

Tolka River

Pumping Station

R157

70X

N3

Terbarch Grove

29

R156

Newtown Bridge

Lutterell Hall

Garnett Hall

Sadleir Hall

SUMMERHILL ROAD

PARK

THE DRIVE

THE AVENUE

THE CRESCENT

THE CLOSE

THE DRIVE

THE COURT

THE GROVE

COURT

COURTHILL DRIVE

ST PETERS PARK

MEADOW VIEW

ST PATRICKS PARK

KILBREW

THE PADDOCKS

THE PADDOCKS

NAHAN

70X

62

ROAD

Temple Manor

OLD FAIRGREEN

CEDAR DRIVE

MAPLE DRIVE

THE ELMS

SILVER BIRCHES CLO

SILVER BIRCHES

SILVER CRES

WILLOW PARK

Millfarm

Sports Gd

Hall

Hall

Grave Yard

Convent

Castleview Estate

Newtown

R157

R157

MAYNOOTH ROAD

Castlefarm House

MAIN ST

Sch

College

Comm Ctr

70

ELTON DR

ELTON COURT

ELTON GROVE

STATION ROAD

Hamilton Hall

Health Centre

Dunboyne Bridge

Dunboyne College

Larchfield

DUBLIN ROAD

R156

70 70X

Loughsallagh Bridge

BROOKE COURT

Woodview Heights

Dunboyne Athletic Club

CORNER HALL

Beechdale

Sports Ground

Chestnut Grove

Sewage Works

St Peter's Dunboyne GAA

Cemetery

The Cottage

Stirling House

Stirling Stud

Sunny Bank

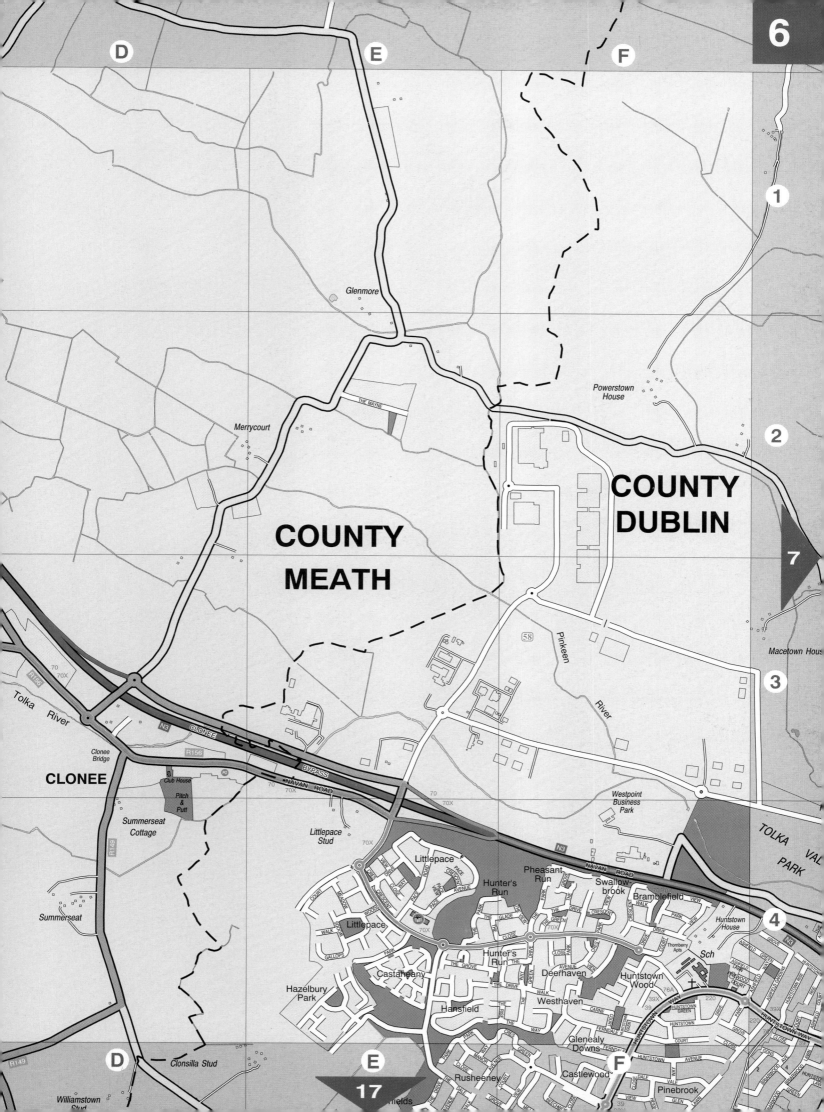

D

E

F

1

2

9

3

4

Pitch
and
Putt

Broghan House

N2

Dunsoghly
Castle

Newtown Cotta

NORTH

Kilmore House

Woodlands

Kilshane
House

ROAD

9

Newtown
House

Open Golf Centre

18

Sports
Ground

Burial
Gd

Cloghran House

Sand &
Gravel Pit

N2

13

Grange House

Kildonan House

Electricity
Station

Rosemount Business
Park

220

238

133

CAPPAGH ROAD

BALLYCOOLIN ROAD

Veterinary Research
Laboratory
(A.I. Station)

Northway
Estate

Cappoge
Cottages

104

D

F

ROUTE

Department of
Marino Fisheries

220

Sports
Groun

DRIVING IS ON THE LEFT THROUGHOUT IRELAND.
SEAT BELTS must be worn by drivers and passengers.
CRASH HELMETS must be worn by motorcyclists and pillion passengers.

WARNING SIGNS
The following are examples of the principal signs.

 TWO-WAY TRAFFIC

Dangerous Corner or Bend Ahead | Series of Dangerous Corners or Bends Ahead | Slippery Stretch of Road Ahead | Sharp Rise Ahead | Sharp Depression Ahead | Series of Bumps or Hollows Ahead

Junction Ahead With Road or Roads of Equal Importance. | Steep Ascent Ahead | Steep Descent Ahead | Road Narrows Dangerously | Roundabout Ahead

Junction Ahead With Roads of Less Importance. (minor roads shown by thin arms) | Unprotected Quay, Canal or River | Road Works Ahead | Children Sign (School etc.) | Traffic Lights Ahead

Junctions Ahead With Roads of Equal Importance | With Roads of Less Importance | Advance Warning of a Major Road Ahead | Low Bridge Ahead | Level Crossing Ahead guarded by gates. | Level Crossing Ahead Unguarded. | End of Dual Carriageway.

EMERGENCY
☎ **999 112**
Police
Ambulance
Fire Brigade
Life Boat
Coastal Rescue

REGULATORY SIGNS
These signs implement road regulations and show the course to follow etc.

 STOP
Give Way
 YIELD RIGHT OF WAY

Traffic must proceed in the direction of the arrow.
    Keep to Left Carriagway

Traffic may not proceed in the direction of the arrow.

Parking
 Parking Permitted | Clearway Stopping or Parking Prohibited (except Buses and Taxis) | Parking Prohibited | TAXI RANK Parking for taxis only.

SPEED LIMITS
MOTORWAY 70 mph/112 kph
NATIONAL LIMIT 60 mph/96 kph
OTHER LIMITS MAY APPLY IN TOWNS, BUILT-UP AREAS AND SOME ROADS AS INDICATED.
  End of Speed Limit

INFORMATION SIGNS
These signs give information regarding direction, distance, place etc. Amenities of particular interest to tourists are displayed in white on a brown background.

 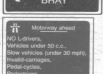   

WEATHERDIAL
FROM THE MET SERVICE
DUBLIN 1550 123 854
MUNSTER 1550 123 850
LEINSTER 1550 123 851
CONNAUGHT 1550 123 852
ULSTER 1550 123 853
SEA AREA 1550 123 855
for the latest weather information.

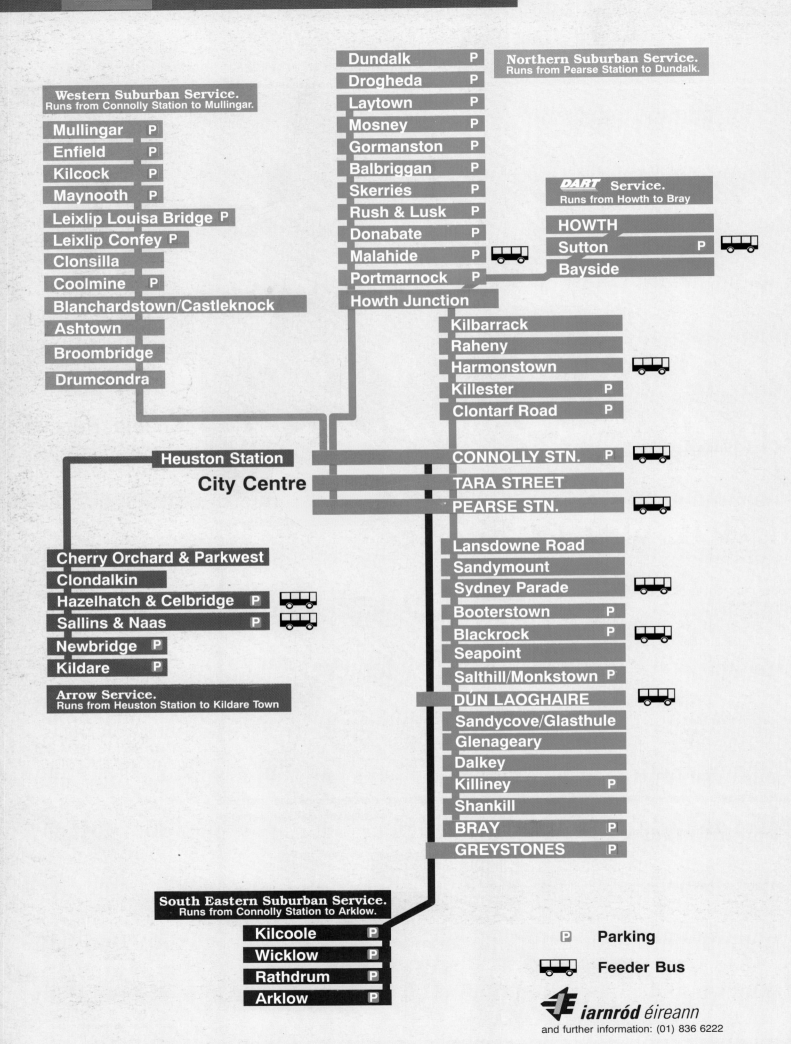

V DART and Suburban Rail Network

Northern Suburban Service.
Runs from Pearse Station to Dundalk.

Dundalk	P
Drogheda	P
Laytown	P
Mosney	P
Gormanston	P
Balbriggan	P
Skerries	P
Rush & Lusk	P
Donabate	P
Malahide	P
Portmarnock	P
Howth Junction	

Western Suburban Service.
Runs from Connolly Station to Mullingar.

Mullingar	P
Enfield	P
Kilcock	P
Maynooth	P
Leixlip Louisa Bridge	P
Leixlip Confey	P
Clonsilla	
Coolmine	P
Blanchardstown/Castleknock	
Ashtown	
Broombridge	
Drumcondra	

DART Service.
Runs from Howth to Bray

HOWTH	
Sutton	P
Bayside	
Kilbarrack	
Raheny	
Harmonstown	
Killester	P
Clontarf Road	P

Heuston Station

City Centre

CONNOLLY STN.	P
TARA STREET	
PEARSE STN.	

Lansdowne Road	
Sandymount	
Sydney Parade	
Booterstown	P
Blackrock	P
Seapoint	
Salthill/Monkstown	P
DÚN LAOGHAIRE	
Sandycove/Glasthule	
Glenageary	
Dalkey	
Killiney	P
Shankill	
BRAY	P
GREYSTONES	P

Cherry Orchard & Parkwest	
Clondalkin	
Hazelhatch & Celbridge	P
Sallins & Naas	P
Newbridge	P
Kildare	P

Arrow Service.
Runs from Heuston Station to Kildare Town

South Eastern Suburban Service.
Runs from Connolly Station to Arklow.

Kilcoole	P
Wicklow	P
Rathdrum	P
Arklow	P

P Parking

🚌 Feeder Bus

iarnród éireann
and further information: (01) 836 6222

The Steer

Tower

Ireland's Eye

Carrigeen Bay

Rowan Rocks

Thulla Rocks

Thulla

Lighthouse

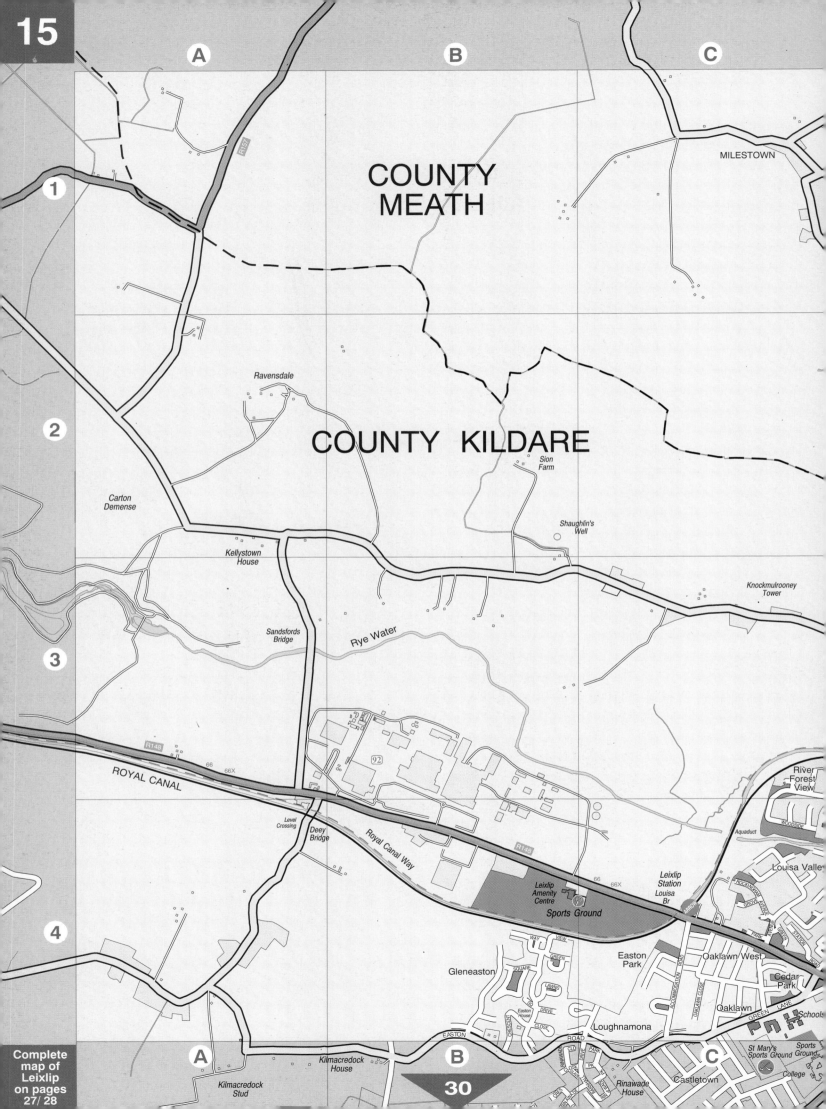

A B C

COUNTY MEATH

COUNTY KILDARE

1

2

3

4

Ravensdale

Sion Farm

Carton Demense

Shaughlin's Well

Kellystown House

Knockmulrooney Tower

Sandsfords Bridge

Rye Water

R148

ROYAL CANAL

66 66X

Level Crossing

Deey Bridge

Royal Canal Way

92

R148

66 66X

Leixlip Amenity Centre

Sports Ground

Leixlip Station Louisa Br

MILESTOWN

River Forest View

WOODSIDE

Aquaduct

Louisa Valley

ROCKINGHAM

GROVE AVENUE

STATION

PARK

GREEN

THE

WAY

VIEW

GREEN

LAWNS

SQUARE

Gleneaston

DRIVE

Easton House

CLOSE

CHESSEL

Easton Park

Oaklawn West

ACCOMMODATION ROAD

OAKLAWN CLOSE

Cedar Park

Oaklawn

EASTON

ROAD

Loughnamona

GREEN LANE

Schools

Kilmacredock House

Kilmacredock Stud

Rinawade House

St Mary's Sports Ground

Castletown

Sports Ground

College

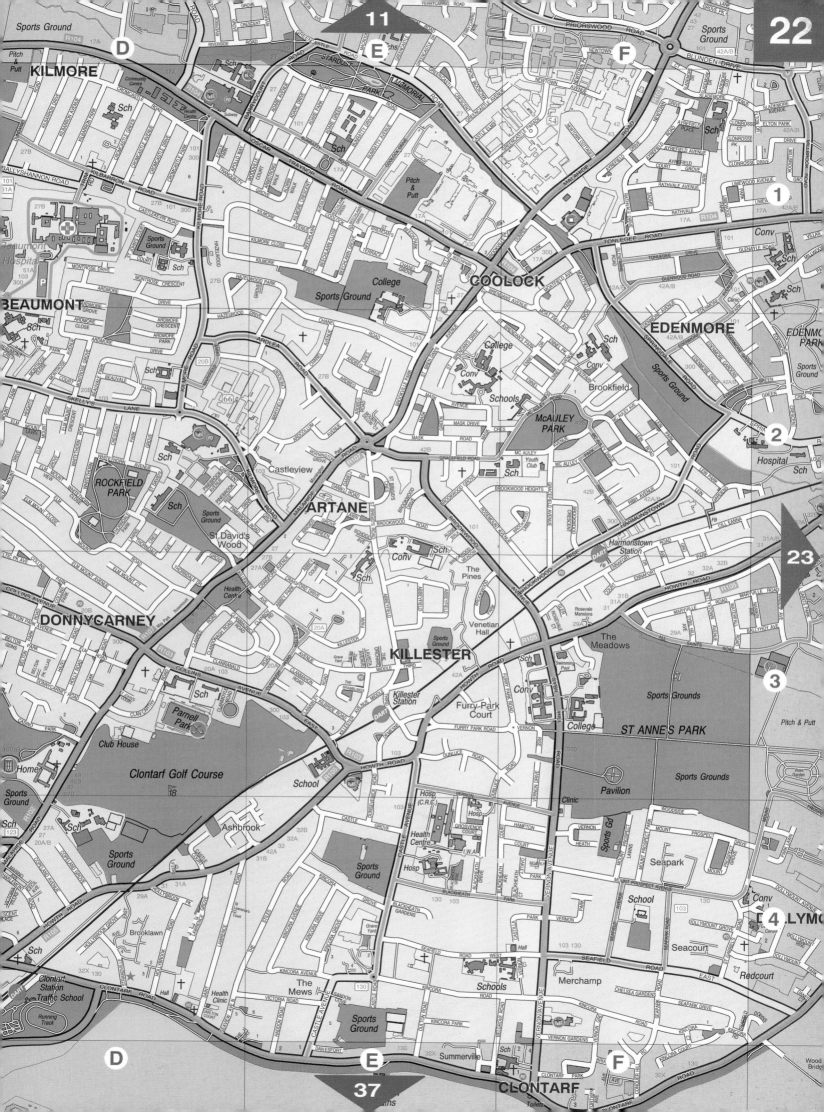

13

GRANGE
Youth ROAD
Club
Georgian
Hamlet Sch
WILLIE NO
Hosp
D
Turnberry
Parkvale
TUSCANY PARK
MEADOWBROOK AVE
School
Moyclare Park
DRIVE AVE
MOYCLARE
Sports
Ground
MOYCLARE CLOSE
Bayside Station
DART
SUTTON
PARK
Sutton Park
Sutton Park
KILBARRACK
Kilbarrack
Cemetery

WARRENHOUSE ROAD
STRAND ROAD
R106
WARREN GREEN
BURROWFIELD
LEVEL
CROSSING
THE CRESCENT
VIEW
RAILWAY AVE
THE COURT
Binn Eadair
View
BALDOYLE ROAD
DUBLIN ROAD
R105

Cush Point
E Club
House

Sutton
Station
DART
STATION ROAD
102
LAUDER LANE
Tramway
Court
Sports
Ground
Club
House
Sch
SUTTON
R105

Sutton

Golf
18

Links School
BURROW ROAD
LEVEL
CROSSING

F

Lifeguard
Station

1

CLAREMONT ROAD

HOWTH ROAD
GREENFIELD ROAD
Sutton
PO 31
Sch
Conv.
Glencarraig
CHURCH ROAD
Santa Sabina
Manor
OFFINGTON PARK
OFFINGTON DRIVE
OFFINGTON AVENUE
OFFINGTON MANOR
Corr Castle
OFFINGTON
LAWN
31
OFFINGTON COURT

Sailing
Club
Slipway Slipway
Sutton
Strand
Sutton
Creek
31B
31A

2
Deer Park Golf
CARRICKBRACK ROAD
OLD CASTLE AVE
Sports
Gd
Duncarraig
CARRICKBRACK HEATH
CARRICKBRACK HILL
Sch
31A
LA VISTA AVENUE
St. Fintans
Cemetery
CARRICKBRACK LAWN
STRAND ROAD
CRESCENT
ST FINTAN'S PARK
Sports
Gd
Sch
31A
FINTAN'S
ST FINTAN'S
CRESCENT
ROAD
GROVE
Slipway
31A
SHIELMARTIN DRIVE
SHIELMARTIN ROAD
South
Hill
R105
31

3
Bottle
Quay
Martello
Tower
Sutton
House
Cliff Walk

BEACH

25

4

D E F

1
2
3
4

Lighthouse

Slipway
WEST PIER
HOWTH HARBOUR
Slipway
Slipway

Slipway
Howth Station
DART
Car Pier
HARBOUR
7 31B
31
R105 ROAD

EAST PIER
Yacht Club
Lifeboat Station
Slipway
Toilets

Baths
Balscadden Bay

Puck's Rocks

Deer

Park

Golf

Course

Reservoir

18
9

EVORA PARK
ST LAWRENCE RD
GRACE O'MALLEY RD
Sch
GRACE O'MALLEY DRIVE
TUCKETTS LANE
11
BALKILL PARK
BALKILL PARK

Tower
9 10 11
2
6
1
Health Centre
ABBEY STREET
CHURCH STREET
ROAD
31B
31
MAIN STREET
31
5
12
13
9
ST PETERS TERRACE
BALGLASS RD
8
14
10

HOWTH
ASGARD PARK
NASHVILLE PARK
NASHVILLE ROAD
ASGARD ROAD
R105
Sch

KILROCK ROAD
BALSCADDEN ROAD
COMBROOTH LANE

Kilrock

Car Park

Nose of Howth

THORMANBY ROAD
BALKILL ROAD
GALGLASS RD
Sports Ground
Club House
Woodside
THORMANBY LAWNS
DUNGRIFFAN ROAD
GREY'S
31B
31
Cannon Rock
MARINERS COVE
Gull Cottage

Cannon Rock Cottage

Casana Rock

Cliff Walk

WOODCLIFF HEIGHTS
CASANA VIEW
Thormanby Woods
Thormanby Lodge

Green Ivy

BALKILL ROAD
WINDGATE ROAD
Ben of Howth
The Green Hallows
Quarry
31
31B
Piper's Gut

KITESTOWN RD
WINDGATE RISE
GLEN RISE
R105
31
The Summit
Fox Hole

Reservoir

Reservoir
Baily Green
Car Park
BAILEY GREEN ROAD
Highroom Bed

Lough Leven

31B
THORMANBY ROAD
ROAD
OLD CARRICKBRACK ROAD
31B
CARRICKBRACK
R105
CEANCHOR ROAD
Earlscliffe
Conv
Gaskin's Leap
Whitewater Brook

Webb's Castle Rock

The Great Baily
Cliff Walk
Hippy Hole
Doldrum Bay
Lion's Head
Glenaveena
The Little Baily

The Needles or Candlesticks

Baily Lighthouse

Drumleck Point

D E F

A B C

1

Reservoir
(Kildare County Council)

R405

67A

M4

MAYNOOTH

ROAD

67
67X

Sports
Ground

Ballygoran
Park

Ballygoran
Stud

Salesian
College

Sports
Ground

Crodaun
Forest
Park

2

Corbally
Stud

LANE

GREEN

Griffinrath
House

Thornhill
Meadows

WOODS
LAWNS
CRES
DRIVE
AVE
VILLAGE
PARK

WAY
RISE
PINE
WALK
CASTLE
VIEW
COURT
CLOSE

BALLYGORAN
COURT

Thornhill
Gardens

Thornhill
Heights

Ashgrove

School
Sports
Ground

3

Oldtown
House

Nursing Home

WILLOW BROOK
WILLOWBROOK PARK
WILLOWBROOK
GROVE

Willowbrook
Lawns

WILLOWBROOK

BEATTY PARK

Celbridge Health Centre

Celbridge Industrial Estate

THE PARK

Vanessa
Lawns

THE DALE

THE GREEN

Sports
Ground

Oldtown Cottages

Sch

THE
COURT

THE
CLOSE

VANESSA CLOSE

St PATRICKS PARK

CHURCH
Cemetery

ROAD

4

Pickering
Forest

PRIORY WAY

PRIORY CLOSE

St RAPHAEL'S

PRIORY
GREEN

PRIORY
COURT

PRIORY DR

Oakleigh

GRATTAN COURT

Sch

St Raphael's

Springfield

Killadoon
Park

Ballymakealy
Grove

Celbridge
Abbey

R403

THE LAWNS

Roselawn

CLANE

ROAD

St. Patricks

Ballymakealy
Lawns

Abbeyfarm

NEWTOWN
ROAD

Temp
Mano

R403

A B C

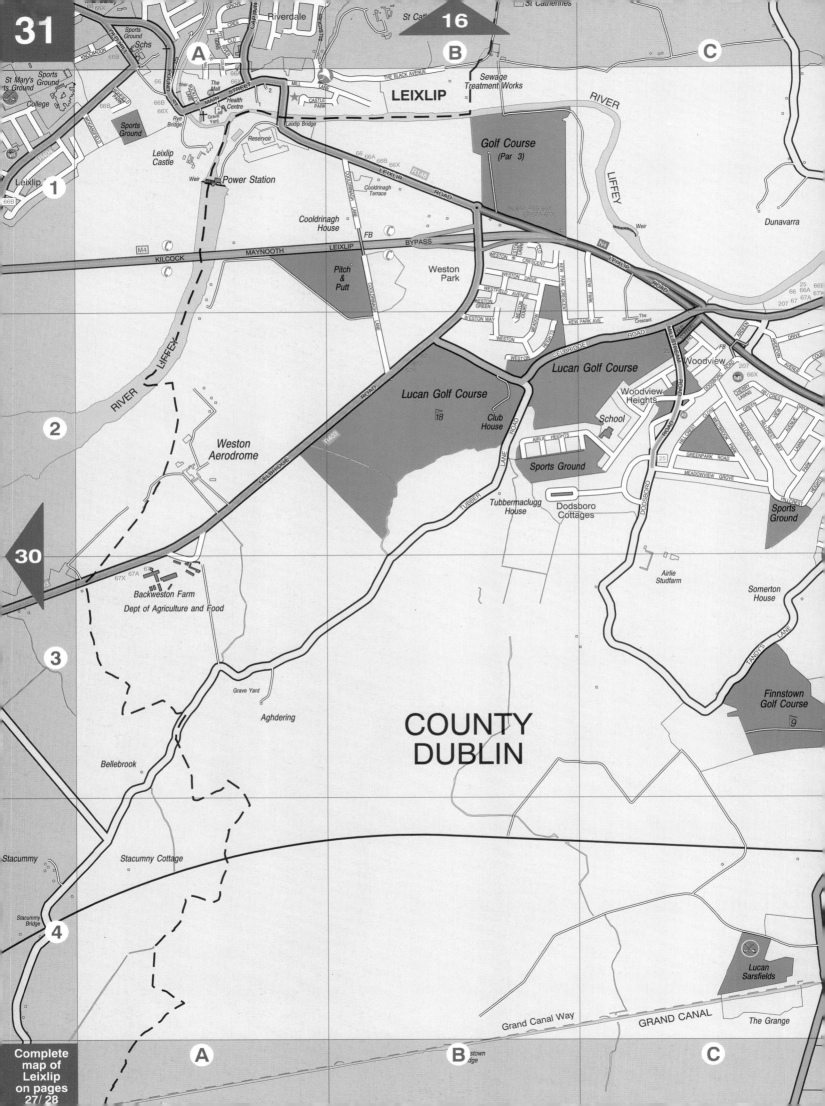

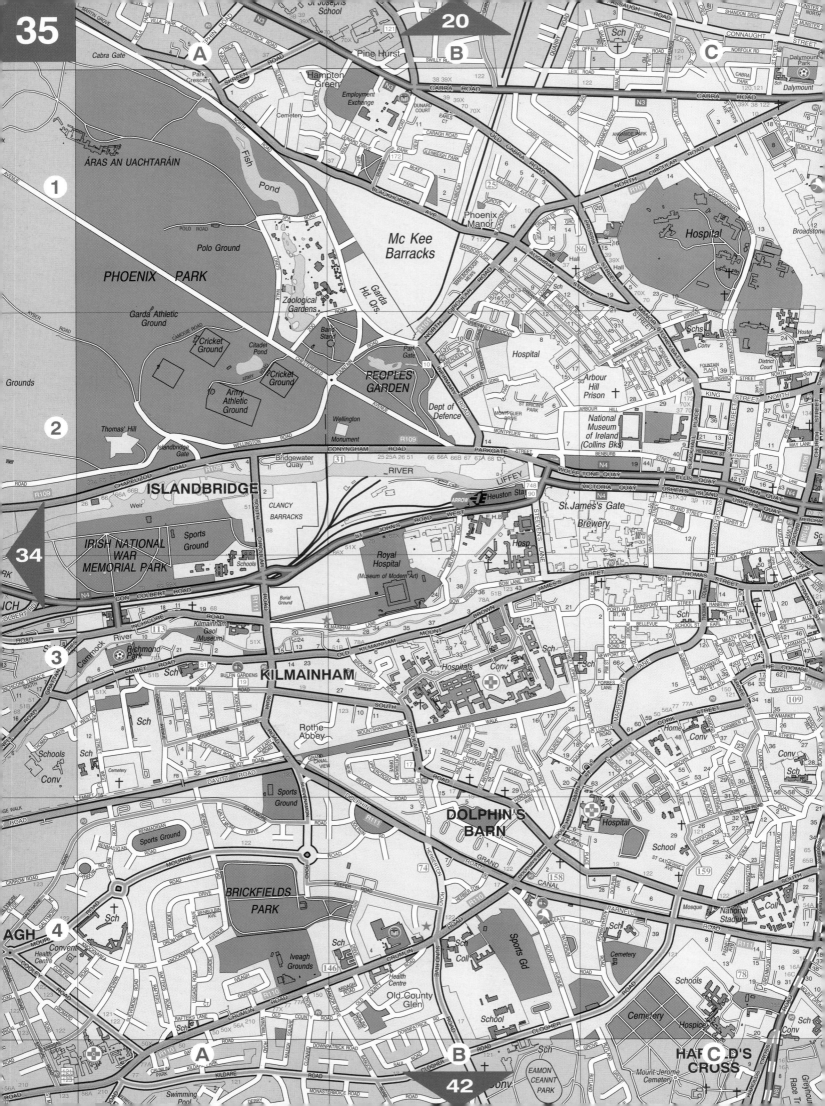

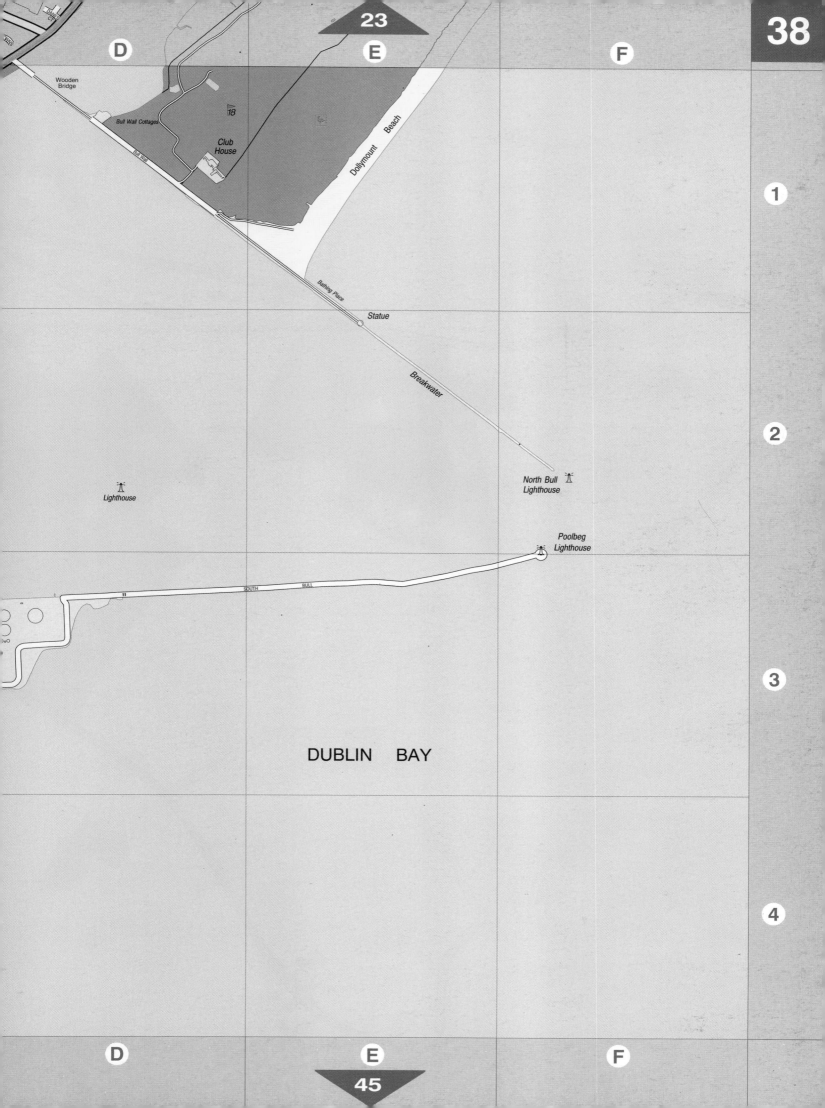

1

Wooden
Bridge

Bull Wall Cottages

Club
House

18

Dollymount   Beach

Bathing Place

Statue

Breakwater

2

North Bull
Lighthouse

Lighthouse

Poolbeg
Lighthouse

SOUTH   BULL

3

DUBLIN   BAY

4

Grange Cottage

GRAND CANAL

A   B   C

1

Sports Ground

School

Westbourne Court

Westbourne Manor

Halting Site

Westbourne Castle

Cherrywood Drive

Sch

Cherrywood Villas

Sch

Cherrywood Park

Sports G

NANGOR   ROAD   68

Kilcarbery House

2

68

Cammock River

Burial Ground

CORKAGH DEMESNE

68

Baldonnell Orchard

Casement Aerodrome and Military Camp

Camac Valley Tourist Caravan and Camping Park

3

Baldonnell House

N7

69

69X

4

Sports Ground

NAAS   ROAD

N82

44

Citywest Bridge

A   NAAS   ROAD   69 69X   B   C

Citywest Business Campus

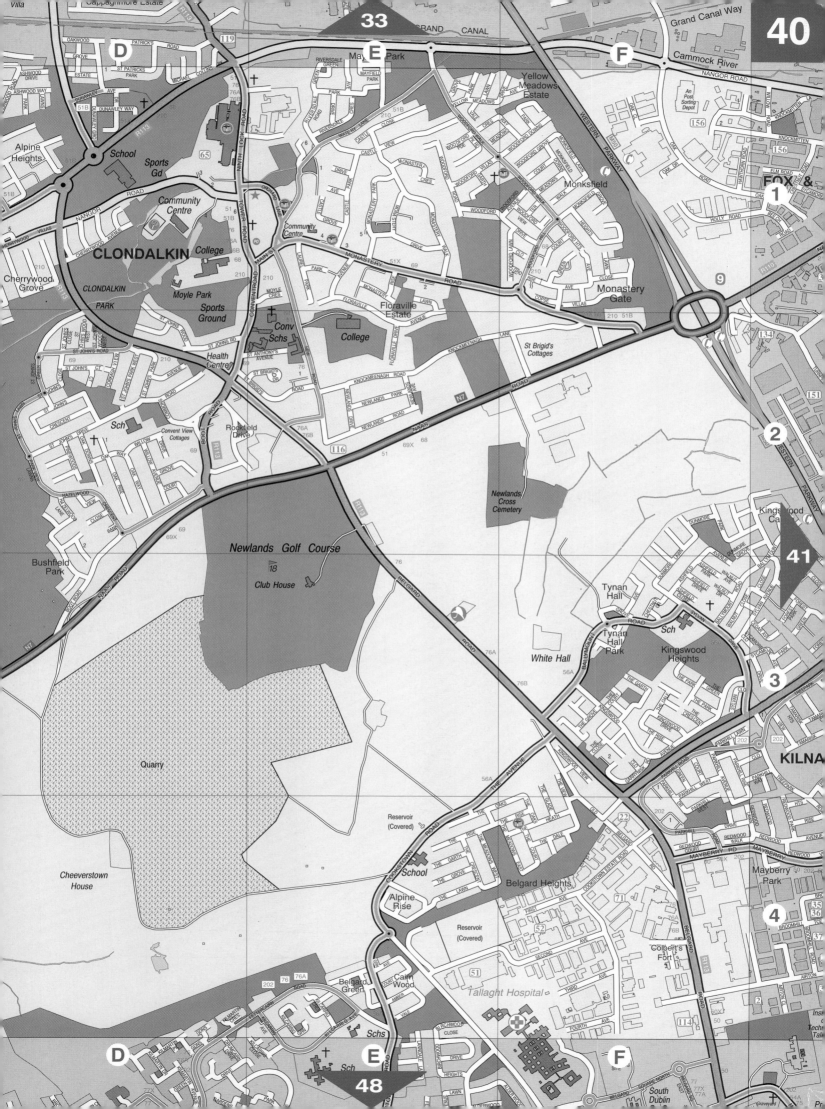

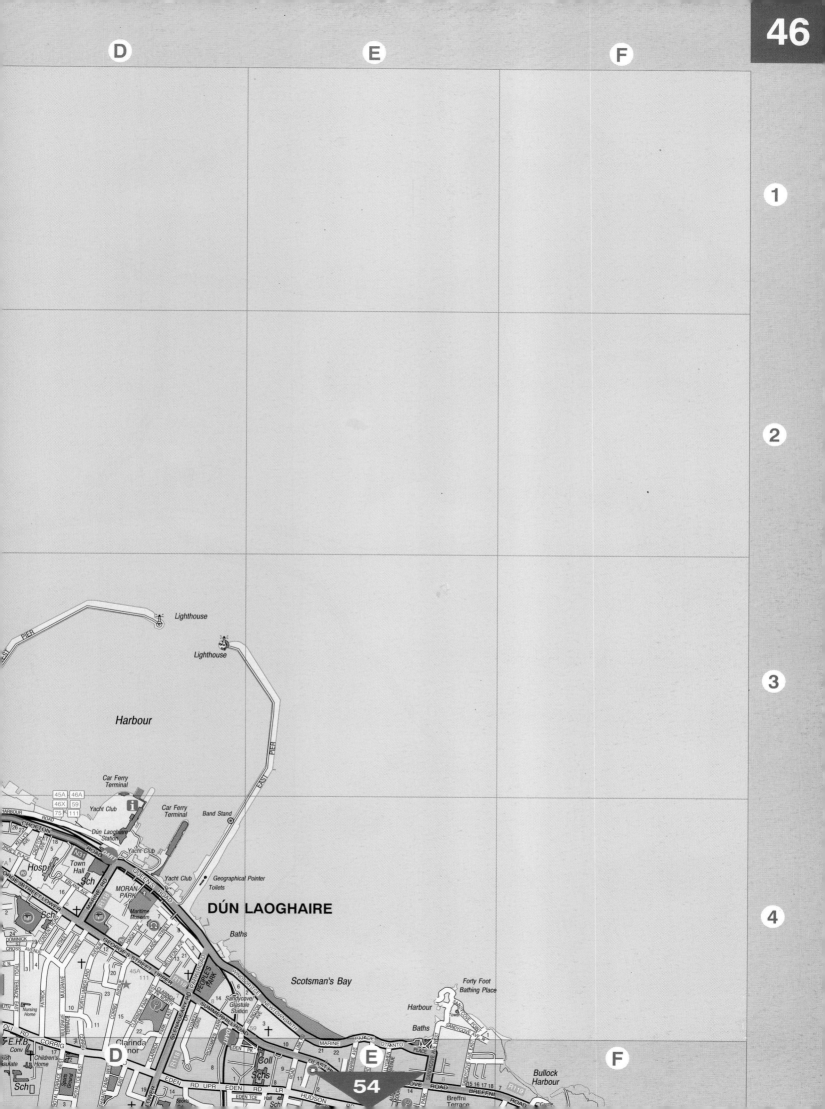

D E F

1

2

3

EAST PIER

Lighthouse

Lighthouse

Harbour

EAST PIER

Car Ferry
Terminal

45A | 46A
46X | 59
75 | 111

Yacht Club

HARBOUR
ROAD

CROFTON

Car Ferry
Terminal

Band Stand

Dún Laoghaire
Station

Yacht Club

Yacht Club

Town
Hall

Hosp

Sch

MORAN
PARK

Yacht Club

Geographical Pointer
Toilets

4

Maritime
Museum

DÚN LAOGHAIRE

Baths

Scotsman's Bay

Forty Foot
Bathing Place

Harbour

Baths

PEOPLES
PARK

Sandycove
Glastule
Station

MARINE PARADE

OTRANTO

E.H.B.
Conv

Clarinda
Manor

Nursing
Home

Children's
Home

Sch

Clarinda

Coll
Schs

MARINE

GLAST

OTRANTO
PLACE

SANDYCOVE

Bullock
Harbour

EDEN
RD UPR

EDEN RD
LR

HUDSON

Breffni
Terrace

R119

Castle

D E **54** F

A   B   39   44   *Citywest Bridge*   C

1   *Sewage Works*   N7   NAAS   ROAD   69   69X   N82   50   65B   *Fortunestown*   *School*

Citywest Golf Course
18
Tassaggart House
Club House
GARTER   LANE
CITYWEST

Sports Ground   FORTUNESTOWN   LANE

Springbank Cottages   MILL   ROAD   69   69X   69 69X   *Cemetery*   **SAGGART**   *Westbrook Glen*   AVENUE   50   65B   ROAD

2   147   *Sch*   *Golf Course*   18   VERSCHOYLE   CLOSE   VERSCHOYLE   PARK   *Westbrook Lawns*
Páirc Mhuire   *Sports Ground*   HEIGHTS   DOWNS   SQUARE   CORBALLY   PARK   HEATH   N82
LAWN   RISE   GLADE   VALE   VALVE   CORBALLY   AVE   WAY   PARK
BLESSINGTON   65   65B   ROAD   50   N81

3   N81   65   *LUGMORE*

BLESSINGTON   ROAD

4   N81   65   *To Blatine*   *St Brigid's Hospital*

A   B   C

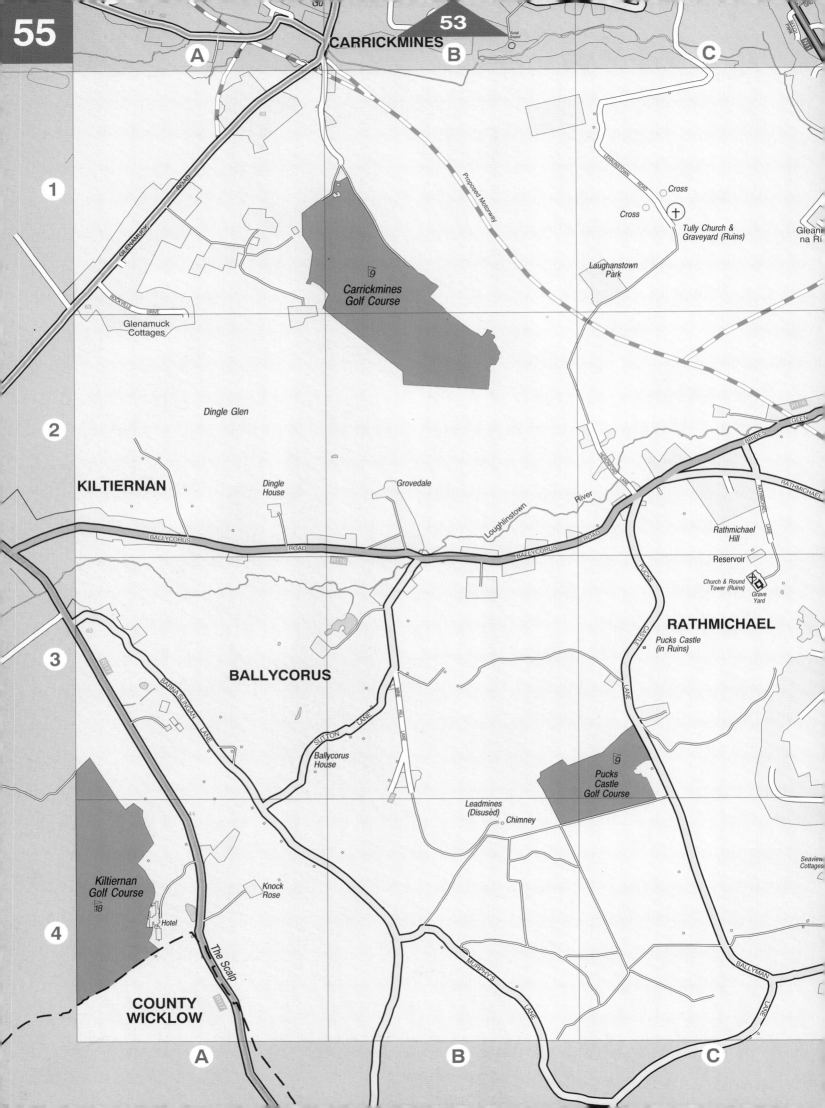

D E F

1

BRAY

2

Toilets
45

Naylor's Cove

Fortenay
Terrace

Cliff Walk

18

Golf Course

Raheenacluig Church
(in Ruins)

Cliff Walk

3

Tunnel

Bray
Head

NEWCOURT

R761

CO. WICKLOW

Cliff Walk

Tunnel

4

84X
84
184

Tunnel
Tunnel

D E F

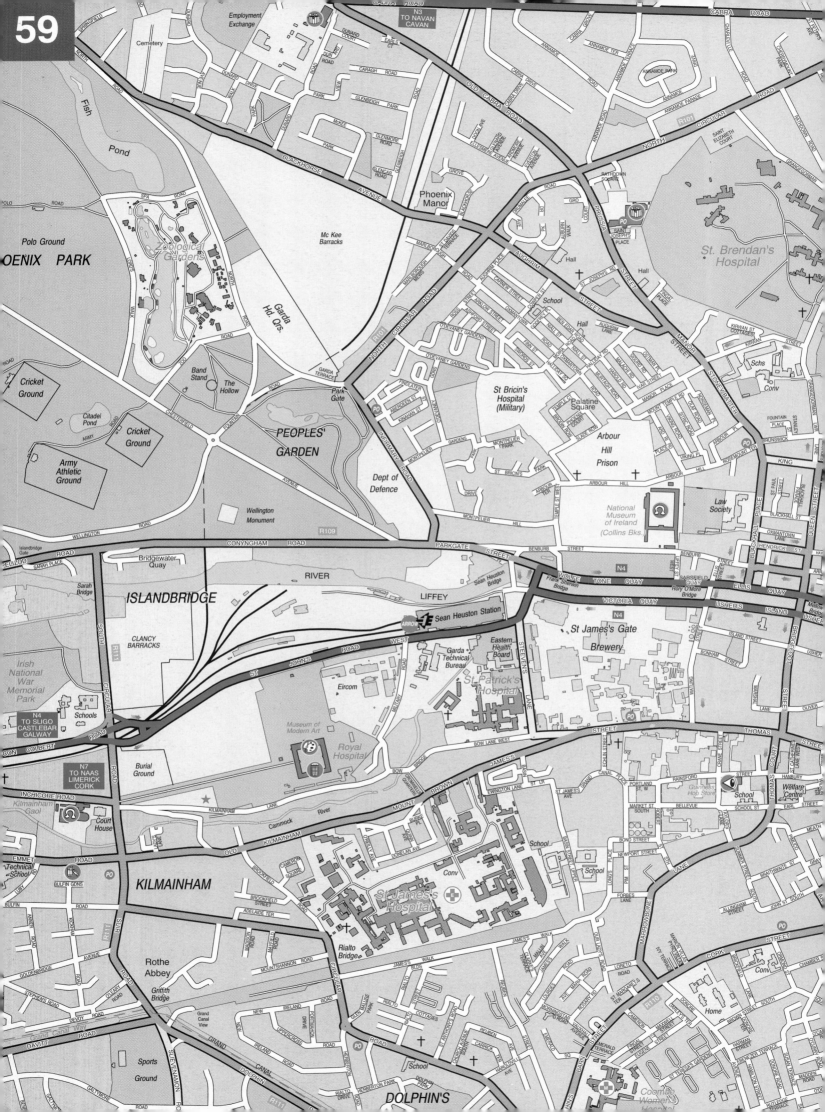

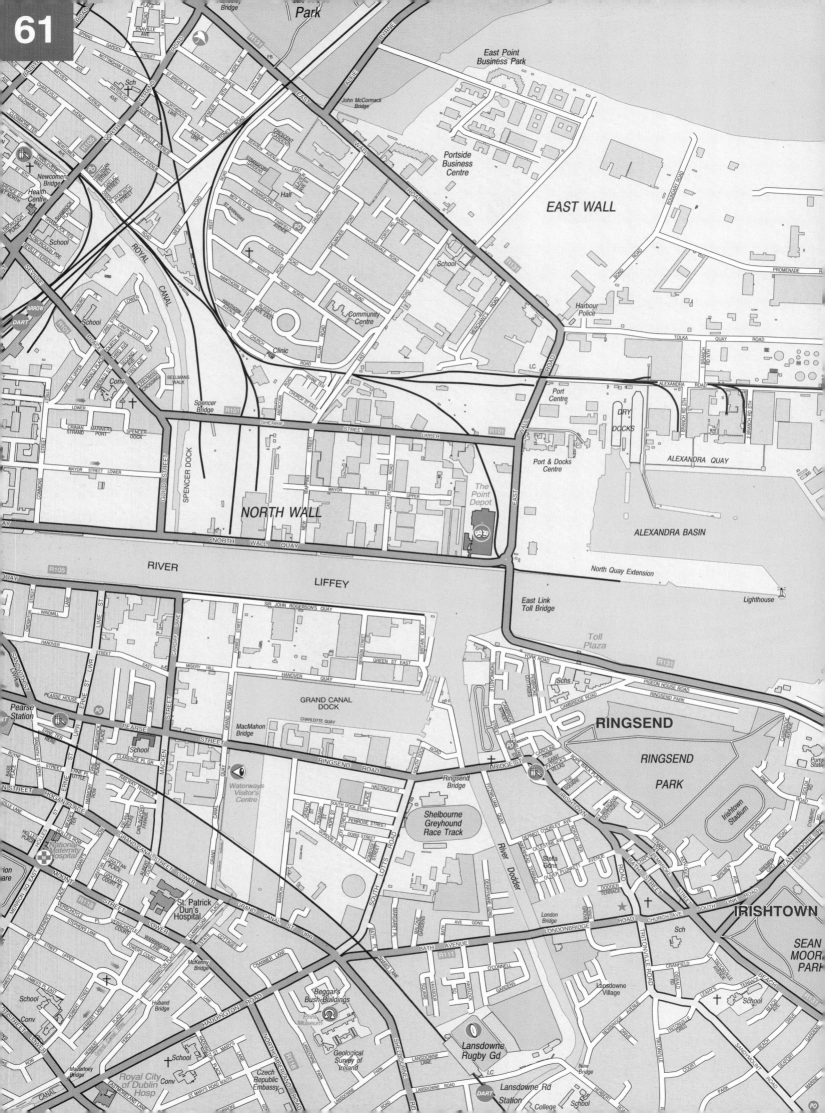

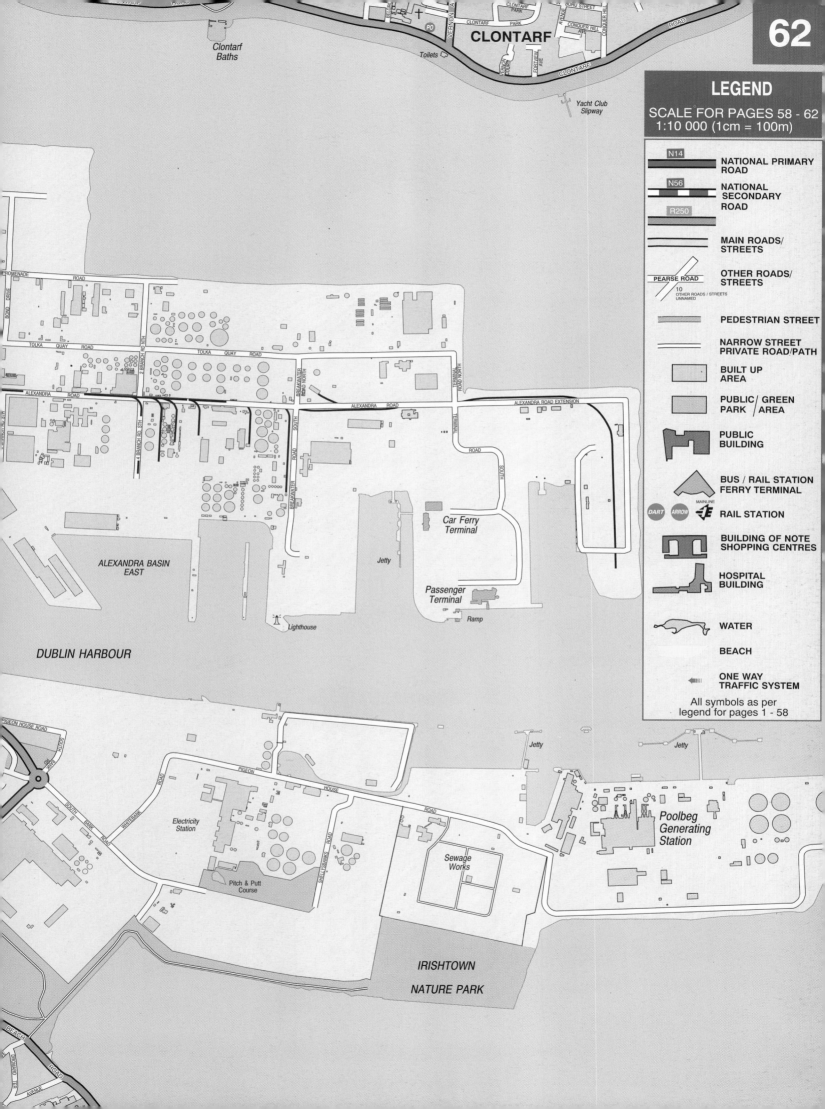

CLONTARF

Clontarf
Baths

Toilets

Yacht Club
Slipway

LEGEND

SCALE FOR PAGES 58 - 62
1:10 000 (1cm = 100m)

N14	NATIONAL PRIMARY ROAD
N56	NATIONAL SECONDARY ROAD
R250	
	MAIN ROADS/ STREETS
PEARSE ROAD 10 OTHER ROADS / STREETS UNNAMED	OTHER ROADS/ STREETS
	PEDESTRIAN STREET
	NARROW STREET PRIVATE ROAD/PATH
	BUILT UP AREA
	PUBLIC/ GREEN PARK / AREA
	PUBLIC BUILDING
	BUS / RAIL STATION FERRY TERMINAL
DART ARROW MAINLINE	RAIL STATION
	BUILDING OF NOTE SHOPPING CENTRES
	HOSPITAL BUILDING
	WATER
	BEACH
	ONE WAY TRAFFIC SYSTEM

All symbols as per
legend for pages 1 - 58

PROMENADE ROAD

BOND DRIVE

TOLKA QUAY ROAD

TOLKA QUAY ROAD

2 BRANCH RD NTH

ALEXANDRA ROAD

4 BRANCH RD. STH

BREAKWATER ROAD NORTH

BREAKWATER ROAD SOUTH

ALEXANDRA ROAD

TERMINAL ROAD NORTH

ALEXANDRA ROAD EXTENSION

TERMINAL ROAD SOUTH

ALEXANDRA BASIN
EAST

Car Ferry
Terminal

Jetty

Passenger
Terminal

Lighthouse

Ramp

DUBLIN HARBOUR

PIGEON HOUSE ROAD

SOUTH BANK ROAD

SOUTH BANK ROAD

WHITEBANK ROAD

PIGEON HOUSE ROAD

SHELLYBANKS ROAD

Electricity
Station

Pitch & Putt
Course

Sewage
Works

Jetty

Jetty

Poolbeg
Generating
Station

IRISHTOWN

NATURE PARK

BEACH

ORCHARD TER.

AVENUE

THE STORY OF DUBLIN

There is evidence of human settlement in the area of present-day Dublin dating back to remote prehistoric times. Ptolemy referred to Dublin as Eblana in A.D. 140 and a number of churches and monasteries existed in the vicinity in the early historic period. Saint Patrick is said to have visited Dublin in A.D. 448 where he made many converts to Christianity.

The history of Dublin as a city starts in A.D. 841, when Norse Vikings established a naval base by the Black Pool or Duibhlinn, which in turn became known by the Norse name of Dyfflin. The present name derives from the early English name of Divelin. Originally the site was below a hurdled ford or 'ath cliath' which is the origin of the current Irish name of Baile Atha Cliath – Town of the Hurdle Ford. An ancient highway south from the capital of Tara crossed the River Liffey at this point, which is now spanned by Father Mathew Bridge.

In A.D. 852-3 the Dublin settlement was the arrival point of further Norse settlers, under the leadership of Olaf the White. The construction of a fortified town followed, being situated on a steep ridge where Christ Church Cathedral and Dublin Castle now stand.

Ivarr the Boneless succeeded Olaf as king of Dublin in A.D. 871. During the following century Dublin became the capital of a small Norse trading and pirate kingdom called Dyfflinarskiri or Dublinshire. There was continual warfare between the Irish and the Danes over the following years. Outstanding events included the Battle of Dublin in A.D. 919 – a disastrous attempt to rid Dublin of its Scandinavian invaders. Niall Blackknee, king of Tara was killed in this battle, which was fought at Cell Mo-Shamhog or Islandbridge. In A.D. 999 Dublin joined in an unsuccessful attempt by the rulers of Leinster to overthrow Brian Boru. Danish power was finally broken when their Dublin/Leinster army, complete with overseas reinforcements, was crushed by the Irish under the leadership of Brian Boru at the Battle of Clontarf in 1014.

After Clontarf, Dublin continued under Danish rule and gained in prosperity, although it remained a small walled town for the following three centuries. When the half-Irish, half-Danish Sigtryggr Silkenbeard died, his dynasty died with him and Danish power began to wane.

Dublin became the seat of King Dermot I of Leinster for a while, and later, at the beginning of the twelfth century, came under the influence of Munster's Turloch Mor O'Brien and other Irish high kings, including the infamous Dermot McMurrough of Leinster. At this time the immediate Norse rulers of Dublin ranked merely as Earls, being subject to Irish rule.

Rory O'Connor, High King of Connacht assumed authority over Dublin in 1166. Under his direction Dermot McMurrough was driven overseas. McMurrough's return shortly afterwards signalled a new chapter in Dublin and Ireland's history, when he brought about the Anglo-Norman invasion of 1169.

McMurrough's son-in-law Richard Strongbow took control of Dublin and Leinster after the king's death. He was later defeated by Henry II of England who arrived in Dublin in 1171, establishing English authority in Ireland and making Dublin the headquarters of England's fluctuating power in Ireland for more than seven centuries. Under Henry II, Dublin received its first charter. Before he left, in 1172, he granted the city as a barony to the citizens of Bristol.

At this stage of Dublin's history the Norse influence and culture had become slight, as their descendants became absorbed into the native population. Whatever survivors were left had settled at Austmannabyr or Ostmaneby. This place later became known as Oxmanstown and was located north of the Liffey in the vicinity of St. Michan's Parish Church.

The Middle Ages saw little change, although the city walls were extended north of the Liffey in 1312. Among the buildings located within the city walls at this time were Dublin Castle, built between 1213 and 1228, Christ Church Cathedral and the churches of St.

Nicholas, St. Werburgh, St. John the Evangelist, St. Michael and St. Mary le Dam. North of the city walls were St. Mary's Abbey, the Dominican friary and the church of St. Michan, which was founded in 1096 by Bishop Samuel O'Hanly. To the south was St. Patrick's Cathedral, St. Bride's Church, the Franciscan friary, the archepiscopal palace of St. Sepulchre, the Carmelite friary, St. Stephen's Leper Hospital and the almshouse of St. Michael de Pole. In the eastern suburbs were St. Andrew's Parish Church, the Augustinian priory of All Hallows and the Augustinian nunnery of St. Mary de Hogge. Outside the western boundaries were St. Lawrence's Leper House, The Augustinian abbey of St. Thomas the Martyr, the hospital of St. John the Baptist, the Crutched friary and the hospital and priory of the Knights of St. John. A visit to the present-day Liberties region of Dublin will recall many associations with those ancient settlements, although much of Dublin's medieval heritage disappeared during the succeeding wartorn centuries.

THE CASTLE

The next era of Dublin's history saw an invasion by Edward and Robert Bruce in 1317, a disastrous Black Death which killed 14,000 in 1348, the 1437 crowning of Lambert Simnel as Edward VI of England in Christ Church Cathedral and the rebellion of Silken Thomas Fitzgerald in 1534. Following these events was the siege of Dublin by Owen Roe O'Neill in 1646 and the surrender of the city to the Parliamentarians by Royalist Ormonde in 1647 – a move designed to prevent Dublin falling into Confederate Catholic hands. Cromwell arrived in 1649 and by the end of the Cromwellian period the city was reduced to ruins, while the population had dwindled to a mere 9,000.

But the eighteenth century brought about a dramatic change under the new Protestant ascendancy. Dublin rapidly became one of Europe's most beautiful capital cities, as it spread out in all directions. This Georgian era was a period of architectural greatness, manifested in the noble squares and thoroughfares which were the setting for hundreds of magnificent private houses and superb public buildings such as the Parliament House in College Green. The arts also found ready encouragement from the wealthy society of the metropolis, who embellished their homes with the work of master stone carvers, painters, glassmakers, silversmiths and continental stucco workers.

A short-lived autonomy was conceded to the Irish Parliament by England in 1783, but this ended in 1800 with the Act of Union which united Ireland and Great Britain. The political unrest of the era culminated in the unsuccessful rising of 1798. A further insurrection by Robert Emmet in 1803 began and ended in failure on the streets of Dublin.

Towards the end of the last century Ireland's capital became the centre of two great cultural movements – the Gaelic League (Conradh na Gaeilge) founded in 1893 in an effort to restore the Irish language and the Irish Literary Renaissance which was dominated by the writings of Yeats and the founding of the Abbey Theatre.

The 1916 Rising, influenced greatly by the Gaelic League movement, was another major milestone. Three years later came the Declaration of Independence adopted in Dublin. The subsequent Anglo-Irish war ended in the Treaty of 1921. Following the setting up of the Irish Free State in 1922 came the tragic Civil War. Dublin once again became a shattered city but eventually recovered and the building of a modern European capital city began in earnest.

PLACES TO VISIT

Phoenix Park Visitor Centre

Located in the Phoenix Park, 5kms from the City Centre. The Tower House possibly dates from the 17th Century, and nearby is the visitor centre. There are exhibitions, a film show, and visitors can view a colourful and realistic historical interpretation of the past.

Visiting times:

Nov.- Mid March	9.30 a.m. - 4.30 p.m. Sat. - Sun.
Mid March - end of March	9.30 a.m. - 5.00 p.m. daily.
April - May	9.30 a.m. - 5.30 p.m. daily.
June - Sept.	10.00 a.m. - 6.00 p.m. daily.
October	9.30 a.m. - 5.00 p.m. daily.

Last admission 45 minutes before closing.
Free guided tours to Áras an Uachtaráin Saturdays only.
Phone 670 9155.

19 C4

Phoenix Park Visitor Centre

Bank of Ireland: (former Parliament House)

College Green.
Origins: Built between 1729 and 1739.
Designed by Sir Edward Lovatt Pearce (1699-1733) and enlarged by James Gandon and Robert Parke between 1785 and 1794.
The Bank of Ireland took over this building in 1804. It had been the scene of many dramatic events in Irish politics up to the passing of the Act of Union in 1800.
Visiting times: Monday, Tuesday, Wednesday and Friday.
10 a.m. – 4 p.m.
Thursday 10 a.m. – 5 p.m.

36 D2

Castletown House

Located in Celbridge, Co. Kildare. Castletown House, designed by Italian architect Alessandro Galilei and Irish architect Sir Edward Lovett Pearce for the speaker of the Irish House of Commons, William Connolly.
Building commenced in 1722, and Castletown House was continuously used by the Connolly family until 1965 when the house and lands were sold.
Castletown House came into state ownership in 1979 under the management of the Office of Public Works.

Visiting times:

April to October	Monday to Friday	10 a.m. – 6 p.m.
	Saturday/Sunday/	
	Bank Holidays	1 p.m. – 6 p.m.
November: Sundays only		1 p.m. – 5 p.m.

Last admission one hour before closing.

30 D2

Bank of Ireland

Celbridge Abbey

Located 12 miles from Dublin, Celbridge Abbey was built by Bartholomew Van Homrigh, Lord Mayor of Dublin in 1697.
The Abbey grounds contain many colourful attractions and are open to the public at the following times.
Visiting times:

Monday to Saturday	10 a.m. – 6 p.m.
Sunday/Bank Holidays	11 a.m. – 6 p.m.

29 C4

Castletown House

Custom House

Custom House

Custom House Quay

Origins: Designed by James Gandon and built between 1781 and 1791.

The building was reduced to a shell when it was gutted by fire during the War of Independence. It was restored by the Office of Public Works after the Irish Free State was established. *36 E2*

Casino Marino

Casino Marino

Malahide Road.

Located just 4kms from the city centre, off the Malahide Road, Dublin 3.

The Casino, has been described as one of the finest 18th century classical buildings in Ireland. Access is by Guided Tour only.

Visiting times: June - Sept.   9.30 a.m. – 6.30 p.m. daily
Oct. and May 10 a.m. - 5 p.m. daily
November   12 noon - 4 p.m. Thursday and Sunday.
Feb.- April   12 noon - 4 p.m. Thursday and Sunday.
Dec.- Jan.   Closed   *22 D3*

City Hall

Lord Edward Street.

Origins: Formerly the Royal Exchange, designed by Thomas Cooley (1740 – 1784) and completed between 1769 and 1779.

This is the headquarters of Dublin's municipal government. Archives dating back to the twelfth century are stored in the Muniment Room. It also houses the mace and sword of the city, along with 102 Royal Charters, including the original charter of 1171 by which Dublin was granted to the men of Bristol by Henry II *36 D2*

Dublinia – Christ Church,

St. Michael's Hill, Dublin 8.

The realistic and novel exhibition that is Dublinia is situated in the old Synod Hall on St. Michael's Hill, alongside of Christ Church Cathedral, to which it is connected by an ornate pedestrian archway over St. Michael's Hill.

The exhibition heralds the arrival of the Anglo-Normans in 1170 through a broad spectrum of Dublin life to the closure of the Monasteries in 1540.

Visiting times: Summer: 10 a.m. – 5 p.m. daily.
Winter: (Oct 1st – March 31st).
Monday – Saturday 11 a.m. – 4 p.m.
Sunday 10 a.m. – 4.30 p.m.
36 D3

Dublin Castle

The main entrance is located at the junction of Cork Hill and Castle Street. Dating from the 13th Century, the site, once a Viking stronghold, has served as a military fortress, prison, courts of law, and the core of British Administration in Ireland until 1922. Dublin Castle is now used for State functions. Guided tours of State Apartments, Chapel Royal and Undercroft.

St. Patrick's Hall

Dublin Castle

Dublin Castle

Visiting times: Monday/Friday   10 a.m. - 5 p.m.
Saturday/Sunday/
Public Holidays   2 p.m. – 5 p.m.

36 D3

The Throne Room

Dublin Castle

Dunsink Observatory

Dunsink Lane, near Castleknock.

Origins: Founded in 1783, this is one of the world's oldest observatories. It formerly belonged to Trinity College but is now the centre of the school of Astronomical Physics of the Dublin Institute for Advanced Studies.

Visiting times: Open to the public on the first and third Wednesday of each month from October to March, at 8.00 p.m.

Admission free on written application to the secretary enclosing stamp-addressed envelope.

19 B2

General Post Office

O'Connell Street.

Origins: Designed by Francis Johnston and built between 1814 and 1818.

The GPO became the focal point of the 1916 Insurrection and the Proclamation of the Irish Republic took place there. Destroyed by fire, it was restored in 1929. In the public office is a noteworthy statue representing the Death of Cuchulainn, the work of Oliver Sheppard R.H.A.

36 D2

Kilmainham Jail

Inchicore Road, Dublin 8.

One of the largest decommissioned jails in Europe, it played its part in some of the most patriotic and tragic episodes that light the path of Ireland's journey to modern nationhood, from the 1780's to 1924. Featuring many exhibitions and a multi-lingual audio-visual show. Access by guided tour only.

Visiting times: Oct - March   Mon. - Fri.   9.30 a.m. – 5 p.m.
                      Sunday   10.00 a.m. – 6 p.m.
                      April - Sept.   9.30 a.m. – 6 p.m. daily.
                      Last admission one hour before closing.

35 A3

Kilmainham Jail

General Post Office

Leinster House

Four Courts
Inns Quay.

Origins: Designed by James Gandon and built between 1785 and 1802. This building, dominated by a great domed central mass, is one of Gandon's masterpieces. The Irish Law Courts and Law Library are housed here. Like the Custom House, Gandon's other great building, it was also destroyed by fire during the struggle for Irish independence. Although significantly altered, the building was completely restored by 1932.

36 D2

Leinster House
Kildare Street.

Origins: Designed by Richard Cassells, building commenced on this fine Georgian mansion in 1745. Originally the residence of the Duke of Leinster, the building became the property of the Royal Dublin Society in 1815. In 1922 it was purchased by the first Irish Free State Government to serve as a Parliament House. Presently it is the meeting place of the Dail (Chamber of Deputies) and Seanad (Senate).

36 E3

Four Courts

Waterways Visitor Centre
Grand Canal Quay, Dublin 2
Located at Grand Canal Docks, beside McMahon Bridge, Pearse Street.
The centre houses an exhibition outlining the history of Ireland's Inland Waterways and the activities and experiences currently available.
Featuring an audio-visual show and working models of various engineering features.
Visiting times: Oct. - May 12.30 p.m. - 5.00 p.m. Wed. - Sun.
June - Sept. 9.30 a.m. – 6.30 p.m. daily.
Last admission 45 minutes before closing.

36 F3

Royal Hospital and Irish Museum of Modern Art

Royal Hospital and Irish Museum of Modern Art

Military Road, Kilmainham.

The most important 17th century building in Ireland has been restored. Guided tours available of the Master's Quarters, the Great Hall with the portrait collection, and the chapel which contains outstanding woodcarving by Tabary and a magnificent Baroque ceiling.

Visiting times: Tuesday – Saturday   10.00 a.m. – 5.30 p.m.
Sunday and Bank Holidays 12 noon – 5.30 p.m.
Closed Monday.   *35 B3*

Trinity College

Mansion House

Trinity College

Main entrance, College Green.

Origins: Trinity College is the sole college of the University of Dublin. Founded by Queen Elizabeth I in 1592, it is built on the site of the Augustinian priory of All Hallows which was founded by Dermot McMurrough. The oldest buildings now surviving are the Rubrics, a range of brick apartments dating from 1700. The Palladian facade was added in 1759. In the same year the Provost's house (facing the northern end of Grafton Street) was built. This is the only great Georgian house in Dublin still being used for its original purpose. Many world-famous men have attended this college over the centuries.

Visiting Times: Monday - Saturday   10.00 a.m. - 5.00 p.m.
See also 'Trinity College Library'.   *36 E2*

Mansion House

Dawson Street.

Origins: This Queen Anne house was built in 1705, the round room having been added in 1821 as the venue for a function to honour King George IV. Built in brick, the building underwent changes during the Victorian era.

Since 1715 the Mansion House has been the residence of Dublin's Lord Mayor. In 1919 the Declaration of Independence was adopted here and here also was signed the truce which ended Anglo-Irish hostilities in 1921.   *36 E3*

SWORDS

Swords is located 12.9 kms north of Dublin City Centre and is situated on the Ward River. Accessible by way of the N1, Swords Town has many features such as St. Colmcille's Well, the Old Constabulary Barracks, St. Columba's Church, Belfry, and Round Tower, and Swords Castle.

Swords Castle

Built in 1183 as a summer palace for the first Norman Archbishop of Dublin, Swords Castle was designed both as a residence and as a place of defence. In 1324 Archbishop de Bicknor left Swords and the castle fell into disrepair. Despite many attempts at renovation over the centuries, it has remained so. Currently in the ownership of Fingal Council, and now in the process of being restored.

Visiting times: Monday, Wednesday and Thursday 10a.m. - 4p.m.

Friday 10a.m. - 3p.m.

2 D2

MALAHIDE

Malahide is a lively, picturesque small town, nestling on the south shore of the Broadmeadow Estuary, in North County Dublin. Located 14.5 kms from Dublin City Centre, it is accessible by the N1, R106, R107 and by direct rail link.

Malahide has many places of note, such as St. Sylvesters Well, Hicks Tower, The Arches, Casino, Robswalls, the most noted of all being Malahide Castle.

Malahide Castle

Built by Sir Richard de Talbot about 1200 and developed over the centuries into the imposing architectural achievement that it is today. The castle houses part of the National Portrait Collection in the Great Hall.

The extensive grounds are open from 9 a.m. - 9 p.m. daily and incorporate the 20 acre Talbot Botanic Garden, which is open to all from 2 p.m. to 5 p.m. daily.

Visiting times: April - Sept. Monday-Saturday 10 a.m. - 5 p.m.

Sunday 11.00 a.m. – 6 p.m.
Closed 12.45 – 2 p.m. daily.
Nov.- March Sat., Sun. and Bank holidays 2 p.m. - 5 p.m.

Also included is the Fry Model Railway Museum, which contains a unique collection of hand-made models showing the history of Irish railways from its inception to the modern day period.

3 A3

Malahide Castle

Howth Castle

The great English architect Sir Edwin Lutyens restyled this 14th century castle overlooking Dublin Bay. The grounds are also noted for its wild rhododendron gardens. The grounds are open daily from 8 a.m. to sunset.

25 C1

Howth Transport Museum

This Museum is located in the grounds of Howth Castle. It features lorries, trucks, fire engines and tractors. Also exhibited is the restored Hill of Howth No.9 Tram.

Visiting times: June - August Monday - Saturday 10 a.m. - 5 p.m.
Sunday / Bank Holidays 2 p.m. - 5 p.m.
October - May Saturday, Sunday and Bank Holidays 2 p.m. - 5 p.m.

25 C1

BRAY

This is one of Ireland's largest and oldest east coast seaside resorts, accommodating business, residential needs and tourist amenities, under the ever dominant Bray Head.

The Courthouse: located on Main Street between Quinsborough Road and Seapoint Road, this building was designed by William Murray, and built in 1841. It is now the location of Bray Heritage Museum, and Bray Tourist Office. Visitors 10 a.m. – 5 p.m. daily

57 C2

The Town Hall: located on Main Street at the junction of Killarney Road and Vevay Road is the jewel in Bray's architectural crown. Designed by Edward G. Dawber for architects Thomas Newenham Deane & Son, it was built in 1884 at the request of Lord and Lady Brabazon for the people of Bray. Currently the seat of Bray Urban District Council.

57 C2

Other notable features include Oldcourt Castle, The Promenade and on the eastern side of Bray Head, the Cliff Walk fringes along a 5km feast of cliff face and sea views into Greystones.

LEIXLIP

What was once the village of Leixlip is now Kildare's youngest and most populous town. Situated on the river Liffey and the river Rye, the Salmon Leap (from which Leixlip gets its name) is overlooked by the 12th century Leixlip Castle. The river Liffey joins the river Rye in the heart of the old village and a lake formed by a hydroelectric dam offers a great opportunity for the angler and water sport enthusiast. The internationally renowned Liffey Descent canoeing event takes place here in September every year.

CHURCHES AND CATHEDRALS

Christ Church Cathedral
Main entrance, Christchurch Place.
Origins: The original church was built about 1030 by Sigtryggr Silkenbeard, Norse King of Dublin. A new church was built in 1173 by Strongbow. The present structure dates mainly from the nineteenth century, although the wonderful medieval crypt still remains. Christ Church contains many interesting historical remains.
Visiting times:

10.00 a.m. to 5.30 p.m. daily
Group tours available on request / application.

36 D3

St. Audoen's Church
High Street
Origins: St. Audoen's dates from medieval times and is the oldest of Dublin's parish churches. The tower houses Ireland's three most ancient bells, dating from 1423. There's a font in the nave dating from 1124. St. Audoen's Arch stands nearby. This is Dublin's only surviving city gate. Built in 1240 it originally led to a strand on the River Liffey.

35 C3

St. Mary's Church
Mary Street.
Origins: Dating from 1627, this was the first Dublin church to be built with galleries. Theobald Wolfe Tone was baptised here in 1763 and Sean O'Casey the playwright in 1880. The Church is now a retail outlet.

36 D2

St. Michan's Church
Church Street
Origins: Founded by the Norse in 1096, the present building dates from 1685-6, having been much restored in 1828. The Church's Harris organ is said to have been used by Handel during his visit to Dublin. Dry magnesium limestone vaults beneath the church contain mummified corpses which may be seen by the public.
Visiting times: Church and Vaults:

April - Oct.	Monday - Friday	10 a.m. - 5 p.m.
Nov. - March	Mon. - Friday	12.30 p.m. - 3.30 p.m.
Saturday	10 a.m. - 1 p.m.	

Vaults closed on Sundays.

35 C2

St. Mary's Pro-Cathedral
Marlborough Street.
Origins: Designed by John Sweetman and built between 1815 and 1825. Originally intended for O'Connell Street but erected on this less suitable site to satisfy Protestant opposition at the time. The interior reveals the inspiration of Chalgin's Church of St. Philippe de Roule, Paris. Some interesting monuments may be seen inside. The metropolitan church of the diocese, it is used for State functions. A Latin Mass is sung each Sunday at 11 a.m. by the Palestrina Choir of which the famous tenor John McCormack was once a member.

36 D2

St. Audoen's Church

St. Werburgh's Church
Werburgh Street, off Christchurch Place.
Origins: Erected in 1715 on the site of the medieval successor to pre-Norman St. Werburgh's. Destroyed by fire in 1754, the church was re-opened in 1759. A spire was added in 1768 but removed in the early nineteenth century by the fearful authorities of Dublin castle, which it overlooked. Until 1790 St. Werburgh's was the Chapel Royal. In the vaults beneath is buried Lord Edward Fitzgerald. His captor Town Major Sirr, is buried in the nearby churchyard.
This fine Georgian building, now well restored, contains many interesting features including an attractive pulpit designed by Francis Johnston and carved by Richard Stewart, as well as a sixteenth-century Fitzgerald tomb located in the porch.
Visiting times: By appointment only. Tel. 478 3710
Monday to Friday   10 a.m. – 4 p.m.
Entrance: North Door, 8 Castle Street.
Main Sunday Service: 10.00 a.m.

36 D3

St. Patrick's Cathedral

St. Patrick's Cathedral
Patrick Street.

Origins: St. Patrick's, Ireland's largest church, was built on the site of the pre-Norman parish church of St. Patrick. The church was rebuilt in 1191 by Archbishop Comyn. In 1213 it gained cathedral status, but later, in 1300 a papal decree gave Christ Church precedence. At the Reformation it became a parish church, but under the Catholic restoration of Philip and Mary it once again became a cathedral.

A university was established there in 1320 but was suppressed later by Henry VIII. The square tower dates from the fourteenth century.

During the wars of the seventeenth century the Cromwellians used the ruinous cathedral as a stable for their horses. But the future saw a great improvement in the fabric of the building. A spire was added by the architect John Semple in 1749 and a general restoration was undertaken between 1844 and 1869 being financed by Sir Benjamin Lee Guinness. Jonathan Swift was Dean of St. Patrick's from 1713 to 1745. His pulpit may still be seen and his tomb, with its famous epitaph is in the south aisle. Buried nearby is Esther (Stella) Johnston one of Swift's two great lovers.

Visiting times:

Monday - Friday	9 a.m. - 6 p.m.
Saturday	9 a.m. - 5 p.m. (4 p.m. Nov. - Mar.)
Sunday	April - Sept. 9.30 a.m. - 5 p.m.
	October- March 10.00 a.m. - 3 p.m.

Except during Sunday service 11 a.m. - 12.45 a.m. and 3 p.m. - 4.15 p.m.

36 D3

LIBRARIES

Chester Beatty Library
Dublin Castle.

One of the world's most valuable private collections of oriental manuscripts and miniatures can be seen here. There are manuscripts of the New Testament, Manichean papyri and Eastern miniatures, as well as picture scrolls, albums and jades from the Far East.

The library is located in the Clock Tower building and will open daily. Admisson free.

Visiting Times: Tuesday - Friday 10.00 a.m. - 5.00 p.m.
Saturday 11.00 a.m. - 5.00 p.m.
Sunday 1.00 p.m. - 5.00 p.m.
For guided tours phone 407 0750.

44 D1

Trinity College Library

Trinity College Library
Main entrance to college from College Green.

Dating from the late sixteenth century, Trinity College Library is Ireland's oldest library. It contains over 1,000,000 volumes and Ireland's most extensive collection of manuscripts and early printed books. Its greatest treasure is the Book of Kells (probably eighth century). This is considered to be the most beautiful illuminated manuscript in existence today. Manuscripts in the library include State letters of Queen Elizabeth I, diaries of Wolfe Tone and manuscripts of the Irish dramatist, John Millington Synge.

The library is housed in two buildings – the Old Library (completed in 1732) and the New Library (1967). Trinity College Library has the right to a copy of any book printed in Ireland or Britain.

Visiting hours: Monday to Saturday 9.30 a.m. to 5.00 p.m.
Sunday October-May 12 noon to 4.30 p.m.
Sunday June-September 9.30 a.m. to 4.30 p.m.

36 E2

Royal Irish Academy Library
19 Dawson Street.

A very extensive collection of ancient Irish manuscripts can be seen in this library. These include the 'Book of the Dun Cow', the 'Book of Ballymote', the 'Speckled Book' and the 'Stowe Missal'. Also to be seen is the Cathach or Battle Book, believed to be the actual copy of the Psalms made in the sixth century by St. Colmcille. An autograph copy of the Annals of the Four Masters made in Donegal between 1632 and 1636 is also there.

Visiting hours: Monday to Friday 10.30 a.m. to 5.00 p.m.
Closed bank holidays and during the last three weeks of August.
Admission free.

36 E3

Marsh's Library
St. Patrick's Close.

This is Ireland's oldest public library, founded in 1701 by Archbishop Narcissus Marsh. The collection consists mainly of theological, medical, ancient historical, Hebrew, Syriac, Greek, French and Latin literature. Still to be seen are the original carved bookcases and the cages into which readers were locked to prevent theft.

Visiting Hours: Weekdays 10 a.m. to 12.45 p.m. – 2 p.m. to 5 p.m.
Saturday 10.30 a.m. to 12.45 p.m.
Closed Tuesdays, Sundays and bank holidays. *36 D3*

National Library
Kildare Street.

Founded in 1877, the National Library is the largest public library in Ireland. Over 500,000 books as well as maps, prints and manuscripts are housed there. Its huge newspaper collection provides a rich source of historical reference. An extensive collection of historical and literary manuscripts relating to Ireland and microfilms of documents from overseas libraries and archives are available for reference. The public service counter is manned by helpful officials.

Visiting hours: Mon. - Wed.(inc) 10 a.m. – 9 p.m.
Thu/Fri 10 a.m. – 5 p.m.
Sat 10 a.m. – 1 p.m.

36 E3

National Library

Dublin City Libraries
There are twenty-eight public libraries maintained by the Corporation of Dublin.

The administrative headquarters for the Dublin Public Libraries is at Fenian Street. It houses special reference collections, including the Gilbert Library of manuscripts and books relating to Dublin. And there are extensive collections of books on Ireland. A collection of W. B. Yeats material contains a full edition of Mosada.

Other Dublin Libraries
Other libraries of note are the King's Inn Library, Henrietta Street; University College Library, Belfield; the Worth Library, Steeven's Hospital; the Franciscan Library, Franciscan House of Studies, Killiney; the Central Catholic Library at 74 Merrion Square; the Royal Dublin Society's Library at Ballsbridge and the library in the Ilac Centre, Henry Street.

ART GALLERIES

Hugh Lane Municipal Gallery of Modern Art.

Charlemont House, Parnell Square.
This building, dating from 1762, was formerly the residence of Lord Charlemont. The collection was originally housed in Harcourt Street, the present gallery dating from 1908. It was Sir Hugh Lane who contributed the nucleus of this collection of pictures. Lane was drowned in the sinking of the Lusitania in 1915. Before his death he left his continental collection to the National Gallery in London but had stipulated in his will that they should return to Dublin. Unfortunately an unwitnessed codicil of his will caused complications and his intentions were declared invalid.
After many years it was agreed in 1959 to divide the pictures between Dublin and London in two groups. The two groups are exchanged every five years. This gallery has an interesting collection of works by nineteenth and twentieth-century artists.

National Gallery

Merrion Lawn, Merrion Square West.
The gallery was officially opened in 1864. It then consisted of only 100 pictures donated by William Dargan and George Mulvany. Dargan was a railway entrepreneur who died in 1867. His statue may be seen on the lawn outside the gallery.
There are now over 2000 pictures in the gallery, representing all the European schools. Donors of pictures include Lady Milltown, Sir Hugh Lane, Edward Martyn, the Friends of the National Collections and Sir Alfred Chester Beatty. Famous works by Poussin, Goya and Gainsborough, may be seen. Irish artists are well represented, in a comprehensive collection which includes works by Ashford, Barry, Barrett, John Butler Yeats, Hone, Osborne, Lavery and Orpen. Part of the National Portrait Gallery provides an interesting survey of personalities spanning 300 years. This is housed under the same roof.

National Gallery

Visiting times:	Monday to Saturday:	10 a.m. – 5.30 p.m.
	Sunday:	2 – 5 p.m.
	Thursday open till 8.15 p.m.	
	Restaurant open during gallery hours.	

Art Reference Library open Monday to Friday: 10 a.m. – 5.15 p.m.
Free public lectures Sundays at 3 p.m. and Tuesdays at 10.30 a.m.
Conducted tours of gallery on Saturdays at 3 p.m. and Sundays at 2.15 p.m., 3 p.m. and 4 p.m. Admission free.

36 E3

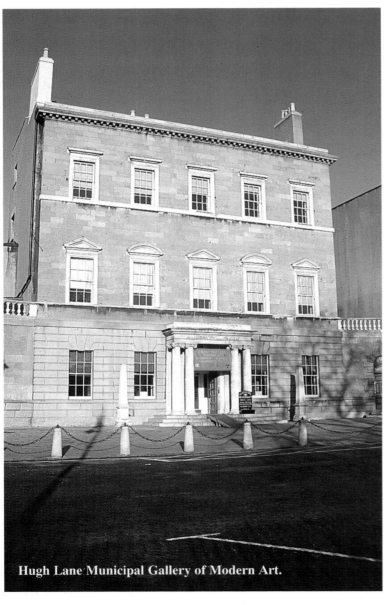

Hugh Lane Municipal Gallery of Modern Art.

Royal Hospital and Irish Museum of Modern Art

Military Road, Kilmainham.
The Irish Museum of Modern Art was established in 1991 and exhibits Irish and International Art of the 20th century

Visiting times:	Tuesday – Saturday	10 a.m. – 5.30 p.m.
	Sundays	12 noon – 5.30 p.m.
	Closed Monday.	

Visiting times:	Tuesday to Friday	9.30 a.m. to 6 p.m.
	Thursday	open until 8 p.m. (summer only)
	Saturday	9.30 a.m. to 5 p.m.
	Sunday	11 a.m. to 5 p.m.
	Closed Monday.	Admission free.

36 D1

35 B3

MUSEUMS

National Museum of Ireland

Kildare Street/Merrion Street.

The contents of this museum comes under three headings – Irish Antiquities, Art and Industrial and Natural History. The Irish antiquities division holds one of Europe's most impressive collections of antiquities. Items displayed cover every age from the Stone Age to medieval times. Gold lunulae, torques and fibulae from the Bronze Age are of particular interest, as well as famous items like the Tara Brooch, the Cross of Cong and the Ardagh Chalice from the early Christian period.

The main entrance is from Kildare Street but part of the natural history division is approached from Merrion Street.

Visiting times: Tuesday to Saturday   10.00 a.m. to 5.00 p.m.
Sunday   2.00 p.m. to 5.00 p.m.
Closed Monday.   *36 E3*

National Museum of Ireland

Collins Barracks
Benburb Street.

Collins Barracks which was acquired by the National Museum in 1994 is Europe's oldest military barracks and the world's oldest continuously occupied barracks .

It houses exhibits of the decorative arts and of the economic, social, political and military history of the state.

Among the exhibits are: Etruscan vases; a pocket book carried by Wolfe Tone during his imprisonment in the barracks in 1798; gauntlets worn by King William at the Battle of the Boyne and a life-belt and oar from the wreckage of the Lusitania.

Visiting Times: Tuesday to Saturday   10.00 a.m. - 5.00 p.m.
Sunday   2.00 p.m. - 5.00 p.m.
Closed Monday
Closed Good Friday
                                                    35 C2

Dublin Civic Museum

South William Street.

Occupying the former City Assembly House, this museum was opened in 1953. It contains a permanent collection of exhibits of antiquarian and historical interest, pertaining to Dublin city. Newspapers and cuttings, as well as maps, prints, and various unique items provide a vivid record of Dublin's past.

Visiting times: Tuesday to Friday   10.00 a.m. - 5.30 p.m.
Saturday   10.00 a.m. – 5.00 p.m.
Sunday   11.00 a.m. - 2.00 p.m.
Closed Weekends, Mondays and Bank Holidays.
Admission free.   *36 D3*

The Writer's Museum

The Writer's Museum

18/19 Parnell Square North.

Opened in 1991 in two restored Georgian houses. It features a display of paintings, photographs, manuscripts and other memorabilia relating to Irish writers such as Shaw, Yeats, Beckett, Wilde, O'Casey, Joyce, Behan and Swift.

Opening hours: Monday to Saturday 10.00 a.m. - 5.00 p.m.
Sundays and Bank Holidays 11.00 a.m. - 5.00 p.m.
                                                    36 D1

Genealogical Office and Heraldic Museum

2 Kildare St. Dublin 2.

The oldest office of state in Ireland, founded in 1552. It contains the unique Heraldic Museum with its colourful display of coats of arms, banners and facility.

The Consultancy Service on ancestry tracing is designed to enable you to undertake on your own the task of uncovering your Irish roots.

Hours of opening: 10.00 a.m. - 12.30 p.m.
2.00 p.m. - 4.30 p.m. Monday - Friday.
                                                    36 E3

Genealogical Office and Heraldic Museum

National Print Museum

Garrison Chapel, Beggars Bush, Dublin 4.

This Museum houses a unique collection of implements, artefacts and machines from all sectors of the printing industry in Ireland. Many of them are still in full working order.

Visiting times:
May - Sept. 10.00 a.m. - 12.30 p.m. and 2.30 p.m. - 5.00 p.m.
Saturday, Sunday and Bank Holidays   12 noon - 5.00 p.m.
Guided tours and audio visual show.
                                                    36 F3

National Wax Museum

Granby Row.

On display are life-size figures of prominent Irish historical, political, theatrical, literary and sporting personalities. Taped narrations on each scene, guide one along. The Chamber of Horrors is a must for all the family.

Visiting times: Monday – Saturday   10.00 a.m. –   5.30 p.m.
Sunday   12 noon   –   5.30 p.m.
                                                    36 D1

SOME FAMOUS DUBLIN PEOPLE

Dublin has produced an amazing number of well-known writers, scientists and scholars. Many of these personalities not only distinguished themselves in their native city, but through their work established their names world-wide.

The following is a brief guide to some of the most famous people who were born in Dublin and/or lived there for a considerable period of time.

THE WORLD OF LETTERS

Samuel Beckett, (1906-1989). Novelist and dramatist, born in Dublin. Novels include 'Murphy','Mollag and Malone Dies'. Plays include 'Waiting for Godot', 'Va et Vient', and 'Silence'. Awarded the Nobel Prize for Literature in 1969.

Brendan Behan, (1923-1964). Dublin-born dramatist. Plays include 'The Quare Fellow' and 'The Hostage'.

Edmund Burke, (1729-1797). Son of a Dublin attorney. Orator, political philosopher and champion of American liberties.

James Joyce, (1882-1941). Poet and writer, born and educated in Dublin. Works include 'A Portrait of the Artist as a Young Man', 'Ulysses' and 'Finnegan's Wake'. The Martello Tower where Joyce lived outside Dublin is now a museum in his memory.

William E.H. Lecky, (1838-1903). Famous Dublin-born historian.

Joseph Sheridan Le Fanu, (1814-1873). Nineteenth-century Dublin novelist, author of 'The House by the Churchyard', among others.

Charles Jones Lever, (1806-1872). A native of Dublin. His novels include 'Harry Lorrequer' and 'Charles O'Malley'.

Edmund Malone, (1741-1812). This great scholar specialised in the study of Shakespeare.

James Clarence Mangan, (1803-1849). Son of a Dublin grocer. His poetry includes 'Dark Rosaleen', 'O'Hussey's Ode to the Maguire' and the autobiographic ballad 'The Nameless One'.

James Joyce

Thomas Moore, (1779-1852). Like Mangan this poet was also a grocer's son. He distinguished himself as an adaptor of traditional airs and as a writer of biographies. Works include 'Moore's Melodies', 'The Twopenny Post Bag' and 'Lalla Rookh'.

Sean O'Casey, (1880-1964). Originally a labourer, O'Casey became one of Ireland's most famous dramatists. Plays include 'The Shadow of a Gunman', 'Juno and the Paycock', 'The Plough and the Stars', 'The Silver Tassie' and 'Purple Dust'.

Birthplace, G.B.Shaw

George Bernard Shaw, (1856-1950). Shaw, a world-famous playwright and wit spent the first twenty years of his life in Dublin, his birthplace. Works include 'John's Bull's Other Island', 'Candida', 'The Doctor's Dilemma', 'Man and Superman', 'Pygmalion', 'Heartbreak House' and 'Saint Joan'. In 1925 he won the Nobel Prize for Literature.

Richard Brinsley Sheridan, (1751-1816). Dramatist and distinguished parliamentary orator. Born in Upper Dorset Street. His three great comedies were 'The Rivals', 'The School for Scandal' and 'The Critic'.

James Stephens, (1882-1950). Novelist and poet. His novels include 'The Crock of Gold', 'The Charwoman's Daughter', 'The Demigods' and 'In the Land of Youth'. Poems include 'The Goat Paths' and 'The Snare'.

Jonathan Swift, (1667-1745). Known mainly as a satirist. Became Dean of St. Patrick's in 1713. Probably best known for 'The Tale of a Tub', the 'Drapier's Letters' and 'Gulliver's Travels'.

John Millington Synge, (1871-1909). Although a Dubliner, this dramatist's first love was the West of Ireland. This is reflected in his work. Best known are 'Playboy of the Western World', 'Riders to the Sea' and 'Deirdre of the Sorrows'.

Sir James Ware, (1594-1666). As an historian and antiquary, Ware is one of Dublin's most distinguished great scholars.

Oscar Wilde, (1854-1900). Born in Dublin and educated at Trinity College, Wilde moved to London when he was twenty-five. His outstanding works are the novel 'The Picture of Dorian Gray', and 'The Importance of being Earnest', his dramatic masterpiece. Also of note is his long letter 'De Profundis' and 'The Ballad of Reading Gaol'.

William Butler Yeats, (1865-1939). Born in London and educated in Dublin, Yeats contributed much to the cultural life of Dublin. He was awarded the Nobel Prize for Literature in 1923. Published works include 'Responsibilities', 'The Tower' and 'The Winding Stair'. This great literary personality played a major part in the establishment of the Abbey Theatre in 1904.

THE WORLD OF MUSIC

Michael William Balfe, (1808-1870). Balfe was famous as a conductor and composer of operas. Works include 'The Bohemian Girl' and 'Il Talismano'.

John Field, (1782-1837). Outstanding as a pianist and romantic composer. His nocturnes are said to have inspired Chopin. Glinka, founder of the Russian school, was taught by Field.

Sir Charles Villiers Stanford, (1852-1924). Composer of opera, songs, symphonies and chamber music.

THE WORLD OF PAINTING

George Barrett, (1732-1784). A founder member of the Royal Academy and landscape painter of note.

Robert Carver, (1750-1791). Carver's work portrays some of the best Irish landscapes of the eighteenth century.

Patrick Vincent Duffy, (1836-1909). Well known for his vivid landscapes.

Nathaniel Hone I, (1718-1784). Portrait painter and a founder member of the Royal Academy, London.

Nathaniel Hone II, (1831-1917). Painter of landscapes and seascapes. Hone II was a member of the Barbizon Group. He was also a founder of the modern school of Irish painting.

Edward Lutterell, (1650-1710). As well as being a painter, Luttrell goes down in the history of Irish art as being one of the earliest exponents of mezzotint engraving.

James Arthur O'Connor, (1791-1841). Landscape painter.

Sir. William Orpen, (1870-1931). Orpen specialised in portrait painting.

Walter Frederick Osborne, (1859-1903). A clear insight into field and street life is made available through the work of Osborne.

Sir Martin Archer Shee, (1869-1950). The work of this portrait artist provides, through his subjects, a unique historical record.

William Sadler, (1782-1839). One of several outstanding landscape painters of the early nineteenth century.

Jack Butler Yeats, (1871-1957). This modern artist painted in a highly original style, his work distinguished by a heavy, unmistakeable texture. His brother was William Butler Yeats.

John Butler Yeats, (1839-1922). Well known as a portrait painter. Father of Jack and William Butler Yeats.

THE WORLD OF MEDICINE AND SCIENCE

Sir Robert Stawell Ball, (1840-1913). Noted astronomer and mathematician.

Abraham Colles, (1773-1843). In the medical world Colles is remembered for 'Colles' Law', 'Colles' fracture' and 'Colles' Fuchsia'.

Sir Dominic Corrigan, (1802-1880). Corrigan specialised in diseases of the aorta. Remembered for 'Corrigan's Disease', 'Corrigan's Pulse'. He also invented 'Corrigan's Button'.

Sir Philip Crampton, (1778-1858). This famous Dublin surgeon played an important role in establishing the fame of the Dublin medical school in the early nineteenth century. He was co-author of a book on bedside teaching with Robert Graves.

George Francis Fitzgerald, (1851-1901). Fitzgerald made a valuable contribution to the study of physics.

Robert Graves, (1796-1853). The concept of bedside teaching was introduced in medical education by Robert Graves. His book 'Clinical Lectures' became an international textbook for medical students.

Sir William Rowan Hamilton, (1805-1865). Hamilton was the discoverer of quaternions. Through his pioneering work he achieved international fame by foreshadowing the quantum theory and later important discoveries in nuclear physics.

Richard Kirwan, (1735-1812). The first systematic textbook in English on mineralogy was written by Kirwan.

Francis Rynd, (1801-1861). A major contribution was made to medical science by Rynd, through his invention of the hypodermic syringe.

George Salmon, (1819-1904). Dublin-born mathematician.

William Stokes, (1804-1878). Stokes is remembered for 'Stokes-Adams Syndrome' and 'Cheyne-Stokes Respiration'. He was the author of 'Diseases of the Chest and Diseases of the Heart and Aorta'.

Sir William Wilde, (1815–1876). Wilde was noted as an ophthalmologist, otologist, and archaeologist. In the medical field he is associated with 'Wilde's Incision' and 'Wilde's Cord'. He was Oscar Wilde's father.

THE WORLD OF STAINED GLASS AND SCULPTURE

Stained glass:
Harry Clarke, (1889-1931).
Michael Healy, (1873-1941).
Evie Hone, (1894-1955).

Sculpture:
John Henry Foley, (1818-1874).
Thomas Kirk, (1777-1845).
Andrew O'Connor, (1874-1941).
Edward Smyth, (1749-1812).

Detail from panel, St. Michan's Church.

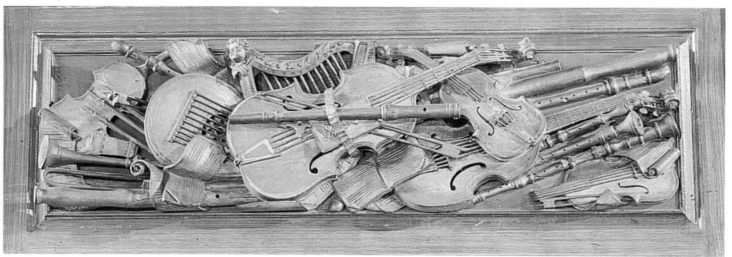

DUBLIN'S PARKS AND GARDENS

Garden of Remembrance
Parnell Square East Dublin 1.
The Garden of Remembrance was designed by Daithí Hanly and is dedicated to the memory of those who died in the cause of Irish freedom. The central theme is peaceful remembrance and reflection, and the sculpture by Oisen Kelly, "Children of Lir" reflects this. The garden is open daily during daylight hours.

36 D1

St. Anne's Park and Gardens
Mount Prospect Avenue, Clontarf.
In a pleasant setting adjacent to Dollymount Strand, the rose gardens in this park cover over three acres alone. The Park and Gardens are open all year round. Admission free. Entrance Howth Road/All Saints Road .

23 A3

Marlay Park
Rathfarnham.
This is the largest park on the south side of the Dublin. It covers three hundred acres in a highly picturesque setting at the foot of the Dublin mountains which is the starting point of the 'Wicklow Way' long distance signposted walk. A craft centre, including workshops, is situated within the area of the park.

51 A2

Merrion Square Park
Merrion Square.
Formerly only for the use of the residents of Merrion Square, this public park is surrounded on all sides by some of Dublin's finest Georgian architecture.

36 E3

National Botanic Gardens

National Botanic Gardens
Botanic Road, Glasnevin.
Covering 19.5 hectares, these beautiful gardens contain a huge assortment of trees, plants and shrubs. Rare blooms and palms are housed in the huge Victorian conservatories. These gardens were founded in 1795 when the estate, on which the gardens now stand, was purchased from the Ticknell family by the Royal Dublin Society.
Visiting times: Monday - Saturday: 9 a.m. – 6 p.m. in summer.
                                    10 a.m. – 4.30 p.m. in winter.
              Sundays: 11 a.m. – 6 p.m. in summer.
                                    11 a.m. – 4.30 p.m. in winter.

              Admission free.

21 A3

Herbert Park
Ballsbridge.
A charming mature park, well laid out with interesting trees, shrubs and flower beds. An attractive feature is the large pond on the eastern side of the park.

36 F4

St. Enda's Park

St. Enda's Park
Grange Road, Rathfarnham.
One of Dublin's most attractive suburban public parks. The park occupies the grounds of St. Enda's, the former school where the patriot Padraic Pearse once taught. The well-restored estate house has been opened as a museum to Pearse's memory.
Visiting hours:

Nov. - January	10 a.m. – 1.00 p.m.	2.00 p.m. – 4.00 p.m.
Feb. - August	10 a.m. – 1.00 p.m.	2.00 p.m. – 5.30 p.m.
Sept. - October	10 a.m. – 1.00 p.m.	2.00 p.m. – 5.00 p.m.

50 F1

St. Stephen's Green
Covering twenty-two acres at the top of Grafton Street, St. Stephen's Green is right in the heart of the city. The varied landscaping of this delightful park includes trees, flower beds, a waterfall and an artificial lake. Several notable monuments and sculptures may also be seen.
Opening Times: During daylight hours.
              Monday to Saturday from 8.00 a.m - 9.00 p.m.
              Sundays and Bank Holidays from 10.00 a.m. *36 D3*

Irish National War Memorial Park.
Islandbridge.
Designed by the English architect Sir Edward Lutyens, these gardens are dedicated to the memory of 49,400 Irish soldiers who died in the First World War. The Gardens are open every day all year round during daylight hours.

35 A2

National War Memorial Gardens,

Phoenix Park

North-western edge of city.

Acknowledged as one of the largest enclosed urban parks in the world, it covers 1,760 acres, with a circumference of seven miles.

Close to the main entrance at Parkgate Street are the People's Gardens and the Zoological Gardens (see separate entry). Within the park are the residence of the President of Ireland (Aras an Uachtarain), the American Ambassador's residence and the Ordnance Survey Office.

In the south-western part of the park is 'The Fifteen Acres', an area of playing fields actually covering two hundred acres. In eighteenth-century Dublin this was used as a duelling ground. During the visit of Pope John Paul II in 1979 it was the site of an outdoor Mass.

Visiting times: Phoenix Park is open to the public at all times but the People's Gardens have their own opening times.

Monday - Friday:	8.30 a.m. - 9.00 p.m.	in summer.
	8.30 a.m. - 4.00 p.m.	in winter.
Saturday - Sunday:	10.00 a.m. - 9.00 p.m.	in summer.
	10.30 a.m. - 4.00 p.m.	in winter.

Admission free.   *35 B2*

Zoological Gardens

Phoenix Park

In these outstanding attractive gardens may be seen a large collection of wild animals and birds from all over the world. Spacious houses and outdoor enclosures add to the total effect. Lion breeding has a long and distinguished history at Dublin Zoo. Two natural lakes house pelicans, flamingoes, ducks and geese.

Visiting hours:	Weekdays	9.30 a.m. – 6 p.m.
	Sundays	10.30 a.m. – 6 p.m.
	Last admission 5.00 p.m. daily.	
	Gardens close at sunset in winter.	

35 A1

Other public parks

Most notable are Corkagh Demesne in Clondalkin, Palmerston Park Dartry, Bushy Park, Terenure, Mountjoy Square Park, Griffeen Valley Park in Lucan and Ward River Valley Park, Swords.

Furry Glen, Phoenix Park

Phoenix Monument, Phoenix Park

DUBLIN AS A SPORTING CENTRE

Dublin has facilities for an amazing variety of sports within a comparatively small area. Outstanding events among the city's sporting events are the Dublin Horse Show, held in August, the national hurling and Gaelic football finals in September in Croke Park and the international rugby games held between January and March in Lansdowne Road, while soccer takes place in Dalymount and Tolka Parks.

The following is a brief guide to the main facilities in city and suburban areas:

For angling enthusiasts: There is fresh water fishing on the River Liffey for salmon, trout, pike and perch. Trout fishing also available on the Rivers Tolka and Dodder.
Sea fishing is available at Dun Laoghaire to the south and at Howth to the north of the city. Fishing permits and bait for sea fishing are obtainable from Dublin fishing tackle shops.

For bowling enthusiasts: There are bowling greens at Herbert Park, Ballsbridge and Willie Pearse Memorial Park, Crumlin. Open 10 a.m. to dusk Monday to Sunday. Nominal fee. Bowling shoes essential. Facilities also at Clontarf Golf Club and Moran Park, Dun Laoghaire.

For golfers: Golfers are well catered for with over 25 G.U.I. affiliated courses (including the internationally renowned Portmarnock links) within a short distance of the city centre. A number of both private and municipal courses also exist. It is advisable to check in advance with the course as green fees and availability of tee time can vary. Generally mid-week is best for visitors. Some clubs have golf clubs and equipment for hire. There are also a number of both par 3 golf and pitch and putt courses throughout Dublin City and district.

For greyhound racing enthusiasts: Racing is held at Shelbourne Greyhound Stadium, Ringsend, on Wednesday, Thursday and Saturday at 8p.m.. Also at Harold's Cross Stadium on Monday, Tuesday and Friday at 8 p.m.

For rowing enthusiasts: The headquarters of most Dublin rowing clubs is at Islandbridge on the River Liffey. This is north of Kilmainham.

For swimmers: Just outside the city area there are beaches at Dollymount to the north and at Sandymount and Merrion to the south. There are numerous bathing places and public baths along the coast. A number of indoor swimming pools and sauna baths are open to the public in the Dublin area. Full details can be obtained from the Dublin tourist information offices.

For tennis players: In return for a nominal fee there are ample facilities on offer at tennis clubs and public courts around Dublin.
Public courts are open at Herbert Park, Ballsbridge; Bushy Park, Terenure; Ellenfield Park, Whitehall; St. Anne's Estate, Dollymount and Johnstown Park, Finglas. Racket hire is not available at these centres.

DUBLIN *ALIVE ALIVE OH!*

Temple Bar

Temple Bar is situated in the heart of Dublin City on the site of one of the first Celtic and Viking settlements.

The area as it is today is the result of an urban renewal program began in 1991. This project has resulted in a vibrant tourist centre with its cobbled streets lined with ethnic restaurants, pubs, nightclubs and small shops.

Alongside these you will find private and public accommodation and open areas such as **Temple Bar Square** and **Meeting House Square** where free concerts, film shows and festival events are held.

In this mainly pedestrianised area you will find some new cultural centres which cater for all age groups. These include: **The Ark Childrens Cultural Centre; The Viking Museum; Multi-Media Centre; Photographic Centre; Music Centre; The Irish Film Centre** and many small galleries. These compliment the long-standing theatres and galleries - **The Olympia Theatre, The Temple Bar Gallery and Studios and The Project Arts Centre.**

Cabaret fans:

A varied programme of cabaret entertainment is available at several Dublin locations. Details from Dublin tourist information offices.

Cinema-goers:

Dubliners are well-known as regular cinema-goers, so the city is well provided with cinemas. O'Connell Street has the Savoy Cinemas 1 to 6. The Ambassador Cinema is in Parnell Street, the Screen Cinema in Townsend Street and a Multiscreen cinema in Parnell Street. More cinemas are located in the suburbs. Full details are published in the evening newspapers.

Night-time revellers:

Ballad singing, jazz, dancing and a host of other musical entertainment is available in pubs, restaurants, hotels and night clubs. Details are published in the evening newspapers.

Outdoor types:

During July and August there are special concerts with an Irish flavour in St. Stephen's Green, as well as regular band recitals in other city parks. Detailed guides to what's on in Dublin are obtainable from Dublin tourist information office in Suffolf Street.

Theatre-goers:

There's a wide choice of theatrical entertainment. The Abbey and the Peacock Theatres are in Lower Abbey Street, the Gaiety Theatre is in South King Street, the Eblana Theatre is located under the Central Bus Station at Store Street, the Gate Theatre is in Parnell Square, the Olympia Theatre is in Dame Street and the Project Arts Centre is located in East Essex Street. Andrews Lane Theatre, Andrews Lane, Tivoli Theatre, Francis St. Also National Concert Hall, Earlsfort Terrace.

Banking Hours:

Monday to Friday 10a.m. - 4p.m.

Most Dublin branches are open until 5p.m. on Thursday. Closed Saturdays, Sundays and Public Holidays.

Dublin Airport Bank open every day for foreign exchange.

Departures:	Sunday to Thursday	5.30 a.m. - 9.00 p.m.
	Friday	6.00 a.m. - 11.00 p.m.
	Saturday	5.30 a.m. - 12 noon
Arrivals:	Monday - Saturday	6.00 a.m. - 10.30 p.m.
	Sunday	6.00 a.m. - 11.30 p.m.

Shopping Hours:

Generally speaking shops are open Monday to Saturday from 9a.m. - 5.30 or 6p.m. Closed all day Sundays and Bank holidays. Shopping centres and some retail outlets remain open until 9p.m. on Wednesday, Thursday and Friday with some opening for a limited period on Sunday.

Apostolic Nunciature
183 Navan Road
Dublin
Tel: 838 0577

20 D4

Argentine Embassy
15 Ailesbury Drive
Dublin 4
Tel: 269 1546
44 D1

Australian Embassy
2nd Floor,
Fitzwilton House
Wilton Terrace, Dublin 2
Tel: 676 1517
36 E4

Austrian Embassy
15 Ailesbury Court Apts.
93 Ailesbury Road
Dublin 4
Tel: 269 4577 / 269 1451
44 D1

Belgian Embassy
2 Shrewsbury Road
Dublin 4
Tel: 269 2082 / 269 1588
44 D1

**Embassy of the
Federative Republic
of Brazil**
Europa House
Harcourt Court
Harcourt Street, Dublin 2.
Tel: 475 6000
36 D4

British Embassy
29 Merrion Road
Dublin 4
Tel: 205 3700
44 D1

Bulgarian Embassy
22 Burlington Road
Dublin 4
Tel: 660 3293
36 E4

Canadian Embassy
4th Floor
65/68 St. Stephen's
Green South
Dublin 2
Tel: 478 1988
36 E3

**Embassy of the
People's Republic
of China**
40 and 77 Ailesbury Road
Dublin 4
Tel: 269 1707 / 269 6756
44 D1

Embassy of Cyprus
71 Lower Leeson Street
Dublin 2
Tel: 676 3060
36 E3

Czech Embassy
57
Northumberland Road
Dublin 4
Tel: 688 1135 / 668 1343
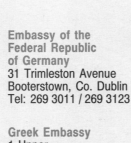
36 F4

**Royal Danish
Embassy**
121/122
St. Stephen's
Green West,
Dublin 2
Tel: 475 6404 / 475 6405
36 D3

**Embassy of the
Arab Republic
of Egypt**
12 Clyde Road
Ballsbridge, Dublin 4
Tel: 660 6566 / 660 6718

36 F4

Estonia Embassy
24 Merlyn Park
Dublin 4
Tel: 269 1552

44 D1

Finnish Embassy
Russell House
Stokes Place
St. Stephen's Green South
Dublin 2
Tel: 478 1344
36 D3

French Embassy
36 Ailesbury Road
Dublin 4
Tel: 260 1666
44 D1

**Embassy of the
Federal Republic
of Germany**
31 Trimleston Avenue
Booterstown, Co. Dublin
Tel: 269 3011 / 269 3123
44 E2

Greek Embassy
1 Upper
Pembroke Street
Dublin 2
Tel: 676 7254 / 676 7255
36 E3

**Embassy of the
Republic of Hungary**
2 Fitzwilliam Place
Dublin 2
Tel: 661 2902 / 661 2905
36 E4

Indian Embassy
6 Leeson Park
Dublin 6
Tel: 497 0843 / 496 6792
/ 496 6787

36 E4

**Embassy of the
Islamic Republic
of Iran**
72 Mount Merrion Avenue
Blackrock, Co. Dublin
Tel: 288 0252 / 288 2967
/ 288 5881

44 F3

Israel Embassy
122 Pembroke Road
Dublin 8
Tel: 668 0303

36 F4

Italian Embassy
63/65
Northumberland Road
Ballsbridge, Dublin 4
Tel: 660 1744

36 F4

Japanese Embassy
Nutley Building
Merrion Centre
Nutley Lane, Dublin 4
Tel: 269 4244 / 269 4033

44 E1

**Embassy of the
Republic of Korea**
20 Clyde Road
Ballsbridge, Dublin 4
Tel: 660 8800

36 F4

Mexican Embassy
43 Ailesbury Road
Dublin 4
Tel: 260 0699

44 D1

**Embassy of the
Kingdom of Morocco**
53 Raglan Road
Dublin 4
Tel: 660 9449
36 F4

Netherlands Embassy
160 Merrion Road
Dublin 4
Tel: 269 3444
44 D1

**Embassy of the
Federal Republic
of Nigeria**
56 Leeson Park
Dublin 6
Tel: 660 4366 / 660 4051
36 E4

**Royal Norwegian
Embassy**
Hainault House
34 Molesworth Street,
Dublin 2
Tel: 662 1800
36 E3

**Embassy of the
Republic of Poland**
5 Ailesbury Road
Dublin 4
Tel: 283 0855
44 D1

Portuguese Embassy
Knocksinna House
Knocksinna Road
Foxrock, Dublin 18
Tel: 289 4416

53 A2

Embassy of Romania
47 Ailesbury Road
Dublin 4
Tel: 269 2852

44 D1

**Embassy of the
Russian Federation**
184/186 Orwell Road
Rathgar, Dublin 14
Tel: 492 3525(Embassy)
Tel: 492 2048(Dip. Consul)
492 3492 (Consular Section)
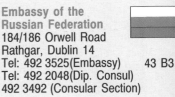
43 B3

Embassy of the Slovak Republic
47 Clyde Road
Dublin 4
Tel: 660 0008
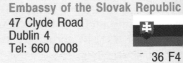
36 F4

**Embassy of
South Africa**
Alexandra House,
Earlsfort Centre,
Earlsfort Terrace, Dublin 2
Tel: 661 5553
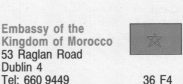
36 E3

Spanish Embassy
17A Merlyn Park
Dublin 4
Tel: 269 1640 / 269 2597

44 E1

Swedish Embassy
Sun Alliance House
13-17 Dawson Street
Dublin 2
Tel: 671 5822

36 E3

Swiss Embassy
6 Ailesbury Road
Ballsbridge
Dublin 4
Tel: 218 6382

44 D1

**Embassy of the
Republic of Turkey**
11 Clyde Road
Ballsbridge, Dublin 4
Tel: 668 5240

36 F4

**Embassy of the
United States
of America**
42 Elgin Road
Ballsbridge, Dublin 4
Tel: 668 8777
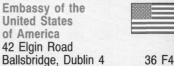
36 F4

*This list contains only those Embassies in the Republic of Ireland. A full list of
Diplomatic and Consular Missions are contained in all Irish Telephone Directories.*

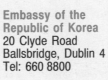
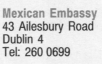

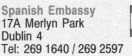

Route Network

Dublin Bus operates the bus network in the greater Dublin area. This network extends from Balbriggan in North County Dublin to Kilcoole in County Wicklow and westwards as far as Kilcock, County Kildare.

Other Services:

In addition to the network described above, Dublin Bus operates the following additional services:

Nitelink – a network of 16 routes radiating from the City Centre which operate every Thursday, Friday and Saturday at 12.30 a.m. and every hour thereafter until 4.30 a.m. - Price £3.00, €3.81. Additional services to Maynooth (Route P) and Balbriggan (Route C) operates at 1.30 a.m. and 3.30 a.m. only Price £4.50, €5.71. A free Shuttle Bus operates every 15 minutes from St. Stephen's Green connecting with the Nitelink services.

Airlink – an Express Bus Service connecting Dublin Airport with Dublin City Centre. The 747 service links Dublin Airport with Bus Aras - Price £3.50, €4.44 . The 748 links Dublin Airport with Heuston Station - Price £3.50, €4.44 .

Private Hire – Double Deck, Single Deck or Minibuses can be hired for group Outings, Parties, Weddings etc.

Sightseeing Tours – Dublin Bus operate a range of tours – see Tours Information section for more details.

Hours of operation

Scheduled services operate from 6.00 a.m. throughout the day with last buses departing the City Centre at around 11.30p.m. In addition to these services a special **Nitelink Network** operates every Thursday, Friday and Saturday night with departures from the City Centre at 12.30 a.m., 1.30 a.m., 2.30 a.m., 3.30 a.m. and 4.30 a.m.

Dublin Bus's Head Office is located at 59 Upper O'Connell Street. Opening hours are from 9.00 a.m. until 5.30 p.m. Monday to Friday and up to 1.00 p.m. on Saturdays. A telephone information service is available on 01-8734222 between 9.00 a.m. and 7.00 p.m. Monday to Saturday.

Timetables are provided on most of the bus stops in the City. In addition, guides and timetables for local areas are available from our Head Offices at 59 Upper O'Connell Street, Dublin 1.

Cash Fares / Autofare System

Fares are charged on the basis of distance travelled and range from 60p €0.76 to £1.30 €1.65 for single journeys. On some longer distance routes, fares of up to £3.50 €4.44 are applicable. Cash fares are paid on entry to the bus. Dublin Bus operates an exact fares system; bank notes can not be accepted.

Autofare - an exact fare system *-how does it work?* Having established the appropriate fare for the journey you propose to take, you insert the exact fare **in coins only** (**bank notes cannot be accepted**) into the top of the fare box. A ticket will then be issued by the ticket machine once the driver is satisfied that the correct fare has been deposited. If you have to deposit more than the exact fare, the driver will issue a passenger change ticket for the overpayment. This passenger change ticket, together with your travel ticket, must be presented at Dublin Bus, 59 Upper O'Connell Street in order to claim a refund of the overpayment.

Prepaid Tickets

Dublin Bus prepaid tickets are available from the Head Office in O'Connell Street as well as from a network of over 270 Ticket Agents throughout the Greater Dublin Area.

2 Easy tickets offer two journeys within 1 month of first validation and are available for adults and school children.

Rambler tickets are also available and offer unlimited bus travel for 1, 3, or 5 days. These Rambler tickets are also valid on the Airlink service.

Transfer 90 Ticket - valid for travel on two bus journeys within 90 minutes of each other inside the Citizone area.

Nitelink tickets - available for single journeys on Dublin Bus Nitelink services.

Bus/Rail Long, Medium and Short Hop Tickets - allows the user to unlimited Bus and Rail/Dart travel within zone.

Tours

Dublin City Hop On Hop Off Tour

The Dublin City Tour is the most popular way for visitors to experience the true delights of Dublin City. This tour allows you the freedom of the city. This 1-hour tour can last all day with buses operating frequently throughout the day. It has 13 specially located bus stops along the route where you are allowed to hop on and off as often as you wish throughout the day to view the Citys major tourist attractions.

Grand Dublin Tour

This tour is the most popular way for visitors to explore Dublin City and the Open Top Bus makes it a dream for the camera enthusiast. This tour takes in some of the citys major tourist attractions. Examples include Trinity College; Guinness Brewery; St. Patricks Cathedral; Christchurch Cathedral and the historic Phoenix Park.

Coast & Castle Tour

Visit the magnificent Malahide Castle set in 250 acres of parkland. View the majestic splendour of Dublin Bay set against the landscape of the Dublin & Wicklow Mountains from the idyllic setting of Howth Summit.

South Coast Tour

Enjoy the elegance of Dun Laoghaires promenade and bustling yacht filled harbour, the charm of Dalkey, panoramic views of Killiney Bay and even more! Return through scenic Dublin and Wicklow Mountains and villages - breathtakingly beautiful.

Ghost Bus Tour

This tour introduces you to the dark romance of a city of gaslight ghosts and chilling legends. You will see haunted houses, learn of Draculas Dublin origins and even a crash course in body snatching. Near journeys end, the lights go out and darkness invites the macabre traditions of the Irish wake. Your host will conclude the tour by explaining the meaning of life and death! Irish style. All tours depart from Dublin Bus's Head Office in 59 O'Connell Street. Prices range from £7.00 €8.89 to £12.00 €15.24 for adults for the above Sightseeing Tours.

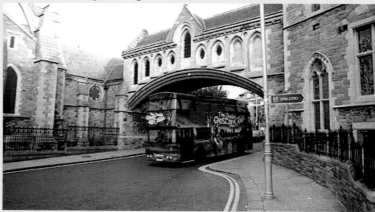

CONTACT DETAILS:
For further information on any of the above,
please contact:- Information Bureau and Customer Service
phone: (01) 873 4222 or visit our Web Site:www.dublinbus.ie

City Centre Termini

Dublin Bus operates the bus network in the greater Dublin area. This network extends from Balbriggan in North County Dublin to Kilcoole in County Wicklow and westwards as far as Kilcock, County Kildare.

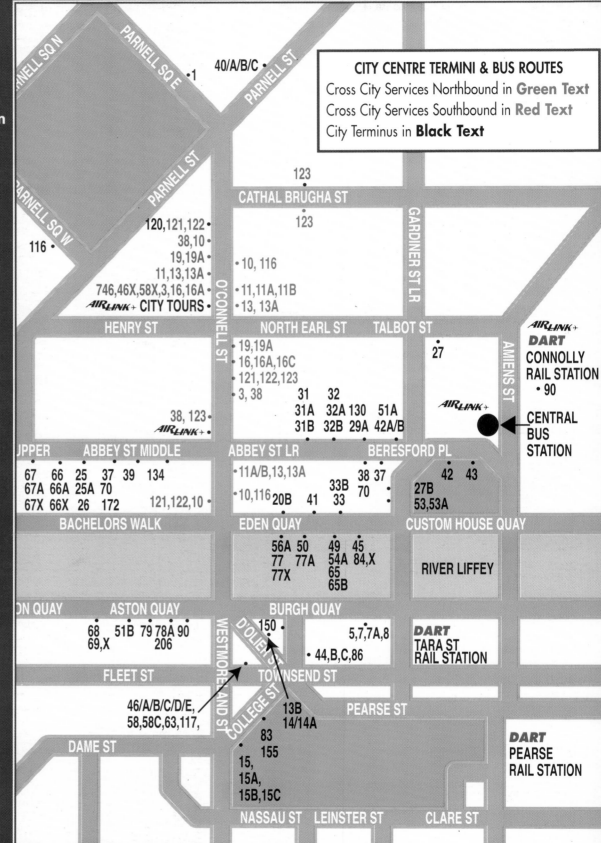

CITY CENTRE TERMINI & BUS ROUTES
Cross City Services Northbound in **Green Text**
Cross City Services Southbound in **Red Text**
City Terminus in **Black Text**

PARNELL SQ N

PARNELL SQ E

PARNELL ST

PARNELL SQ W

• 1

40/A/B/C

123

CATHAL BRUGHA ST

123

116 •

120,121,122
38,10
19,19A
11,13,13A
746,46X,58X,3,16,16A
AIRLINK+ CITY TOURS •

• 10, 116

• 11,11A,11B
• 13, 13A

GARDINER ST LR

HENRY ST

NORTH EARL ST   TALBOT ST

• 19,19A
• 16,16A,16C
• 121,122,123
• 3, 38   31   32
             31A   32A 130   51A
             31B   32B 29A   42A/B

38, 123 •
AIRLINK+

AIRLINK+
DART
CONNOLLY
RAIL STATION
• 90

AMIENS ST

• 27

AIRLINK+

● CENTRAL BUS STATION

UPPER   ABBEY ST MIDDLE

67   66   25   37   39   134
67A   66A 25A 70
67X   66X 26   172   121,122,10 •

ABBEY ST LR   BERESFORD PL

• 11A/B,13,13A

• 10,116 20B   41   33B
                   33
                   38 37
                   70

42   43

27B
53,53A

BACHELORS WALK   EDEN QUAY   CUSTOM HOUSE QUAY

56A 50   49   45
77 77A   54A 84,X
77X   65
          65B

RIVER LIFFEY

ON QUAY   ASTON QUAY   BURGH QUAY

68   51B 79 78A 90
69,X   206

WESTMORELAND ST

D'OLIER ST

150

• 5,7,7A,8

• 44,B,C,86

DART
TARA ST
RAIL STATION

FLEET ST

COLLEGE ST

TOWNSEND ST

13B
14/14A

PEARSE ST

46/A/B/C/D/E,
58,58C,63,117,

• 83

155

DAME ST

15,
15A,
15B,15C

DART
PEARSE
RAIL STATION

NASSAU ST   LEINSTER ST   CLARE ST

Sept. 2000

Dublin Bus

PLACE NAME	SERVED BY BUS NO.
Abbey Pk. (Baldoyle)	32B
Abbey Pk. (Blackrock)	46A, 746
Abbotstown Ave.	40A, 220
Adelaide Rd.	14, 14A, 15, 15A, 15C, 15B, 44, 44B, 44C, 48A
Ailesbury Rd.	3, 5, 7, 7A, 8
Albert Rd.	8, 59
Alexandra Rd.	53A
All Saints' Rd.	29A
Allenton Estate	49A
Amiens St.	20B, 90, 130
Angelsea Rd.	46, 63, 84
Annamoe Rd.	10
Anne Devlin Pk.	15B
Appian Way	11, 11A, 11B, 13B, 18
Ardee St.	50, 56A, 150
Ardlea Rd.	20B, 27B
Artane S.Centre	20B, 103
Artane	27, 42, 42B
Arthur Griffith Pk.(Lucan)	25A
Ashtown	37, 38, 39, 70
Aughrim St.	10, 37, 38, 39
Baggot St.	10, 18
Balbriggan	33
Balbutcher	13, 13A, 220
Baldonnel	68
Baldoyle	32, 32A, 32B, 102
Balgaddy	78A
Balgriffin	42, 43
Ballinclea Rd.	7, 45A, 86
Ballinteer	48A, 75
Ballsbridge	5, 7, 7A, 8, 18, 45
Ballybrack	7, 45A, 46, 111
Ballyboden	15C, 161
Ballybough	51A, 123
Ballydowd	25, 66, 66A, 67, 67A
Ballyfermot	18, 76, 76A, 76B, 78A, 79
Ballygall Rd. East	19, 134
Ballygall Rd. West	17A, 19A, 134, 103
Ballyknockan	65
Ballymore Eustace	65
Ballymount Rd.	56A
Ballymun	13, 13A 17A, 103, 104, 220
Ballymun Rd.	11, 11A, 11B, 13, 19A
Ballyroan	15B
Ballyshannon	27B
Ballywaltrim	145
Balrothery (Tallaght)	65
Baltiboys (Ballyknockan)	65
Bangor Rd.	17, 18, 83, 121
Barnaculla	44B
Barry's Bridge	84,184
Bawnogue	51B, 210
Bawnville Rd.	76B, 77A
Beaumont Ave.(Churchtown)	14, 14A, 16A
Beaumont Rd.(Whitehall)	16, 16A, 16C, 20B, 51A, 103, 104
Beaumont Hospital	27B, 51A, 103, 104
Beechwood Ave.	11, 11A, 11B, 13, 48A
Belcamp Rd.	42
Belfield (U.C.D.)	2, 3, 10, 11, 11B, 17, 46, 46A, 46B
Belgard Rd.	50, 76, 76A, 76B
Belgrave Square	13B, 18
Berkeley Rd.	10, 38, 120
Binn's Bridge	11, 11A, 13, 13A, 16,16A, 16C, 40, 40A, 40B
Bird Ave.	11, 11A, 48A
Biscayne(Malahide)	32A, 42, 102, 230
Blackhall Place	37, 39, 70
Blackhorse Ave.	10, 37
Blackrock	7, 7A, 8, 17, 45, 114
Blakestown	39, 76A, 220
Blanchardstown	38, 39, 70, 76A, 237, 239
Blessington	65
Blessington St.	10, 38, 120
Bluebell	51, 51B, 68, 69
Blunden Drive	42A, 42B
Bohernabreena	49A
Bolbrook	76B, 77A
Booterstown	5, 7, 7A, 8, 45
Botanic Gardens	13, 19, 134
Botanic Rd.	13, 19, 19A, 134
Braemor Rd.	14
Brandon Rd.	122, 123
Bray	45, 45A, 84, 145, 184, 185
Brewery Rd.	46A, 86
Brittas	65
Broadford	48A, 75
Broadstone	19, 19A, 134
Brookfield	56A, 77, 202
Brookwood Ave.	42B, 104
Broombridge Rd.	120
Bulfin Rd.	19,
Bull Wall	130

PLACE NAME	SERVED BY BUS NO.
Burgage	65
Bushy Park	15B
Bushy Pk. Rd.	15C, 16, 16A
Butterfield Ave.	15B, 16, 16A, 17, 75
Cabinteely	45, 46, 84, 86
Cabra	120, 121, 122
Camden St.	16, 16A, 19, 19A, 83, 122,155,
Cappagh Hospital	40A, 220
Cappagh Rd.	40, 40A, 220
Cappaghmore	51
Captain's Rd.	54A, 83, 155
Cardiffsbridge Rd.	40, 220
Carnlough Rd.	120, 121, 122
Carpenterstown	37, 239
Carrickmines	63, 86
Carysfort Ave.	7A, 8, 17, 114
Casement Park	40, 40A
Cashel Rd.	17, 18, 83, 155,
Castle Ave.	29A, 31, 103, 104, 130
Castleknock	37, 38, 237, 239
Castle Lawns	65, 65B, 77A
Castletimon Rd.	27B
Cedarwood Rd.	19, 19A
Celbridge	67, 67A, 67X
Chapelizod	25, 25A, 26, 66, 66A, 66B, 67, 67A
Charlemont St.	44, 48A
Chelmsford Rd.	11, 11A, 13B, 18, 48A
Cherry Orchard	18, 76, 76A, 76B, 78A
Christchurch Place	50, 51B, 54A, 56A, 78A, 123
Churchtown	14, 14A
Church St.	134
Clanbrassil St.	49, 54A
Clogher Rd.	121
Cloghran	33, 41, 41B, 41C, 230
Clondalkin	51, 51B, 68, 69, 76, 76A, 76B, 210
Clonburris	51, 76, 76A, 76B
Clonee	70
Clonkeen Rd.	45
Clonsilla	39, 39X, 220, 237, 239
Clonskea	11, 11A, 17
Clontarf Castle	130, 103, 104
Clontarf Rd.	103, 104, 130
Cloverhill Rd.	79
Colberts Rd.	50
Coldcut	18, 76, 76A, 76B, 78A
Collinstown	16A, 33, 41, 41B, 41C, 746
Collins Ave.	3, 16, 16A, 20B, 42A, 103
Connolly Station	20B, 90, 130
Conyngham Rd.	25, 25A, 26, 51, 66, 67
Cooldrinagh Rd.	66, 67
Cooley Rd.	18, 50, 56A, 122, 123, 150
Coombe, The	50, 56A, 77, 77A, 150, 210
Coolmine Cross Rd.	39, 76A, 220
Coolock	17A, 27, 42A, 42B
Coolock Lane	16A, 17A, 41, 41B, 746
Corduff	38, 220, 238
Cornelscourt Centre	46, 84, 86, 45
Cowper Rd.	13B
Croke Park	3, 11, 11A, 16, 16A, 51A
Cromcastle Drive	27B, 103, 104
Cromwellsfort Rd.	155
Crooksling	65
Cross Chapel	65
Crumlin Village	17, 18, 150
Crumlin Rd.(Shopping Centre)	50, 56A, 77, 77A, 150, 210
Cushlawn	65B, 201
Dalkey	8
Dalymount Park	10, 19, 19A, 38,120, 121, 122, 134
Danieli Rd.	27, 42, 42B
Darndale	27, 42, 42A, 42B, 43
Dartry Rd.	14A
Deansgrange	45, 46A, 75
Deanstown Ave.	40C, 220
Delgany	184
Distillery Rd.	51A
Dodsboro'	25, 66, 67
Dollymount	130
Dolphin's Barn	17, 19, 50, 56A, 122, 150, 210
Donabate	33B
Donaghies	29A
Donaghmede S.C	29A
Donomore	65
Donnybrook	10, 46, 46A, 46B, 746
Donnycarney	20B, 27, 27B, 42, 42B, 43, 103
Donore Ave.	19, 121, 122
Dorset St.	3, 11, 11A, 13, 13A, 16, 16A, 122, 746
Drimnagh	121, 122, 123
Drimnagh Rd.	18, 50, 56A, 77, 150
Drumcondra	3, 11, 11A, 13A, 16, 16A, 746
Drumfin Rd.	18, 76, 76A, 76B, 78A

PLACE NAME	SERVED BY BUS NO.
Dubber Cross	40B
Dublin Airport	16A,16C, 41, 41B, 41C 230, 746, 747, 748
Dunboyne	70
Dundrum	17, 44, 44B, 44C, 48A, 75
Dungriffin Rd.	31B
Dun Laoghaire(S.C.)	7, 7A, 8, 45A, 46A, 59, 75,111, 746
Dunsink Drive	40C
Earlsfort Terrace	14, 14A, 15, 15A, 15B 15C, 44, 44B, 44C, 48A
East Wall Rd.	53
Edenmore	42A, 42B
Edmonstown	161
Embankment(Tallaght)	65
Enniskerry	44, 185
Errigal Rd.	50, 56A, 123
Exchequer St.	16, 19, 83, 122, 155
Fairview	20B, 29A, 31, 32, 130
Faussagh Ave.	120, 121, 122
Feltrim Lane	43
Fettercairn	56A, 65, 65B, 76, 77, 202
Finglas	17A, 40, 40A, 40B, 40C, 104, 134 220
Finglas South	40A, 40C, 220
Firhouse	49, 49A, 75
Fitzwilliam Sq.	11, 11A, 13B, 46A, 746
Fortfield Rd.	54A
Foster Ave.	11A, 17, 46B
Four Courts	25, 26
Fox & Geese	51, 51B, 68, 69, 210
Foxrock	63, 86
Galtymore Rd.	123
George's St. Sth.	16, 19, 65, 65B, 83, 122, 155
Gilford Rd.	2, 3
Glasanaon Rd.	19, 134
Glassmore	41, 41X
Glasnevin	13, 19, 134
Glasnevin Ave.	13, 13A, 17A, 19, 19A
Glasnevin Cemetery	40, 40A, 40B, 40C
Glasthule	8, 59
Glenageary Rd. Lr.	7, 7A, 45A, 111
Glenamuck	63
Glencullen	44B
Glen O'The Downs(Willow Gr.)	184
Glenview	54A, 65, 65B, 76B
Goatstown	11
Gracefield Rd.	42B
Gracepark Rd.	51A
Grand Canal St.	7, 7A, 8, 45
Grange Rd.(Rathfarnham)	16, 16C, 75
Grange X Rd.(Raheny)	29A
Granville Park	46A, 114, 746
Greencastle Rd.	27
Greenhills Rd.	50, 77
Greenpark(Walkinstown)	15A, 77, 77A
Greystones	84, 184
Griffith Ave.	11, 11A, , 13A,19A
Griffith Ave.(Extension)	40C, 220
Griffith Ave.(Whitehall)	3, 13A, 16,16A, 41, 746
Griffith Ave.(Marino)	20B, 123
Grove Rd.(Finglas)	17A, 19, 19A
Guild St.	53A
Haddington Rd.	7, 7A, 8, 45
Haddon Rd.	103, 104, 130
Halfway House(Walkinstown)	18, 50, 77, 77A, 210
Hanlon's Corner	10, 39, 70
Harcourt St.	14, 14A, 15, 15A, 15B, 15C, 48A
Harrington St.	16, 16A, 19, 122, 155
Hatch St.	14, 14A, 15, 15A, 15B, 15C, 48A
Harmonstown Rd.	42A, 42B
Harold's Cross	16, 16A, 49, 49A, 54A, 155
Hartstown	39, 220
Herbert Pk.	7A, 8, 10, 46A
Herbert St.	3
Heuston Station	25/A/X, 26, 46A/X,51/X,66/A/B/X, 67/A/X, 79, 90, 748
Highfield Rd.	14A, 15A, 15B
Holles St.	5, 7, 7A, 7X, 8, 13, 13A
Hollybank Rd.	3, 11, 11A, 13A, 16, 16A, 41, 41C, 746
Homefarm Rd.	3, 11, 11A, 13A, 16, 16A, 41, 41C, 746
Howth	31, 31B
Howth Rd.	29A, 31, 31A, 32, 32A, 32B
Howth Summit	31B
Hume St.(off St. Stephen's Gr.)	14, 14A, 15, 15A, 15B, 15C, 44, 44B, 44C, 48A
Huntstown	39, 76A, 220
Iona Rd.	13, 13A, 19, 19A, 134
Inchicore	51, 51B, 68, 69
Irishtown	1, 2, 3
Islandbridge	25, 25A, 26, 51, 68, 69

PLACE NAME	SERVED BY BUS NO.
James' St.	51B, 78A, 123
Jamestown Rd.(Finglas)	40B, 104, 220,134
Jamestown Rd.(Inchicore)	51, 51B, 68, 69
Jobstown	50, 65, 65B, 77, 201
Jones Rd.	51A
Kenilworth Park	16, 16A, 18, 49, 49A, 83
Kennelsfort Rd.	26
Kilbarrack	17A, 29A, 31, 31A, 32, 32A, 32B
Kilbarron	27B
Kilcock	66
Kilcoole	84
Kilcross	44, 44B, 44C, 114
Kilcroney	44, 185
Kildare Rd.	121
Kildonan Rd.	17A, 40, 40A
Kill Avenue	46A, 74B
Killester	29A, 31, 31A, 31B, 32, 32A, 32B, 42A, 103
Killester Ave.	27, 27B
Killinarden	50,65, 65B, 77, 201
Killincarrick	84, 184
Killiney	59
Killiney Camp Site	45A
Killiney S.C.	7, 45A, 86
Kill O'The Grange	46A, 746
Kilmacud	5,11, 75, 86
Kilmainham	51B, 78A, 206
Kilmainham Jail	68, 69, 79
Kilmore	27B, 103
Kilnamanagh	50, 51B, 206
Kilternan	44, 63
Kimmage Rd. Lr.	54A, 155
Kimmage Rd. West	15A, 17, 155
Kingswood Heights	56A, 76, 76A, 76B
Kinsealy	42, 43
Kinvara Park	37, 38, 39, 70, 122
Knockmore	65B, 77, 201
Kylemore Rd.	18, 68, 68A, 69, 79
Lady's Well	38, 220, 238
Lakelands Park	15, 15B, 49, 65, 65B
Lamb, The	65
Lambert Estate	14A
Lamb's Cross	44, 44B, 44C
Landscape Rd.	14
Lansdowne Rd.	5, 7, 7A, 8
Larchill	3, 16, 16A, 41, 41B, 41C, 103, 746
Larkhill	
Larkfield Gardens	18, 54A, 83, 155
Laurel Lodge	37, 237, 239
Leeson St.	11, 11A, 13B, 46A, 46B, 746
Leinster Rd.	14, 14A,15, 15A, 15B, 15C, 49, 49A, 83
Leixlip	66, 66A, 66B, 66X
Leonard's Corner	16, 16A, 16C, 19, 19A, 122, 155
Leopardstown Rd	46, 46A, 63, 86, 746
Liam Mellowes Rd.	17A, 40
Limekiln Rd.	15A, 54A, 150
Lissenhall Bridge	33, 33B
Londonbridge Rd	2, 3
Long Mile Rd.	18, 56A, 210
Lord Edward St.	50, 54A, 56A, 150
Loughlinstown	45, 84
Loughshinney	33
Lucan	25, 66, 66A, 67, 67A
Lusk	33
Luttrellstown	239
Macken St.	1, 2, 3
Macroom Rd.	27
Malahide	32A, 42, 102, 230
Malahide Rd.	20B, 27,27B, 42, 42B, 43, 103
Manor St.	37, 39, 70
Marian Park(Baldoyle)	32B
Marian Park(Templeogue)	15B
Marino	123
Marley Grange	16C
Mather Rd. Nth.	11A
Maynooth	66, 67A
Meadow Grove(Churchtown)	14, 14A
Mellowes Rd.	17A, 40
Merchant's Quay	25, 25A, 26, 51B, 79, 90
Merrion Rd.	5, 7, 7A, 8, 45
Merrion Row	10, 11, 13B
Merrion Sq.	5, 7, 7A, 8, 13, 13A, 45
Milltown	44, 44B, 44C, 48A, 86
Milltown Cross	68
Mobhi Rd.	11, 11A, 19A
Monkstown	7A, 8
Morehampton Rd.	10, 46A, 46B, 746
Mt. Jerome Cemetery	16, 16A, 16C, 54A, 155
Mount Merrion	5, 46, 46A, 46B, 63, 746
Mount Merrion Ave.	5, 17
Mt Prospect Ave.	130, 104
Mountown	46A, 746
Mount St.	5, 7, 7A, 8, 45
Mount Anville	11
Mourne Rd.	122
Mulhuddart	38, 220, 238
Murphystown	44
McKee Ave.	134
McKee Rd.	19A
McKelvey Ave.	134
Naas Rd.	18, 51, 51B, 68, 69, 210
National Stadium	19, 122
Navan Rd.	37, 38, 39, 70, 122
Neilstown	51, 76, 76A, 76B, 210
Newcastle(Co. Dublin)	68
Newcastle(Co. Wicklow)	84
Newgrove Cross	29A
Newlands Cross	51, 76, 76A, 76B
Newtown Park Ave	45, 114
Nth. Circular Rd.	10, 38, 120, 121, 122
North Rd. (Finglas)	40A, 134
Northside S.C.	17A, 27, 27B, 42, 42A, 42B, 104
North Strand Rd.	20B, 27, 27B, 31, 31A, 31B, 32, 32A, 32B, 42, 42A, 42B, 43, 130
North Wall	53A
Nutgrove S.C.	16A, 17, 75, 161
Nutley Lane	2, 3, 5, 7, 7A, 8, 46, 46A, 46B, 63, 746
Old Bawn Rd.	49, 49A, 75
Old Cabra Rd.	39, 70
Oldcourt (Bray)	45, 145
Omni Park S.C.	16A,41, 41B, 41C, 103, 104, 746
Orwell Park Estate	54A, 150
Orwell Rd.	14, 14A
Oscar Traynor Rd.	17A, 27, 27B, 104
Oxmanstown Rd.	10
Palmerston Park	13B
Palmerston Rd.	13B
Palmerston	18, 25, 25A, 26, 66, 67, 76A
Parkgate St.	25, 25A, 26, 68, 69
Patrick St.	50, 54A, 56A, 150
Peamount	68
Pearse St.	1, 2, 3
Peck's Lane	37, 38, 39, 70
Pelican House(Mespil Rd.)	10, 11, 11A, 11B
Pembroke Park	10, 46A, 746
Pembroke Rd.	5, 7, 7A, 8, 10, 18
Pembroke St.	10, 11, 11A, 13B, 46A, 46B, 746
Phibsboro	10, 19, 19A, 38, 120, 121, 122, 134
Philipsburgh Ave.	123
Phoenix Park(N.C.R. Gate)	10
Phoenix Park(Parkgate St.)	25, 25A, 26, 66, 66A, 67, 67A, 68, 69
Plunkett Rd.	40, 40A
Poppintree(Ballymun)	13, 13A, 104, 220
Porterstown	239
Portmarnock	32, 32A, 32X, 102, 230
Portrane	33B, 33C
Powerscourt(Enniskerry)	44, 185
Priorswood	27, 42A, 42B
Quarry Rd.	120, 121, 122
Raheen(Tallaght)	56A, 65, 76, 77
Raheny	29A, 31, 31A, 31B, 32, 32A, 32B
Ranelagh	11, 11A, 13B, 18, 48A, 86
Rathbeale	41B
Rathcoole	69
Rathfarnham	15C, 16, 16A, 16C, 17
Rathfarnham S.C.	15B, 16, 75
Rathgar	15A, 15B
Rathmines	14, 14A, 15, 15A, 15B, 15C, 18, 83
Ratoath Rd.	40C, 120, 121, 122
R.D.S. (Ballsbridge)	7, 7A, 8, 18, 45
Rialto	17, 19
Richmond Rd.	3, 11, 11A, 13A, 16, 16A, 746
Ringsend	1, 2, 3
Riverside (Coolock)	27
Rivervalley (Swords)	41C, 230
Robinhood	51, 51B, 68, 69, 210
Rochestown Ave.	7, 45A, 86, 111
Rockbrook	161
Roebuck Rd.	11, 11A, 17
Rolestown	41B
Rowlagh	76, 76A, 76B, 78A
Rush	33
St. Anne's Estate	29A
St. Assam's Ave.	31, 31A, 31B, 32, 32A, 32B
St. Brendan's Cres.	155
St. Maelruan's Park	49, 49A, 75
St. Margaret's Rd.	40A, 134
St. Pappin's Rd.	11
St. Patrick's Coll(Drumcondra)	3, 11, 11A, 13A, 16, 16A, 41, 41B, 41C, 746
St. Peter's Rd.(Walkinstown)	155
St. Stephen's Green	10, 11, 13B, 15, 15A, 15B, 15C
Saggart	69
Sallynoggin	7, 7A, 45A, 111
Sandford Rd.	11, 11A, 48A
Sandycove	8
Sandyford	44
Sandyford Ind. Est.	5, 11, 75, 114
Sandymount Ave.	5, 7, 7A, 8, 18
Sandymount Green	2, 3, 18
Sandymount Tower	2, 3, 18 (Sun)
Santry	16, 16A, 33, 41, 41B,41C, 746
Santry Ave.	17A, 41, 41A, 103, 104
Sarsfield Rd.	78A, 79
Scalp, The	44
Scholarstown	15
Seamount	42
Seskin View Rd.	76B, 77A
Shankill	45, 45A, 46, 84
Shanard Rd.	16
Shanboley Rd.	16, 16A, 103, 104
Shangan	13A
Shanganagh Cliffs Estate	45A
Shanowen Rd.	16
Sheepmoor	39, 76A, 220
Shop River(Enniskerry)	185
Sillogue	13
Skerries	33
Spiddal Park	79
Springfield Estate(Tallaght)	50, 65, 76, 77, 201
Stannaway Rd.	18, 83
Stepaside	44
Stillorgan S.C.	46, 46A, 63, 75, 84, 86, 746
Stradbrook	45
Strand Rd. (Sutton)	31A, 31B
Strand Rd.(Sandymount)	2, 3
Sth. Circular Rd.	16, 16A, 19, 122
Sth. Richmond St.	14, 14A, 15, 15A, 15B, 15C, 83
Suir Rd.	123
Sundrive Rd.	17, 18, 50, 54A, 56A, 83, 150
Sutton Cross	31, 31A, 31B
Swords	33, 41, 41B, 41C, 230
Sycamore Rd.	19A, 104, 220
Sylvan Drive	56A
Tallaght	49, 50, 65, 76, 77, 77A
Templeogue	15B, 49, 65
Templeville Rd.	54A
Terenure	15A, 15B, 16, 16A, 17, 49, 49A
The Rise(Mt. Merrion)	46A, 46B, 746
Thomas St.	51B, 78A, 123
Tibradden	161
Tinode	65
Toberburr	40B
Tolka Estate	19
Tonlegee Rd.	17A, 29A
Tritonville Rd.	2, 3
Tymon North	77A
Valleymount(Ballyknockan)	65
Vernon Ave.	103, 104, 130
Villa Park	37, 38, 39, 70, 122
Wadelai Estate	11
Walkinstown Ave.	18, 56A
Walkinstown Cross	50, 56A, 77, 77A, 155
Waterloo Rd.	10, 18
Willington	54A, 150
Werburg St.	50, 56A, 150
Westland Row Stn.(Pearse Stn)	1, 2, 3, 48A
Wellmount Rd.	40A, 40C
Weston Ave.	14A
West Rd.	53
Wexford St.	16, 16A, 19, 19A, 83, 122, 155
Whitechurch	15C, 116
Whitehall(Drumcondra)	3, 16, 16A, 33, 41, 41B, 41C, 746
Whitehall Rd.(Terenure)	15A
Whitestown	39
Whitworth Rd.	13, 40, 40A, 40B, 40C
Willbrook	15C
Willow Grove	184
Windgates	184
Woodford	51B, 210
Woodlawn(Firhouse)	49, 75
Wyattville Rd.	7, 111
Yellow Walls Rd.	42, 102, 230
Zion Rd.	15C

COLOUR CODES : ■ = Peripheral Service - does not operate via City Centre

Name	Page	Grid Ref	No.
Airport Industrial Estate	10	E4/F4	1
Airton Close	41	A4	2
Airton Road	41	A4	3
Airton Terrace	41	A4	4
Airways Industrial Estate	10	F4	5
Allied Industrial Estate	34	E4	6
Ardee Court	57	B2	7
Ashgrove Industrial Estate	53	C1	8
Avonbeg Industrial Estate	41	B1	9
Baldoyle Industrial Estate	23	C1	10
Balheary Industrial Park	2	D1	11
Ballyboggan Industrial Estate	20	D3	12
Ballycoolin Business Park	8	D4	13
Ballymount Business Park	41	B2	14
Ballymount Cross Ind Estate	41	A2	15
Ballymount Industrial Estate	41	B2	16
Ballymount Industrial Park	41	B2	17
Ballymount Trading Centre	41	B2	18
Ballymun Industrial Estate	10	D4	19
Beechlawn Industrial Complex	41	B2	20
Beechwood Close Industrial Estate	57	C4	21
Belgard Industrial Estate	40	F4	22
Bellevue Industrial Estate	20	E3	23
Benson Street Enterprise Centre	36	F2	24
Blackhorse Industrial Estate	35	B1	25
Blanchardstown Industrial Park	7	C4	26
Bluebell Business Centre	34	E4	27
Bluebell Industrial Estate	34	D4	28
Bracetown Business Park	5	C1	29
Bray Industrial Estate	57	B3	30
Bridgewater Business Centre	35	A2	31
Bridges Industrial Estate	41	A1	32
Broombridge Close	20	E3	33
Broombridge Industrial Estate	20	E3	34
Broomhill Close	41	A4	35
Broomhill Drive	41	A4	36
Broomhill Road	41	A4	37
Broomhill Terrace	41	A4	38
Burton Hall Road	52	E2	39
Carriglea Industrial Estate	41	B1	40
Castleforbes Industrial Estate	36	F2	41
Cherry Orchard Industrial Estate	33	C2/C3	42
Cian Park Industrial Estate	21	B4	43
Citywest Business Campus	39	B4	44
Clondalkin Commercial Park	33	B4	45
Clondalkin Industrial Estate	33	B4	46
Clonshaugh Industrial Estate	11	A4	47
Cloverhill Industrial Estate	33	B4	48
Collinstown Cross	10	F2	49
Collinstown Park	10	F3	50
Cookstown Enterprise Park	40	E4	51
Cookstown Industrial Estate	40	F4	52
Coolmine Industrial Estate	18	D2	53
Coolock Industrial Estate	22	F1	54
Croke Park Industrial Estate	36	E1	55
Crossbeg Industrial Estate	41	A2	56
Crosslands Industrial Park	41	A2	57
Damastown Business Park	6	E3	58
Deans Grange Industrial Estate	53	B1/B2	59
Doyles Industrial Estate	41	B1	60
Dublin Industrial Estate (Glasnevin)	20	E3	61
Dunboyne Industrial Estate	5	B2	62
Dun Laoghaire Industrial Estate	53	B2/C2	63
East Road Industrial Estate	36	F1	64
Elmfield	40	D1	65
Fairdale Industrial Estate	22	D2/E2	66
Feltrim Industrial Estate	2	E3	67
Finches Industrial Park	41	B1	68
Fingal Enterprise Centre	20	E2	69
Gaywood Industrial Estate	7	B3	70
Glen Abbey Complex	40	F4	71
Glen Industrial Centre	20	E3	72
Glen Industrial Estate	20	E3	73
Glenview Industrial Estate	35	B4	74
Glenville Industrial Estate	44	E3	75
Goldenbridge Industrial Estate	34	F3/F4	76
Greenhills Industrial Estate	41	C2	77
Greenmount Industrial Estate	35	C4	78
Grove Industrial Estate	20	E1	79
Grove Industrial Estate (2)	20	E1	80
Harbour Industrial Estate	57	C1	81
Hibernian Industrial Estate	41	A4	82
Hills Industrial Centre	28	D1	83
I.D.A. Centre	36	E1	84
I.D.A. Enterprise Centre	36	F3	85
I.D.A. Industrial Centre	35	C1	86
I.D.A. Small Industries Centre	36	F1	87
I.D.A. Small Industries Centre	11	A4	88
I.D.A. Tallaght Business Park	48	F2	89
Industrial Garden Estate	34	E2	90
Industrial Yarns Complex	57	B1	91
INTEL Collinstown Industrial Park	15	B3	92
Irish Farm Centre	34	E4	93
Jamestown Industrial Estate	34	E4/F4	94
Jamestown Little Industrial Estate	34	E4/F4	95
J.F.K. Avenue	41	A1	96
J.F.K. Drive	41	B1	97
J.F.K. Park	34	D4	98
J.F.K. Road	34	D4	99
KCR Industrial Estate	42	E2	100
Kilbarrack Industrial Estate	23	C1	101
Kylemore Industrial Estate	34	D4	102
Kylemore Park N	34	D3	103
Kylemore Park S	34	D4/E4	104
Kylemore Park W	34	D4	105
Landy's Industrial Estate	50	D1	106
Lansdowne Valley	41	C1	107
Leopardstown Retail Park	52	E2	108
Liberties Craft & Small Industries Centre	35	C3	109
Lilmar Industrial Estate	10	F4	110
Loughlinstown Industrial Estate	56	D1	111
McGarveys Industrial Park	41	B2	112
Metropolitan Industrial Estate	35	A3	113
Monarch Industrial Estate	40	F4	114
Mulcahy Keane Estate	41	C2	115
Newlands Business Park	40	E2	116
Newtown Industrial Estate	11	C4	117
North Richmond Industrial	36	E1	118
Oakfield Industrial Estate	33	A4	119
Old Court Industrial Estate	57	B4	120
Old Sawmills Industrial Estate	41	C2	121
Ossory Business Park & Ind. Est.	36	F1	122
Parkmore Industrial Estate	41	B1	123
Phoenix Industrial Estate	19	B3	124
Pineview Industrial Estate	49	C1	125
Pinewood Close Industrial Estate	57	C4	126
Poppintree Industrial Centre	9	B4	127
Richmond Road Industrial Estate	21	B4	129
Riversdale Industrial Estate	34	E4	130
Robinhood Industrial Estate	41	B1	131
Rohan Industrial Estate	34	F4	132
Rosemount Industrial Park	8	D4	133
St. Joans Industrial Estate	41	A2	134
Sallynoggin Industrial Estate	54	D2	134A
Sandyford Industrial Estate	52	E2	135
Sandyford Office Park	52	E2	136
Sandyford Business Park	52	E2	137
Santry Avenue Industrial Estate	10	E4	138
Santry Hall Industrial Estate	21	B1	139
Seaview Industrial Complex	57	C2	140
Shankill Business Centre	56	E2	141
Shanowen Road	21	B2	142
South County Business	52	F2	143
Stag Industrial Estate	20	E3	34
Stillorgan Industrial Park	52	D2	144
Sunbury Industrial Estate	41	B2	145
Sunshine Industrial Estate	35	A4/B4	146
Swiftbrook Industrial Estate	47	A2	147
Swords Business Park	2	D1	148
Tallaght Enterprise Centre	49	A1	149
The Liffey Enterprise Centre	36	F2	150
Tolka Industrial Park	20	E3	34
Turnpike Industrial Estate	41	A2	151
Unidare Industrial Estate	20	E1	152
Weatherwell Industrial Estate	33	A4	153
West Link Industrial Estate	34	E3	154
Western Industrial Estate (2)	40	F1	156
Western Parkway Business Centre	41	B2	157
White Heather Industrial Estate	35	B4	158
White Swan Business Centre & Industrial Estate	35	C4	159
Whitestown Industrial Estate	48	F1	160
W.I.L. Industrial Complex	20	E1	161
Woodlawn Industrial Estate	10	F3	162

Last updated 1997

Name	Phone Number	Page	Grid Ref.
Beaumont Hospital	809 3000	**22**	D1
Blackrock Clinic	283 2222	**44**	F3
Bloomfield Hospital (Donnybrook)	668 3815	**43**	B1
Bon Secours Private (St. Joseph's Glasnevin)	837 5111	**21**	A3
Cappagh National Orthopaedic (Finglas)	834 1211	**19**	C1
Central Mental Hospital (Dundrum)	298 9266	**43**	C3
Cheeverstown (Templeogue)	490 4681	**42**	D4
Cheery Orchard (Ballyfermot)	626 4702	**33**	C3
Children's Hospital (Temple Street)	874 8763	**36**	D1
City of Dublin Skin and Cancer (Hume Street)	676 6935	**36**	E3
Clonskeagh (Vergemount)	269 7877	**43**	C2
Coombe Women's Hospital (Dolphin's Barn)	408 5200	**35**	C4
Dental Hopstital (Lincoln Place)	612 7200	**36**	E3
Gascoigne Home (Camden Row)	475 3574	**36**	D4
Highfield Hospital (Whitehall)	837 4444	**21**	B3
James Connolly Memorial Hostipal (Blanchardstown)	821 3844	**18**	F1
Leopardstown Park (Foxrock)	295 5055	**52**	E3
Mater Misericordiae (Eccles Street)	803 2000	**36**	D1
Mount Carmel (Braemor Park)	492 2211	**43**	A3
National Maternity (Holles Street)	637 3100	**36**	E3
National Rehabilitation Hospital (Dun Laoighaire)	285 4777	**53**	C2
Orthopaedic Hospital of Ireland (Clontarf)	833 2521	**22**	E4
Our Lady's Hospital for Sick Children (Crumlin)	409 6100	**42**	D1
Our Lady's Hospice (Harold's Cross)	479 2101	**35**	C4
Rotunda (Maternity), (Parnell Street)	873 0700	**36**	D1
Royal City of Dublin (Baggot Street)	668 1577	**36**	F4
Royal Hospital (Donnybrook)	497 2844	**43**	B1
Royal Victoria Eye and Ear (Adelaide Road)	678 5500	**36**	E4
St. Bricin's Military (Infirmary Road)	677 6112	**35**	B2
St. Brigid's Home (Crooksling)	458 2123	**47**	A4
St. Clare's (Griffith Avenue)	837 3617	**21**	A2
St. Edmundsbury Hospital (Lucan)	628 0221	**32**	E1
St. James Hospital (James's Street)	410 3000	**35**	B3
St. John of God (Stillorgan)	288 1781	**52**	F1
St. Joseph's (Clonsilla)	821 7177	**17**	B2
St. Joseph's (Raheny)	847 8433	**23**	A2
St. Luke's (Oakland, Highfield Road)	406 5000	**43**	A2
St. Mary's Orthopaedic (Baldoyle)	832 3056	**13**	A4
St. Mary's Hospital (Phoenix Park)	677 8132	**34**	E2
St. Michael's Hospital (Dun Laoighaire)	280 6901	**46**	D4
St. Patrick's (James Street)	677 5423	**35**	B3
St. Paul's (Beaumont)	837 7673	**21**	C1
St. Vincent's (Elm Park, Merrion Road)	269 4533	**44**	E1
St. Vincent's (Richmond Road)	884 2400	**21**	B4
Simpson's Hospital (Dundrum)	298 4322	**51**	B2
Stewart's Hospital (Palmerston)	626 4444	**33**	C1
Tallaght Hospital	414 2000	**48**	F1
Verville Retreat (Vernon Avenue)	833 2598	**22**	E4

STREET NAME	PAGE/GRID REFERENCE	STREET NAME	PAGE/GRID REFERENCE	STREET NAME	PAGE/GRID REFERENCE	STREET NAME	PAGE/GRID REFERENCE
A		Adare Park	22 E1	Alderwood Park	48 F1	*Appian Close (on Leeson Park)	36 E4
1 Branch Road North	37 A2	Adare Road	22 E1	Alderwood Rise	48 E1	Apples Road	52 D2
1 Branch Road South	37 A2	Addison Place	21 A3 [9]	Alderwood Way	48 F1	Aran Avenue	56 E1
2 Branch Road North	37 B2	Addison Road	21 C4	Aldrin Walk	22 E1	Aran Close	56 E1
2 Branch Road Nth Extension	37 B1	Adelaide Court	36 D4	Alexander Terrace	57 C2 [43]	Aran Drive	56 E1
2 Branch Road South	37 A2	Adelaide Court	36 D4 [57]	Alexander Terrace (North Wall)	36 F2 [11]	Aranleigh Court	50 F1
3 Branch Road South	37 A2	Adelaide Mews	44 E1	Alexandra Quay	37 A2 [2]	Aranleigh Dell	51 A1
4 Branch Road South	37 B2	Adelaide Road	57 C2	Alexandra Quay	37 A2	Aranleigh Gardens	50 F1
Abberley	56 E1	Adelaide Road	54 E1	Alexandra Road	37 A2	Aranleigh Mount	50 F1
Abbey Cottages	36 D2 [43]	(Dun Laoghaire)		Alexandra Road Extension	37 C2	Aranleigh Park	51 A1
Abbey Court	22 E3	Adelaide Road (Leeson Street)	36 D4	Alexandra Terrace (Dundrum)	43 C4	Aranleigh Vale	50 F1
Abbey Court	29 C4	Adelaide Street	46 D4	Alexandra Terrace (Portobello)	36 D4 [45]	Aravon Court	58 D2
Abbey Court (Monkstown)	53 B1 [7]	Adelaide Terrace	54 E1 [28]	Alexandra Terrace (Terenure)	42 F2	Arbour Hill	35 C2
Abbey Drive	20 D3	(Dun Laoghaire)		Alexandra Villas	43 C4 [3]	Arbour Place	35 C2
Abbey Green	29 C4	*Adelaide Terrace	35 B3	Alfie Byrne Road	36 F1	Arbour Terrace	35 B2 [6]
Abbey Lane	29 C4	(off Brookfield Road)		All Saints Drive	23 A3	Arbutus Avenue	35 C4 [8]
Abbey Park (Baldoyle)	23 C1	Adelaide Villas	54 E1 [27]	All Saints Park	23 A3	Arbutus Grove	57 B1 [4]
Abbey Park (Kill o' the Grange)	53 B1	Adelaide Villas	57 C2	All Saints Road	22 F3	Arbutus Place	36 D4 [51]
Abbey Park (Killester)	22 E3	Admiral Park	13 A4	Allen Park Drive	52 E1	Ard Lorcain	52 F1
Abbey Road	53 B1 [8]	Adrian Avenue	42 F1	Allen Park Road	52 E1	Ard Lorcain Villas	52 F1 [2]
Abbey Road	53 B1	Aideen Avenue	42 E2	*Allen Terrace	35 C1	Ard Mhacha	48 F2
Abbey Street (Howth)	26 D1	Aideen Drive	42 E2	(off Avondale Avenue)		Ard Mhuire Park	54 E2
Abbey Street Lower	36 E2	Aideen Place	42 E2	Allenton Avenue	49 A3	Ard Na Greine	43 A3 [11]
Abbey Street Middle	36 D2	Aikenhead Terrace	37 A3	Allenton Crescent	49 A2 [3]	Ard na Mara	3 A3
Abbey Street Old	36 E2 [19]	Ailesbury	21 B1 [1]	Allenton Drive	49 A3	Ard na Meala	10 D4
Abbey Street Upper	36 D2	Ailesbury Drive	44 D1	Allenton Gardens	49 A3	Ard Ri Road	35 C2
Abbey Terrace	26 D1 [11]	Ailesbury Gardens	44 E1	Allenton Green	49 A3	Ard Righ Place	35 C2 [2]
Abbey View	53 B1	Ailesbury Grove (Donnybrook)	44 D1	Allenton Lawns	49 A2	Ardagh Avenue	53 A1
Abbeydale	32 F3	Ailesbury Grove (Dundrum)	51 B1	Allenton Park	49 A2	Ardagh Close	53 A1 [6]
Abbeydale Close	32 F3	*Ailesbury Lane	44 D1	Allenton Road	49 A1 [1]	Ardagh Court	52 F1
Abbeydale Crescent	32 F3	(off Ailesbury Road)		Allenton Way	49 A3	Ardagh Crescent	53 A1
Abbeydale Gardens	32 F3	Ailesbury Lawn	51 B1	Allingham Street	35 C3 [15]	Ardagh Drive	53 A1
Abbeydale Park	32 F3	Ailesbury Mews	44 E1	Alma Park	45 C4 [30]	Ardagh Grove	53 A1
Abbeydale Rise	32 F3	Ailesbury Park	44 E1	Alma Place	45 C4 [14]	Ardagh Park	53 A1
Abbeydale Walk	32 F3	Ailesbury Road	44 D1	Alma Road	45 B4	Ardagh Park Road	53 A1
Abbeyfarm	29 C4	Airfield Court	44 D2	Alma Terrace	43 A1 [13]	Ardagh Road	35 B4
Abbeyfield	22 E3	Airfield Drive	43 B4 [13]	Almeida Avenue	35 B3 [26]	Ardara Avenue	12 D4 [.]
Abbeyfield	43 B2	Airfield Park	44 D2	Almeida Terrace	35 B3 [27]	Ardbeg Crescent	22 E2
Abbeylea Avenue	1 C1	Airfield Road	42 F2	Alone Walk	22 E2	Ardbeg Drive	22 E2
Abbeylea Close	1 C1	Airlie Heights	31 B2	Alpine Heights	40 D1	Ardbeg Park	22 E2
Abbeylea Drive	1 C1	Airton Close	41 A4	Alpine Rise	40 E4	Ardbeg Road	22 E2
Abbeylea Green	1 C1	Airton Road	41 A4	Altadore	54 D2	Ardbrugh Close	54 F2 [31]
Abbeyvale Avenue	1 B1	Airton Terrace	41 A4	Alton Terrace	54 F2	Ardbrugh Road	54 F2
Abbeyvale Close	1 B1	(off Greenhills Rd)		Alverno	37 B1 [1]	Ardbrugh Villas	54 F2 [21]
Abbeyvale Court	1 B1	Albany Avenue	45 B4	Amber Vale	40 E4	Ardcian Park	1 C1
Abbeyvale Crescent	1 B1	Albany Court	56 E1	Amiens Street	36 E2	Ardcollum Avenue	22 E2
Abbeyvale Drive	1 B2	Albany Road	43 B1	Anastasia Lane	54 F2 [3]	Ardee Road	36 D4
Abbeyvale Green	1 B2	Albert Avenue	58 D2	Anglesea Avenue	45 A3	Ardee Row	35 C3 [34]
Abbeyvale Grove	1 B1	Albert College Avenue	21 A2	Anglesea Lane	46 D4 [20]	Ardee Street	35 C3
Abbeyvale Lawn	1 B1	Albert College Crescent	21 A2	Anglesea Park	54 E2	Ardee Street	57 B2
Abbeyvale Place	1 B1	Albert College Drive	21 A2	Anglesea Road	43 C1	Ardeen	31 C2
Abbeyvale Rise	1 B1	Albert College Grove	21 A2	Anglesea Row	36 D2 [7]	Ardeevin Avenue	31 C2
Abbeyvale View	1 B2	Albert College Lawn	21 A2	Anglesea Street	36 D2	Ardeevin Court	31 C2
Abbeyvale Way	1 B2	Albert College Park	21 A2	Ann Devlin Avenue	42 E4	Ardeevin Drive	31 C2
Abbeywood	32 F3	Albert Court	36 F3 [30]	Ann Devlin Drive	42 E4	Ardeevin Road	54 F2
Abbeywood Avenue	32 E3	Albert Court	36 F4	Ann Devlin Park	50 E1	*Ardeevin Terrace	54 F2
Abbeywood Close	32 F3	Albert Court	54 E1	Ann Devlin Road	42 E4	(off Ardeevin Road)	
Abbeywood Court	32 F3	*Albert Court	36 F4	Anna Villa	43 B1	Ardenza Park	45 B3 [3]
Abbeywood Crescent	32 F3	(off Grand Canal St)		Annabeg	54 D4 [1]	Ardenza Terrace	45 B3 [1]
Abbeywood Park	32 F3	Albert Park	54 E1 [3]	Annadale	43 B4 [16]	Ardglas Estate	51 C1
Abbeywood Way	32 F3	Albert Place East	36 F3 [14]	Annadale Avenue	21 C4 [1]	Ardilaun	12 F1
Abbotstown Avenue	19 C2	Albert Place West	36 D4 [15]	Annadale Crescent	21 C3	Ardilaun Road	36 E1 [3]
Abbotstown Drive	20 D2	Albert Road Lower	54 E1	Annadale Drive	21 C3	*Ardilaun Square	36 E1
Abbotstown Road	20 D2	Albert Road Upper	54 E2	Annaly Road	20 F4	(off Sackville Avenue)	
Abercorn Road	36 F2	Albert Terrace	36 D4 [18]	Annamoe Drive	35 C1	Ardilea Downs	44 D4
Abercorn Square	34 F3 [19]	Albert Terrace	46 D4 [27]	Annamoe Parade	35 C1 [2]	Ardlea Road	22 E2
Abercorn Terrace	34 F3 [10]	Albert Walk	57 C2	Annamoe Park	35 C1	Ardlui Park	53 A1
Aberdeen Street	35 B2	Aldborough Parade	36 E1 [17]	Annamoe Road	35 B1	Ardmeen Park	53 A1
Accommodation Road	15 C4	Aldborough Place	36 E1	Annamoe Terrace	35 C1	Ardmore Avenue	35 B1 [4]
Achill Road	21 B3	*Aldborough Square	36 E1	Annaville Avenue	53 A1	Ardmore Close	22 D2
Achill Road	56 E1	(off Aldborough Place)		Annaville Grove	43 C3 [1]	Ardmore Crescent	22 D2
Acorn Drive	51 B1	Aldemere	17 B2	Annaville Park	43 C3	Ardmore Crescent	57 B2
Acorn Road	51 B1	Alden Drive	23 C1	Annaville Terrace	43 C4	Ardmore Drive	22 D1
Acres Road	34 F2	Alden Park	23 C1	Anne Street North	36 D2 [5]	Ardmore Grove	22 D1
Adair	37 A4 [14]	Alden Road	23 C1	Anne Street South	36 D3	Ardmore Lawn	57 B3
*Adair Lane (Dorset Street)	36 D1	Alder Court	4 D4 [1]	Anner Road	35 A3	Ardmore Park	57 B2
*Adair Terrace	36 D1	Alderpark Court	48 F1	Anne's Lane	36 D3 [33]	Ardmore Park (Artane)	22 D2
(on St Joseph's Parade)		Alderwood Avenue	48 E1	Annesley Avenue	36 F1 [9]	Ardmore Park	53 C1
*Adam Court (off Grafton St)	36 D3	Alderwood Close	48 E1	Annesley Bridge Road	36 F1	(Kill o' the Grange)	
Adamstown Road	32 D2	Alderwood Court	48 E1	Annesley Park	43 B1	Ardmore Wood	57 B3
Adare Avenue	22 E1	Alderwood Drive	48 F1	Annesley Place	36 F1	Ardpatrick Road	20 D4
Adare Drive	22 E1	Alderwood Green	48 E1	Annsbrook	43 C2	Ardtona Avenue	43 B4 [6]
Adare Green	22 E1	Alderwood Grove	48 F1	Annville Drive	52 E1	Arena Road	52 E2
		Alderwood Lawn	48 E1	Apollo Way	22 D1	Argyle Road	36 F4

STREET NAME	PAGE/GRID REFERENCE
Arkendale Court	54 E1 [26]
Arkendale Road	54 E1
Arkendale Woods	54 E1 [25]
Arkle Road	52 E2
Arkle Square	52 F2 [6]
Arklow Street	35 B1 [13]
Armagh Road	42 D1
Armstrong Street	35 C4 [37]
*Armstrong Street (off Harold's Cross Road)	35 C4
Armstrong Walk	22 E1
Army Road	35 A2
Arnold Grove	54 D2
Arnold Park	54 D2
Arnott Street	36 D3
Arran Green	57 C2
Arran Quay	35 C2
Arran Quay Terrace	35 C2 [10]
Arran Road	21 B3
Arran Street East	36 D2
Arran Street West	35 C2 [17]
Arranmore Avenue	36 D1 [36]
Arranmore Road	43 C1
Artane	22 E2
Artane Cottages Lower	22 E2 [2]
Artane Cottages Upper	22 E2 [3]
Arthur Griffith Park	32 D3
Arundel	45 B4 [19]
*Asdill's Row (off Temple Bar)	36 D2
Asgard Park	26 D2
Asgard Road	26 D2
*Ash Grove (Meath Street)	35 C3
Ash Park Avenue	32 E3
Ash Park Court	32 E3
Ash Park Grove	32 E2
Ash Park Heath	32 E2
Ash Street	35 C3
Ashberry	32 D3
Ashbrook	19 C3
Ashbrook	22 D4
*Ashbrook Terrace (Ranelagh)	43 B1
*Ashbrook Villas (Ranelagh)	43 B1
Ashbury Park	57 C2
Ashcroft	23 A2
Ashcroft Grove	23 A2
Ashdale Avenue	42 F2
Ashdale Close	2 E3
Ashdale Gardens	42 F2
Ashdale Park	42 F2 [1]
Ashdale Road	42 F2
Ashdale Road (Swords)	2 E3
Ashfield	42 D4
Ashfield Avenue (Clondalkin)	40 F3
Ashfield Avenue (Ranelagh)	43 B1
Ashfield Close (Clondalkin)	40 F3
Ashfield Close (Templeogue)	42 D4
Ashfield Court	7 A4
Ashfield Drive	40 F3
Ashfield Gardens	7 A4
Ashfield Green	6 F4
Ashfield Grove	7 A4
Ashfield Lawn	6 F4
Ashfield Park (Booterstown)	44 E2
Ashfield Park (Clondalkin)	40 F3
Ashfield Park (Mulhuddart)	7 A4
Ashfield Park (Templeogue)	42 D4
Ashfield Park (Terenure)	42 F2
Ashfield Road (Ranelagh)	43 B1
Ashfield Way	6 F4
Ashford Cottages	35 B1 [17]
*Ashford Cottages (off Ross Street)	35 B1
Ashford Place	35 B1 [16]
*Ashford Place (off Ross Street)	35 B1
Ashford Street	35 B1 [10]
Ashgrove	29 C2
Ashgrove (Kill o' the Grange)	53 C1
Ashgrove (Tallaght)	48 E1
Ashgrove Court	51 C1 [8]
Ashgrove Lodge	19 C4 [4]
Ashgrove Terrace	51 C1 [2]
*Ash-Hurst	54 E4
Ashington Avenue	20 D3
Ashington Close	20 D3
Ashington Court	20 D3
Ashington Crescent	19 C3
Ashington Dale	20 D3
Ashington Gardens	20 D3
Ashington Green	20 D3
Ashington Grove	20 D3
Ashington Heath	20 D3
Ashington Mews	20 D3
Ashington Park	20 D3
Ashington Rise	19 C3
Ashlawn	51 C1
Ashlawn Court	57 B2
Ashlawn Park	54 D4
Ashleigh Green	18 F3
Ashleigh Grove	18 F3
Ashleigh Lawn	3 B3
Ashley Avenue	2 D2
Ashley Drive	2 D2
Ashley Grove	2 D2
Ashley Heights	57 B2 [4]
Ashley Rise	4 D4
Ashling Close	35 B4
Ashling Heights	18 E1
Ashmount	7 A4
Ashmount Court	35 A3 [23]
Ashton Avenue	50 D1
Ashton Close	50 D1
Ashton Grove	50 D1
Ashton Lawn	50 D1
Ashton Park	45 B4
Ashton Wood	57 A4
Ashtown	19 C3
Ashtown Gate Road	19 B4
Ashtown Grove	19 C4
Ashtown Road	19 B3
*Ashtown Villas	19 C4
Ashurst	44 E4 [3]
Ashurst	54 E4
Ashwood Avenue	39 C1
Ashwood Close	39 C1
Ashwood Drive	40 D1
Ashwood Lawns	40 D1
Ashwood Park	40 D1
Ashwood Road	40 D1
Ashwood Way	40 D1
*Ashworth Place (off Mount Drumond Avenue)	35 C4
Aspen Drive	2 E3
Aspen Park	2 E3
Aspen Park	53 C1 [11]
Aspen Road	2 E3
Assumpta Park	56 E3
Aston Place	36 D2 [39]
Aston Quay	36 D2
Athgoe Drive	56 E2 [4]
Athgoe Road	56 E2
Atlumney Villas	36 D4 [12]
Atmospheric Road	54 E1 [29]
Aubrey Grove	56 E3
Aubrey Park	56 E3
Auburn Avenue (Cabinteely)	54 D3
Auburn Avenue (Castleknock)	19 A3
Auburn Avenue (Donnybrook)	43 C1
Auburn Close	19 A3
Auburn Close	54 D3
Auburn Drive (Cabinteely)	54 D3
Auburn Drive (Castleknock)	19 A3
Auburn Green	19 A3
Auburn Grove	3 A3
Auburn Road	54 D3
Auburn Road (Cabinteely)	54 D3 [1]
Auburn Road (Donnybrook)	43 C1 [11]
Auburn Street	36 D1
*Auburn Terrace (Old Kilmainham)	35 B3
Auburn Villas	43 A2
Auburn Villas	57 B2 [1]
Auburn Walk	35 B1 [18]
Aughavannagh Road	35 C4
Aughrim Court	35 C1 [21]
Aughrim Lane	35 C1 [1]
Aughrim Place	35 B1 [8]
Aughrim Street	35 B1
Aughrim Villas	35 B1 [12]
Augustine Villas	57 C2 [30]
Aulden Grange	10 F4
Aungier Lane	36 D3 [23]
Aungier Place	36 D3 [10]
Aungier Street	36 D3
Austin's Cottages	36 F1 [23]
Avalon	53 A3 [3]
Avalon Apts.	25 B1 [2]
Ave Maria Road	35 B3 [18]
Avenue Road	36 D4 [26]
Avila Park	19 C1
Avoca Avenue	44 F4
Avoca Avenue	57 C3
Avoca Hall	45 A4 [10]
Avoca Park	44 F4
Avoca Place	45 A3
Avoca Road	44 F4
Avonbeg Drive	49 A1
Avonbeg Gardens	49 B1
Avonbeg Park	49 A1
Avonbeg Road	49 B1
Avondale	16 D4
Avondale Avenue	35 C1
Avondale Court	54 E1
Avondale Crescent	54 E2
Avondale House	36 E1 [63]
Avondale Lawn	45 A4
Avondale Lawn Extension	45 A4
Avondale Park	57 B3
Avondale Park (Dalkey)	54 E2
Avondale Park (Dun Laoghaire)	45 A4 [1]
Avondale Park (Raheny)	23 A2
Avondale Road (Dalkey)	54 D2
Avondale Road (Phibsborough)	35 C1
Avondale Terrace	41 C2
Avonmore	53 A2
Avonmore Avenue	49 B1 [5]
Avonmore Close	49 B1
Avonmore Drive	49 B1
Avonmore Grove	49 B1
Avonmore Park	49 B1
Avonmore Road	49 B1
Aylesbury (Estate)	49 A2
Ayrefield Avenue	22 F1
Ayrefield Court	22 F1
Ayrefield Drive	22 F1
Ayrefield Grove	22 F1
Ayrefield Park	22 F1 [2]
Ayrefield Place	22 F1
Ayrefield Road	22 F1

B

STREET NAME	PAGE/GRID REFERENCE
Bachelor's Walk	36 D2
Bachelors Way	36 D2 [30]
Back Lane (Baldoyle)	13 A4 [3]
Back Lane (High Street)	36 D3
*Back Lane (off Sandwith St Upr)	36 E3
Back Road	3 B4
Baggot Court	36 E3 [9]
Baggot Lane	36 F4
Baggot Street Lower	36 E3
Baggot Street Upper	36 E4
Baggot Terrace	19 C4 [1]
Baggotrath Place	36 E3 [28]
Bailey Green Road	26 E3
Bailey View	54 F1 [15]
Bailey's Row	36 E1 [11]
Balally Avenue	52 D1
Balally Close	52 D1
Balally Drive	52 D1
Balally Grove	52 D2
Balally Hill	52 D2
Balally Park	52 D1
Balally Road	51 C1
Balally Terrace	52 D2 [1]
Balbutcher Drive	9 C4
Balbutcher Lane	9 C4
Balbutcher Way	9 C4
Balcurris Gardens	10 D4
Balcurris Road	10 D4
Baldoyle	13 A4
Baldoyle Road	24 D1
Balfe Avenue	41 C1
Balfe Gardens	30 D4 [1]
Balfe Road	41 C1
Balfe Road East	42 D1
Balfe Street	36 D3 [29]
Balglass Road	26 D2
Balgriffin	12 D3
Balgriffin Cottages	12 D3
Balgriffin Road	12 D3
Balheary Road	2 D1
Balkill Park	26 D2
Balkill Road	26 D2
Ballawley Court	51 C2
Ballinclea Heights	54 E3
Ballinclea Road	54 D3
Ballinteer	51 B2
Ballinteer Avenue	51 B2
Ballinteer Close	51 B2
Ballinteer Court	51 B2 [2]
Ballinteer Crescent	51 B2
Ballinteer Drive	51 B2
Ballinteer Gardens	51 C2
Ballinteer Grove	51 B2
Ballinteer Park	51 B2
Ballinteer Park	51 B2 [3]
Ballinteer Road	51 C1
Ballintrane Wood	1 C2
Ball's Lane	36 D2 [23]
Ballsbridge	36 F4
Ballsbridge Avenue	37 A4 [26]
Ballsbridge Gardens	37 A4 [25]
Ballsbridge Park	37 A4 [23]
Ballsbridge Terrace	36 F4 [14]
Ballsbridge Wood	36 F4
Ballyboden	50 E1
Ballyboden Crescent	50 E1
Ballyboden Road	50 E1
Ballyboggan Road	20 E3
Ballybough Avenue	36 E1 [42]
Ballybough Court	36 E1 [43]
Ballybough Lane	36 E1 [43]
Ballybough Road	36 E1
Ballybrack	54 E4
Ballybride Road	56 D3
Ballycoolin Road	8 D4
Ballycorus	55 A3
Ballycorus Road	55 A2
Ballycullen Avenue	49 B2
Ballycullen Drive	49 B2
Ballycullen Drive	49 B2
Ballycullen Road	49 C1
Ballycullen View	49 B2
Ballycullen View	49 C2
Ballydowd Grove	32 E1
Ballyfermot	34 D3
Ballyfermot Avenue	34 D3
Ballyfermot Crescent	34 D3
Ballyfermot Drive	34 D3
Ballyfermot Parade	34 D3
Ballyfermot Road	33 C3
Ballyfermot Road	34 D3
Ballygall Avenue	20 E1
Ballygall Crescent	20 E2
Ballygall Parade	20 E2
Ballygall Place	20 E2 [1]
Ballygall Road	20 E2
Ballygall Road East	20 F2
Ballygall Road West	20 E1
Ballygihen Avenue	54 E1
Ballygihen Villas	54 E1 [20]
Ballygoran Court	29 C2
Ballygoran View	29 C2
Ballygorten	29 C2
Ballyhoy Avenue	23 A3
Ballymace Green	42 E4
Ballymadrough Road	2 F1
Ballymakeally Lawns	29 C4
Ballymakealy Crescent	32 F1
Ballymakealy Grove	29 C4
Ballyman Lane	55 C1
Ballyman Road	57 A1
Ballymana	48 E1
Ballymanagin Lane	33 A4 [1]
Ballymorris	57 B4
Ballymoss Parade	52 F2 [5]

STREET NAME	PAGE/GRID REFERENCE	STREET NAME	PAGE/GRID REFERENCE	STREET NAME	PAGE/GRID REFERENCE	STREET NAME	PAGE/GRID REFERENCE
Ballymoss Road	52 E2	Barry Green	20 D1	Beaumont Grove	21 C2	Belclare Avenue	9 C4
Ballymount Cottages	41 A2	Barry Park	20 D1	Beaumont Road	21 C2	Belclare Crescent	9 C4
Ballymount Drive	41 B2	Barry Hall	20 D1	Beaumont Hall	21 C2 [7]	Belclare Drive	9 C4
Ballymount Road	40 F3	Barryscourt Road	22 E1	Beaupark Downs	45 B4 [15]	Belclare Green	9 C4
Ballymount Road Lower	41 B2	Barton Avenue	50 F1	Beauvale Park	22 D2	Belclare Grove	9 C4
Ballymount Road Upper	41 A2	Barton Court	51 A1 [3]	Beaver Close	36 E1 [51]	Belclare Lawns	9 C4
Ballymun	21 A1	Barton Drive	50 F1	Beaver Row	43 C1	Belclare Park	9 C4
Ballymun Road	21 A1	Barton Road East	51 B1	Beaver Street	36 E1	Belclare Terrace	9 C4
Ballyneety Road	34 F3	Barton Road Extension	51 A1	Beckett Way	33 C4	Belclare Way	9 C4
Ballynoe Court	57 B3 [1]	Barton Road West	50 F1	Bedford Court	42 E1 [5]	Belfield Close	43 B3 [8]
Ballyogan Avenue	52 F4	Bartra Rock (Apts.)	54 F1 [18]	*Bedford Lane (off Aston Quay)	36 D2	Belfield Court	44 D2
Ballyogan Close	52 F4	Basin Street Lower	35 B3	Bedford Row (off Aston Quay)	36 D2	Belfield Downs	43 C4
Ballyogan Court	52 F4	Basin Street Upper	35 B3	Beech Drive	51 B1	Belfield Park	44 E3
Ballyogan Crescent	52 F4	*Basin View (off Basin St Upr)	35 B3	Beech Grove (Blackrock)	44 F2	Belgard Close	40 F3 [2]
Ballyogan Drive	52 F4	Baskin Cottages	11 C1	Beech Grove (Lucan)	32 E2	Belgard Green	40 E4
Ballyogan Estate	52 F4	Baskin Lane	11 B1	Beech Hill	43 C2	Belgard Heights	40 F4
Ballyogan Green	52 F4	Bass Place	36 E3 [3]	Beech Hill Avenue	43 C2	Belgard Road	40 E3
Ballyogan Lawn	52 F4	Bath Avenue (Malahide)	3 C2	Beech Hill Crescent	43 C2 [3]	Belgard Square East	48 F1
Ballyogan Park	52 F4 [1]	Bath Avenue (Sandymount)	36 F3	Beech Hill Drive	43 C2	Belgard Square North	48 F1
Ballyogan Road	52 F4 [1]	Bath Avenue Gardens	36 F3	Beech Hill Road	43 C2	Belgard Square South	48 F1
Ballyolaf Manor	51 C1 [6]	Bath Avenue Place	36 F3 [10]	Beech Hill Terrace	43 C2 [4]	Belgard Square West	48 F1
Ballyoulster Park	30 E3	Bath Lane	36 D1 [42]	Beech Hill Villas	43 C2 [2]	Belgrave Avenue	43 B1
Ballyowen Avenue	32 F1	Bath Place	45 A3 [8]	Beech Lawn	51 B1	Belgrave Place (Monkstown)	45 B4 [10]
Ballyowen Court	32 F1	Bath Street	37 A3	Beech Park (Cabinteely)	53 C4	Belgrave Place (Rathmines)	43 A1 [15]
Ballyowen Crescent	32 F1	Bawnlea Avenue	48 D2	Beech Park (Castleknock)	18 F3	Belgrave Road (Monkstown)	45 B4
Ballyowen Drive	32 F1	Bawnlea Close	48 D2	Beech Park (Lucan)	32 E1	Belgrave Road (Rathmines)	43 A1
Ballyowen Green	32 F1	Bawnlea Crescent	48 D2	Beech Park Avenue	19 A3	Belgrave Sq. (Monkstown)	45 B4
Ballyowen Grove	32 F1	Bawnlea Drive	48 D2	(Blanchardstown)		Belgrave Sq. (Rathmines)	43 A1
Ballyowen Lane	32 F1	Bawnlea Green	48 D2	Beech Park Avenue	53 B2	Belgrave Sq. East	43 A1
Ballyowen Lane	32 F2	Bawnogue Cottages	39 C1 [1]	(Deans Grange)		Belgrave Sq. East (Monkstown)	45 B4
Ballyowen Lawn	32 F1	Bawnville Avenue	49 A2	Beech Park Crescent	19 A3 [1]	Belgrave Sq. North	43 A1
Ballyowen View	32 F1	Bawnville Close	49 A2	Beech Park Drive	53 B2	Belgrave Sq. North (Monkstown)	45 B4
Ballyowen Way	32 F1	Bawnville Drive	49 B2	Beech Park Grove	53 B2	Belgrave Sq. South	43 A1
Ballyroan Court	50 D1 [3]	Bawnville Park	49 B2	Beech Park Lawn	19 A3	Belgrave Sq. South (Monkstown)	45 B4
Ballyroan Crescent	50 E1	Bawnville Road	49 A2	Beech Park Road	53 B2	Belgrave Sq. West	43 A1
Ballyroan Heights	50 E1	Baymount Park	23 A4	Beech Road	41 A1	Belgrave Sq. West (Monkstown)	45 B4
Ballyroan Park	50 D1	Bayshore Lane	56 E1	Beech Road	57 B2	Belgrave Terrace	58 D2 [2]
Ballyroan Road	50 E1	Bayside Boulevard North	23 C1	Beech Row	33 A4	Belgrave Terrace (Monkstown)	45 B4
Ballyshannon Avenue	21 C1	Bayside Boulevard South	23 C1	Beech Row	40 D1 [3]	*Belgrave Tce (On Meath Road)	57 C2
Ballyshannon Road	22 D1	Bayside Crescent	23 C1 [1]	Beech Walk	50 E2 [4]	Belgrave Villas	58 D2 [9]
Ballytore Road	42 F3	Bayside Park	23 C1	Beechbrook Grove	12 D4 [4]	*Belgrave Villas (On Meath Road)	57 C2
Ballywaltrim Cottages	57 B4 [1]	Bayside Square East	23 C1	Beechdale	5 B3	Belgrave Villas (Rathmines)	43 B1 [16]
Ballywaltrim Heights	57 B4	Bayside Square North	23 C1	Beechdale Mews	43 B1 [19]	Belgrove Lawn	34 D2
Ballywaltrim Road	57 A4	Bayside Square South	23 C1	Beeches Park	54 E1	Belgrove Park	34 D2
Balnagowan	43 B2 [4]	Bayside Square West	23 C1	Beeches Road	52 D1	Belgrove Road	22 F4
Balrothery Estate	41 B4	Bayside Walk	23 C1	Beechfield Avenue	41 C2	*Bella Avenue (off Bella St)	36 E1
Balscadden Road	26 E1	Bayswater Terrace	54 F1 [7]	Beechfield Close	42 D2	*Bella Place (off Bella St)	36 E1
Bancroft Avenue	49 A1	Bayview	56 E1	Beechfield Haven	56 E2 [3]	Bella Street	36 E1 [27]
Bancroft Close	49 B1	Bayview	57 C2 [51]	Beechfield Manor	56 E2	Belleville Avenue	43 A2
Bancroft Crescent	41 B4	*Bayview (On Seapoint Road)	57 C2	Beechfield Mews	42 D2 [4]	Bellevue	35 C3
Bancroft Grove	49 B1	Bayview Avenue	36 E1	Beechfield Road	41 C2	Bellevue Ave (Merrion)	44 E2
Bancroft Park	49 A1	Bayview Close	56 E1	Beechlawn	44 F3	Bellevue Avenue (Dalkey)	54 E2
Bancroft Road	49 B1	Bayview Court	56 E1	Beechlawn Avenue	22 E1	Bellevue Copse	44 E2
Bangor Drive	35 B4	Bayview Crescent	56 E1	Beechlawn Avenue (Ballinteer)	51 B1	Bellevue Cottages	20 F3 [4]
Bangor Road	42 E1	Bayview Drive	56 E1	Beechlawn Close	22 E1	Bellevue Court	44 E2 [2]
Bankside Cottages	43 B2	Bayview Glade	56 E1 [12]	Beechlawn Green	22 E1	Bellevue Park	44 E2
Bann Road	20 E3	Bayview Grove	56 E1	Beechlawn Grove	22 E1	Bellevue Park Avenue	44 E2
Bannaville	36 D4 [41]	Bayview Lawn	56 E1	Beechlawn Manor	42 F2 [20]	Bellevue Road	54 D2
Bannow Road	20 E4	Beach Avenue	37 A3	Beechlawn Mews	42 F2 [21]	Bellman's Walk	36 F2 [2]
Bantry Road	21 A3	Beach Drive	37 A3	Beechmount Dr. (Windy Arbour)	43 C3	Bell's Lane	36 E3 [30]
Barberstown Lane	1 A4	Beach Park	13 A1	Beechpark Avenue	22 E1	*Belmont	52 F1
Barclay Court	45 A3	Beach Road	37 A3	Beechpark Close	19 A3 [3]	*Belmont	53 A1
Bargy Road	36 F1	Beach View	23 C2	Beechpark Court	22 E1	*Belmont	57 C4
Barnacoille Park	54 F1	*Beacon Hill (off Nerano Road)	54 F2	Beechurst	57 B2	Belmont Avenue	43 C1
Barnamore Crescent	20 D3	Beaconsfield Court	35 A3 [18]	Beechview Court	50 E2 [1]	*Belmont Court (off Belmont Ave)	43 C1
Barnamore Grove	20 D3	Bearna Park	52 D3	Beechwood Avenue Lower	43 B1	Belmont Gardens	43 C1
Barnamore Park	20 D3	Beatty Grove	30 D2	Beechwood Avenue Upper	43 B1	Belmont Green	52 F1
Barnaslingan Lane	55 A3	Beatty Park	30 D3	Beechwood Close	17 C1	Belmont Green	53 A1
Barnhall Drive	30 F1	Beatty's Avenue	36 F4 [8]	Beechwood Close	57 C4	Belmont Grove	52 F1
Barnhill Avenue	54 E2	Beaucourt	21 B3 [4]	Beechwood Court	54 D3	Belmont Lawn	52 F1
Barnhill Cross Road	32 D1	Beaufield Manor	44 E4	Beechwood Downs	17 C1	Belmont Park	23 A2
Barnhill Grove	54 F2 [7]	Beaufield Mews	44 E4 [2]	Beechwood Grove	54 D1 [11]	Belmont Park	43 C1 [3]
Barnhill Lawn	54 E2 [1]	Beaufield Park	44 E4	Beechwood Lawn	54 D1	*Belmont Place	36 E1
Barnhill Park	54 E2 [3]	Beaufort	54 E1 [19]	Beechwood Park (Dun Laoghaire)	54 D1	(off Gardiner St Middle)	
Barnhill Road	54 E2	Beaufort Court	42 F4 [10]	Beechwood Park (Rathmines)	43 B1 [7]	*Belmont Terrace	52 F1
*Barnhill Villas (on Barnhill Rd)	54 F2	Beaufort Downs	42 F4	Beechwood Road	43 B1	(off Stillorgan Road)	
*Barrack Lane (off Irishtown Rd)	37 A3	Beaufort Villas	42 F4 [3]	Beggar's Bush Buildings	36 F3	Belmont Villas	43 C1
Barrett Street	45 C4 [2]	Beaumont	22 D1	Beggars Bush Court	36 F3 [48]	Belton Park Avenue	22 D3
Barron Place	21 A3 [4]	Beaumont Avenue	43 B4	Belcamp Avenue	11 B4	Belton Park Gardens	22 D3
Barrow Road	20 E3	Beaumont Close	43 B4 [3]	Belcamp Crescent	11 B4	Belton Park Road	22 D3
Barrow Street	36 F3	Beaumont Cottages	32 D2	Belcamp Gardens	11 B4	Belton Park Villas	22 D3
Barry Avenue	20 D1	Beaumont Crescent	22 D2	Belcamp Green	11 B4	Belton Terrace	57 C2 [44]
*Barry Close(off Barry Drive)	20 D1	Beaumont Drive	43 B4	Belcamp Grove	11 B4	Belvidere Avenue	36 E1 [19]
Barry Drive	20 D1	Beaumont Gardens	44 F4	Belcamp Lane	11 C4	Belvidere Court	36 D1 [11]

STREET INDEX

STREET NAME	PAGE/GRID REFERENCE	STREET NAME	PAGE/GRID REFERENCE	STREET NAME	PAGE/GRID REFERENCE	STREET NAME	PAGE/GRID REFERENCE
Belvidere Place	36 D1	Birchfield Avenue	43 B4	Boden Dale	50 F1	Brandon Terrace	35 B3 [32]
Belvidere Road	36 E1	Birchfield Court	43 B4	Boden Mill	50 E2	Bray	58 D1
Ben Edar Road	35 B1	Birchfield Heights	43 B4	Boden Park	50 E1	Bray Commons	57 B2
Ben Inagh Park	45 A3 [3]	Birchfield Lawn	43 B4	Boden Wood	42 F4	Bray Head Terrace	57 C3 [20]
Benbulbin Avenue	35 A4	Birchfield Park	43 B4	Boeing Road	10 F4	Bray Road	53 B2
Benbulbin Road	35 A4	Birch's Lane	43 C4	Boghall Road	57 B4	Bray Road	53 C4
Benburb Street	35 C2	Birchview Avenue	41 A4	Bohernabreena Road	49 A3	Bray Southern Cross Route	57 B4
Beneavin Court	20 F2	Birchview Close	41 A4	Bolbrook Avenue	49 B1 [3]	Breakwater Road North	37 B2
Beneavin Drive	20 F2	Birchview Court	41 A4	Bolbrook Close	49 B1 [4]	Breakwater Road South	37 B2
Beneavin Park	20 F1	Birchview Drive	41 A4	Bolbrook Drive	49 B1 [1]	Breffini Terrace	54 E1
Beneavin Road	20 F1	Birchview Heights	41 A4	Bolbrook Grove	49 B1	Breffni Gardens	13 A4 [5]
Bengal Terrace	20 F4 [4]	Birchview Lawn	41 A4	Bolbrook Park	49 B1	Breffni Road	54 E1
Benmadigan Road	35 A4	Birchview Rise	41 A4	Bolbrook Villas	49 B1	Bregia Road	20 F4
Benson Street	36 F2	Birchwood Close	40 E4	Bolton Street	36 D2	Brehon's Chair	51 A3
Bentley Avenue	57 C4 [3]	Birchwood Drive	48 E1	Bond Drive	37 A1	Bremen Avenue	37 A3
Bentley Park	57 C4	Birchwood Heights	48 E1	Bond Road	37 A1	Bremen Grove	37 A3
Bentley Road	57 C4	Bird Avenue	43 C3	Bond Street	35 C3	Bremen Road	37 A3
Bentley Villas	45 C4 [17]	Biscayne	3 C3	Bonham Street	35 C2	Brendan Behan Court	36 E1 [3]
Beresford	21 B3	Bishop Street	36 D3	Boolavogue Road	36 F1 [13]	Brendan Road	43 C1
Beresford Avenue	21 B3	Bisset's Strand	3 B2	Boot Road	40 D2	Brennan's Cottages	36 D4
Beresford Green	21 B3	Black Street	35 B2 [9]	Booterstown	44 E2	(Synge Street)	
Beresford Lane	36 E2 [9]	Blackberry Lane	13 A1	Booterstown Avenue	44 F3	Brennans Parade	58 D2 [14]
Beresford Lawn	21 B3	Blackberry Lane	36 D4 [8]	*Booterstown Grove	44 F2	Brennans Terrace	58 D2 [4]
Beresford Place	36 E2	Blackberry Rise	13 A1	(off Booterstown Avenue)		Brennanstown Road	53 B4
Beresford Street	36 D2	Blackburn Square	42 F4 [15]	Booterstown Park	44 F3	Brennanstown Vale	53 B4
Berkeley Avenue	36 D1 [55]	Blackcourt Road	18 E1	Boroimhe Cedars	1 C3	Brewery Road	52 F2
Berkeley Place	36 D1 [57]	Blackditch Drive	33 C3	Boroimhe Elms	1 C3	Brian Avenue	21 C4
Berkeley Road	36 D1	Blackditch Road	33 C3	Boroimhe Maples	1 C3	Brian Boru Avenue	37 C1
Berkeley Street	36 D1	Blackglen Court	52 D3	Boroimhe Oaks	1 C3	Brian Boru Street	37 C1
Berkeley Terrace	36 F3 [36]	Blackglen Road	51 C3	Boroimhe Pines	1 C3	Brian Road	21 C4
Bernard Curtis House	34 F4 [2]	Blackhall Parade	35 C2 [4]	Boroimhe Poplars	1 C3	Brian Terrace	21 C4
Berryfield	32 D3	Blackhall Place	35 C2	Boroimhe Willows	1 C3	Briansboro Terrace	35 C4 [23]
Berryfield Crescent	20 D2	Blackhall Street	35 C2 [13]	Botanic Avenue	21 A4	Briar Walk	4 D4
Berryfield Drive	20 D2	Blackheath Avenue	22 F4	Botanic Park	21 A4 [14]	Briarfield Grove	23 B1
Berryfield Road	20 D2	Blackheath Court	22 F4	Botanic Road	21 A4	Briarfield Road	23 B2
Berwick Avenue	1 B2	Blackheath Drive	22 E4	Botanic Villas	21 A4 [10]	Briarfield Villas	23 B1
Berwick Court	1 B1	Blackheath Gardens	22 E4	Boundary Road	37 A1	Briarly Court	43 B4 [4]
Berwick Crescent	1 B1	Blackheath Grove	22 E4	Bow Bridge	35 B3	Briarsfield Walk	23 B1 [4]
Berwick Drive	1 B1	Blackheath Park	22 E4	Bow Bridge Place	35 B3	Briarwood Avenue	18 D1
Berwick Grove	1 B1	Blackhorse Avenue	35 B1	Bow Lane East	36 D3 [37]	Briarwood Close	7 A4
Berwick Hall	43 A4	Blackhorse Grove	35 B1	Bow Lane West	35 B3	Briarwood Gardens	18 D1
Berwick Lawn	1 B1	Blackpitts	35 C3	Bow Street	35 C2	Briarwood Green	18 D1
Berwick Place	1 B1	Blackrock	45 A3	Boyne Court	35 C4 [31]	Briarwood Lawn	18 D1
Berwick Rise	1 B2	Blackthorn Avenue	52 E2	Boyne Lane	36 E3 [2]	Briarwood Park	18 D1 [2]
Berwick View	1 B1	Blackthorn Close	4 D4	Boyne Road	20 E3	Briarwood Road	18 D1 [4]
Berwick Walk	1 B2	Blackthorn Close	52 D2 [7]	Boyne Street	36 E3	Brickfield	57 B3
Berwick Way	1 B1	Blackthorn Court	52 D2 [4]	Brabazon Cottages	57 C2 [16]	Brickfield Drive	35 B4
Berystede	36 E4 [25]	Blackthorn Drive	52 D2	Brabazon Place	35 C3 [35]	Brickfield Lane	35 C3 [48]
Bessborough Avenue	36 F1	Blackthorn Green	52 D2 [6]	Brabazon Row	35 C3 [18]	Bride Close	36 D3 [59]
Bessborough Parade	36 D4 [9]	Blackthorn Grove	52 D2 [3]	Brabazon Square	35 C3 [40]	Bride Road	36 D3
Besser Drive	33 B4	Blackthorn Road	52 D2	Brabazon Street	35 C3 [17]	Bride Street	36 D3
Bethany House	37 B4 [4]	Blackwater Road	20 E3	Bracken Drive	4 D4	Bride Street New	36 D3
Bethesda Place	36 D1 [58]	Blackwood Lane	3 C4	Bracken Road	52 D2	Brides Glen	55 C2
Bettyglen	23 B2	*Blakes Villas	35 C1	Brackenbush Park	54 D4	Bridge Street	2 D2
Bettysford	40 E1 [3]	(on Grangegorman Lower)		Brackenbush Road	54 D4	Bridge Street	37 A3
Bettystown Avenue	22 F3	Blakesfield	17 C1	Bracken's Lane	36 E2 [28]	Bridge Street Lower	35 C2
Beverly Avenue	50 D1	Blakestown Cottages	18 D1	Brackenstown Avenue	1 C2	Bridge Street Upper	35 C3
Beverly Court	22 F4	Blakestown Drive	18 D1	Brackenstown Road	1 C2	Bridgefoot Street	35 C2
Beverly Crescent	49 C2	Blakestown Road	18 D1	Braemor Avenue	43 A3	Bridgewater Quay	35 A2
Beverly Downs	49 C2	Blakestown Way	18 D1	Braemor Drive	43 A3	Brighton Avenue	53 A4
Beverly Drive	50 D2	Blanchardstown	18 F2	Braemor Grove	43 A3	Brighton Avenue (Clontarf)	22 D4 [1]
Beverly Green	49 C2	Blanchardstown Bypass	18 F2	Braemor Park	43 A3	Brighton Avenue (Monkstown)	45 B4
Beverly Grove	50 D1	Blanchardstown ByPass	18 F2	Braemor Road	43 A3	Brighton Avenue (Rathgar)	42 F2
Beverly Heights	50 D2	Blanchardstown Road North	7 B4	Braithwaite Street	35 C3	Brighton Cottages	53 A3 [1]
Beverly Lawns	50 D2	Blanchardstown Road South	18 D2	Bramblefield Court	6 F4	Brighton Court	53 A4
Beverly Park	49 C1	Blarney Park	42 E1	Bramblefield Crescent	6 F4	Brighton Gardens	42 F2
Beverly Rise	49 C2	Blessington Court	36 D1 [56]	Bramblefield Drive	6 F4	Brighton Green	42 F2 [1]
Bewley	32 E2	Blessington Lane	36 D1 [53]	Bramblefield Park	6 F4	Brighton Hall	53 A4
Bewley Avenue	32 E2	*Blessington Place	36 D1	Bramblefield View	6 F4	Brighton Lane	45 B4 [22]
Bewley Drive	32 E2	(off St Joseph's Parade)		Bramblefield Walk	6 F4	Brighton Lodge	53 A3 [4]
Bewley Grove	32 E2	Blessington Road	47 C2	Bramley Avenue	18 E3	Brighton Road (Foxrock)	53 A3
Bewley Lawn	32 E2	Blessington Road (Tallaght)	48 D2	Bramley Court	18 E3	Brighton Road (Terenure)	42 F2
Big Lane	30 D3	Blessington Street	36 D1	Bramley Crescent	18 E3	Brighton Square	42 F2
Bigger Road	41 C2	Bloomfield Avenue (Donnybrook)	36 E4	Bramley Garth	18 E3	Brighton Terrace	45 B4 [4]
Binn Eadair View	25 A1	Bloomfield Avenue (Portobello)	36 D4	Bramley Green	18 E3	Brighton Terrace	54 E1 [13]
Birch Avenue	52 D2	Bloomfield Cottages	36 D4 [49]	Bramley Grove	18 E3	(Dun Laoghaire)	
Birch Dale	53 A2 [9]	Bloomfield Park	36 D4 [46]	Bramley Heath	18 E3	Brighton Vale	45 B3
Birch Dale	53 C1 [12]	Bluebell	34 E4	Bramley Park	18 E3	Britain Place	36 D1 [47]
Birch Grove	53 C1	Bluebell Avenue	34 E4	Bramley Road	18 E3	Britain Quay	36 F2
Birchdale Close	2 E3	Bluebell Road	34 E4	Bramley View	18 E3	Broadford Avenue	51 B2
Birchdale Drive	2 E3	Blunden Drive	11 C4	Bramley Walk	18 E3	Broadford Close	51 B2
Birchdale Park	2 F3	Blythe Avenue	36 F2 [4]	Bramley Way	18 E3	Broadford Crescent	51 B2
Birchdale Road	2 E3	*Boardman's Lane	35 C3	Brandon Road	34 F4	Broadford Drive	51 B2
Birches Road	52 D1	(off Cork Street)		Brandon Road	41 C1	Broadford Hill	51 B2

STREET NAME	PAGE/GRID REFERENCE
Broadford Lawn	**51** B2
Broadford Park	**51** B2
Broadford Rise	**51** B2
Broadford Road	**51** B2
Broadford Walk	**51** B2
Broadmeadow	**1** C1
Broadstone Avenue	**36** D1 [68]
*Broadstone Avenue	**36** D1
(off Royal Canal Bank)	
*Broadstone Place	**36** D1
(off Royal Canal Bank)	
Broadway Drive	**18** E2
Broadway Grove	**18** E2
Broadway Park	**18** E2
Broadway Road	**18** E2
Brodin Row	**35** B2 [15]
Brompton Court	**18** E3
Brompton Court	**18** E3
Brompton Green	**18** E2
Brompton Green	**18** E3
Brompton Grove	**18** E3
Brompton Lawn	**18** E2
Brook Court	**45** B4
Brookdale	**49** A2
Brookdale Avenue	**1** B3
Brookdale Close	**1** B2
Brookdale Court	**1** B3
Brookdale Drive	**1** B2
Brookdale Green	**1** B2
Brookdale Grove	**1** B2
Brookdale Lawns	**1** B2
Brookdale Park	**1** B2
Brookdale Road	**1** B2
Brookdale Walk	**1** B2
Brookdale Way	**1** B2
Brookdene	**56** E2
Brookfield	**32** D3
Brookfield	**43** C1 [19]
Brookfield (Blackrock)	**44** F3
Brookfield (Coolock)	**22** F2
Brookfield (Milltown)	**43** B2
Brookfield Avenue	**45** A4
Brookfield Avenue	**58** D3 [4]
Brookfield Court	**42** E2 [6]
Brookfield Estate	**42** E2
Brookfield Green	**42** E2 [5]
Brookfield Place	**45** A4
Brookfield Road (Kilmainham)	**35** B3
Brookfield Road (Tallaght)	**48** D1
Brookfield Street	**35** B3
Brookfield Terrace	**45** A4
Brookhaven Drive	**18** E1
Brookhaven Grove	**18** E1
Brookhaven Lawn	**18** E1
Brookhaven Park	**18** E1
Brookhaven Rise	**18** E1
Brooklands	**44** E1
Brooklawn	**32** D3
Brooklawn (Blackrock)	**44** F3
Brooklawn (Clontarf)	**22** D4
Brooklawn Avenue	**45** B4 [12]
Brooklawn Wood	**45** B4 [13]
Brookmount Avenue	**49** C1
Brookmount Lawns	**49** C1 [1]
Brookpark	**32** D3
Brookstone Lane	**13** A4 [6]
Brookstone Road	**13** A4
Brookvale	**32** D1 [8]
Brookvale Downs	**42** F3
Brookvale Road (Donnybrook)	**43** C1 [8]
Brookvale Road (Rathfarnham)	**42** F3
Brookview Avenue	**48** D1
Brookview Close	**48** D1
Brookview Crescent	**48** D1
Brookview Drive	**48** D1
Brookview Gardens	**48** D1
Brookview Green	**48** D1
Brookview Green	**48** D1
Brookview Grove	**48** D1
Brookview Lawns	**48** D1
Brookview Park	**48** D1
Brookview Rise	**48** D1
Brookview Terrace	**48** D1
Brookview Way	**48** D1

STREET NAME	PAGE/GRID REFERENCE
Brookville	**20** D1
Brookville Crescent	**22** E1 [2]
Brookville Park (Artane)	**22** E2
Brookville Park (Coolock)	**22** E1
Brookville Park (Dean's Grange)	**53** B1
Brookwood	**50** E2
Brookwood Avenue	**22** E2
Brookwood Crescent	**22** F2
Brookwood Drive	**22** E2
Brookwood Glen	**22** F3
Brookwood Grove	**22** E2
Brookwood Heights	**22** F2
Brookwood Lawn	**22** F2
Brookwood Meadow	**22** E2
Brookwood Park	**22** E3
Brookwood Rise	**22** F3
Brookwood Road	**22** E2
Broombridge Road	**20** E4
Broomfield	**3** B4
Broomfield Court	**56** E2
Broomhill Close	**41** A4
Broomhill Drive	**41** A4
Broomhill Road	**41** A4
Broomhill Terrace	**41** A4
(Off Broomhill Road)	
Brown Street North	**35** C2 [5]
Brown Street South	**35** C3
Brunswick Place	**36** F3 [22]
Brunswick Street North	**35** C2
Brunswick Villas (Pearse Street)	**36** E2 [30]
Brusna Cottages	**45** A3 [12]
Buckingham St Lower	**36** E1
Buckingham St Upper	**36** E1
Buckingham Village	**36** E1 [56]
Buckleys Lane	**31** A1
Bulfin Gardens	**35** A3
Bulfin Road	**35** A3
Bull Alley Street	**36** D3
*Bull Lane (Off Main Street)	**57** C2
Bull Wall Cottages	**38** D1
Bullock Steps	**54** F1 [8]
Bunratty Avenue	**22** E1
Bunratty Drive	**22** E1
Bunratty Road	**22** E1
Bunting Road	**41** C1
Burdett Avenue	**54** E1
Burgess Lane	**35** C2 [18]
Burgh Quay	**36** E2
Burke Place	**35** B3 [42]
*Burke Place (off Mount Brown)	**35** B3
Burleigh Court	**36** E4 [34]
Burlington Gardens	**36** E4 [33]
Burlington Road	**36** E4
Burmah Close	**54** F2 [22]
Burnell Park Avenue	**18** E4
Burnell Park Green	**18** E4
Burren Court	**9** C4
*Burris Court (off High Street)	**36** D3
Burrow Court	**13** A1
Burrow Road (Stepaside)	**52** D4
Burrow Road (Sutton)	**25** B1
Burrowfield Road	**24** D1
Burton Hall Avenue	**52** E2
Burton Hall Road	**52** E2
Burton Road	**54** F2
Bushfield Avenue	**43** B1 [8]
Bushfield Park	**40** D3
Bushfield Place	**43** B1 [17]
Bushfield Square	**21** C4 [15]
Bushfield Terrace	**43** B1
Bushy Park Gardens	**42** F3
Bushy Park Road	**42** F3
Buttercup Close	**11** C4
Buttercup Drive	**11** C4
Buttercup Park	**11** C4
Buttercup Park	**11** C4
Buttercup Square	**11** C4
Butterfield Avenue	**42** E4
Butterfield Close	**42** E4
Butterfield Court	**42** F4
Butterfield Crescent	**42** F4
Butterfield Drive	**42** F4
Butterfield Grove	**42** E4
Butterfield Orchard	**42** E4

STREET NAME	PAGE/GRID REFERENCE
Butterfield Park	**42** E4
*Byrne's Cottages (Francis St)	**35** C3
Byrne's Lane (Jervis St)	**36** D2 [31]
*Byrne's Lane (Pearse Sq West)	**36** F2

C

STREET NAME	PAGE/GRID REFERENCE
Cabinteely	**53** C4
Cabinteely Avenue	**53** C3
Cabinteely Bypass	**53** C3
Cabinteely Close	**53** C3
Cabinteely Court	**53** C3 [4]
Cabinteely Court	**53** C3 [5]
Cabinteely Crescent	**53** C3
Cabinteely Drive	**53** C3
Cabinteely Green	**53** C3
Cabinteely Grove	**53** C3
Cabinteely Park	**53** C3 [2]
Cabinteely Way	**53** C3
Cabra Drive	**35** B1
Cabra Grove	**35** C2
Cabra Park	**20** F4
Cabra Road	**35** B1
Cadogan Road	**21** C4
Cairn Court	**10** D4
Cairn Hill	**53** B2
Cairnwood Avenue	**40** E4
Cairnwood Court	**40** E4
Cairnwood Green	**40** E4
Calderwood Avenue	**21** C3
Calderwood Grove	**21** C3 [3]
Calderwood Road	**21** C3
Caledon Court	**36** F1 [25]
Caledon Road	**36** F1
Callary Road	**44** D3
Camac Close	**35** A3 [6]
Camac Court	**35** A3 [10]
Camac Park	**34** E4
Camac Terrace	**35** B3
Camac View (Bow Bridge)	**35** B3
Camaderry Road	**58** D3
Camberley	**43** B4
Camberley Oaks	**43** B4
Cambridge Avenue	**37** A3 [7]
Cambridge Court	**37** A3 [24]
Cambridge Park	**37** A3 [27]
Cambridge Road (Rathmines)	**43** A1
Cambridge Road (Ringsend)	**37** A3
Cambridge Street	**37** A3 [1]
Cambridge Terrace	**45** C4 [24]
(Dun Laoghaire)	
Cambridge Terrace (Ranelagh)	**36** E4 [7]
Cambridge Villas	**43** A1 [16]
Camden Buildings	**36** D3 [54]
Camden Court	**36** D4 [30]
Camden Lock	**36** F3 [39]
Camden Market	**36** D4 [28]
Camden Place	**36** D3
Camden Row	**36** D3
Camden Street Lower	**36** D3
Camden Street Upper	**36** D4
Camden Villas	**36** D3 [22]
Cameron Square	**35** B3 [5]
Cameron Street	**35** C3
Camogie Road	**35** A2
Campbell's Court	**36** D2 [34]
Campbell's Lane	**36** E1 [71]
(off Belvidere Ave)	
Campbell's Row	**36** E1 [69]
(off Portland Street N)	
Campfield Terrace	**51** C1
Canal Road	**36** D4
Canal Terrace	**34** E4
Canal Turn	**33** B4
Cannon Mews East	**36** F3 [47]
Cannon Rock View	**26** E2 [1]
Cannonbrook	**32** D2
Cannonbrook Lawn	**32** D2
Cannonbrook Park	**32** D2
Canon Lillis Avenue	**36** F1
Canon Mooney Gardens	**37** A3 [15]
Canonbrook Avenue	**32** D2
Canonbrook Court	**32** D2
Capel Street	**36** D2
Cappagh Avenue	**20** D1

STREET NAME	PAGE/GRID REFERENCE
Cappagh Drive	**20** D2
Cappagh Green	**20** D1
Cappagh Road	**20** D1
Cappaghmore Estate	**33** A4
Cappoge Cottages	**8** E4
Captain's Avenue	**42** D1
Captain's Drive	**42** D2
Captain's Hill	**16** D4
Captain's Road	**42** D2
Cara Park	**11** B3
Caragh Court	**21** C4 [12]
Caragh Road	**35** B1
Carberry Road	**21** C3
Carbury Place	**45** A3 [20]
Carbury Terrace	**36** F2 [9]
Cardiff Castle Road	**20** D2
Cardiff Lane	**36** F2
Cardiffs Bridge	**20** D3
Cardiffsbridge Avenue	**20** D2
Cardiffsbridge Grove	**20** D1 [1]
Cardiffsbridge Road	**20** D2
Card's Lane (Pearse St)	**36** E2 [13]
Careys Lane	**2** F4
Carfdiff Castle Road	**20** D1
Carleton Road	**21** C4
Carlingford Parade	**36** F3 [4]
Carlingford Road	**21** A4
Carlisle Avenue	**43** B1
Carlisle Street	**36** D4
Carlisle Terrace	**54** D1 [17]
Carlisle Terrace (Malahide)	**3** B3
*Carlisle Terrace (Off N C Rd)	**35** C1
*Carlisle Terrace	**57** C2
(On Seymour Road)	
*Carlisle Terrace (on Tivoli Road)	**54** D1
Carlton Court	**2** D2
Carlton Court	**22** D4
Carlton Terrace	**57** C2 [41]
Carlton Villas	**36** F4 [6]
Carlton Villas	**57** C2 [42]
Carmanhall Road	**52** E2
Carman's Hall	**35** C3
Carna Road	**33** C3
Carndonagh Drive	**23** B1
Carndonagh Lawn	**23** B1
Carndonagh Park	**23** B1
Carndonagh Road	**23** B1
Carne Court	**6** F4
Carnew Street	**35** B1 [9]
Carnlough Road	**20** E4
Caroline Row	**37** A3 [16]
Carpenterstown	**18** D3
Carpenterstown Avenue	**18** E3
Carpenterstown Park East	**18** E3
Carpenterstown Road	**18** E4
Carraig Glen	**53** C4
Carraroe Avenue	**23** A1
Carrick Court	**12** F1
Carrick Lawn	**52** D1 [2]
Carrick Terrace	**35** B3 [29]
Carrickbrack Heath	**25** B2
Carrickbrack Hill	**25** B2
Carrickbrack Lawn	**25** B2
Carrickbrack Park	**25** B2
Carrickbrack Road	**25** B2
Carrickbrennan Lawn	**45** C4
Carrickbrennan Road	**45** C4
Carrickfoyle Terrace	**35** A3 [9]
Carrickhill Close	**4** D4
Carrickhill Drive	**13** A1
Carrickhill Heights	**13** A1
Carrickhill Rise	**4** D4
Carrickhill Road	**13** A1
Carrickhill Road Middle	**13** A1
Carrickhill Road Upper	**3** C4
Carrickhill Walk	**4** D4
Carricklea Court	**53** C1 [14]
Carrickmines	**53** B4
Carrickmines Little	**53** A4
Carrickmines Wood	**53** B4
Carrickmount Avenue	**51** B1
Carrickmount Drive	**51** A1
Carrig Road	**9** C4
Carrigallen Drive	**20** E3

STREET INDEX

STREET NAME	PAGE/GRID REFERENCE
Carrigallen Park	20 E3
Carrigallen Road	20 E3
Carriglea Avenue	49 B2
Carriglea Avenue	53 C2
Carriglea Court	49 B2
Carriglea Downs	53 C2
Carriglea Drive	49 B2
Carriglea Gardens	53 C1
Carriglea Grove	49 B2
Carriglea Rise	49 B2
Carriglea View	49 B2
Carriglea Walk	49 B2
Carrigmore Drive	48 F2
Carrigmore Park	48 F3
Carrigmore Road	48 F2
Carrigwood	49 C2
Carrow Road	34 F4
Carysfort Avenue	45 A4
Carysfort Downs	52 F1
Carysfort Downs	53 A1
Carysfort Drive	54 F1 [1]
Carysfort Grove	53 A1
Carysfort Hall	45 A4
Carysfort Park	45 A4
Carysfort Road	54 F1
Casana View	26 E2
*Casement Close (off Barry Road)	20 D1
Casement Drive	20 D1
Casement Green	20 D1
Casement Grove	20 D1
Casement Park	20 D1
Casement Road	20 D1
Casement Road	20 D2
Casement Villas	53 B1
Cashel Avenue	42 E2
Cashel Road	42 D1
Casimir Avenue	42 F1
*Casimir Court (off Casimir Avenue)	42 F1
Casimir Road	42 F1
Casino Park	22 D3
Casino Road	21 C4
Castaheany	6 E4
Castilla Park	22 F4
Castle Avenue (Clondalkin)	40 E1
Castle Avenue (Clontarf)	22 E4
Castle Avenue (Swords)	2 D2
Castle Close (Clondalkin)	40 E1
Castle Close (Dalkey)	54 F1
Castle Court	42 F4 [1]
Castle Court	43 A4
Castle Court	56 E1
Castle Court (Booterstown)	44 F2
Castle Court (Clontarf)	22 D4
*Castle Court (off Cypress Lawn)	42 D4
Castle Court Dundrum	51 C1 [4]
Castle Cove	3 A2
Castle Cove	54 F2 [32]
Castle Crescent	40 E1 [4]
Castle Down Croft	2 F2
Castle Down Grove	2 F2
Castle Down Road	2 F2
Castle Drive	40 E1
Castle Drive (Swords)	2 D2
Castle Elms	22 E1
Castle Grove (Clondalkin)	40 E1
Castle Grove (Clontarf)	22 E4
Castle Grove (Swords)	2 D2
Castle Lawns	2 F2
Castle Lawns	41 B4
*Castle Market (off Drury St)	36 D3
Castle Park	31 A1
Castle Park	41 B4
Castle Park (Clondalkin)	40 E1
Castle Park (Monkstown)	45 C4
Castle Park (Swords)	2 D2
Castle Park Estate (Tallaght)	49 B1
Castle Place	29 C2
*Castle Place (on Breffni Road)	54 F1
Castle Riada Avenue	32 E3
Castle Riada Crescent	32 E2
Castle Riada Drive	32 E3
Castle Riada Grove	32 E2
Castle Road	22 E4
Castle Road	32 E2
Castle Rosse	12 F4
*Castle Steps (off Castle St)	36 D3
Castle Street	57 C2
Castle Street (Cork Hill)	36 D3 [3]
Castle Street (Dalkey)	54 F2
Castle Terrace	3 B2
*Castle Terrace (off Ulverton Rd)	54 F1
Castle Terrace (Phibsborough Ave)	35 C1 [17]
*Castle Terrace(off Castle St)	57 C2
Castle View	40 E1
Castle Village	29 C2
Castle Village Avenue	29 C2
Castle Village Close	29 C2
Castle Village Court	29 C2
Castle Village Crescent	29 C2
Castle Village Drive	29 C2
Castle Village Lawns	29 C2
Castle Village Park	29 C2
Castle Village Rise	29 C2
Castle Village Walk	29 C2
Castle Village Way	29 C2
Castle Village Woods	29 C2
Castle Villas	54 F2
Castlebrook	51 C1
Castlebyrne Park	45 A4
Castledawson Avenue	44 F3
Castlefarm	1 C1
Castlefarm	56 E3
Castlefield	49 C2
Castlefield Avenue	49 C1
Castlefield Court	17 C2
Castlefield Court	49 C1
Castlefield Drive	49 C2
Castlefield Drive	49 C2
Castlefield Green	49 C2
Castlefield Green	49 C2
Castlefield Grove	49 C2
Castlefield Grove	49 C2
Castlefield Lawn	49 C1
Castlefield Manor	3 B3
Castlefield Manor (Firhouse)	49 C1
Castlefield Park	17 B1
Castlefield Park	49 C2
Castlefield Way	49 C2
Castlefield Woods	17 B1
Castleforbes Road	36 F2
Castlegrange Avenue	2 D1
Castlegrange Close	2 D1
Castlegrange Heights	2 D1
Castlegrange Hill	2 D1
Castlegrange Road	2 D1
Castlegrange Way	2 D1
Castlekevin Road	22 D1
Castleknock	18 F3
Castleknock Avenue	18 F3
Castleknock Brook	18 F3
Castleknock Close	18 E3
Castleknock Court	18 F3 [2]
Castleknock Crescent	18 F3
Castleknock Dale	18 F3
Castleknock Downs	18 E3
Castleknock Drive	18 F3
Castleknock Elms	18 F3
Castleknock Gate	19 B4 [1]
Castleknock Glade	18 F3
Castleknock Grange	18 F3
Castleknock Green	19 A3
Castleknock Grove	18 F3
Castleknock Laurels	18 F3
Castleknock Lodge	19 A4
Castleknock Manor	19 A3 [5]
Castleknock Meadows	18 F3
Castleknock Oaks	18 F3
Castleknock Park	19 A3
Castleknock Parklands	18 F3
Castleknock Rise	18 E3
Castleknock Road	18 F3
Castleknock Road	19 A4
Castleknock Vale	18 F3
Castleknock View	18 F3
Castleknock Walk	18 E3
Castleknock Way	18 F3
Castleknock Wood	18 F3
Castlelands	54 F1 [16]
Castlelands Grove	54 F1 [12]
Castlepark Road	54 E1
Castlerosse Crescent	12 F4
Castlerosse Drive	12 F4
Castlerosse View	12 F4
Castleside Drive	42 F3
Castletimon Avenue	21 C1
Castletimon Drive	21 C1
Castletimon Gardens	21 C1
Castletimon Green	21 C1
Castletimon Park	21 C1
Castletimon Road	21 C1
Castletown	30 F1
Castletown Court	30 D3
Castletown Drive	30 D3
Castletown Grove	30 D3
Castletown Lawn	30 D3
Castleview	5 B3
Castleview	22 E2
Castleview	51 C1 [7]
Castleview Park	3 A3
Castlewood	17 C1
Castlewood Avenue	43 A1
Castlewood Close	43 A1 [24]
*Castlewood Close (on Castlewood Ave)	43 A1
Castlewood Park	43 A1
Castlewood Place	43 A1 [6]
Castlewood Terrace	43 A1 [5]
Cathal Brugha Street	36 D2
Cathedral	36 D2
Cathedral Lane	36 D3 [5]
Cathedral View Court	36 D3 [43]
Cathedral View Walk	36 D3 [44]
*Catherine Court (off William Street N)	36 E1
Catherine Lane	35 C3 [22]
Catherine Street (Swift's Alley)	35 C3 [45]
Cats Ladder	54 F2 [5]
Causeway Road	23 B3
Cavendish Row	36 D1 [21]
Cave's Strand	3 A2
Ceanchor Road	26 D4
*Ceannt Fort (off Mount Brown)	35 B3
Cecil Avenue	22 D4
*Cecilia Street (off Temple Bar)	36 D2
Cedar Avenue	41 A3
Cedar Court	42 F2
Cedar Court	56 D1
Cedar Drive	5 B2
Cedar Drive	33 B2
Cedar Grove	17 C2 [2]
Cedar Hall	43 C1 [16]
Cedar Park	15 C4
Cedar Park	23 A1
Cedar Square	44 F4 [4]
Cedar Walk	23 B2
Cedarmount Road	44 E4
Cedarwood	30 D3
Cedarwood Avenue	20 F1
Cedarwood Close	20 F1
Cedarwood Green	20 F1
Cedarwood Grove	20 F1
Cedarwood Park	20 F1
Cedarwood Rise	20 F1
Cedarwood Road	20 F1
Celbridge	30 D3
Celbridge Abbey	29 C4
Celbridge Road (Leixlip)	30 F2
Celbridge Road (Lucan)	31 A2
*Celestine Avenue (off Dermot O'Hurley Ave)	37 A3
Celtic Park Avenue	21 C2
Celtic Park Road	21 C2
Chalet Gardens	32 E1
Chalfont Avenue	3 B2
Chalfont Park	3 B2
Chalfont Place	3 B2
Chalfont Road	3 A2
*Chamber Court (Chamber St)	35 C3
Chamber Street	35 C3
Champions Avenue	36 E2 [32]
Chancery Lane	36 D3
Chancery Place	36 D2
Chancery Street	36 D2
Chanel Avenue	22 E2
Chanel Grove	22 E1
Chanel Mews	20 D4
Chanel Road	22 E2
*Chapel Avenue (off Bath St)	37 A3
Chapel Lane	57 B1
Chapel Lane (Parnell Street)	36 D2 [13]
Chapel Lane (Swords)	2 D2
Chapel Road	12 D1
Chapelizod	34 E2
Chapelizod Bypass	34 E2
Chapelizod Court	34 E2
Chapelizod Hill Road	34 E2
Chapelizod Road	34 F2
Charlemont	21 C3
Charlemont Avenue	46 D4 [5]
Charlemont Gardens	36 D4 [20]
Charlemont Mall	36 D4
Charlemont Parade	36 E1 [1]
Charlemont Place	36 E4
Charlemont Road	22 D4
Charlemont Street	36 D4
Charlemont Terrace	46 D4 [18]
Charles Lane	36 E1
*Charles Sheils Houses	52 F2
Charles Street Great	36 E1
*Charles Street West (off Ormond Quay Upper)	36 D2
Charleston Avenue	43 B1
Charleston Court Flats	43 B1 [9]
Charleston Road	43 B1
Charleville	43 B4
Charleville Avenue	36 E1
Charleville Close	43 A1
Charleville Mall	36 E1
*Charleville Rd (Phibsborough)	35 C1
Charleville Road (Rathmines)	43 A1
Charleville Terrace (on Charleville Rd)	35 C1
Charlotte Quay	36 F3
Charlotte Terrace	54 F2 [18]
Charlotte Way	36 D4 [32]
Charlton Lawn	44 D4
Charnwood	17 B1
Charnwood	57 C3
*Chatham Court (on Chatham St.)	36 D3
*Chatham Lane (off Chatham St.)	36 D3
Chatham Row	36 D3
Chatham Street	36 D3 [35]
*Chaworth Terrace (Hanbury Lane)	35 C3
Cheeverstown Road	48 D1
Chelmsford Avenue	36 E4 [8]
Chelmsford Lane	43 B1 [15]
Chelmsford Road	43 B1
Chelsea Gardens	22 F4
Cheltenham Place	36 D4 [13]
Cherbury Court	44 F3
Cherbury Gardens	44 F3
Cherbury Mews	44 F3 [4]
Cherbury Park Avenue	32 D2
Cherbury Park Road	32 D2
Cherries Road	52 D2
Cherrington Close	56 E3
Cherrington Drive	56 E3
Cherrington Road	56 E3
Cherry Avenue	18 E3
Cherry Avenue (Swords)	1 C3
Cherry Court	42 F2
Cherry Court	56 D1 [1]
Cherry Drive	18 E3
Cherry Garth	44 E4
Cherry Garth (Swords)	1 B2
Cherry Grove	41 C2
Cherry Grove (Swords)	1 B3
Cherry Lawn	18 E3
Cherry Lawns	31 C2
Cherry Orchard Avenue	33 C3
Cherry Orchard Crescent	33 C4

STREET NAME	PAGE/GRID REFERENCE	STREET NAME	PAGE/GRID REFERENCE	STREET NAME	PAGE/GRID REFERENCE	STREET NAME	PAGE/GRID REFERENCE
Cherry Orchard Drive	33 C4	Church Road (Finglas)	20 D2	Claremount Pines	53 B4	Clonshaugh Avenue	11 A4
Cherry Orchard Drive	34 D3	Church Road (Killiney)	54 D3	Claremount Terrace	58 D2 [11]	Clonshaugh Close	11 B4
Cherry Orchard Green	33 C3	Church Road (Malahide)	3 B3	Clarence Mangan Road	35 C3	Clonshaugh Court	11 B4
Cherry Orchard Grove	33 C4	Church Road (Mulhuddart)	7 A4	*Clarence Mangan Square	36 D3	Clonshaugh Crescent	11 A4
Cherry Park	18 E3	Church Road (Sutton)	25 B1	(off John Dillon St)		Clonshaugh Drive	11 B4
Cherry Park (Swords)	1 B3	Church Street	35 C2	Clarence Place Great	36 F3 [1]	Clonshaugh Green	11 B4
Cherry Tree Drive	57 C3 [1]	Church Street (Finglas)	20 E2	Clarence St Great North	36 E1 [67]	Clonshaugh Grove	11 B4
Cherry Wood	56 D1	Church Street (Howth)	26 D1	Clarence St Great Nth	36 E1	Clonshaugh Heights	11 A4
Cherryfield Avenue	41 C2	Church Street East	36 F2	*Clarendon Market	36 E1	Clonshaugh Lawns	11 B4
Cherryfield Avenue Lr	43 B1	Church Street New	35 C2 [11]	(off William St)		Clonshaugh Meadow	11 A4
Cherryfield Avenue Upr	43 B1	Church Street Upper	35 C2	*Clarendon Row	36 D3	Clonshaugh Park	11 B4
Cherryfield Close	17 B1	Church Terrace	57 C2 [45]	(off King St South)		Clonshaugh Rise	11 B4 [2]
Cherryfield Court	17 B1	*Church Tce (off Church Street)	35 C2	Clarendon Street	36 D3	Clonshaugh Road	11 A4
Cherryfield Drive	41 C2	Church View (Clondalkin)	40 D2 [1]	Clareville Court	20 F4 [7]	Clonshaugh Walk	11 B4
Cherryfield Lawn	17 C1	Church View (Finglas)	20 D2 [7]	Clareville Grove	20 F4	Clonsilla	17 C2
Cherryfield Park	17 C1	Church View (Harold's Cross)	42 F1	Clareville Road	42 F1	Clonsilla Close	18 E2
Cherryfield Road	41 C2	Church Walk	20 D4	Clarinda Manor	46 D4 [22]	Clonsilla Park	18 E2
Cherryfield View	17 B1	Churchfields	43 C2	Clarinda Manor	54 D1	Clonsilla Road	18 E2
Cherryfield Walk	17 B1	Churchgate Avenue	37 C1 [1]	Clarinda Park East	54 D1	Clonskeagh	43 C2
Cherrymount Crescent	22 D3 [1]	Churchill Mews	54 F1 [17]	Clarinda Park North	46 D4	Clonskeagh Drive	43 C2 [6]
Cherrymount Grove	22 D3 [2]	Churchill Terrace	37 A4 [6]	Clarinda Park West	46 D4	Clonskeagh Road	43 C2
Cherrymount Park	35 C1 [3]	Churchtown	43 B4	Clarke Terrace	35 B3 [16]	Clonskeagh Square	43 C2 [7]
Cherrywood	30 D3	Churchtown Avenue	43 B3	Clarkeville Terrace	33 C1 [3]	Clontarf	37 C1
Cherrywood Avenue	40 D1	Churchtown Close	43 B3	Claude Road	21 A4	Clontarf Park	37 C1
Cherrywood Crescent	39 C1	Churchtown Drive	43 B3	Clayton Terrace	34 E2 [8]	Clontarf Road	22 D4
Cherrywood Drive	39 C1	Churchtown Road Lower	43 B3	Cleggan Avenue	33 C3	Clonturk Avenue	21 B3 [1]
Cherrywood Grove	40 D1	Churchtown Road Upper	43 A4	Cleggan Park	33 C3	Clonturk Court	21 B3 [6]
Cherrywood Lawn	39 C2	Churchtown Road Upper	43 B4	Cleggan Road	33 C3	Clonturk Gardens	21 B4 [3]
Cherrywood Park	39 C2	Churchview Avenue	54 D3	Clifden Drive	33 C3	Clonturk Park	21 B4
Cherrywood Park	56 D1	Churchview Drive	54 D3	Clifden Road	34 D3	Cloonlara Crescent	20 E3
Cherrywood Road	56 D2	Churchview Park	54 D3	Cliff Terrace	54 E1 [18]	Cloonlara Drive	20 E2
Cherrywood Villas	40 D1 [6]	Churchview Road	54 D3	Clifton Avenue	45 C4 [11]	Cloonlara Road	20 E2
Cherrywood Villas	40 D1	Cian Park	21 B4	Clifton Lane	45 C4 [10]	Cloonmore Avenue	48 D2
Chester Downs	54 D1	Cianlea	1 B1	Clifton Park	56 E2	Cloonmore Close	48 D2
Chester Road	43 B1	Cill Cais	48 F2	Clifton Terrace	45 C4 [13]	Cloonmore Crescent	48 D2
Chester Square	54 E1 [23]	Cill Eanna	22 F2	Cliftonville Road	21 A4	Cloonmore Drive	48 D2
Chesterfield Avenue	19 B4	Cill Manntan Park	57 C2 [9]	Clinch's Court	36 E1 [7]	Cloonmore Gardens	48 D2
Chesterfield Ave (Phoenix Park)	34 F1	Cill Sarain	57 B3	Clogher Road	42 E1	Cloonmore Green	48 D2
Chesterfield Close	19 B4	City Quay	36 E2	Clogher Road	42 E1	Cloonmore Grove	48 D2
Chesterfield Copse	19 B3	Citywest Road	47 C1	Cloghran	1 C4	Cloonmore Lawn	48 D2
Chesterfield Grove	19 B4	Claddagh Green	33 C3	Cloister Avenue	45 A4	Cloonmore Park	48 D2
Chesterfield Park	19 B3	Claddagh Road	33 C3	Cloister Court	20 D3	Cloonmore Road	48 D2
Chesterfield View	19 B3	Claddagh Terrace	58 D2 [15]	Cloister Gate	45 A4	Cloragh Road	50 E4
Chestnut Court	21 C1 [1]	*Claddagh Tce (On Albert Ave)	57 C2	Cloister Green	45 A4	Clover Hill	57 A3
Chestnut Grove (Ballinteer)	51 B2	Clanawley Road	22 E3	Cloister Grove	45 A4	Clover Hill Drive	34 D3
Chestnut Grove (Celbridge)	30 D3	Clanboy Road	22 E3	Cloister Square	45 A4	Clover Hill Road	34 D4
Chestnut Grove (Clondalkin)	40 F3	Clanbrassil Close	35 C4 [17]	Cloister Way	45 A4	Cloverhill Road	33 A4
Chestnut Grove (Dunboyne)	5 B3	Clanbrassil Street Lower	35 C4	Cloister Way	45 A4	Cloyne Road	42 E1 [1]
Chestnut Park	53 A2 [5]	Clanbrassil Street Upper	35 C4	Clonard Avenue	51 C2	Cluain Mhuire	54 D1
Chestnut Road (Clondalkin)	41 A1	Clancarthy Road	22 D3	Clonard Close	51 C2	Cluain Mhuire	45 B4
Chestnut Road (Mount Merrion)	44 E3	Clancy Avenue	20 E1	Clonard Drive	51 C2	(Newtown Park Avenue)	
Christchurch Place	36 D3	Clancy Road	20 E1	Clonard Grove	51 C2	Cluain Rì	32 F2
Christchurch Square	36 D3 [51]	Clandonagh Road	22 D3	Clonard Lawn	51 C2	Club Road	41 A1
Church Avenue	12 F2 [2]	Clane Road	29 B4	Clonard Park	51 C2	Clune Road	20 E1
Church Ave. (Blanchardstown)	18 F2	Clanfadda Wood	44 F3	Clonard Road (Crumlin)	42 D1	Cluny Grove	54 D3
Church Ave. (Glasnevin)	21 A3 [2]	Clanhugh Road	22 E3	Clonard Road (Sandyford)	51 C2	Cluny Park	54 E2
Church Ave. (Irishtown)	37 A3	Clanmahon Road	22 E3	Clonasleigh	56 E2 [2]	Clyde Lane	36 F4
Church Ave. (Killiney)	54 E4	Clanmaurice Road	22 D3	Clondalkin	40 D1	Clyde Road	36 F4
Church Ave.(Rathmines)	43 A1	Clanmawr	56 E2	Clonee	6 D3	Coast Road	13 A4
Church Ave Nth (Drumcondra)	21 B3	Clanmoyle Road	22 D3	Clonfert Road	42 E1	Coast Road (Malahide)	3 C2
Church Ave Sth (Dolphin's Barn)	35 B3 [22]	Clanranald Road	22 D3	Clonkeen Crescent	53 B2	Coburg Place	36 E1
Church Ave West (Church Street)	35 C2 [25]	Clanree Road	22 D3	Clonkeen Drive	53 B2	*Coghill's Court (off Dame St)	36 D2
*Church Ave(off Irvine Street)	36 F2	Clanwilliam Place	36 F3	Clonkeen Grove	53 B2	Cois Coillte	56 D1 [3]
Church Court	18 F3	Clanwilliam Square	36 F3 [41]	Clonkeen Lawn	53 B3 [5]	Cois Na hAbhann	48 F2
Church Gardens	43 A1	Clanwilliam Terrace	36 F3 [40]	Clonkeen Road	53 B2	Cois Sleibhe	57 B4
Church Green	42 F1	Clare Hall	12 D4	Clonlara Road	37 A3 [12]	Coke Lane	35 C2 [42]
Church Grove	49 A2	Clare Lane	36 E3 [14]	Clonlea	51 C2	*Coke Lane (off Arran Quay)	35 C2
Church Lands	57 C3	Clare Park Villas	21 B3 [3]	Clonlea Wood	51 C2 [1]	Colbert's Fort	40 F4
Church Lane (College Green)	36 D2 [41]	Clare Road	21 B3	Clonliffe Avenue	36 E1	*Colbert's Fort	35 B3
Church Lane (Rathfarnham)	42 F3	Clare Street	36 E3	Clonliffe Gardens	21 B4	(off St James Walk)	
Church Lane Sth	36 D3 [53]	Claremont Avenue	21 A3 [1]	Clonliffe Road	21 B4	Coldcut Road	33 B2
*Church Lane Sth (off Kevin St)	36 D3	Claremont Close	20 F4	Clonmacnoise Grove	42 E1 [4]	Coldwell Street	54 D1
Church Park	42 F1	Claremont Court	20 F4	Clonmacnoise Road	42 E1	Colepark Avenue	34 D3
Church Park Avenue	42 F1	Claremont Court	37 A4 [21]	Clonmel Road	21 A2	Colepark Drive	34 D3
Church Park Court	42 F1	Claremont Crescent	20 F4	Clonmel Street	36 D3 [18]	Colepark Green	34 D3
Church Park Drive	42 F1	Claremont Drive	20 F2	Clonmellon Grove	12 D4 [3]	Colepark Road	34 D3
Church Park Lawn	42 F1	Claremont Grove	54 E3	Clonmore Court	21 A3 [11]	Coleraine Street	36 D2
Church Park Way	42 F1	Claremont Lawn	20 F4	Clonmore Road (Ballybough)	36 E1	Coliemore Road	54 F2
*Church Place (off Irvine Tce)	36 F2	Claremont Park	37 A4	Clonmore Road (Goatstown)	44 E4	Coliemore Villas	54 F2 [14]
Church Road	2 D2	Claremont Road (Killiney)	54 E3	Clonmore Terrace	36 E1 [6]	College Crescent	42 D3
Church Road (Bray)	57 C3	Claremont Road (Sandymount)	37 A4	Clonmore Villas	36 E1 [39]	College Drive	42 E3
Church Road (Celbridge)	30 D4	Claremont Road (Sutton)	25 B1	Clonrosse Court	22 F1	College Gate	18 F3
Church Road (Dalkey)	54 F1	Claremont Terrace	43 C4 [7]	Clonrosse Drive	22 F1	College Green	36 D2
Church Road (East Wall)	36 F1	Claremont Villas	54 E1 [4]	Clonrosse Park	22 F1	College Grove	18 F4

STREET INDEX

STREET NAME	PAGE/GRID REFERENCE	STREET NAME	PAGE/GRID REFERENCE	STREET NAME	PAGE/GRID REFERENCE	STREET NAME	PAGE/GRID REFERENCE
College Lane	36 E3 [19]	Convent Road (Dun Laoghaire)	46 D4	Corduff Gardens	18 F1	Cremore Park	21 A3
College Manor	21 B4 [8]	Convent View Cottages	20 D4 [2]	Corduff Green	18 F1	Cremore Road	20 F3
College Mews	21 B4 [11]	Convent View Cottages	40 D2	Corduff Grove	7 B4	Cremore Villas	20 F3 [5]
College Park (Castleknock)	19 A4	Convent View Crescent	20 D4 [3]	Corduff Park	7 B4	Cremorne	50 D1
College Park (Kimmage)	42 E3	Convey Way	20 D4	Corduff Place	18 F1	Cremorne (Terenure Road East)	42 F2
College Park Avenue	51 C2	Conway Court	36 F3 [23]	Corduff Way	18 F1	Crescent Gardens	36 F1 [11]
College Park Close	51 C2	Conyngham Road	35 B2	*Cork Hill (off Dame St)	36 D2	Crescent House	22 D4 [6]
College Park Court	51 C2 [2]	Cook Street	36 D2	Cork Street	35 C3	Crescent Place	22 D4
College Park Drive	51 C2 [4]	Cooks Road	1 A4	Corkagh View	40 D2	Crescent Villas	21 A4
College Park Drive	51 C2 [3]	Cookstown Estate Road	40 F4	Corke Abbey	57 C1	Crestfield Avenue	21 B2
College Park Grove	51 C2	Cookstown Road	40 E4	Corke Abbey Avenue	57 B1	Crestfield Close	21 B2
College Park Way	51 C2	Cookstown Way	40 E4	Cormac Terrace	42 F2	Crestfield Drive	21 B2
College Rd. (Castleknock)	18 F4	Coolamber Court	50 D1 [1]	Corn Exchange Place	36 E2 [24]	Crestfield Park	21 B2
College Rd. (Whitechurch Road)	51 A3	Coolamber Park	50 D1	Cornelscourt	53 B3	Crestfield Road	21 B2
College Street	13 A4 [8]	Coolatree Close	21 C2	Cornelscourt Hill Road	53 B3	Crinan Strand	36 E2 [31]
College Street	36 E2	Coolatree Park	21 C2	Cornmarket	35 C3	Crinken Glen	56 E3
College Street (Baldoyle)	13 A4	Coolatree Road	21 C2	Corporation Street	36 E2	Crinken Lane	56 D4
Collier's Avenue	43 B1 [3]	Cooldrinagh Lane	31 B1	Corrbridge Terrace	25 B1 [1]	Croaghpatrick Road	20 D4
Collins Avenue	21 C2	Cooldrinagh Terrace	31 B1	(off Claremont Road)		Crodaun Court	29 C2 [1]
Collins Avenue East	22 D3	Cooleen Avenue	21 C1	Corrib Road	42 E2	Crodaun Forest Park	30 D2
Collins Avenue Extension	21 A2	Coolevin (Ballybrack)	54 D4	Corrib Road	42 F2	Crofton Avenue	46 D4
Collins Avenue West	21 B2	Coolevin Road	36 D3 [49]	Corrig Avenue	46 D4	Crofton Road	46 D4
Collins Court	21 C3 [6]	Cooley Road	34 F4	Corrig Close	41 B3	*Crofton Mansions	46 D4
Collins Court	45 A3 [13]	Coolgariff Road	21 C1	Corrig Park	46 D4	(Crofton Rd Dun Laoghaire)	
Collins Drive	20 E1	Coolgreena Close	21 C2	Corrig Road (Dalkey)	54 F1	Crofton Road	46 D4
Collins Green	20 E1	Coolgreena Road	21 C1	Corrig Road (Dun Laoghaire)	54 D1	Crofton Terrace	45 C4 [6]
Collins Park	22 D3	Coolkill	52 D3	Corrig Road (Stillorgan)	52 E2	Crofton Terrace	46 D4 [25]
Collins Place	20 E1	Coolmine Boulevard	18 E2	Corrybeg	42 D4	Croftwood Crescent	33 C3
Collins Row	20 E2 [6]	Coolmine Close	18 D2	Coulson Avenue	42 F2	Croftwood Drive	33 C3
Collinstown Crescent	33 A3 [1]	Coolmine Cottages	7 A4	Coultry Avenue	21 B1	Croftwood Gardens	33 C3
Collinstown Grove	33 B3	Coolmine Court	18 E2	Coultry Crescent	10 D4	Croftwood Green	34 D3
Collinstown Road	33 A3	Coolmine Green	18 D3	Coultry Drive	10 D4	Croftwood Grove	33 C3
Collinswood	21 C2	Coolmine Lawn	18 D2	Coultry Gardens	10 D4	Croftwood Park	34 D3
Colthurst Close	32 F2	Coolmine Mews	18 D2 [1]	Coultry Grove	10 E4	Croke Villas	36 E1 [68]
Colthurst Crescent	32 F2	Coolmine Park	18 E2	Coultry Lawn	10 E4	Cromcastle Avenue	22 D1
Colthurst Crescent	32 F2	Coolmine Road	18 E3	Coultry Park	10 E4	Cromcastle Close	22 D1 [2]
Colthurst Gardens	32 F2	Coolmine Woods	18 E2	Coultry Road	10 D4	Cromcastle Court	22 D1 [6]
Colthurst Green	32 F2	Coolnevaun	52 E1	Coultry Way	21 B1	Cromcastle Drive	22 D1
Colthurst Mews	32 F2	Coolock	22 E1	Coundon Court	54 E4	Cromcastle Green	22 D1
Colthurst Park	32 F2	Coolock Drive	22 E1	Courthill Drive	5 B2	Cromcastle Park	22 D1
Colthurst Rise	32 F2	Coolock Green	22 E1	Courtlands	53 C3	Cromcastle Road	22 D1
Colthurst Road	32 F2	Coolock Lane (Santry)	10 F4	Courtney Place	36 F1 [8]	Cromlech Court	9 C4
Colthurst Way	32 F2	Coolock Village	22 E1	Cow Parlour	35 C3 [24]	Cromlech Fields	56 E1
Comeragh Road	34 F4	Coolrua Drive	21 C1	Cowbooter Lane	26 E2	Cromwell's Quarters	35 B3 [3]
Commons East	2 D2	Coombe Court	35 C3 [62]	Cowper Downs	43 A1	Cromwellsfort Road	41 C2
Commons Road	40 D2	Cope Street	36 D2 [22]	Cowper Drive	43 B2	Cross Avenue (Booterstown)	44 F3
Commons Road	56 E2	Copeland Avenue	22 D4	Cowper Gardens	43 B2	Cross Avenue (Dun Laoghaire)	46 D4
Commons Street	36 E2	Copeland Grove	22 D4	Cowper Mews	43 A2 [4]	Crosstrees Court	26 D2 [13]
Comyn Place	21 A3 [5]	*Copper Alley	36 D3	Cowper Road	43 B2	Crosthwaite Park East	54 D1
Con Colbert Road	35 A3	(off Lord Edward St)		Cowper Street	35 B1	Crosthwaite Park South	54 D1
Confey	16 D4	Copper Beech Grove	57 B2 [6]	Cowper Village	43 A2	Crosthwaite Park West	54 D1
Congress Gardens	54 E1 [2]	Coppinger	45 A4	Crag Avenue	33 B4	Crosthwaite Terrace	46 D4 [15]
Congress Hall	5 B3	Coppinger Close	44 F4	Crag Crescent	33 B4	*Crostick Alley (off Meath St)	35 C3
Congress Park	5 B3	Coppinger Glade	44 F4	Crag Terrace	33 B4	Crotty Avenue	41 C1
Connaught Parade	20 F4 [6]	Coppinger Row	36 D3 [34]	Craigford Avenue	22 E3	*Crow Street (off Dame St)	36 D2
Connaught Place	46 D4 [26]	Coppinger Walk	45 A4	Craigford Drive	22 E3	*Crown Alley (Off Temple Bar)	36 D2
*Connaught Place (Crofton Rd)	46 D4	Coppinger Wood	44 F4	Craiglands	54 F2 [26]	Croydon Gardens	21 C4
Connaught Street	20 F4	Corbally Avenue	47 C2	Craigmore Gardens	45 A3 [5]	Croydon Green	21 C4
Connawood Copse	57 B1	Corbally Close	47 C2	Crampton Avenue	36 F4 [16]	Croydon Park Avenue	21 C4
Connawood Crescent	57 B1	Corbally Down	47 C2	*Crampton Court (off Dame St)	36 D2	Croydon Terrace	21 C3 [4]
Connawood Drive	57 B1	Corbally Drive	47 C2	Crampton Quay	36 D2 [40]	Crumlin	42 D1
Connawood Green	57 B1	Corbally Glade	47 C2	*Crane Lane (off Dame Street)	36 D2	Crumlin Park(off Crumlin Road)	42 D1
Connawood Grove	57 B1	Corbally Heath	47 C2	Crane Street	35 C3	Crumlin Road	35 B4
Connawood Lawn	57 B1	Corbally Lawn	47 C2	Cranfield Place	37 A3	Cuala Grove	58 D3
Connawood Walk	57 B1	Corbally Park	47 C2	Cranford Court	44 D2	Cuala Road	20 F4
Connawood Way	57 B1	Corbally Rise	47 C2	Cranmer Lane	36 F3 [19]	Cuala Road	58 D3
Connolly Avenue	3 A4	Corbally Square	47 C2	Crannagh	43 C2 [9]	Cuan na Mara	26 D1 [10]
Connolly Avenue	35 A3	Corbally Vale	47 C2	Crannagh Castle	42 F3	Cuckoo Lane	36 D2
Connolly Gardens	35 A3 [3]	Corbally Way	47 C2	Crannagh Court	42 F3	Cuffe Lane	36 D3
Conor Clune Road	19 C4	Corbawn Avenue	56 E2	Crannagh Grove	43 A3	Cuffe Street	36 D3
Conquer Hill Avenue	37 C1	Corbawn Close	56 F2	Crannagh Park	42 F3	Cul na Greine	48 F2
Conquer Hill Road	37 C1	Corbawn Court	56 F2	Crannagh Road	42 F3	Cullen's Cottages	45 A4 [7]
Constellation Road	10 F4	Corbawn Dale	56 F2	Crannagh Way	43 A3 [8]	*Cullenswood Court	43 B1
Constitution Hill	36 D2	Corbawn Drive	56 F2	Crannogue Close	9 C4	(off Cullenswood Park)	
Convent Avenue	21 B4	Corbawn Glade	56 E3	Crannogue Road	9 C4	Cullenswood Gardens	43 B1
Convent Avenue	58 D3	Corbawn Grove	56 F2	Crawford Avenue	21 A4	Cullenswood Park	43 B1
Convent Close	36 E3 [40]	Corbawn Lane	56 E2	*Crawford Tce (off Kings Ave)	36 E1	Cullenswood Road	43 B1 [11]
Convent Court	52 E1 [4]	Corbawn Lawn	56 E3	Creighton Street	36 E2	Culmore Park	33 C2 [1]
Convent Lane	4 D4	Corbawn Wood	56 E2	Cremona Road	34 E3	Culmore Road	33 C2
Convent Lane	42 F4	Corduff	18 F1	Cremore Avenue	20 F3	*Cumberland PlaceNorth	35 C1
Convent Place	36 E4 [12]	Corduff Avenue	18 F1	Cremore Crescent	20 F3	(on North Circular Road)	
Convent Road (Blackrock)	45 A4	Corduff Close	18 F1	Cremore Drive	20 F3	Cumberland Road	36 E4
Convent Road (Clondalkin)	40 E2	Corduff Cottages	18 E1	Cremore Heights	20 F2	Cumberland Street	45 C4
Convent Road (Dalkey)	54 F2	Corduff Crescent	18 F1	Cremore Lawn	20 F3	Cumberland Street North	36 E1
						Cumberland Street South	36 E3 [1]

STREET NAME	PAGE/GRID REFERENCE
Cunningham Drive	54 F2
Cunningham Road	54 F2
Curlew Road	34 F4
Curracloe Drive	23 A1 [4]
Curraghcloe Drive	12 D4 [5]
Curzon Street	36 D4
Cushlawn Park	48 F2
Custom House Harbour	36 E2 [27]
Custom House Quay	36 E2
Cymric Road	37 A3
Cypress Avenue	50 E2 [2]
Cypress Court	56 E1
Cypress Drive	42 D3
Cypress Garth	42 D4
Cypress Grove North	42 D3
Cypress Grove Road	42 D3
Cypress Grove South	42 D4
Cypress Lawn	42 D4
Cypress Park	42 D4
Cypress Road	44 E3

D

STREET NAME	PAGE/GRID REFERENCE
*Daisy Market (on Parnell St)	36 D2
Dakota Avenue	10 F4
Dal Riada	3 C4
Dalcassian Downs	20 F4
Dale Close	52 E1 [1]
Dale Drive	52 E1
Dale Road	52 E1
Dale Tree Avenue	49 B2
Dale Tree Drive	49 C2
Dale Tree Grove	49 C2
Dale Tree Park	49 C3
Dale Tree Road	49 C3
Dale View	54 E4
Dale View Park	54 E4 [2]
Dale View Road	1 C1
Dalepark Road	49 A2
Daletree Crescent	49 C2
Daletree Road	49 C2
Dalkey	54 F1
Dalkey Avenue	54 F2
Dalkey Court	54 F2 [23]
Dalkey Grove	54 F2 [6]
Dalkey Park	54 E2
Dalkey Rock	54 F2
Dalymount	35 C1
Dame Court	36 D3 [16]
Dame Lane	36 D2 [42]
Dame Lane	36 D3 [7]
Dame Street	36 D2
Dane Road	9 C4
Danes Court	23 A4
Danesfort	37 B1
Daneswell Road	21 A4
Dangan Avenue	42 D2
Dangan Drive	42 D2
Dangan Park	42 D2
Daniel Street	36 D3
Danieli Drive	22 E2
Danieli Road	22 E2
Dara Court	30 D3
Dara Crescent	30 D3
Dargan Court	58 D2 [6]
Dargan Street	57 B2 [10]
Dargle Crescent	57 B2 [5]
Dargle Drive	51 A1
Dargle Heights	57 B2
Dargle Road (Dean's Grange)	53 A1
Dargle Road (Drumcondra)	21 A4
*Dargle Terrace (On Lower Dargle Road)	57 B2
Dargle Valley	51 A1
Dargle View	51 A1
Dargle Wood	50 D1
Darley Cottages	57 C2 [15]
Darley Street	35 C4 [40]
Darley Street	36 D4
Darley's Terrace	35 C3 [9]
Darling Estate	19 C4
Dartmouth Lane	36 E4 [6]
Dartmouth Place	36 E4 [4]
Dartmouth Road	36 E4
Dartmouth Square East	36 E4 [16]
Dartmouth Square North	36 E4 [14]
Dartmouth Square South	36 E4 [15]
Dartmouth Square West	36 E4 [17]
Dartmouth Terrace	36 E4 [5]
Dartry Cottages	43 B2 [1]
Dartry Park	43 A2
Dartry Road	43 A2
David Park	21 A4
David Road	21 A4
*Davis Place (off Thomas Davis St Sth)	35 C3
Davitt Park	54 D4
Davitt Road	34 F4
Davitt Road	57 C2
Dawson Court	44 F3
*Dawson Court (off Stephen St Lower)	36 D3
Dawson Lane	36 E3 [18]
Dawson Street	36 E3
De Burgh Road	35 B2 [14]
De Courcy Square	21 A4 [2]
De Selby Close	48 D2
De Selby Close	48 D2
De Selby Lawns	48 D2
De Selby Park	47 C2
De Valera Place	36 D1 [19]
*De Vesci Court (Flats) (off Sloperton)	45 C4
De Vesci Terrace	45 C4
Dean Street	36 D4
Dean Swift Green	21 A2
Dean Swift Road	21 A2
Dean Swift Square	35 C3
Deans Court	53 B1 [10]
Deans Grange	53 B2
Dean's Grange Road	53 B1
Deansrath Avenue	32 F4
Deansrath Crescent	39 C1
Deansrath Green	39 C1
Deansrath Grove	32 F4
Deansrath Lawn	32 F4
Deansrath Park	39 C1
Deansrath Road	39 C1
Deanstown Avenue	20 D2
Deanstown Drive	20 D2
Deanstown Green	20 D2
Deanstown Park	20 D2
Deanstown Road	20 D2
Decies Road	34 E3
Deerhaven	6 F4
Deerhaven Avenue	6 F4
Deerhaven Close	6 F4
Deerhaven Crescent	6 F4
Deerhaven Green	6 F4
Deerhaven Park	6 F4
Deerhaven View	6 F4
Deerhaven Walk	6 F4
Deerpark	57 B4
Deerpark Avenue	19 A4
Deerpark Close	19 A3
Deerpark Drive	19 A3
Deerpark Lawn	19 B3
Deerpark Road	44 D4
Deerpark Rd (Castleknock Rd)	19 A3
Del Val Avenue	23 C2
Del Val Court	23 C2 [2]
Delaford Avenue	49 C1
Delaford Drive	49 C1
Delaford Grove	49 C1
Delaford Lawn	49 C1
Delaford Park	49 C1
Delbrook Manor	51 C2 [5]
Delbrook Park	51 C2 [4]
Delbrook Park	51 C2
Delville Road	21 A2
Delvin Road	20 F4 [3]
Delwood Close	18 E3
Delwood Drive	18 E3
Delwood Grove	18 E3
Delwood Lawn	18 E3
Delwood Park	18 E3
Delwood Road	18 E3
Delwood Walk	18 E3
Demesne	22 E3
Denmark Street Great	36 D1
Denville Court	54 D4
Denzille Lane	36 E3
*Derby Square (off Werburgh St)	36 D3
Dermot O'Hurley Avenue	37 A3
Derravaragh Road	42 E2
Derry Drive	42 D1
Derry Park	42 D1
Derry Road	42 D1
Derrynane Gardens	37 A3
Derrynane Parade	36 D1 [33]
Deselby	48 D2
Desmond Avenue	46 D4 [3]
Desmond Cottages	54 F2 [20]
Desmond Street	36 D4 [2]
Devenish Road	42 E1
Deverell Place	36 E2 [5]
Devery's Lane	21 A4 [4]
Devitt Villas	54 E1 [8]
Devlin's Place	36 E3 [22]
Devon Close	53 B1 [11]
Devoy Road	35 A3
Dewberry Park	4 D4
Dexter Terrace	36 E4 [29]
Diamond Terrace	57 B2 [15]
Digges Lane	36 D3 [38]
Digges Street Upper	36 D3
*Dillon Place South (off John Dillon St)	36 D3
Dingle Road	20 E4
Dispensary Lane (Lucan)	32 D1 [6]
Dispensary Lane (Willbrook)	42 F4
Distillery Lane	16 D4
Distillery Road	21 B4
Diswellstown Cottages	18 E4
Dixon Villas	54 E1 [9]
Dodder Avenue	49 B2
Dodder Court	49 B2
Dodder Crescent	49 B2
Dodder Dale	42 F4
Dodder Green	49 B2
Dodder Lawn	49 B2
Dodder Park Drive	42 F3 [3]
Dodder Park Grove	42 F3
Dodder Park Road	42 F3
Dodder Road Lower	43 A3
Dodder Terrace	37 A3 [18]
Dodder View Cottages	36 F4 [9]
Doddervale	43 A3
Dodsboro Cottages	31 B2
Dodsboro Road	31 C2
D'Olier Street	36 E2
Dollymount	23 A4
Dollymount Avenue	23 A4
Dollymount Grove	22 F4
Dollymount Park	23 A4
Dollymount Rise	23 A4
Dolmen Court	10 D4
Dolphin Avenue	35 C4
Dolphin Court	35 B4 [7]
Dolphin House	35 B4 [1]
*Dolphin Market (off Dolphin's Barn St)	35 B4
Dolphin Park	35 B4 [5]
Dolphin Road	35 B4
Dolphin's Barn	35 B4
Dolphin's Barn Street	35 B4
Domhnach's Well	24 D1 [3]
Dominick Lane	36 D2 [35]
Dominick Place	36 D1
Dominick Street	46 D4
Dominick Street Lower	36 D2
Dominick Street Upper	36 D1
Domville Drive	42 D4
Domville Green	42 D4
Domville Grove	56 E1 [9]
Domville Road	42 D4
Donaghmede	12 E4
Donaghmede Avenue	23 B1
Donaghmede Drive	23 B1
Donaghmede Park	23 B1
Donaghmede Road	23 B1
Donard Road	34 F4
Donmore Green	42 E2
Donnellan Avenue	35 B3 [7]
Donnybrook	43 C1
Donnybrook Green	44 D2 [3]
Donnybrook Manor	43 C1
Donnybrook Road	43 C1
Donnycarney	22 D3
Donnycarney Road	22 D3
Donomore Avenue	48 E2
Donomore Crescent	48 E2
Donomore Green	48 E2
Donomore Park	48 E2
Donore Avenue	35 C3
Donore Road	35 C3
Donore Terrace	35 C3 [55]
Donovan Lane	35 C4 [21]
Doon Avenue	35 B1 [6]
Doon Court	9 C4
Doonamana Road	54 D3
Doonanore Park	54 D3
Doonsalla Drive	54 D3
Doonsalla Park	54 D3
Doris Street	36 F3
Dornden Park	44 E2
Dorney Court	56 E3
Dorset Lane	36 D1
*Dorset Place (off Dorset Street Lower)	36 D1
Dorset Street Lower	36 D1
Dorset Street Upper	36 D1
Dowland Road	42 D1
Dowling's Court	36 E2 [15]
Downpatrick Road	35 B4
Downpatrick Road	42 E1
Dowth Avenue	20 F4
Drapier Green	20 F2 [1]
Drapier Road	20 F2
Drayton Close	45 B4 [16]
Drimnagh	34 F4
Drimnagh Road	41 C1
Drimnigh Road	12 E3
Drinagh Avenue	52 F4
Drinagh Close	52 F4
Drinagh Court	52 F4
Drinagh Park	52 F4
Drinaghmore	52 F4
Dromard Road	34 F4
Dromard Terrace	37 A4 [17]
Dromard Terrace	37 B4 [17]
Dromawling Road	21 C2
Drombawn Avenue	21 C2
Dromcarra Avenue	48 E2
Dromcarra Drive	48 E2
Dromcarra Green	48 D2
Dromcarra Grove	48 E2
Dromeen Avenue	21 C2
Dromheath Avenue	7 B4
Dromheath Drive	7 B4
Dromheath Gardens	7 B4
Dromheath Grove	7 B4
Dromheath Park	7 B4
Dromlee Crescent	21 C2
Dromnanane Park	21 C2 [2]
Dromnanane Road	21 C2 [1]
Dromore Road	35 A4
Druid Court	9 C4
Druid Valley	56 D1
Drumahill	52 D1
Drumalee Avenue	35 B1
Drumalee Court	35 B1 [14]
Drumalee Drive	35 B1
Drumalee Grove	35 B1
Drumalee Park	35 B1
Drumalee Road	35 B1
Drumcairn Avenue	48 D1
Drumcairn Drive	48 D1
Drumcairn Gardens	48 D1
Drumcairn Green	48 E1
Drumcairn Park	48 E1
Drumcliffe Drive	20 E4
Drumcliffe Road	20 E4
Drumcondra	21 B4
Drumcondra Park	36 E1 [18]
Drumcondra Road Lower	21 B4
Drumcondra Road Upper	21 B3

STREET INDEX

STREET NAME	PAGE/GRID REFERENCE	STREET NAME	PAGE/GRID REFERENCE	STREET NAME	PAGE/GRID REFERENCE	STREET NAME	PAGE/GRID REFERENCE
Drumfinn Avenue	33 C2	Dunsink Avenue	20 D2	Eden Park Avenue	52 D1	Elm Mount View	22 D2
Drumfinn Park	34 D3	Dunsink Drive	20 D2	Eden Park Drive	44 D4	Elm Park	44 D1
Drumfinn Road	34 D2	Dunsink Gardens	20 D2	Eden Park Road	52 D1	Elm Park (Celbridge)	30 D3
Drumkeen Manor	54 D3	Dunsink Green	20 D2	Eden Quay	36 E2	Elm Park Terrace	42 F2
Drummartin Close	44 D4	Dunsink Lane	19 A2	Eden Road Lower	54 D1	Elm Road (Donnycarney)	22 D3
Drummartin Crescent	52 D1 [1]	Dunsink Park	20 D2	Eden Road Upper	54 D1	Elm Road (Fox & Geese)	41 A1
Drummartin Park	52 D1	Dunsink Road	20 D2	*Eden Terrace (Botanic Ave)	21 A4	Elm Vale	32 E3
Drummartin Road	44 D4	Dunsoghly Avenue	19 C1	Eden Terrace (Dun Laoghaire)	54 D1	Elm Way	32 E3
Drummartin Terrace	44 D4	Dunsoghly Drive	19 C1	Eden Villas	54 D1 [5]	Elm Way	51 A2 [3]
*Drummond Place	35 C4	Dunsoghly Park	19 C1	Edenbrook Court	50 F1 [5]	Elm Wood	32 E3
(off Mount Drummond Ave)		Dunville Avenue	43 B1	Edenbrook Drive	42 E4	Elmbrook	32 E2
Drury Street	36 D3	Durham Place	54 D1 [18]	Edenbrook Park	42 E4	Elmbrook Crescent	32 E2
Drynam Court	2 D2	Durham Road	37 B4	Edenmore Avenue	22 F1	Elmbrook Lawn	32 E2
Drynam Lane	2 E2	Durrow Road	42 E1	Edenmore Crescent	23 A2	Elmbrook Walk	32 E2
Drynam Road	2 D2	Dwyer Park	57 C1	Edenmore Drive	22 F2	Elmcastle Close	41 A3
Drysdale Close	49 A2	**E**		Edenmore Gardens	22 F2	Elmcastle Court	41 A3
Dublin Road	5 C3	Eagle Hill	45 A3 [15]	Edenmore Green	22 F2	Elmcastle Drive	41 A3
Dublin Road	25 A1	Eagle Hill Avenue	42 F2 [4]	Edenmore Grove	22 F2	Elmcastle Green	41 A3
Dublin Road	44 F4	Eagle Park	22 D1	Edenmore Park	22 F2	Elmcastle Park	41 A3
Dublin Road (Bray)	57 B1	Eagle Terrace	51 C1 [3]	Edenvale Road	43 B1	Elmcastle Walk	41 A3
Dublin Road (Celbridge)	30 D3	*Eagle Terrace (Dalkey)	54 F2	Edenwood	44 D4 [1]	Elmdale Crescent	33 C3
Dublin Road (Kilbarrack)	23 C2	(Sorrento Rd)		Edgewood	21 B4 [10]	Elmdale Drive	33 C3
Dublin Road (Malahide)	3 A3	Earl Place	36 D2 [19]	Edgewood Lawns	18 E1	Elmdale Park	33 C3
Dublin Road (Shankill)	56 E3	Earl Street North	36 D2	Edmondsbury Court	32 E1 [1]	Elmfield Avenue	12 D4
Dublin Road (Swords)	1 C3	Earl Street South	35 C3	Edmondstown	50 E3	Elmfield Close	12 D4
Dublin Street (Baldoyle)	13 A4	Earls Court	35 B1	Edmondstown Green	50 E3	Elmfield Close	12 E4
Dublin Street (Swords)	2 D2	Earls Court	42 F2 [15]	Edmondstown Road	50 E3	Elmfield Court	12 D4
Dufferin Avenue	35 C4	Earlscroft	57 C4	Edward Road	58 D3	Elmfield Drive	12 E4
Duke Lane Lower	36 E3 [17]	Earlsfort	32 F3	*Edward Tce (Off Nerano Rd)	54 F2	Elmfield Green	12 D4
Duke Lane Upper	36 D3 [32]	Earlsfort Avenue	32 F3	Edwin Court	54 E2 [5]	Elmfield Grove	12 D4
Duke Row	36 E1 [57]	Earlsfort Close	32 F3	Effra Road	43 A1	Elmfield Lawn	12 E4
Duke Street	36 D3	Earlsfort Court	32 F2	Eglington Road	57 C2 [3]	Elmfield Rise	12 D4
Dun an Oir	48 F2	Earlsfort Drive	32 F3	Eglinton Court	43 C1	Elmfield Vale	12 E4
Dun Aonghasa	48 F2	Earlsfort Gardens	32 F2	Eglinton Park (Donnybrook)	43 C1	Elmfield Walk	12 D4
Dun Emer Drive	51 C1	Earlsfort Green	32 F3	Eglinton Road	43 C1	Elmfield Way	12 D4
Dun Emer Park	51 C1	Earlsfort Grove	32 F3	Eglinton Square	43 C1 [13]	Elmgrove	45 A4
Dun Emer Road	51 C1	Earlsfort Lane	32 F3	*Eglinton Terrace (Donnybrook)	43 C1	Elmgrove	54 D4
Dun Laoghaire	46 D4	Earlsfort Lawn	32 F2	Eglinton Terrace (Dundrum)	43 C4	Elmgrove Terrace	57 C2 [22]
Dunamase	44 F3	Earlsfort Meadows	32 F2	Eglinton Tce (Royal Canal Bank)	36 D1	Elmpark Avenue	43 B1
Dunard Avenue	35 A1	Earlsfort Park	32 F2	Eglinton Wood	43 C1 [22]	Elms	44 F3
Dunard Court	35 B1	Earlsfort Rise	32 F3	Elderberry	32 D3	Elmwood	17 B1
Dunard Drive	35 B1	Earlsfort Road	32 F2	Elderwood Road	33 B2	Elmwood Avenue Lower	43 B1
Dunard Park	35 B1	Earlsfort Terrace	36 E4	*Elford Terrace (off Donore Ave)	35 C3	Elmwood Avenue Upper	43 B1
Dunard Road	35 B1 [11]	Earlsfort Vale	32 F3	Elgin Heights	57 A4	Elmwood Court	1 C1 [1]
Dunard Road	35 B1	Earlsfort View	32 F3	Elgin Road	36 F4	Elmwood Drive	1 C1
Dunard Walk	35 B1	Earlsfort Way	32 F3	Elgin Wood	57 A4	Elmwood Park	1 C1
Dunawley Avenue	40 D1	East Pier (Dun Laoghaire)	46 E3	Elizabeth Street	21 B4	Elmwood Road	1 C1
Dunawley Drive	40 D1	East Pier (Howth)	26 D1	Elkwood	50 E1	Elner Court	4 D4
Dunawley Grove	40 D1	East Road	36 F2	Ellenfield Road	21 C2	Elton Court	22 F1 [1]
Dunawley Way	40 D1	East Wall	36 F1	Ellensborough	48 F3	Elton Court	30 F1
Dunbo Hill	26 D1 [4]	East Wall Road	36 F1	Ellensborough Avenue	48 F3	Elton Court (Dunboyne)	5 C3
Dunbo Terrace	26 D1 [1]	Eastmoreland Lane	36 F4 [2]	Ellensborough Close	48 F3	Elton Drive	23 A1
Dunboyne	5 B2	Eastmoreland Place	36 F4 [1]	Ellensborough Court	48 F3	Elton Drive (Dunboyne)	5 B2
Dunbro Lane	9 C1	Easton Park	15 C4	Ellensborough Crescent	48 F3	Elton Drive (Dunboyne)	5 C2
Dunbur Terrace	57 C2 [21]	Easton Road	30 F1	Ellensborough Green	48 F3	Elton Grove (Dunboyne)	5 C3
Duncairn Avenue	57 C2	Eastwood	19 C2 [1]	Ellensborough Grove	48 F3	Elton Park (Coolock)	23 A1
Duncairn Terrace	57 C2	Eaton Brae	43 A3	Ellensborough Park	48 F3	Elton Park (Dalkey)	54 E1
Duncarraig	25 B2	Eaton Brae	56 E2	Ellensborough Rise	48 F3	Elton Walk	23 A1 [1]
Dundaniel Road	22 D1	Eaton Court	42 F2 [22]	Ellensborough View	48 F3	Ely Close	49 B3
Dundela Avenue	54 E1	Eaton Court	58 D3 [1]	Ellensborough Walk	48 F3	Ely Crescent	49 B3 [1]
Dundela Crescent	54 E1	Eaton Hall	42 F2 [18]	Ellesmere	52 F2 [4]	Ely Drive	49 B3
Dundela Haven	54 E1 [24]	Eaton Place	45 B4	Ellesmere Avenue	35 B1	Ely Green	49 B3 [1]
Dundela Park	54 E1	Eaton Road	42 F2	Ellis Court	35 C2 [38]	Ely Grove	49 B3 [1]
Dundrum	51 C1	Eaton Square (Monkstown)	45 B4	Ellis Court	35 C2 [44]	Ely Place	36 E3
Dundrum Road	43 C3	Eaton Square (Terenure)	42 F2	Ellis Quay	35 C2	Ely Place Upper	36 E3 [31]
Dundrum Wood	51 B1	Eaton Wood Avenue	56 E3	*Ellis Street (off Benburb Street)	35 C2	Ely View	49 B3
Dunedin Court	53 C1	Eaton Wood Court	56 E3	Elm Close	32 E3	Embassy Lawn	43 C2
Dunedin Drive	53 C1 [8]	Eaton Wood Green	56 E3	Elm Court	32 E3	Emerald Cottages	36 F3 [34]
Dunedin Terrace	53 C1	Eaton Wood Grove	56 E3	Elm Dene	32 E3	Emerald Place	36 E2 [23]
Dungar Terrace	46 D4 [12]	Ebenezer Terrace	35 C3 [53]	Elm Drive	32 E3	Emerald Square	35 B3 [20]
Dungriffan Road	26 D2	Eblana Avenue	46 D4	Elm Green	32 E3	Emerald Street	36 F2 [1]
Dungriffan Villas	26 D2 [8]	Eblana Villas	36 F3 [2]	Elm Grove	32 E3	Emerald Terrace	35 C3 [63]
Dunleary Hill	45 C4	(Lr Grand Canal St)		*Elm Grove Cottages	19 C4	Emmet Court	35 A3
Dunleary Road	45 C4	*Eblana Villas (off Arbour Hill)	35 B2	Elm Mount Avenue	21 C2	Emmet Road	35 A3
Dunluce Road	22 E3	Eccles Court	36 D1 [20]	Elm Mount Close	22 D2	Emmet Square	44 F3
Dunmanus Road	20 E4	Eccles Place	36 D1	Elm Mount Court	22 D3	Emmet Street (Harold's Cross)	35 C4 [10]
Dunmore Grove	40 F2	Eccles Street	36 D1	Elm Mount Crescent	22 D2	Emmet Street (Nth Circular Rd)	36 E1
Dunmore Lawn	40 F3	Echlin Street	35 C3	Elm Mount Drive	22 D2	Emmet Street (Sallynoggin)	54 D1 [4]
Dunmore Park	40 F2	Eden Avenue	51 A1	Elm Mount Grove	22 D2	Emor Street	36 D4
Dunne Street	36 E1	Eden Court	51 A1	Elm Mount Heights	22 D2	Emorville Avenue	36 D4
Dunree Park	22 F1	Eden Crescent	51 A1	Elm Mount Lawn	22 D2	Empress Place	36 E1
Dunsandle Court	19 A3	Eden Grove	51 A1	Elm Mount Park	22 D2	*Enaville Avenue	36 F1
Dunsandle Grove	19 A3	Eden Park	54 D1	Elm Mount Rise	22 D2	(off Annesley Place)	
Dunseverick Road	22 E4			Elm Mount Road	22 D2	Enaville Road	36 F1 [10]

STREET NAME	PAGE/GRID REFERENCE	STREET NAME	PAGE/GRID REFERENCE	STREET NAME	PAGE/GRID REFERENCE	STREET NAME	PAGE/GRID REFERENCE
*Engine Alley (off Meath St)	35 C3	Fade Street	36 D3 [39]	Fernwood Court	48 E1	Fleurville	45 A4
English Row	30 D4	Fair Haven	3 B2 [1]	Fernwood Lawn	48 E1	Floraville Avenue	40 E1
Ennafort Avenue	22 F2	Fairbrook Lawn	42 F4	Fernwood Park	48 E1	Floraville Drive	40 E2
Ennafort Court	22 F3	Fairfield Avenue	36 F1	Fernwood Way	48 E1	Floraville Estate	40 E1
Ennafort Drive	22 F3	Fairfield Park	43 A2	Ferrard Road	42 F2	Floraville Lawn	40 E1
Ennafort Grove	22 F2	Fairfield Road	21 A4	Ferrycarrig Avenue	11 B4	Floraville Road	43 C1 [8]
Ennafort Park	22 F3	Fairgreen Court	57 C2 [50]	Ferrycarrig Drive	11 B4	Florence Road	57 C2
Ennafort Road	22 F2	Fairgreen Road	57 B2 [11]	Ferrycarrig Green	11 B4 [3]	Florence Street	36 D4 [17]
Ennel Avenue	22 F2	Fairgreen Terrace	57 C2 [32]	Ferrycarrig Park	11 B4	Florence Terrace	57 C2 [39]
Ennel Court	56 E1 [6]	Fairhaven	3 B2	Ferrycarrig Road	11 B4	*Florence Terrace	36 E4
Ennel Drive	22 F2	Fairlawn Park	20 E2	Ferryman's Crossing	36 F2 [14]	(Leeson Park Avenue)	
Ennel Park	22 F2	Fairlawn Road	20 E2	Fertullagh Road	20 F4 [5]	Florence Villas	57 C2 [40]
Ennis Grove	37 A3 [19]	Fairlawns	54 E2 [6]	Fettercairn Road	40 E4	*Florence Villas (Sandymount)	37 A4
Enniskerry Road (Phibsborough)	21 A4 [3]	Fairview	21 C4	Fey Yerra	52 F2 [8]	Flower Grove	54 D2
Enniskerry Road (Sandyford)	52 D4	Fairview Avenue Lower	21 C4	Fforester	32 E2	Foley Street	36 E2
Erne Place	36 F3 [21]	Fairview Avenue Upper	21 C4	Fforester Close	32 E2	Fontenoy Street	36 D1
Erne Place Little	36 E3 [4]	Fairview Court	21 C4 [14]	Fforester Court	32 E2	Fontenoy Terrace	58 D3
Erne Place Lower	36 E2 [2]	Fairview Green	21 C4 [7]	Fforester Lawn	32 E2	Fonthill Abbey	50 F1 [3]
Erne Street Lower	36 E2	Fairview Lawn	56 D1	Fforester Park	32 E2	Fonthill Park	50 F1
Erne Street Upper	36 E3	Fairview Passage	21 C4 [10]	Fforester Walk	32 E2	Fonthill Road (Clondalkin)	33 A2
Erne Terrace Front	36 E3 [20]	Fairview Strand	21 C4	Field Avenue	41 C1 [1]	Fonthill Road (Rathfarnham)	50 F1
Erne Terrace Rere	36 E3 [21]	Fairview Terrace	21 C4 [11]	Field's Terrace	43 B1 [5]	Forbes Lane	35 C3
Errigal Gardens	41 C1	Fairways	42 E4	Fieldview Cottages	45 A4 [6]	Forbes Street	36 F2
Errigal Road	34 F4	Fairway's Avenue	20 F2	Findlater Place	36 D2 [25]	Forest Avenue	1 B3
Erris Road	20 E4	Fairway's Green	20 F2	Findlater St (Dun Laoghaire)	54 E1 [7]	Forest Avenue	41 A3
Esker Drive	32 D2	Fairways Grove	20 E2	Findlater St (Nth Circular Rd)	35 B2 [10]	Forest Boulevard	1 B3
Esker Lane	32 E1	Fairway's Park	20 F2	Fingal Place	35 C1 [5]	Forest Close	41 A3
Esker Lane	32 E2	Fairyhill	53 A1	Fingal Street	35 C3 [11]	Forest Court	1 B2
Esker Lawns	32 D1	Fairyhill	57 B3	Finglas	20 D1	Forest Crescent	1 B3
Esker Lodge	32 E2	Faith Avenue	36 F1	Finglas East	20 E1	Forest Dale	1 B2
Esker Lodge	32 E2	Falcarragh Road	21 B2	Finglas Park	20 E1	Forest Drive	1 B3
Esker Lodge Avenue	32 E2	Falls Road	56 D2	Finglas Place	20 E2	Forest Drive	41 A3
Esker Lodge Close	32 E2	Farmhill Drive	43 C4	Finglas Road	20 E2	Forest Fields	1 C3
Esker Lodge View	32 E2	Farmhill Park	43 C4	Finglas Road Old	20 F3	Forest Fields Road	1 C3
Esker Meadow	32 E2	Farmhill Road	43 C4	Finglas South	20 E2	Forest Green	1 B3
Esker Meadow Close	32 E2	Farmleigh Avenue	52 F1	Finglas West	20 D1	Forest Green	41 A3
Esker Meadow Court	32 E2	Farmleigh Close	52 F1	Finglaswood Road	20 D2	Forest Grove	1 B3
Esker Meadow Green	32 E2	Farmleigh Park	52 F1	Finn Street	35 B2 [12]	Forest Lawn	41 A2
Esker Meadow Grove	32 E2	Farney Park	37 A4	Finneber Fort	20 E2	Forest Park	1 B2
Esker Meadow Lawn	32 E2	Farnham Crescent	20 E2	Finnscourt	32 D3	Forest Park	30 F1
Esker Meadow Rise	32 E2	Farnham Drive	20 E2	Finnsgreen	32 D3	Forest Park	41 A3
Esker Meadow View	32 E2	Farrenboley Cottages	43 B3	Finnsgrove	32 D3	Forest Road	1 B4
Esker Park	32 E2	Farrenboley Park	43 B3	Finnslawn	32 D3	Forest View	1 B3
Esker Road	32 D3	Fassaroe	57 A2	Finnspark	32 D3	Forest Walk	1 C3
Esker South	32 D3	Fassaroe Lane	57 A3	Finnstown Fairways	32 D3	Forest Way	1 C3
Esker Villas	43 A1 [11]	Father Colohan Terrace	57 C2 [11]	Finnsvale	32 D3	Fortfield Avenue	42 E3
Esker Wood Close	32 E2	Father Mathew Square	35 C2 [26]	Finnsview	32 D3	Fortfield Court	42 E3 [2]
Esker Wood Court	32 E2	Fatima Mansions	35 B3 [23]	Finnswalk	32 D3	Fortfield Drive	42 E3
Esker Wood Drive	32 E2	(off James's Walk)		Finnswood	32 D3	Fortfield Gardens	43 A2
Esker Wood Grove	32 E2	Fatima Terrace	57 C2	Finsbury Park	43 B4	Fortfield Grove	42 E3
Esker Wood Rise	32 E2	Faughart Road	42 E1 [3]	Firgrove	54 E4 [8]	Fortfield Park	42 E3
Esker Wood View	32 E2	Faussagh Avenue	20 E4	Firhouse	49 C1	Fortfield Road	42 E2
Esker Wood Walk	32 E2	Faussagh Road	20 F4	Firhouse Road	49 B2	Fortfield Road	42 E3
Esker Woods	32 E2	Feltrim	3 A4	Firhouse Road West	49 A2	Fortfield Terrace	43 A2
Esmond Avenue	21 C4	Feltrim Road	2 F4	First Avenue	40 F4	Forth Road	36 F1
Esmonde Terrace	57 B2 [18]	Fenian Street	36 E3	First Avenue (Sarsfield Road)	34 F3	Forthill Court	50 F1 [4]
Esplanade Terrace	58 D2 [3]	Fergus Road	42 F2	First Avenue (Seville Place)	36 F2 [3]	Fortlawn Avenue	18 D1
Esposito Road	41 C1 [5]	Ferguson Road	21 A3	Fishamble Street	36 D2	Fortlawn Drive	18 D1
*Essex Gate (off Essex Quay)	36 D2	Fern Court	49 B3	Fishermans Wharf	37 A2 [1]	Fortlawn Park	18 D1
Essex Quay	36 D2	Ferncarrig Avenue	52 D3	Fitzgerald Park	53 C1 [6]	Fortlawns	54 E2
Essex Street East	36 D2	Ferncarrig Court	52 D3	Fitzgerald Street	36 D4 [1]	Fortrose Park	42 E4
*Essex Street West	36 D2	Ferncarrig Rise	52 D3	Fitzgibbon Lane	36 E1 [21]	Fortunestown	47 C1
(off Fishamble St)		Ferncourt Avenue	49 B3	Fitzgibbon Street	36 E1	Fortunestown Close	47 C1
Estate Avenue	44 E1	Ferncourt Close	49 B3	Fitzmaurice Road	20 F2	Fortunestown Crescent	47 C1
Estate Cottages	36 F3 [16]	Ferncourt Crescent	49 B3 [5]	Fitzpatrick's Cottages	42 F1 [6]	Fortunestown Lane	47 B1
(Northumberland Rd)		Ferncourt Drive	49 B3 [4]	Fitzroy Avenue	21 B4	Fortunestown Road	48 D2
Estate Cottages (Shelbourne Rd)	36 F4 [13]	Ferncourt Green	49 B3	Fitzwilliam Court	36 E3 [38]	Fortunestown Way	48 D1
Estuary Court	2 D1	Ferncourt Park	49 B3	Fitzwilliam Lane	36 E3	Fortview Avenue	37 C1
Estuary Road	2 F2	Ferncourt View	49 B3	Fitzwilliam Place	36 E3	Foster Place North	36 E1 [41]
Estuary Row	3 B2	Ferndale	6 F4	Fitzwilliam Place North	35 C2 [23]	Foster Place South (College Grn)	36 D2 [38]
Eugene Street	35 C3	Ferndale	17 C1	(Grangegorman)		Foster Terrace	36 E1
Eustace Street	36 D2	Ferndale	49 A2	Fitzwilliam Quay	37 A3	Fosterbrook	44 E3
Everton Avenue	35 B1 [3]	Ferndale Avenue	20 F2	Fitzwilliam Square East	36 E3	Fosters Avenue	44 E2
Evora Park	26 D1	Ferndale Road	20 F2	Fitzwilliam Square North	36 E3	Fountain Place	35 C2
Evora Terrace	26 D1 [2]	Ferndale Road (Bray)	57 A1	Fitzwilliam Square South	36 E3	Fountain Road	35 B2
Ewington Lane	35 B3 [12]	Ferndale Road (Shankill)	56 D3	Fitzwilliam Square West	36 E3	Fourth Avenue	40 F4
*Exchange St. Lr	36 D2	Fernhill Avenue	41 C3	Fitzwilliam Street (Ringsend)	37 A3 [2]	Fourth Avenue (Seville Place)	36 F2 [8]
(off Wood Quay)		Fernhill Park	41 C3	Fitzwilliam Street Lower	36 E3	*Fownes Street Lower	36 D2
*Exchange St. Upr	36 D2	Fernhill Road	41 C3	Fitzwilliam Street Upper	36 E3	(off Temple Bar)	
(off Lord Edward St)		*Fernleigh (Est)	52 D3	Fitzwilliam Terrace	58 D2 [21]	Fownes Street Upper	36 D2 [47]
Exchequer Street	36 D3	Ferns Road	42 E1	Fleet Street	36 D2	*Fownes Street Upper	36 D2
		Fernvale Drive	42 D1	Fleming Road	21 A3	(off Dame St)	
F		Fernwood Avenue	48 E1	Fleming's Place	36 E4	Fox and Geese	41 A1
Faber Grove	53 B1 [9]	Fernwood Close	48 E1	Flemingstown Park	43 B4	Foxborough Avenue	32 E3

STREET INDEX

STREET NAME	PAGE/GRID REFERENCE
Foxborough Close	32 F3
Foxborough Court	32 F3
Foxborough Downes	32 E3
Foxborough Drive	32 E3
Foxborough Gardens	32 F3
Foxborough Glen	32 F3
Foxborough Green	32 F3
Foxborough Grove	32 F3
Foxborough Hall	32 F3 [1]
Foxborough Heights	32 F3
Foxborough Hill	32 E3
Foxborough Lane	32 F3
Foxborough Lawn	32 F3
Foxborough Meadows	32 E3
Foxborough Park	32 E3
Foxborough Place	32 E3
Foxborough Rise	32 E3
Foxborough Road	32 E3
Foxborough Road	32 E3
Foxborough Row	32 F3
Foxborough Villas	32 F3
Foxborough Walk	32 F3
Foxdene Avenue	32 F3
Foxdene Drive	32 F3
Foxdene Gardens	32 F3
Foxdene Green	32 F3
Foxdene Grove	32 F3
Foxdene Park	32 F3
Foxes Grove	56 E3
Foxfield	32 D3
Foxfield Avenue	23 B2
Foxfield Crescent	23 B2
Foxfield Drive	23 B2
Foxfield Green	23 B2
Foxfield Grove	23 B2
Foxfield Heights	23 B2
Foxfield Lawn	23 B2
Foxfield Park	23 B2
Foxfield Road	23 B2
Foxfield St John	23 B2
Foxford	32 F2
Foxhill Avenue	23 A1
Foxhill Close	23 A1
Foxhill Court	23 A1
Foxhill Crescent	23 A1
Foxhill Drive	23 A1
Foxhill Green	12 D4
Foxhill Grove	23 A1
Foxhill Lawn	23 A1
Foxhill Park	23 A1
Foxhill Way	23 A1
Foxpark	32 D3
Foxrock	53 A3
Foxrock Avenue	53 A2
Foxrock Close	53 B2
Foxrock Court	53 A2
Foxrock Crescent	53 B2
Foxrock Green	53 A2
Foxrock Grove	53 B2
Foxrock Manor	52 F2
Foxrock Mount	53 A2 [4]
Foxrock Park	53 A2
Foxrock Wood	53 B2
Fox's Lane	23 B2
Foxwood	2 D2
Foxwood	32 D3
Foyle Road	21 C4
Fr Kitt Court	42 D1 [3]
Francis Street	35 C3
Frankfort	43 B4 [10]
Frankfort Avenue	43 A2
Frankfort Cottages	36 E1
Frankfort Court	42 F2 [8]
Frankfort Flats	42 F2 [9]
Frankfort Park	43 B4
Frascati Park	45 A3
Frascati Road	45 A3
Frederick Court	36 D1 [46]
Frederick Lane North	36 D1 [14]
Frederick Street North	36 D1
Frederick Street South	36 E3
Frenchman's Lane	36 E2 [20]
Friar's Walk	40 E1 [5]
Friarsland Avenue	43 C3 [3]

STREET NAME	PAGE/GRID REFERENCE
Friarsland Road	43 C3
Friary Avenue	35 C2 [6]
Friary Grove	35 C2 [41]
*Friary Grove (off Friary Ave)	35 C2
Fumbally Lane	36 D3
Furry Park	22 E3
Furry Park Court	22 E3
Furry Park Road	22 E3
Furze Road	34 E1
Furze Road	52 E2

G

STREET NAME	PAGE/GRID REFERENCE
Gables	23 A1 [6]
Gaelic Street	36 F1 [6]
Gainsborough Avenue	2 F3
Gainsborough Close	2 F3
Gainsborough Court	2 F3
Gainsborough Crescent	2 F3
Gainsborough Downs	2 F3
Gainsborough Green	2 F3
Gainsborough Lawn	2 F3
Gainsborough Park	2 F3
Gallanstown Drive	33 C4
Gallanstown Green	33 C4
Gallanstown Lower	33 C4
Gallanstown Way	33 C4 [1]
Gallaun Road	9 C4
Galloping Green	52 F1
Galloping Green	53 A1 [9]
Galmoy Road	20 F4
Galtrim Park	57 C2
Galtrim Road	57 C2
Galtymore Close	34 F4
Galtymore Drive	35 A4
Galtymore Park	34 F4
Galtymore Road	35 A4
Gandon Close	42 F1 [9]
Gandon Mews	32 D1 [10]
Garden Lane	35 C3 [21]
*Garden Terrace	35 C4
(off Clanbrassil St Upper)	
Garden View	36 D4 [42]
Gardiner Lane	36 E1
Gardiner Place	36 D1
Gardiner Row	36 D1 [40]
Gardiner St Middle	36 E1
Gardiner Street Lower	36 E1
Gardiner Street Upper	36 D1
Garnett Hall	5 A2
Garrynisk Close	40 F3
Garrynisk Road	40 F3
Garryowen Road	34 E3
Gartan	2 E1
Gartan Avenue	21 A4
Gartan Court	2 E1
Gartan Drive	2 E1
Garter Lane	47 B1
Garville Avenue	43 A2
Garville Avenue Upper	42 F2
Garville Court	43 A2 [10]
Garville Drive	43 A2 [6]
*Garville Drive (off Garville Ave)	43 A2
Garville Lane	43 A2
Garville Place	43 A2 [5]
Garville Road	43 A2
Gas Yard Lane	3 B2
Gaybrook Lawns	3 A3
Geoffrey Keating Road	35 C3 [30]
*George Reynolds Flats	37 A3
(off Oliver Plunkett Ave)	
George's Avenue (Blackrock)	45 A3
George's Hill	36 D2 [6]
George's Lane	35 C2 [3]
George's Place	36 D1 [43]
George's Place (Blackrock)	45 A3 [6]
George's Place (Dun Laoghaire)	46 D4
George's Quay	36 E2
Georges Road	20 E1 [1]
George's Street Great North	36 D1
George's Street Great South	36 D3
George's Stt Lr (Dun Laoghaire)	46 D4
George's Stt Upr (Dun Laoghaire)	46 D4
Georgian Hamlet	13 A4
Georgian Village	19 A4

STREET NAME	PAGE/GRID REFERENCE
Gerald Street	36 F3 [9]
Geraldine Street	36 D1
Gertrude Terrace	57 B2 [25]
Gilbert Road	35 C4 [12]
Gilford Avenue	37 B4
Gilford Court	37 A4 [10]
Gilford Drive	37 A4
Gilford Park	37 A4
Gilford Place	36 E1 [30]
Gilford Road	37 A4
Gilford Terrace	37 B4 [1]
Glandore Park	53 C1
Glandore Road	21 C3
Glasanaon Court	20 E2
Glasanaon Park	20 E2
Glasanaon Road	20 E2
Glasaree Road	20 E2
Glasilawn Avenue	20 F2
Glasilawn Road	20 F2
Glasmeen Road	20 F2
Glasmore Park	1 C1
Glasnamana Place	20 F2 [2]
Glasnamana Road	20 F2
Glasnevin	20 F3
Glasnevin Avenue	20 F1
Glasnevin Court	20 E3
Glasnevin Downs	20 F3
Glasnevin Drive	21 A1
Glasnevin Hill	21 A3
Glasnevin North	20 F1
Glasnevin Oaks	20 F3 [3]
Glasnevin Park	20 F1
Glasnevin Woods	20 E3
Glasson Court	43 B3
Glasthule Buildings	54 E1 [11]
Glasthule Road	54 E1
Gleann na Rí	55 C1
Gleann na Smol	45 B4
Gleann na Smol	48 F2
Glebe View	20 E2 [7]
Gledswood Avenue	43 C3
Gledswood Close	43 C3
Gledswood Drive	43 C3 [5]
Gledswood Park	43 C3
Glen Avenue	53 B3
Glen Close	53 B3
Glen Dale	53 B3
Glen Drive	53 B3
Glen Druid	56 E1 [11]
Glen Ellan Avenue	1 C1
Glen Ellan Close	1 C1
Glen Ellan Court	1 C1
Glen Ellan Crescent	1 C1
Glen Ellan Drive	1 C1
Glen Ellan Gardens	1 C1
Glen Ellan Green	1 C1
Glen Ellan Grove	1 C1
Glen Ellan Park	1 C1
Glen Ellan Pines	1 C1
Glen Ellan Walk	1 C1
Glen Garth	53 B3
Glen Grove	53 B3
Glen Lawn Drive	53 B3
Glen na Smol	57 C4
Glen Terrace	54 E1 [10]
Glen Walk	53 B3
Glenaan Road	21 B2
Glenabbey Road	44 E4
Glenageary Avenue	54 D2
Glenageary Court	54 D2
Glenageary Hall	54 E2
Glenageary Lodge	54 D2
Glenageary Park	54 D2
Glenageary Road Lower	54 D1
Glenageary Road Upper	54 D1
Glenageary Woods	54 D1
Glenagle Grove	56 E1
Glenalbyn Road	52 F1
Glenalua Heights	54 E3
Glenalua Road	54 E3
Glenalua Terrace	54 E3
Glenamuck Cottages	55 A1
Glenamuck Road	55 A2
Glenann	42 F4 [4]

STREET NAME	PAGE/GRID REFERENCE
Glenanne	42 E2
Glenard Avenue	35 B1 [5]
Glenard Avenue	57 C2
Glenard Hall	43 B3 [7]
Glenarm Avenue	21 B4
Glenarriff Road	19 C3
Glenart Avenue	44 F4
Glenaulin	34 D2
Glenaulin Drive	34 D2
Glenaulin Green	33 C2 [2]
Glenaulin Park	34 D2
Glenaulin Road	33 C2
Glenavon Park	56 D1
Glenavy Park	42 E2
Glenayle Road	22 F1
Glenayr Road	42 E2
Glenbeigh Park	35 B1
Glenbeigh Road	35 B1
Glenbourne Avenue	52 F4
Glenbourne Close	52 F4
Glenbourne Crescent	52 F4
*Glenbourne Drive	52 F4
Glenbourne Green	52 F4
Glenbourne Grove	52 F4
Glenbourne Park	52 F4
Glenbourne Road	52 F4
Glenbourne View	52 F4
Glenbourne Walk	52 F4
Glenbourne Way	52 F4
Glenbower Park	43 B4 [1]
Glenbrook Park	42 F4
Glenbrook Road	19 C3
Glenburgh Terrace	57 B2 [1]
Glencairn	52 E3
Glencairn Avenue	52 E3
Glencairn Chase	52 E3
Glencairn Close	52 E3
Glencairn Copse	52 E3
Glencairn Court	52 E4
Glencairn Crescent	52 E3
Glencairn Dale	52 E3
Glencairn Drive	52 E3
Glencairn Garth	52 E3 [1]
Glencairn Glade	52 E3
Glencairn Glen	52 F4
Glencairn Green	52 E3
Glencairn Grove	52 F4
Glencairn Heath	52 E3 [2]
Glencairn Heath	52 E3
Glencairn Heights	52 E3
Glencairn Lawn	52 E3
Glencairn Oaks	52 E3
Glencairn Park	52 E3
Glencairn Place	52 E3
Glencairn Rise	52 E3
Glencairn Road	52 E3
Glencairn Thicket	52 F3
Glencairn View	52 E3
Glencairn Walk	52 E3
Glencairn Way	52 E3
Glencar Road	35 B1 [1]
Glencarr Court	56 E1 [8]
Glencarr Lawn	56 E1
Glencarraig	25 B1
Glencarrig Court	49 B2
Glencarrig Drive	49 B2
Glencarrig Green	49 B2
Glencloy Road	21 B2
Glencorp Road	21 C2
Glencourt Estate	57 B3
Glendale	16 D4
Glendale Drive	57 C3
Glendale Meadows	16 E4
Glendale Park	42 D3
Glendalough Road	21 A4 [6]
*Glendenning Lane	36 D3
(off Wicklow Street)	
Glendhu Park	19 C3
Glendhu Road	19 C3
Glendoher Avenue	50 F1
Glendoher Close	50 F1
Glendoher Drive	50 F1
Glendoher Park	50 E1
Glendoher Road	50 E1

STREET NAME	PAGE/GRID REFERENCE	STREET NAME	PAGE/GRID REFERENCE	STREET NAME	PAGE/GRID REFERENCE	STREET NAME	PAGE/GRID REFERENCE
Glendoo Close	41 B3	Glenville Drive	18 E3	Grange Brook	50 F2	Green Acre Court	50 D1
Glendown Avenue	42 D3	Glenville Garth	18 E3	Grange Close	23 C1	Green Isle Court	40 D2 [2]
Glendown Close	42 D3	Glenville Green	18 E2	Grange Cottages	53 B1 [6]	Green Lane	29 A2
Glendown Court	42 D3	Glenville Grove	18 E2	Grange Court	51 A1	Green Lane (Leixlip)	15 C4
Glendown Crescent	42 D3	Glenville Lawn	18 E2	Grange Crescent	53 B2	Green Park (Rathgar)	43 B3
Glendown Drive	42 D3	Glenville Road	18 E3	Grange Downs	51 A1	Green Park Road	57 B2
Glendown Green	42 D3	Glenville Terrace	43 C4 [8]	Grange Drive	23 C1	Green Road (Blackrock)	44 F3
Glendown Grove	42 D3	Glenville Way	18 E2	Grange Grove	53 B1 [2]	Green Street	36 D2
Glendown Lawn	42 D3	Glenwood	57 B2	Grange Manor	32 D3	Green Street East	36 F2
Glendown Park	42 D3	Glenwood Road	22 F1	Grange Manor Avenue	51 A1	Green Street Little	36 D2 [8]
Glendown Road	42 D3	Glin Avenue	11 B4	Grange Manor Close	51 A1	Greencastle Avenue	22 E1
Glendun Road	21 B2	Glin Crescent	11 B4	Grange Manor Drive	51 A1	Greencastle Crescent	22 E1
Glenealy Downs	6 F4	Glin Drive	11 B4	Grange Manor Grove	51 A1	Greencastle Drive	11 B4
Glenealy Road	35 B4	Glin Grove	11 B4	Grange Manor Road	51 A1	Greencastle Parade	22 F1
Gleneaston	15 B4	Glin Park	11 B4	Grange Parade	23 C1	Greencastle Park	11 B4
Gleneaston	15 B4	Glin Road	11 B4	Grange Park (Baldoyle)	12 F4	Greencastle Road	22 E1
Gleneaston Close	15 B4	Gloucester Diamond	36 E1 [52]	Grange Park (Cornelscourt)	53 B2	Greendale Avenue	23 C2
Gleneaston Crescent	15 B4	*Gloucester Lane	36 E1	Grange Park (Willbrook)	50 F1	Greendale Court	23 B2 [2]
Gleneaston Drive	15 B4	(off Sean McDermott Street Lr)		Grange Park Avenue	23 A2	Greendale Road	23 B2
Gleneaston Green	15 B4	Gloucester Place	36 E1 [25]	Grange Park Close	23 B2	Greenfield Crescent	44 D2
Gleneaston Lawns	15 B4	Gloucester Place Lower	36 E1 [53]	Grange Park Crescent	23 B2	Greenfield Manor	44 D2 [4]
Gleneaston Square	15 B4	Gloucester Place Lower	36 E1 [54]	Grange Park Drive	23 A2	Greenfield Park	44 D2
Gleneaston View	15 B4	Gloucester Place Upper	36 E1 [24]	Grange Park Green	23 B2	Greenfield Park	49 C2
Gleneaston Way	15 B4	Gloucester Street South	36 E2	Grange Park Grove	23 A2	*Greenfield Place	35 C4
Glenfarne Road	22 F1	Glovers Alley	36 D3 [28]	Grange Park Rise	23 B1	(off Mount Drummond Ave)	
Glenfield Avenue	33 A2	*Glovers Court (off York Street)	36 D3	Grange Park Road	23 A2	Greenfield Rd (Mount Merrion)	44 E3
Glenfield Close	33 A2	Goatstown	44 D4	Grange Park View	23 B1	Greenfield Rd (Sutton)	25 B1
Glenfield Drive	33 A2	Goatstown Avenue	43 C4	Grange Park Walk	23 A2	Greenfort Avenue	33 A2
Glenfield Grove	33 A2	Goatstown Road	43 C4	Grange Rise	12 F4	Greenfort Close	33 A2
Glenfield Park	33 A2	*Godfrey Place	35 B1	Grange Road (Baldoyle)	12 F4	Greenfort Crescent	33 A2
Glengara Close	54 D1 [15]	(off Oxmanstown Road)		Grange Road (Marley Park)	51 A1	Greenfort Drive	33 A2
Glengara Park	54 D1	Gofton Hall	20 E1 [2]	Grange Road (Rathfarnham)	42 F4	Greenfort Gardens	33 A2
Glengariff Parade	36 D1 [64]	Golden Lane	36 D3	Grange Road (The Priory)	50 F1	Greenfort Lawns	33 A2
Glengarriff Crescent	36 D1 [18]	Goldenbridge Avenue	35 A3	Grange View Close	39 B1	Greenfort Park	33 A2
Glengarriff Parade	36 D1	Goldenbridge Gardens	35 A3 [4]	Grange Way	23 C1	Greenhills	41 B3
Glenhill Avenue	20 E2	Goldenbridge Terrace	35 A3 [5]	Grange Wood (Ballinteer)	51 A2	Greenhills Road	41 A4
Glenhill Court	20 E2	Goldenbridge Walk	34 F4	Grangebrook Avenue	50 F2	Greenlands	52 D2
Glenhill Drive	20 E2	Goldenbridge Walk	35 A3 [16]	Grangebrook Close	50 F2	Greenlands	52 D2
Glenhill Grove	20 E2	Goldsmith Street	36 D1	Grangebrook Park	50 F2	Greenlawns	11 B4 [1]
Glenhill Road	20 E2	Goldsmith Terrace	57 C2 [25]	Grangebrook Vale	50 F2	Greenlea Avenue	42 E2
Glenhill Villas	20 E2 [2]	Gordon Avenue	53 A3	Grangegorman Lower	35 C2	Greenlea Drive	42 E2
Glenlucan	57 B2	Gordon Place	36 D4 [23]	Grangegorman Upper	35 C1	Greenlea Grove	42 E2
Glenlyon	49 C2	Gordon Street	36 F3	*Grangegorman Villas	35 C1	Greenlea Park	42 E3
Glenlyon Crescent	49 C2	Gorsefield Court	22 F2 [1]	(Grangegorman Upper)		Greenlea Place	42 F2 [12]
Glenlyon Grove	49 C2	Gort na Mona Drive	53 B3	Grangemore	12 E4	Greenlea Road	42 E3
Glenlyon Park	49 C2	Gortbeg Avenue	20 E3	Grangemore Avenue	12 D4	Greenmount Avenue	35 C4 [9]
Glenmalure Park	35 B3 [13]	Gortbeg Drive	20 E3	Grangemore Court	12 D4	Greenmount Court	35 C4 [19]
Glenmalure Square	43 B2	Gortbeg Park	20 E3	Grangemore Court	12 D4	Greenmount Lane	35 C4
*Glenmalure Villas (Rialto)	35 B3	Gortbeg Road	20 E3	Grangemore Crescent	12 D4	Greenmount Lawns	42 F2
Glenmaroon Park	33 C2	Gortmore Avenue	20 E2	Grangemore Drive	12 E4	Greenmount Road	42 F2
Glenmaroon Road	33 C2	Gortmore Drive	20 E2	Grangemore Grove	12 E4	Greenmount Square	35 C4 [14]
Glenmore Court	50 F2	Gortmore Park	20 E3	Grangemore Lawn	12 E4	Greenore Terrace	36 F3 [26]
Glenmore Park	50 F2	Gortmore Road	20 E3	Grangemore Park	12 E4	Greenpark Road	31 C2
Glenmore Road	35 B1 [1]	Gosworth Park	54 E1	Grangemore Rise	12 D4	Greenridge Court	18 E1
Glenmurry Park	41 C3 [2]	Gowrie Park	54 D1	Grangemore Road	12 D4	Greentrees Drive	41 C2
Glenomena Grove	44 E2	Grace O'Malley Drive	26 D2	Grangewood	53 C1	Greentrees Park	41 C2
Glenomena Park	44 E2	Grace O'Malley Road	26 D2	(Kill O' The Grange)		Greentrees Road	41 C2
Glenpark Close	33 B1	Grace Park Avenue	21 B4	Granite Hall	54 D1 [7]	Greenville Avenue	35 C4 [11]
Glenpark Drive	33 B1	Grace Park Court	21 C2	Granite Place	36 F4 [10]	*Greenville Parade (Blackpitts)	35 C3
Glenpark Road	33 B1	Grace Park Gardens	21 B4	Granite Terrace	34 F3 [11]	Greenville Place	35 C4 [35]
Glenshane Close	48 D1	Grace Park Heights	21 C3	Granitefield	53 C3	Greenville Road	45 B4
Glenshane Crescent	48 D1	Grace Park Meadows	21 C3	Granitefield	54 D3	Greenville Terrace	35 C4
Glenshane Drive	48 D1	Grace Park Road	21 C3	Grantham Place	36 D4	Greenwood Avenue	12 D4
Glenshane Gardens	48 D1	Grace Park Terrace	21 C3	Grantham Street	36 D4	Greenwood Close	12 D4
Glenshane Green	48 D1	Gracefield Avenue	22 F2	Grant's Row	36 E3 [5]	Greenwood Court	12 D4
Glenshane Grove	48 D1	Gracefield Road	22 E2	Granville Close	54 D3	Greenwood Drive	12 D4
Glenshane Lawns	48 D1	Grafton Street	36 D3	Granville Crescent	54 D3 [2]	Greenwood Park	12 D4
Glenshane Park	48 D1	Graham Court	36 D1 [13]	Granville Park	53 A1	Greenwood Walk	12 D4
Glenshesk Road	21 C2	Graham's Row	36 D1 [54]	Granville Road (Cabinteely)	53 C3	Greenwood Way	12 D4
Glenside Villas	33 C1 [2]	Graigue Court	9 C4	Granville Road (Deans Grange)	53 A2	Grenville Lane	36 D1 [15]
Glenthorn	57 B3	Granby Lane	36 D1	Grattan Court	29 C4	Grenville Street	36 D1
Glenties Drive	20 D2	Granby Place	36 D2	Grattan Court East	36 F3 [28]	Greygates	44 E4
Glenties Park	20 D2	Granby Row	36 D1	Grattan Crescent	34 F3	Greygates	44 E4 [1]
Glentow Road	21 B2	Grand Canal Docks	36 F3	Grattan Hall	12 E4	Grey's Lane	26 D2
Glentworth Park	23 A1 [2]	Grand Canal Place	35 C3 [2]	Grattan Lodge	12 E4	Greythorn Park	54 D1
Glenvale	32 E3	Grand Canal Quay	36 F3	Grattan Parade	21 A4	Griffeen	32 E3
Glenvar Park	44 F3	Grand Canal Street Lower	36 F3	Grattan Place	36 F3 [29]	Griffeen Avenue	32 D3
Glenvara Park	49 C2	Grand Canal Street Upper	36 F3	Grattan Street	36 E3	Griffeen Glen Avenue	32 E3
Glenview	54 D3	Grand Canal View	35 A3	Gray Square	35 C3 [41]	Griffeen Glen Chase	32 E3
Glenview Drive	49 B1 [2]	Grand Parade	36 E4	*Gray Street (off Meath St)	35 C3	Griffeen Glen Court	32 E3
Glenview Lawns	49 B1	Grange Abbey Crescent	12 E4	Great Western Avenue	35 C1 [18]	Griffeen Glen Crescent	32 E3
Glenview Park	49 B1	Grange Abbey Drive	12 E4	Great Western Square	35 C1 [8]	Griffeen Glen Dene	32 E3
Glenville Avenue	18 E2	Grange Abbey Grove	12 E4	Great Western Villas	35 C1 [9]	Griffeen Glen Drive	32 E3
Glenville Court	18 E3	Grange Avenue	12 F4	Greek Street	36 D2	Griffeen Glen Green	32 E3

STREET NAME	PAGE/GRID REFERENCE	STREET NAME	PAGE/GRID REFERENCE	STREET NAME	PAGE/GRID REFERENCE	STREET NAME	PAGE/GRID REFERENCE
Griffeen Glen Grove	32 E3	Hainault Road	53 A3	Hastings Street	36 F3 [5]	Hempenstal Terrace	37 B4 [5]
Griffeen Glen Lawn	32 E3	Halliday Road	35 C2	Hastings Terrace	54 E1 [12]	Hendrick Place	35 C2 [9]
Griffeen Glen Park	32 E3	Halliday Square	35 B2 [2]	Hatch Lane	36 E4 [2]	Hendrick Street	35 C2
Griffeen Glen Road	32 D3	Halston Street	36 D2	Hatch Place	36 E4 [13]	Henley Court	43 B4 [8]
Griffeen Glen Road	32 E3	Hamilton Court (Dunboyne)	5 B3 [3]	Hatch Street Lower	36 E4	Henley Park	43 B4
Griffeen Glen Vale	32 E3	*Hamilton Court	36 D2	Hatch Street Upper	36 D4	Henley Villas	43 B4
Griffeen GlenWay	32 E3	(off Strand St Little)		Hatter's Lane	35 C4 [15]	Henrietta Lane	36 D1
Griffeen Way	20 E2	Hamilton Hall	5 B3	Havelock Square	36 F3	Henrietta Place	36 D2
Griffith Avenue	21 B3	Hamilton Street	35 C4 [1]	Havelock Terrace	37 A3 [17]	Henrietta Street	36 D2
Griffith Close	20 F2	Hammond Lane	35 C2	Haven View	3 B2 [2]	Henry Place	36 D2 [16]
Griffith Court	21 C4	Hammond Street	35 C3 [56]	Haverty Road	21 C4	Henry Street	36 D2
Griffith Downs	21 B3	Hampstead Avenue	21 A2	Hawkins Street	36 E2	Herbert Avenue	44 E1
Griffith Drive	20 F2	Hampstead Court	21 A2	Hawthorn Avenue	36 F1	Herbert Cottages	36 F4 [4]
Griffith Lawns	21 A3	Hampstead Park	21 A3	Hawthorn Drive	51 B1 [2]	Herbert Crescent	18 F2 [1]
Griffith Parade	20 F2	Hampton Court	34 F3 [16]	Hawthorn Lawn	18 F3	Herbert Lane	36 E3 [41]
Griffith Road	20 F2	Hampton Crescent	44 E3	Hawthorn Lodge	18 F3	Herbert Park	36 F4
Griffith Square	35 C4 [22]	Hampton Estate	22 F4	Hawthorn Manor	53 A1 [4]	Herbert Park	57 B3
Grosvenor Avenue	58 D3 [3]	Hampton Green	35 B1	Hawthorn Park	1 C2	Herbert Park Lane	36 F4
Grosvenor Court	22 E4	Hampton Park	44 E3	Hawthorn Road	40 F1	Herbert Place	36 E3
Grosvenor Court	42 D3	Hanbury Lane (Lucan)	32 D1 [3]	Hawthorn Road	57 B1	(Baggot Street Lower)	
Grosvenor Lane	43 A1	Hanbury Lane (The Coombe)	35 C3	Hawthorn Terrace	36 F1	*Herbert Place (off Bath St)	37 A3
Grosvenor Lodge	43 A1	Hannaville Park	42 F2	Hawthorn View	30 D2	Herbert Road	57 B3
Grosvenor Park	43 A1 [7]	Hanover Lane	36 D3 [1]	Hawthorns Road	52 D2	Herbert Road (Blanchardstown)	18 F2
Grosvenor Place	43 A1	Hanover Quay	36 F2	Hayden's Lane	32 D3	Herbert Road (Sandymount)	37 A4
Grosvenor Road	43 A1	Hanover Square	36 D3 [47]	Haydens Park	32 D3	Herbert Street	36 E3
Grosvenor Square	43 A1	Hanover Street East	36 E2	Haymarket	35 C2	Herbert View	57 B2 [26]
Grosvenor Terrace (Dalkey)	54 F2 [17]	Hanover Street West	35 C3 [47]	Hazel Avenue	52 D1	Herberton Drive	35 B4
Grosvenor Terrace	45 C4 [9]	Hansfield	6 E4	Hazel Court	12 F2 [7]	Herberton Park	35 B3 [15]
(Dun Laoghaire)		Harbour Court	36 E2 [18]	Hazel Grove	12 F2	Herberton Road	35 B4
*Grosvenor Villas (Dalkey)	54 F2	Harbour Crescent	54 F1	Hazel Grove	48 D2	Hermitage Avenue (Grange Road)	50 F1
(Off Sorrento Rd)		Harbour Master Place	36 E2 [34]	Hazel Lawn	18 E2	Hermitage Close (Grange Road)	50 F1
Grosvenor Villas (Rathmines)	43 A1	Harbour Road (Dalkey)	54 F1	Hazel Lawn	53 C2 [4]	Hermitage Court (Grange Road)	51 A1
Grotto Avenue	44 F2	Harbour Road (Dun Laoghaire)	46 D4	Hazel Park	42 E2 [2]	Hermitage Crescent (Lucan)	32 F1
Grotto Place	44 F2	Harbour Road (Howth)	26 D1	Hazel Road	22 D3	Hermitage Downs	51 A1
Grove Avenue	3 C3	Harbour Terrace	45 C4 [8]	Hazel Villas	52 D1	Hermitage Drive (Grange Road)	50 F1
Grove Avenue (Finglas)	20 E1	Harbour View	26 D1 [6]	Hazelbrook Court	42 E2	Hermitage Garden (Lucan)	32 F1
Grove Avenue (Harold's Cross)	36 D4 [47]	Harcourt Lane	36 D4 [14]	Hazelbrook Drive	42 E2	Hermitage Green (Lucan)	32 F1
Grove Avenue (Mount Merrion)	44 F4	Harcourt Lodge	35 A3 [22]	Hazelbrook Road	42 E2	Hermitage Grove (Grange Road)	50 F1
Grove Court	1 A2 [1]	Harcourt Road	36 D4	Hazelcroft Gardens	20 E2	Hermitage Lawn (Grange Road)	50 F1
Grove Court	34 F4 [4]	Harcourt Street	36 D3	Hazelcroft Park	20 E2	Hermitage Manor (Lucan)	32 F1
Grove House Gardens	44 F4 [5]	Harcourt Terrace	36 E4	Hazelcroft Road	20 E2	Hermitage Park (Grange Road)	50 F1
Grove Lane	11 C4	*Harcourt Villas	43 C3	Hazeldene	43 C1	Hermitage Park (Lucan)	32 F1
Grove Lawn	44 F4	(off Dundrum Rd/Mulvey Pk)		Hazelwood (Bray)	57 B2	Hermitage Place (Lucan)	32 F1
Grove Lawns (Malahide)	3 C3	Hardebeck Avenue	41 C1	Hazelwood (Shankill)	56 E2	Hermitage Road (Lucan)	32 F1
Grove Paddock	44 F4	Hardiman Road	21 A3	Hazelwood Avenue	17 C1	Hermitage Valley (Lucan)	32 F1
Grove Park	11 C4	*Hardwicke Arch	36 D1	Hazelwood Bank	40 D2	Hermitage View (Grange Road)	50 F1
Grove Park (Rathmines)	36 D4	(off Hardwicke St)		Hazelwood Close	40 D2	Hermitage Way (Lucan)	32 F1
Grove Park Avenue	20 F1	Hardwicke Lane	36 D1 [45]	Hazelwood Court	17 C1	Heronford Lane	55 C2
Grove Park Crescent	20 F1	Hardwicke Place	36 D1 [12]	Hazelwood Court	22 D1	Heuston Square	35 A3 [11]
Grove Park Drive	20 F1	Hardwicke Street	36 D1	Hazelwood Crescent	17 C1	*Hewardine Terrace	36 E1
Grove Park Road	20 F1	Harelawn Avenue	33 A3	Hazelwood Crescent	40 D2	(off Killarney Street)	36 F4
Grove Road (Finglas)	20 E1	Harelawn Crescent	33 A3	Hazelwood Drive	22 D2	Heytesbury Lane	36 D3
Grove Road (Malahide)	3 C3	Harelawn Drive	33 A2	Hazelwood Green	17 C1	Heytesbury Street	
Grove Road (Rathmines)	36 D4	Harelawn Green	33 A3	Hazelwood Grove	22 E1	Hibernian Avenue	36 F1 [1]
Grove Wood	20 E1	Harelawn Grove	33 A2	Hazelwood Lane	40 D2	Hibernian Terrace	34 E2 [3]
Grovedale	55 B2	Harelawn Park	33 A2	Hazelwood Park	22 E1	High Park	21 C2
Guild Street	36 F2	Harlech Crescent	44 D3	Hazelwood View	40 D2	High Street	36 D3
Guilford Terrace	56 E3 [1]	Harlech Downs	43 C3	Hazlebrook Apartments	42 E2 [7]	High Street	49 A1 [1]
Gulistan Cottages	43 A1	Harlech Grove	44 D3	Hazlebury Park	6 E4	Highbridge Green	52 E1
Gulistan Place	43 A1	Harlech Villas	43 C3 [4]	Headford Grove	43 B4	Highfield Avenue (Dundrum)	51 A2
Gulistan Terrace	43 A1	Harman Street	35 C3 [54]	Healthfield Road	42 F2	Highfield Close	1 C2
Gurteen Avenue	34 D3	Harmonstown Road	22 F2	*Healy Street	36 E1	Highfield Court	43 A2 [3]
Gurteen Park	34 D3	Harmony Avenue	43 C1 [5]	(off Rutland Place North)		Highfield Crescent	1 C2
Gurteen Road	34 D2	Harmony Row	36 E3 [23]	Heany Avenue	54 F2 [19]	Highfield Downs	1 C2
		Harold Bridge Court	35 C4 [36]	Heather Close	51 A2	Highfield Drive	51 A2
H		*Harold Crescent	54 E1	Heather Drive	51 A2	Highfield Green	1 C2
Hacketsland	56 E1	(off Eden Rd Lower)		Heather Gardens	4 D4	Highfield Grove	43 A2
Haddington Lawns	54 E2	Harold Road	35 C2	Heather Grove (Ballinteer)	51 B2	Highfield Lawn	1 C2
Haddington Park	54 E2	Harold Ville Avenue	35 B3	Heather Grove (Palmerston)	33 B2	Highfield Park	31 A1
Haddington Place	36 F3 [18]	Harold's Cross	42 F1	Heather Lawn	51 A2	Highfield Park	43 B3
Haddington Road	36 F3	Harold's Cross Cottages	35 C4 [18]	Heather Park	51 B2	Highfield Road	43 A2
Haddington Terrace	46 D4 [7]	Harold's Cross Cottages	36 D4 [54]	Heather Road	51 A2	Highland Avenue	53 B3
Haddon Court	37 B1 [2]	Harold's Cross Road	42 F1	Heather Road	52 E2	Highland Grove	53 B3
Haddon Park	22 D4 [5]	Harold's Grange Road	51 B3	Heather View Avenue	48 F2	Highland Lawn	53 B3
Haddon Road	22 E4	Harrington Street	36 D4	Heather View Close	48 F2	Highland View	53 B3
Hadleigh Court	19 A3	Harrison Row	42 F2	Heather View Drive	48 F2	Highthorn Park	53 C1
Hadleigh Green	19 A3 [2]	Harry Street	36 D3 [17]	Heather View Lawn	48 F2	Highthorn Woods	53 C1 [10]
Hadleigh Park	19 A3	Hartstown	17 B1	Heather View Park	48 F2	Hill Cottages	54 E3 [1]
Hagan's Court	36 E3 [39]	Hartstown Road	17 C1	Heather View Road	48 F2	Hill Court	12 F1
Haigh Terrace	46 D4	Harty Avenue	41 C1	Heather Walk	4 D4	Hill Drive	3 B3
Hainault Drive	53 B3	Harty Court	41 C1 [8]	Heatherwood	57 B4	Hill Street	36 D1
Hainault Grove	53 B3 [2]	*Harty Court (off Daniel Street)	36 D3	Heathfield	45 B4 [17]	Hill View (Ballinteer)	51 B1
Hainault Lawn	53 B3 [3]	Harty Place	36 D3	*Heatley Villas (on Pearse Road)	53 C2	Hill View Court	51 B1
Hainault Park	53 A3	Harvard	44 D3	Heidelberg	44 D3	Hillcourt Park	54 D2

STREET NAME	PAGE/GRID REFERENCE
Hillcourt Road	54 D2
Hillcrest	3 A2
Hillcrest	32 D2
Hillcrest (Templeogue)	42 D4 [1]
Hillcrest Avenue	31 C2
Hillcrest Close	31 C2
Hillcrest Court	32 D2
Hillcrest Downs	52 D3
Hillcrest Drive	31 C2
Hillcrest Green	31 C2
Hillcrest Grove	32 D2
Hillcrest Heights	31 C2
Hillcrest Lawns	31 C2
Hillcrest Manor	42 D4 [2]
Hillcrest Park	20 F2
Hillcrest Park	31 C2
Hillcrest Road (Lucan)	32 D2
Hillcrest Road (Sandyford)	52 D3
Hillcrest View	31 C2
Hillcrest Walk	31 C2
Hillcrest Way	31 C2
Hillsbrook Avenue	42 D2
Hillsbrook Crescent	42 D2
Hillsbrook Drive	42 D2
Hillsbrook Grove	42 D2
Hillside	54 E2
Hillside Drive	43 A3
Hillside Park	50 E1
Hillside Terrace	26 D2 [7]
Hilltop Lawn	56 D3
Hilltown	1 B3
Hilltown Close	1 C2
Hilltown Court	1 C2
Hilltown Green	1 C2
Hilltown Grove	1 C2
Hilltown Lawn	1 C2
Hilltown Park	1 C2
Hilltown Road	1 C2
Hilltown Way	1 C2
Hillview Cottages	53 C2 [1]
Hillview Drive	53 C2
Hillview Glade	51 B1 [5]
Hillview Grove	51 B1 [6]
Hillview Lawn	53 C2
Hilton Gardens	51 C2
*Hoeys Court (off Werburgh St)	36 D3
Hogan Avenue	36 F3 [27]
Hogan Place	36 E3
Holles Place	36 E3 [34]
Holles Row	36 E3 [7]
Holles Street	36 E3
Holly Avenue	52 D1
Holly Court	56 D1 [4]
Holly Court	56 D1
Holly Park	56 E2
Holly Park Avenue	53 A1
Holly Road (Donnycarney)	22 D3
Holly Road (Fox and Geese)	40 F1
Hollybank Avenue Lower	43 B1
Hollybank Avenue Upper	43 B1
Hollybank Road	21 A4
Hollybrook Court	22 D4 [3]
Hollybrook Court Drive	22 D4 [2]
Hollybrook Grove	22 D4
Hollybrook Park	22 D4
Hollybrook Park	57 C4
Hollybrook Road	22 D4
Hollybrooke	34 E4 [4]
Hollystown	7 B1
Hollyville Lawn	33 C1
Hollywood Drive	44 D4
Hollywood Park	44 D4
*Holme's Cottages (Church Ave Rathmines)	43 A1
Holmston Avenue	54 D1
Holmwood	53 B4
Holycross Avenue	21 B4 [5]
*Holycross Cottages (off Holycross Avenue)	21 B4
Holyrood Park	37 A4
Holywell	52 D1
Holywell Avenue	23 B1
Holywell Crescent	23 B1
Holywell Road	23 B1

STREET NAME	PAGE/GRID REFERENCE
Home Farm Park	21 B3
Home Farm Road	21 A3
Home Villas	43 C1
Homelawn Avenue	49 B1
Homelawn Drive	49 B1
Homelawn Gardens	49 B1
Homelawn Road	49 B1
Homelawn Villas	49 A1
*Homelawn Villas (Homelawn Rd)	49 A1
Homelee	37 A4 [11]
Homeleigh	18 D4
Homeville	43 A1
Homeville	49 C1 [4]
Homeville Court	49 C1 [3]
Honey Park	54 D2 [1]
Hope Avenue	36 F1
*Hope Street (off Gordon Street)	36 F3
Horton Court	42 F2
Hospital Lane	35 A2 [2]
Hotel Yard	36 D2 [29]
Houghton Terrace	35 C2 [28]
*Howard Street (off Gordon St)	36 F3
Howth	26 D2
Howth Junction Cottages	23 B1 [1]
Howth Road (Howth)	25 C1
Howth Road (Killester)	22 E3
Howth Road (Marino)	22 D4
Howth Road (Raheny)	22 F3
Howth Road (Raheny)	23 B2
Howth Road (Sutton)	25 B1
Howth Terrace	26 D1 [5]
Howth View Park	23 B1
Huband Road	34 F4
Hudson Road	54 E1
Hughes Road East	41 C1
Hughes Road North	41 C1
Hughes Road South	41 C1
Hume Street	36 E3
Hunters Run	6 E4
Hunters Run The Close	6 E4
Hunters Run The Drive	6 E4
Hunters Run The Glade	6 E4
Hunters Run The Grove	6 E4
Hunters Run The Park	6 E4
Hunters Run The Rise	6 F4
Hunters Run The View	6 F4
Hunters Run The Way	6 F4
Huntstown Avenue	17 C1
Huntstown Close	6 F4
Huntstown Court	6 F4
Huntstown Drive	6 F4
Huntstown Glen	6 F4
Huntstown Green	6 F4
Huntstown Grove	6 F4
Huntstown Lawn	18 D1 [1]
Huntstown Park (Mulhuddart)	6 F4
Huntstown Rise	7 A4
Huntstown Road	17 C1
Huntstown Way	7 A4
Huntstown Wood	6 F4
Hutchinson's Strand	2 E1
Huxley Crescent	35 C3 [8]
Hyacinth Street	36 F1 [7]
Hybreasal	35 A3 [1]
Hyde Park (Dalkey)	54 E1
Hyde Park (Templeogue)	42 E3
Hyde Park Avenue	44 F3
Hyde Park Gardens	44 F3
Hyde Road	54 F1

I

STREET NAME	PAGE/GRID REFERENCE
Idrone Avenue	50 D1
Idrone Close	50 D1
Idrone Drive	50 D1
Idrone Mews	45 A3 [11]
Idrone Park	50 D1
Idrone Terrace	45 A3
Imaal Road	35 C1
Inagh Court	56 E1
Inagh Road	34 D3
Inbhir Ide	3 A2
Inbhir Ide Close	3 A2
Inbhir Ide Drive	3 A2

STREET NAME	PAGE/GRID REFERENCE
Inchicore	34 F3
Inchicore Road	35 A3
Inchicore Square	34 F3 [13]
Inchicore Terrace North	34 F3 [3]
Inchicore Terrace South	34 F3
Infirmary Road	35 B2
Inglewood Close	17 C2
Inglewood Crescent	17 C2
Inglewood Drive	17 C2
Inglewood Road	17 C2
Ingram Road	35 C4 [2]
Inis Fail	48 F2
Inis Thiar	48 F2
*Inkerman Cottages (off Amiens Street)	36 E2
Innisfallen Parade	36 D1
Innishmaan Road	21 B2
*Innishmore Tce (St Mary's Rd)	42 D1
Innismore	42 D1
*Inns Court (on Winetavern St)	36 D2
Inver Road	20 E4
Invermore Grove	23 A1 [3]
Inverness Road	21 C4
Iona Crescent	21 A4
Iona Drive	21 A4
Iona Park	21 A4
Iona Road	21 A4
Iona Villas	21 A4
Iris Grove	44 E3
Irishtown	37 A3
Irishtown (Bray)	57 C4
Irishtown Road	37 A3
Irvine Cottages	36 F2 [10]
Irvine Terrace	36 F2
Irwin Court	35 B3 [24]
Irwin Street	35 B3 [1]
Island Street	35 C2
Island View	3 C3
Island View Apts.	26 D1 [9]
Island Villa	36 F3 [3]
Islandbridge	35 A2
Islandbridge Court	35 A2 [1]
Islington Avenue	46 E4
Isolda Road	37 A3
Isolde Gardens	34 E2 [6]
Ivar Street	35 C2
Iveagh Buildings	36 D3 [4]
Iveagh Gardens	35 A4 [1]
Iveagh Gardens	35 A4
Iveleary Road	21 B2
Iveragh Court	36 F4 [17]
Iveragh Road	21 B2
Ivy Court	21 C1
Ivy Terrace	35 C3 [61]

J

STREET NAME	PAGE/GRID REFERENCE
James Connolly Park	33 A4
James Connolly Square	57 C2 [5]
James Everett Park	57 B2
James Larkin Road	23 B2
James McCormack Gardens	25 A1 [1]
James's Place East	36 E3
James's Street	35 B3
James's Street East	36 E3
James's Street North	36 F1 [20]
James's Terrace	3 B2
Jamestown Avenue	34 F4
Jamestown Court	34 F4
Jamestown Road (Finglas)	20 E1
Jamestown Road (Inchicore)	34 F4
*Jane-Ville (Off Tivoli Road)	46 D4
Jervis Lane Lower	36 D2 [11]
Jervis Lane Upper	36 D2 [10]
Jervis Street	36 D2
Jobstown	48 D2
Jobstown Road	48 D2
John Dillon Street	36 D3
John F Kennedy Avenue	41 A1
John F Kennedy Drive	41 A1
John F Kennedy Park	34 D4
John F Kennedy Road	34 D4
John Field Road	36 D3 [40]
John MacCormack Avenue	41 C1
*John Street Nth (off Ellis Quay)	35 C2

STREET NAME	PAGE/GRID REFERENCE
John Street South	35 C3
John Street West	35 C3
John's Lane East	36 D3 [13]
John's Lane West	35 C3 [50]
Johnsbridge	32 D3
Johnsbridge Avenue	32 D3
Johnsbridge Close	32 D3
Johnsbridge Green	32 D3
Johnsbridge Grove	32 D3
Johnsbridge Meadows	32 D3
Johnsbridge Park	32 D3
Johnsbridge Walk	32 D3
Johnson Place	36 D3 [36]
Johnson's Court	36 D3 [30]
Johnstown Avenue	53 C3
Johnstown Court	53 C2
Johnstown Gardens	20 E2 [5]
Johnstown Grove	53 C3
Johnstown House	20 F2 [3]
Johnstown Lane	53 C3
Johnstown Park (Cornelscourt)	53 C3
Johnstown Park (Glasnevin)	20 F2
Johnstown Road	53 C3
Jones Terrace	58 D2 [18]
Jones's Road	36 E1
Josephine Avenue	36 D1 [25]
*Joy Street (off Gordon Street)	36 F3
Joyce Avenue	53 A3
Joyce Road	21 A3
Joyce Way	33 C4
Jugback Close	1 C1
Jugback Crescent	1 C1
Jugback Lane	1 C1

K

STREET NAME	PAGE/GRID REFERENCE
Keadeen Avenue	41 B2
Kearn's Place	35 A3 [7]
*Keegan's Cottages (off Merrion Rd)	44 E1
Keeper Road	35 B4
Kells Road	42 E1
Kelly's Avenue	46 D4
Kelly's Lane	36 D1 [22]
Kelly's Row	36 D1
Kellystown Road	51 B4
Kelvin Close	4 D4
Kempton	19 C3
Kempton Avenue	19 C3
Kempton Court	19 C3
Kempton Green	19 C3
Kempton Grove	19 C3
Kempton Heath	19 C3
Kempton Lawn	19 C3
Kempton Park	19 C3
Kempton Rise	19 C3
Kempton View	19 C3
Kempton Way	19 C3
Kenah Court	54 E3
Kengar Mews	42 F1 [14]
Kenilworth Lane	42 F1
Kenilworth Manor	42 F1 [11]
Kenilworth Park	42 F1
Kenilworth Road	43 A1
Kenilworth Square	42 F1
Kenilworth Square East	43 A1
Kenilworth Square North	42 F1
Kenilworth Square South	42 F1
Kenilworth Square West	42 F1
Kenmare Parade	36 D1 [31]
Kennedy Court	37 A3 [31]
Kennedy Park	57 C3 [5]
Kennedy's Villas	35 B3 [2]
Kennelsfort Green	33 B2
Kennelsfort Road Lower	33 C1
Kennelsfort Road Upper	33 C2
Kennington Close	41 C4
Kennington Crescent	41 C4
Kennington Lawn	41 C4
Kennington Road	41 C3
*Kent Terrace (on Barnhill Road Dalkey)	54 F2
Kentfield	56 E2
Kerlogue Road	37 A3
Kerrymount Avenue	53 A4

STREET NAME	PAGE/GRID REFERENCE	STREET NAME	PAGE/GRID REFERENCE	STREET NAME	PAGE/GRID REFERENCE	STREET NAME	PAGE/GRID REFERENCE
Kerrymount Close	53 B3 [1]	Killakee Avenue	49 B2	Kilmartin Green	48 D1	Kingston Park	51 B3
Kerrymount Green	53 B3	Killakee Avenue	49 B2	Kilmartin Park	48 D1	Kingston Rise	51 B3
Kerrymount Mall	53 B3	Killakee Court	49 B2	Kilmashogue Close	41 B3	Kingston View	51 B3
Kerrymount Rise	53 B3	Killakee Gardens	49 B2	Kilmashogue Drive	41 B3	Kingston Walk	51 B3
Kettles Lane	2 E4	Killakee Green	49 B2	Kilmashogue Grove	41 B3	Kingswood Avenue	40 F3
*Kevin Barry(off Church St Upr)	35 C2	Killakee Grove	49 B2	Kilmashogue Lane	50 F3	Kingswood Castle	41 A2
*Kevin Street Cross	36 D3	Killakee Lawns	49 B2	Kilmore	22 D1	Kingswood Drive	40 F3
(on Bride St New)		Killakee Park	49 B2	Kilmore Avenue (Coolock)	22 E1	Kingswood Heights	40 F3
Kevin Street Lower	36 D3	Killakee View	49 B2	Kilmore Avenue (Killiney)	54 E4	Kingswood View	40 F3
Kevin Street Upper	36 D3	Killakee Walk	49 B2	Kilmore Close	22 E1	Kinsaley	12 D1
Kew Park	31 C1	Killakee Way	49 B2	Kilmore Court	22 D1 [5]	Kinsaley Lane	3 A4
Kew Park Avenue	31 B2	Killala Road	20 E4	Kilmore Crescent	22 E1	Kinsealy Court	2 E3
Kew Park Crescent	31 B1	Killan Road	36 F2	Kilmore Drive	22 E1	Kinsealy Downs	2 E3
Kickham Road	35 A3	Killarney Avenue	36 E1 [13]	Kilmore Road	22 D1	Kinvara Avenue	20 D4
Kilakee Close	41 B3	Killarney Glen	57 B2	Kilmorony Close	23 A1	Kinvara Drive	19 C4
Kilakee Drive	41 B3	Killarney Heights	57 B3	Kilnamanagh	41 A3	Kinvara Grove	19 C4
Kilakee Road	50 D4	Killarney Lane	57 B3	Kilnamanagh Road	41 C1	Kinvara Park	20 D4
Kilbarrack	23 C1	Killarney Parade	36 D1 [30]	Kilohan Grove	41 B3	Kinvara Road	19 C4
Kilbarrack Avenue	23 C2	Killarney Park	57 B3	Kilrock Road	26 E2	Kippure Avenue	41 B3
Kilbarrack Gardens	23 C2	Killarney Road	57 B3	Kilronan Court	22 D4 [7]	Kippure Park	20 D3
Kilbarrack Grove	23 C2	Killarney Street	36 E1	Kilshane Road	19 C2	Kirkfield	18 D2 [2]
Kilbarrack Parade	23 B1	Killarney Villas	57 C2 [48]	Kiltalown	48 D3	Kirkpatrick Avenue	18 D3
Kilbarrack Road	23 B1	Killary Grove	23 B1	Kiltalown Avenue	48 D2	Kirkpatrick Drive	18 D3
Kilbarrack Way	23 B1	Killeck	1 A2	Kiltalown Close	48 D2	Kirkwood	37 A4
Kilbarron Avenue	22 D1	Killeck Lane	1 A3	Kiltalown Court	48 D2	Kirwan Street	35 C2
Kilbarron Court	22 D1 [1]	Killeen	2 F3	Kiltalown Crescent	48 D2	Kirwan Street Cottages	35 C1 [10]
Kilbarron Drive	22 D1	Killeen Avenue	2 F3	Kiltalown Drive	48 D2	Kitestown Road	26 E3
Kilbarron Park	22 D1	Killeen Court	2 F3	Kiltalown Green	48 D2	Knapton Court	45 C4 [21]
Kilbarron Road	22 D1	Killeen Crescent	2 F3	Kiltalown Grove	48 D2	Knapton Lawn	45 C4 [22]
Kilbegnet Close	54 F2 [24]	Killeen Mews	3 B3	Kiltalown Heights	48 D2	Knapton Road	45 C4
Kilbogget Grove	53 C4	Killeen Park	2 F3	Kiltalown Park	48 D2	Knapton Terrace	45 C4 [27]
Kilbogget Villas	53 C4 [1]	Killeen Road	34 D4	Kiltalown Road	48 D2	Knapton Villas (Knapton Road)	45 C4
*Kilbride Cottages	57 B3	Killeen Road (Fox and Geese)	41 A1	Kiltalown View	48 D2	Knights Bridge	22 E4 [4]
(Killarney Road)		Killeen Road (Rathmines)	43 B1	Kiltalown Walk	48 D2	Knights Wood	10 F4
Kilbride Court (Killarney Road)	57 B3	Killeen Terrace	3 B2	Kiltalown Way	48 D2	Knockaire	50 D1
Kilbride Grove	57 B3	*Killery Terrace	57 B2	Kilteragh Drive	53 A3	Knockaulin	16 D4
Kilbride Lane	57 B3	(Upper Dargle Road)		Kilteragh Pines	53 A3 [2]	Knockcullen	50 D1
Kilbride Road	22 E3	Killester	22 E3	Kilteragh Road	53 A3	Knockcullen Drive	50 D1
Kilbrina	5 B2	Killester Avenue	22 E3	Kiltiernan	55 A2	Knockcullen Lawn	50 D1
Kilcarrig Avenue	40 E4	Killester Court	22 E3 [4]	Kiltipper	48 F3	Knockcullen Park	50 D1
Kilcarrig Close	48 E1	Killester Park	22 E3	Kiltipper Avenue	49 A2	Knockcullen Rise	50 D1
Kilcarrig Crescent	40 E4	KillesterPark	22 E3 [5]	Kiltipper Close	49 A2	Knockdara	3 C3
Kilcarrig Green	40 E4	Killinarden	48 E3	Kiltipper Drive	49 A2	Knockfield Manor	49 C1
Kilclare Avenue	48 E2	Killinarden Estate	48 E2	Kiltipper Road	49 A3	Knocklyon	50 D1
Kilclare Crescent	48 E2	Killinarden Heights	48 E2	Kiltuck Park	56 E4 [1]	Knocklyon Avenue	49 C1
Kilclare Drive	48 E2	Killinarden Heights	48 E2	Kilvere	42 E4	Knocklyon Close	50 D1
Kilclare Gardens	48 E2	Killinarden Road	48 E3	Kilworth Road	34 F4	Knocklyon Court	50 D1
Kilcock Maynooth Leixlip ByPass	30 E1	Killiney	54 E3	Kimmage	42 D2	Knocklyon Drive	50 D1
Kilcolman Court	54 E2 [4]	Killiney Avenue	54 E4 [7]	Kimmage Court	42 E2 [3]	Knocklyon Green	50 D1
Kilcronan Avenue	32 E4	Killiney Avenue	54 E4	Kimmage Grove	42 E2	Knocklyon Grove	50 D1
Kilcronan Close	32 E4	Killiney Court	56 E1 [1]	Kimmage Road Lower	42 F1	Knocklyon Heights	49 C1
Kilcronan Crescent	32 E4	Killiney Gate	54 E4	Kimmage Road West	42 D2	Knocklyon Mews	49 C1 [2]
Kilcronan Grove	32 E4	Killiney Grove	54 E2	Kinahan Street	35 B2 [4]	Knocklyon Park	49 C1
Kilcroney Lane	57 A4	Killiney Heath	54 E4	Kincora Avenue	22 E4	Knocklyon Road	49 C1
Kilcross Avenue	52 D3	Killiney Hill Road	54 E3	Kincora Court	37 C1	Knocklyon Road	50 D1
Kilcross Close	52 D3	Killiney Hill Road	56 E1	Kincora Drive	22 E4	Knockmaroon Hill	34 D1
Kilcross Court	51 C3	Killiney Oaks	56 E1 [2]	Kincora Grove	22 E4	Knockmaroon Road	34 D1
Kilcross Crescent	51 C3	Killiney Road	54 E2	Kincora Park	22 E4	Knockmeenagh Lane	40 E2
Kilcross Drive	51 C3	Killiney Terrace	54 E1 [15]	Kincora Road	22 E4	Knockmeenagh Road	40 E2
Kilcross Grove	51 C3	Killiney Towers	54 E2 [2]	King Edward Court	57 C2 [53]	Knockmitten Close	40 F1 [1]
Kilcross Lawn	52 D3	Killiney View	54 E1	King Edward Lawn	57 C2	Knockmitten Lane	41 A1
Kilcross Park	51 C3	Killiney View (off Albert Road)	54 E1	King Edward Park	57 B2	Knockmitten Lane North	40 F1 [1]
Kilcross Road	52 D3	Kilmacud Avenue	52 E1	King Edward Road	57 B2	Knockmore Avenue	48 E2
Kilcross Way	51 C3	Kilmacud Park	52 E1	King Street North	35 C2	Knockmore Crescent	48 E2
Kildare Park	42 D1	Kilmacud Road Upper	52 E1	King Street South	36 D3	Knockmore Drive	48 E2
Kildare Place	36 E3 [25]	Kilmahuddrick Avenue	39 B1	Kingram Place	36 E4	Knockmore Gardens	48 E2
Kildare Road	42 D1	Kilmahuddrick Close	39 B1	King's Avenue	36 E1	Knockmore Green	48 E2
Kildare Street	36 E3	Kilmahuddrick Court	39 B1	King's Court	35 C1 [19]	Knockmore Grove	48 E2
Kildonan Avenue	20 D1	Kilmahuddrick Crescent	39 B1	Kings Inns	36 D2	Knockmore Park	48 E2
Kildonan Drive	20 D1	Kilmahuddrick Drive	39 B1	King's Inns Street	36 D2	Knock-na-Cree Grove	54 F2
Kildonan Road	20 D1	Kilmahuddrick Green	39 B1	Kingsland Parade	36 D4 [5]	Knocknacree Park	54 F2
Kilfenora Drive	23 A1	Kilmahuddrick Grove	39 B1	Kingsland Park Avenue	36 D4 [4]	Knock-na-Cree Park	54 F2
Kilfenora Road	42 E1	Kilmahuddrick Lawn	39 B1	Kingsmill Road	57 C2	Knock-na-Cree Road	54 F2
Kilgobbin Heights	52 E4	Kilmahuddrick Place	39 B1	Kingston	51 B3	Knocknarea Avenue	35 A4
Kilgobbin Lane	52 D4	Kilmahuddrick Road	39 B1	Kingston Avenue	51 B3	Knocknarea Road	35 A4
Kilgobbin Road	52 E3	Kilmahuddrick Walk	39 B1	Kingston Close	51 B3	Knocknarrow Terrace	35 B3 [34]
Kilkieran Court	20 E4 [1]	Kilmahuddrick Way	39 B1	Kingston Court	50 F2	Knocknashee	43 C4
Kilkieran Road	20 E4	Kilmainham	35 A3	Kingston Crescent	51 B3	Knocknashee	44 D4
Kill Abbey	53 B1	Kilmainham Lane	35 A3	Kingston Drive	51 C3	Knocksinna	53 A2
Kill Avenue	53 B1	Kilmantain Place	57 C2 [10]	Kingston Green	51 B3	Knocksinna Court	53 A2 [1]
Kill Avenue	53 C1	Kilmartin Avenue	48 D1	Kingston Grove	51 B3	Knocksinna Crescent	53 A2
Kill Lane	53 B2	Kilmartin Crescent	40 D4	Kingston Heights	51 C3	Knocksinna Grove	53 A2 [1]
Kill O' the Grange	53 C1	Kilmartin Drive	48 D1	Kingston Lawn	51 B3	Knocksinna Park	53 A2
Killadoon Park	29 C4	Kilmartin Gardens	48 D1	Kingston Lodge	21 B4 [4]	Knowth Court	9 C4

STREET NAME	PAGE/GRID REFERENCE
Kyber Road	34 F2
Kyle-Clare Road	37 A3 [13]
Kylemore Avenue	34 D3
Kylemore Drive	34 D3
Kylemore Park North	34 D4
Kylemore Park South	34 D4
Kylemore Park West	34 D4
Kylemore Road	34 D2

L

STREET NAME	PAGE/GRID REFERENCE
La Touche Court	34 F4 [3]
La Touche Court	51 B2
La Touche Drive	34 E4
La Touche Road	34 F4
La Vista Avenue (Howth)	25 B2
Labre Park	34 E4
Laburnum Road	43 C2
Laburnum Walk	33 B2
Lad Lane	36 E3
Lad Lane Upper	36 E4
Lady's Lane	35 A3 [13]
Lady's Well Road	7 A4
Lagan Road	20 E3
Lakelands Avenue	52 D1
Lakelands Close	52 D1
Lakelands Crescent	52 E1
Lakelands Drive	52 E1
Lakelands Grove	52 D1
Lakelands Lawn	52 D1
Lakelands Park	42 E3
*Lakelands Place	52 D1
Lakelands Road	52 E1
Lally Road	34 E3
Lamb Alley	35 C3
Lambay Close	56 E1
Lambay Court	3 C3
Lambay Drive	56 E1
Lambay Road	21 A3
Lambourne Avenue	17 C2
Lambourne Court	17 C2
Lambourne Drive	17 C2
Lambourne Park	17 C2
Lambourne Road	17 C2
Lambourne Village	22 E4 [3]
Lambourne Wood	53 C4
Lamb's Brook	52 D3 [1]
*Lamb's Court (off James Street)	35 B3
Landen Road	34 E3
Landore	43 A3 [9]
Landscape Avenue	43 A3
Landscape Crescent	43 A4
Landscape Gardens	43 B4
Landscape Park	43 A4
Landscape Road	43 A3
Landsdowne Valley	41 C1 [6]
Landsdowne Valley Park	34 F4 [5]
Lanesville	53 B1
Langrishe Place	36 E1 [23]
Lanndale Lawn	48 E1
Lansdowne Crescent	36 F3 [43]
Lansdowne Gardens	36 F4 [7]
Lansdowne Hall	37 A3 [25]
Lansdowne Lane	36 F3 [20]
Lansdowne Park (Ballsbridge)	36 F3
Lansdowne Park (Templeogue)	50 D1
Lansdowne Road	36 F4
Lansdowne Square	37 A4 [24]
Lansdowne Terrace	36 F3 [37]
Lansdowne Village	37 A3
Lansdowne Villas	36 F3 [44]
Laracor Gardens	23 A1 [5]
Laragh	54 E4
Laragh (Flats)	21 C2 [4]
Laragh Close	23 A1
Laragh Grove	23 A1
Larch Drive	50 E2 [3]
Larch Grove (Clonsilla)	17 C2
Larch Grove (Donnybrook)	43 B1
Larchfield	43 C4
Larchfield (Dunboyne)	5 C3
Larchfield Park	43 C4
Larchfield Road	43 C4
Larkfield	32 F2
Larkfield Avenue	32 F2
Larkfield Avenue	42 F1
Larkfield Close	32 F2
Larkfield Court	32 F2
Larkfield Gardens	42 F1
Larkfield Green	32 F2
Larkfield Grove	42 F1
Larkfield Mews	30 D3
Larkfield Park	42 F1
Larkfield Rise	32 F2
Larkfield Way	32 F2
Larkhill Road	21 B2
Lauderdale Estate	57 C3
Lauderdale Terrace	57 C3 [16]
*Lauderdale Terrace (on New Row South)	36 D3
Lauder's Lane	25 A1
Laundry Lane	42 F1
Laurel Avenue	51 B1
Laurel Avenue	56 E1
Laurel Court	18 E3
Laurel Drive	51 B1 [6]
Laurel Hill	54 D1
Laurel Lodge Road	18 F3
Laurel Park	40 E1
Laurel Road	51 B1
Laurelton	42 F3
Laurence Brook	34 E2
Laurence Place East	36 F2 [5]
Laurleen	52 F1
Lavarna Grove	42 E2
Lavarna Road	42 E2
Laverna Avenue	18 E3
Laverna Dale	18 E3
Laverna Grove	18 E3
Laverna Way	18 E3
Lavery Avenue	33 C4
Lavista Avenue (Killester)	22 E3
Lawnswood Park	52 F1
Lawrence Grove	22 D4
Lawson Spinney	3 A3
Lawson Terrace	54 E1 [14]
Le Bas Terrace	42 F1 [2]
Le Brett Terrace	42 F3 [7]
Le Fanu Drive	34 D3 [1]
Le Fanu Road	34 D3
Le Vere Terrace	35 C4 [38]
*Le Vere Terrace (off Harold's Cross Road)	42 F1
Lea Crescent	37 B4
Lea Road	37 B4
Leahy's Terrace	37 A3
Lealand Avenue	39 C1
Lealand Close	39 C1
Lealand Crescent	39 C1
Lealand Drive	39 C1
Lealand Gardens	39 C1
Lealand Grove	39 C1
Lealand Road	39 C1
Lealand Walk	39 C1
Ledwidge Crescent	57 B1
Lee Road	20 E3
Leeson Close	36 E4 [1]
Leeson Lane	36 E3 [16]
Leeson Park	36 E4
Leeson Park Avenue	36 E4
Leeson Place	36 E4 [3]
Leeson Street Lower	36 E3
Leeson Street Upper	36 E4
Leeson Village	36 E4 [30]
Leeson Walk	36 E4 [19]
Lehaunstown Road	55 C1
Leicester Avenue	43 A1
Leighlin Road	42 E1
Lein Gardens	22 F2
Lein Park	22 F2
Lein Road	22 F2
Leinster Avenue	36 F1
Leinster Lane	36 E3 [13]
Leinster Lawn	43 C3
Leinster Market	36 E2 [11]
*Leinster Market (off d'Olier Street)	36 E2
Leinster Place	42 F1
Leinster Road	43 A1
Leinster Road West	42 F1
Leinster Square	43 A1 [2]
Leinster Street East	36 F1 [21]
Leinster Street North	20 F4
Leinster Street South	36 E3
Leinster Terrace	40 D1 [2]
Leitrim Place	36 F3 [33]
Leix Road	35 C1
Leixlip	31 B1
Leixlip Park	30 F1
Leixlip Road	31 B1
Lemon Street	36 D3 [31]
Lennox Place	36 D4
Lennox Street	36 D4
Lennox Terrace	36 D4 [31]
Lentisk Lawn	23 A1
Leo Avenue	36 D1 [24]
Leo Street	36 D1
Leonard's Court	35 C4 [34]
Leopardstown	52 F3
Leopardstown Avenue	52 F2
Leopardstown Court	52 F2 [1]
Leopardstown Drive	52 F2
Leopardstown Gardens	52 F2
Leopardstown Grove	52 F2
Leopardstown Heights	52 E3
Leopardstown Lawn	52 F2 [2]
Leopardstown Oaks	52 F2
Leopardstown Park	52 F2
Leopardstown Rise	52 E3
Leopardstown Road	52 F2
Leopardstown Valley	52 F4
Leslie Avenue	54 F1
Leslie's Buildings	35 C1 [7]
Leukos Road	37 A3 [11]
Liberty House	36 E1 [64]
Liberty Lane	36 D3 [20]
Library Road	46 D4
Library Road	56 E2
Library View Villas	36 D1 [61]
Liffey Close	32 F2
Liffey Drive	32 F2
Liffey Junction	20 E3
Liffey Lawn	32 F2
Liffey Street Lower	36 D2
Liffey Street South	34 F3
Liffey Street Upper	36 D2
Liffey Street West	35 C2 [19]
Liffey Terrace	34 E2 [7]
Liffey Valley Ave	32 F2
Liffey View	32 F2
Liffey View Apts	31 A1 [2]
Liffey Walk	32 F2
Liffey Way	32 F2
Lime Street	36 E2
Limekiln Avenue	41 C3
Limekiln Close	41 C3
Limekiln Drive	41 C3
Limekiln Green	41 B3
Limekiln Grove	41 C2
Limekiln Lane (Harold's Cross)	35 C4 [16]
Limekiln Lane (Kimmage)	41 C2
Limekiln Park	41 C3
Limekiln Road	41 C3
Limes Road	52 D2
Limetree Avenue	3 C4
Limewood Avenue	22 F1
Limewood Park	22 F1
Limewood Road	23 A1
Lincoln Lane	35 C2 [43]
*Lincoln Lane (off Arran Quay)	35 C2
Lincoln Place	36 E3
Linden Grove	44 F4
Linden Lea Park	52 F1
Lindenvale	45 A4 [4]
Lindisfarne Avenue	39 C1
Lindisfarne Drive	39 C1
Lindisfarne Green	39 C1
Lindisfarne Grove	39 C1
Lindisfarne Lawns	39 C1
Lindisfarne Park	32 F4
Lindisfarne Park	32 F4
Lindisfarne Vale	39 C1
Lindisfarne Walk	39 C1
Lindsay Road	21 A4
Linenhall Parade	36 D2 [4]
*Linenhall Street (off King Street North)	36 D2
Linenhall Terrace	36 D2 [1]
Link Road	54 E1
Lios na Sidhe	48 F2
Lisburn Street	36 D2 [2]
Liscannor Road	20 E4
Liscanor	54 F1 [9]
Liscarne Court	33 A3
Liscarne Gardens	33 A3
Lisle Road	42 D1
Lismeen Grove	22 E1 [1]
Lismore Road	42 E1
Lissadel Avenue	35 A4
Lissadel Court	35 A4
Lissadel Crescent	2 F2
Lissadel Drive	35 A4
Lissadel Grove	2 F2
Lissadel Park	2 F2
Lissadel Road	35 A4
Lissen Hall	2 D1
Lissenfield	36 D4 [53]
Lissenhall Avenue	2 D1
Lissenhall Court	2 D1
Lissenhall Drive	2 D1
Lissenhall Park	2 D1
Little Britain Street	36 D2
Little Fitzwilliam Place	36 E3 [29]
Little Meadow	53 C3 [1]
Littlepace	6 E4
Littlepace Close	6 E4
Littlepace Court	6 E4
Littlepace Crescent	6 E4
Littlepace Drive	6 E4
Littlepace Gallops	6 E4
Littlepace Meadow	6 E4
Littlepace Park	6 E4
Littlepace View	6 E4
Littlepace Walk	6 E4
Littlepace Way	6 E4
Littlepace Woods	6 E4
Litton Lane	36 D2 [18]
*Litton Lane (off Bachelors Walk)	36 D2
Llewellyn Close	51 A1
Llewellyn Court	51 A1
Llewellyn Grove	51 A1
Llewellyn Lawn	51 A1
Llewellyn Park	51 A1
Llewellyn Way	51 A1
Lock Road	32 D3
Loftus Lane	36 D2
Loftus Square	42 F4 [14]
Lohunda Crescent	17 C2
Lohunda Dale	18 D2
Lohunda Downs	18 D2
Lohunda Drive	18 D2
Lohunda Grove	18 D2
Lohunda Park	17 C2
Lohunda Road	18 D2
Lombard Court	36 E2 [33]
Lombard Street East	36 E2
Lombard Street West	36 D4
Lomond Avenue	21 C4
Londonbridge Drive	37 A3 [20]
Londonbridge Road	37 A3
Long Lane	36 D3
Long Lane (New Street)	36 D1 [49]
*Long Lane Close (off Long Lane)	36 D3
Long Mile Road	41 B1
Longford Lane	36 D3 [45]
Longford Place	45 C4
Longford Street Great	36 D3 [8]
Longford Street Little	36 D3 [9]
Longford Terrace	45 C4
Longlands	2 D2
Longmeadow	53 C3
Long's Place	35 C3 [5]
Longwood Avenue	36 D4
Longwood Park	42 F4
Lorcan Avenue	21 C1

STREET NAME	PAGE/GRID REFERENCE	STREET NAME	PAGE/GRID REFERENCE	STREET NAME	PAGE/GRID REFERENCE	STREET NAME	PAGE/GRID REFERENCE
Lorcan Crescent	21 C1	Luttrellstown Chase	18 D4	*Malpas Place	36 D3	Marino	21 C4
Lorcan Drive	21 B1	Luttrellstown Close	18 E4	(off Malpas Street)		Marino Avenue	21 C4
Lorcan Green	21 C1	Luttrellstown Court	18 D4	*Malpas Street	36 D3	Marino Avenue East	54 E4
Lorcan Grove	21 C1	Luttrellstown Dale	18 D4	Malpas Terrace	36 D3 [46]	Marino Avenue West	54 E4 [4]
Lorcan O'Toole Court	42 D2 [2]	Luttrellstown Drive	18 D4	Mander's Terrace	36 E4 [10]	Marino Court	21 C4 [13]
Lorcan O'Toole Park	42 D2	Luttrellstown Glade	18 D4	Mangerton Road	34 F4	Marino Crescent	22 D4
Lorcan Park	21 C1	Luttrellstown Green	18 D4	Mannix Road	21 A4	Marino Green	21 C4
Lorcan Road	21 B1	Luttrellstown Grove	18 D4	Manor Avenue	42 E3	Marino Mart	21 C4 [9]
Lorcan Villas	21 C1	Luttrellstown Heath	18 D4	Manor Close	51 A2	Marino Park	21 C4
Lord Edward Street	36 D3	Luttrellstown Heights	18 D4	Manor Crescent	17 B1	Marino Park Avenue	21 C4
Lordello Road	56 D3	Luttrellstown Lawn	18 D4	Manor Drive	12 D4	Marion Villas	35 C3 [59]
Lords Walk	35 A1	Luttrellstown Oaks	18 D4	Manor Green	51 A2	Mark Street	36 E2 [26]
Loreto Avenue	43 A4	Luttrellstown Park	18 D4	Manor Grove	42 D2	Market Square	57 C2 [49]
Loreto Avenue (Dalkey)	54 F1	Luttrellstown Place	18 D4	Manor Heath	51 A1	Market Street South	35 C3 [4]
Loreto Court	43 A4	Luttrellstown Rise	18 D3	Manor Park (Ballinteer)	51 A2	Mark's Alley West	35 C3 [22]
Loreto Crescent	43 A4	Luttrellstown Thicket	18 D4	Manor Park (Palmerston)	33 C2	Mark's Lane	36 E2 [4]
Loreto Grange	57 C3	Luttrellstown View	18 E4	Manor Place	35 C2	Marlborough Court	36 E2 [35]
Loreto Park	43 A4	Luttrellstown Walk	18 D4	Manor Rise	51 A2	Marlborough Mews	35 B1
Loreto Road	35 C3	Luttrellstown Way	18 D4	Manor Road	33 C2	Marlborough Park	54 D1 [9]
Loreto Row	43 A4	Luttrellstown Wood	18 E4	Manor Street	35 C2	Marlborough Place	36 E2 [7]
Loreto Terrace	42 F4	Lyllymore Terrace	35 C4 [6]	Manor Villas	42 F1 [4]	Marlborough Rd (Donnybrook)	43 C1
Loretto Avenue	57 C2 [34]	Lynches Lane	32 D2	Manorfields	17 B1	Marlborough Rd (Glenageary)	54 E1
Loretto Terrace	57 C2 [35]	Lynch's Lane	34 E3 [2]	Mantua Park	2 D1 [2]	Marlborough Road	35 B1
Loretto Villas	57 C2 [54]	Lynch's Place	36 D1 [2]	Maolbuille Road	21 A2	(Nth Circular Rd)	
*Lorne Terrace	35 B3	Lyndon Gate	20 D4 [4]	Mapas Avenue	54 E2	Marlborough Street	36 D2
(off Almeida Avenue)		Lynton Court	37 A4 [12]	Mapas Road	54 E2	Marlborough Terrace	58 D2 [16]
Lotts	36 D2	Lynwood	51 C1	Maple Avenue	18 E3	Marley Avenue	51 A1
Lough Conn Avenue	34 D2			Maple Avenue	52 D2	Marley Close	51 A1
Lough Conn Drive	34 D2	**M**		(off Blackthorn Drive)		Marley Court North	51 A1
Lough Conn Road	34 D2			Maple Close	18 E3	Marley Court South	51 A1
Lough Conn Terrace	34 D2	Mabbot Lane	36 E2 [17]	Maple Drive	5 B2	Marley Drive	51 A1
Lough Derg Road	23 A2	Mabel Street	21 B4	Maple Drive	18 E3 [6]	Marley Grove	51 A1
Loughlinstown	56 D1	Macken Street	36 F3	Maple Drive	42 F2	Marley Lawn	51 A1
Loughlinstown Drive	56 D1	Macken Villa	36 F3 [31]	Maple Glen	18 E3	Marley Rise	51 A1
Loughlinstown Park	56 D1	Mackies Place	36 E3 [33]	Maple Green	18 E3	Marley Villas	51 A1 [1]
Loughlinstown Wood	56 D1	Mackintosh Park	53 C2	Maple Grove	18 E3	Marley Walk	51 A1
Loughnamona	15 C4	Macroom Avenue	11 B4	Maple Grove	57 B2	Marlfield	53 C3
Louis Lane	43 A1 [23]	Macroom Road	11 B4	Maple Lawn	18 E3	Marlfield Gardens	53 C3
*Louis Lane	43 A1	Madden Road	35 C3 [31]	Maple Manor	53 C3	*Marmion Court	35 C2
(off Leinster Road)		*Madden's Court	35 C3	Maple Road	43 C2	(on Blackhall Street)	
Louisa Vally	15 C4	(off Thomas Street)		Maples Road	52 D2	Marne Villas	35 C1 [13]
Lourdes House	36 E1 [61]	Madden's Lane	54 E4	Maplewood Avenue	48 E1	Marrowbone Lane	35 C3 [66]
Lourdes Road	35 B3	Madison Road	35 B3 [10]	Maplewood Close	48 E1	Marrowbone Lane	35 C3
Louvain	44 D3	*Magdalen Terrace	37 A3	Maplewood Court	48 E1	*Marrowbone Lane Close	35 C3
Louvain Glade	44 D3	(off Oliver Plunket Ave)		Maplewood Drive	48 E1	(off Marrowbone Lane)	
Love Lane East	36 F3 [15]	Magennis Place	36 E2 [3]	Maplewood Green	48 E1	Marshal Lane	35 C3 [1]
Lower Dargle Road	57 B2	Magennis Square	36 E2 [29]	Maplewood Lawn	48 E1	Marshalsea Lane	35 C2 [12]
Lower Glen Road	34 D1	Magenta Crescent	21 B1	Maplewood Park	48 E1	Marsham Court	52 E1
Lr Kilmacud Road (Goatstown)	44 D4	Magenta Hall	21 B1	Maplewood Road	48 E1	Mart Lane	53 B3
Lr Kilmacud Road (Stillorgan)	52 D1	Magenta Place	54 D1 [8]	Maplewood Way	48 E1	Martello Avenue	46 D4 [14]
Lr Lucan Road	17 C4	Maher's Terrace	43 C4	Maretimo Gardens East	45 A3	Martello Court	4 D4
Lr Road (Shankill)	56 E3	(Main Street Dundrum)		Maretimo Gardens West	45 A3 [4]	Martello Mews	44 E1
Lr Road (Strawberry Beds)	33 B1	Maidens Row	34 E2 [2]	Maretimo Place	45 A3 [17]	Martello Terrace	25 B3 [2]
Luby Road	35 A3	Main Street	5 B2	Maretimo Road	45 A3 [2]	Martello Terrace	57 C1 [2]
Lucan	32 D2	Main Street	57 C2	Maretimo Terrace	45 A3 [16]	Martello Terrace (Booterstown)	44 F3 [1]
Lucan Bypass	32 D2	Main Street (Baldoyle)	13 A4	Maretimo Villas	45 A3 [18]	Martello Terrace (Dun Laoghaire)	46 E4 [2]
Lucan Heights	32 E1	Main Street (Blackrock)	45 A3	Margaret Place	36 F3 [11]	Martello View	37 B4 [3]
Lucan Newlands Road	32 D2	Main Street (Blanchardstown)	18 F2	Marguerite Road	21 A4	Martello Wood	37 B4 [6]
Lucan Road (Chapelizod)	34 D2	Main Street (Celbridge)	30 D3	Marian Crescent	42 E4	Martin Grove	20 D4
Lucan Road (Lucan)	32 D1	Main Street (Clondalkin)	40 E1	Marian Drive	42 E4	Martin Savage Park	19 C3
Lucan Road (near Qaurryvale)	33 A1	Main Street (Dundrum)	43 C4	Marian Grove	42 E4	*Martin Savage Road	19 C4
Lucan Road (Palmerston)	33 C1	Main Street (Finglas)	20 E2	Marian Park (Baldoyle)	23 C1	Martin Street	36 D4 [34]
Lucan-Newlands Road	33 A4	Main Street (Howth)	26 D2	Marian Park (Blackrock)	53 A1	Martin White Chalets	37 A4 [4]
Ludford Drive	51 B1	Main Street (Leixlip)	31 A1	Marian Park (Templeogue)	42 E4	Martin's Row	34 E2
Ludford Park	51 B1	Main Street (Lucan)	32 D1	Marian Road	42 E4	*Martin's Terrace	36 E2
Ludford Road	51 B2	Main Street (Raheny)	23 A2	Marie Villas	57 C2 [55]	(off Hanover Street East)	
Lugmore	48 D3	Main Street (Rathfarnham)	42 F4	Marigold Court	11 C4	Mary Street	36 D2
Lugmore Lane	47 C3	Main Street (Swords)	2 D2	Marigold Court	11 C4	Mary Street Little	36 D2 [32]
Lugnaquilla Avenue	41 B3	Main Street (Tallaght)	49 A1	Marigold Crescent	11 C4	Maryfield Avenue	22 E2 [1]
Luke Street	36 E2 [25]	Main Street (Tallaght)	49 A1	Marigold Grove	11 C4	Maryfield Crescent	22 E2
Lurgan Street	36 D2 [3]	Maitland Street	57 B2	Marigold Park	11 C4	Maryfield Drive	22 D2
Lutterell Hall	5 A2	Malachi Place	36 F1 [18]	Marina Village	3 B2	Maryland	56 E1 [5]
Luttrell Park	18 D3	Malachi Road	35 C2 [45]	Marine Avenue	54 E1	Mary's Abbey	36 D2
Luttrell Park Close	18 D3	*Malachi Road	35 C2	Marine Court	54 E1	Mary's Lane	36 D2
Luttrell Park Court	18 D3	(off Halliday Road)		Marine Drive	37 A4	Maryville Road	22 F3
Luttrell Park Crescent	18 E3	Malahide	3 C2	Marine Parade	46 E4	Mask Avenue	22 E2
Luttrell Park Drive	18 E3	Malahide Road	2 E2	Marine Road	46 D4	Mask Crescent	22 E2
Luttrell Park Green	18 E3	Malahide Road (Artane)	22 E2	Marine Terrace	46 D4 [9]	Mask Drive	22 E2
Luttrell Park Grove	18 D3	Malahide Road (Balgriffin)	12 D3	Marine Terrace	58 D2 [17]	Mask Green	22 E2
Luttrell Park Hall	18 D3	Malahide Road (Coolock)	22 F1	Marine View	44 F3	Mask Road	22 E2
Luttrell Park Heath	18 E3	Malahide Road (Marino)	22 D4	Marine Villas	26 D1 [7]	Mather Road North	44 E3
Luttrell Park Lawn	18 D3	Malborough Court	54 E2 [8]	Mariners Court	23 C2 [1]	Mather Road South	44 D3
Luttrell Park View	18 D3	Mallin Avenue	35 B3 [17]	Mariners Cove	26 E2	Matt Talbot Court	36 E1 [28]
Luttrellstown Avenue	18 E4	Malone Gardens	36 F3 [12]	Mariner's Port	36 F2 [16]	Maunsell Place	36 D1 [52]
		Malpas Court	36 D3 [50]				

STREET NAME	PAGE/GRID REFERENCE	STREET NAME	PAGE/GRID REFERENCE	STREET NAME	PAGE/GRID REFERENCE	STREET NAME	PAGE/GRID REFERENCE
Maxwell Court	43 A1 [18]	Mellowes Avenue	20 D1	Millbrook Grove	23 A1	Monksfield	40 F1
Maxwell Lane	43 A2	Mellowes Court	20 D2 [3]	Millbrook Lawns	49 A1	Monksfield Court	40 F1
Maxwell Road	43 A1	Mellowes Crescent	20 D2 [4]	Millbrook Road	23 A1	Monksfield Downs	40 F1
Maxwell Street	35 C3 [10]	Mellowes Park	20 D1	Millbrook Terrace	35 A3 [24]	Monksfield Grove	40 F1
May Lane	35 C2	Mellowes Road	20 D1	Millbrook Village	43 C1 [17]	Monksfield Heights	40 F1
May Park	22 D3	Melrose Avenue (Clondalkin)	39 C1	Millfarm	5 C2	Monksfield Lawn	40 F1
*May Street (off Fitzroy Ave)	21 B4	Melrose Avenue (Fairview)	21 C4	Millgate Drive	41 C3	Monksfield Meadows	40 F1
Mayberry Park	41 A4	Melrose Crescent	39 C1	Millmount Avenue	21 A4	Monksfield Walk	40 F1
Mayberry Road	41 A4	Melrose Green	32 F4	Millmount Grove	43 B3	Monkstown	45 B4
Mayfair	3 C2	Melrose Green	39 C1	Millmount Place	21 B4	Monkstown Avenue	53 B1
Mayfield	43 A2	Melrose Grove	39 C1	Millmount Terrace (Drumcondra)	21 B4	Monkstown Crescent	45 C4
Mayfield Park	33 B4	Melrose Lawn	32 F4	Millmount Villas	21 A4 [1]	Monkstown Farm	53 C1
Mayfield Road (Kilmainham)	35 B3 [11]	Melrose Park	2 E3	Millrose Estate	34 E4 [2]	Monkstown Gate	45 C4 [29]
Mayfield Road (Terenure)	42 F2	Melrose Park	39 C1	Millstead	18 F2	Monkstown Grove	53 C1
Mayfield Terrace	57 C3 [17]	Melrose Road	32 F4	Millstream Road	31 C2	Monkstown Road	45 B4
Mayfield Terrace (Ballinteer)	51 C2	Melvin Road	42 F2	Milltown	43 C2	Monkstown Valley	45 B4
Mayne Road	12 E3	Memorial Road	35 A3 [9]	Milltown Bridge Road	43 C2	Montague Court	36 D3 [25]
Maynooth Road	5 A3	Memorial Road	36 E2	*Milltown Collonade	43 B2	Montague Lane	36 D3 [13]
Maynooth Road (Celbridge)	29 C1	Mercer Street Lower	36 D3	(on Milltown Road)		Montague Place	36 D3 [26]
Mayola Court	43 B3	Mercer Street Upper	36 D3	Milltown Drive	43 A3	Montague Street	36 D3
Mayor Street Lower	36 E2	Merchamp	22 F4	Milltown Grove	43 A3	Monte Vella	54 F2 [9]
Mayor Street Upper	36 F2	*Merchants Arch	36 D2	Milltown Grove	43 B2 [6]	Montebello Terrace	58 D2 [2]
Mayville Terrace	54 F1 [11]	(off Temple Bar)		Milltown Hill	43 B2 [7]	Montpelier Drive	35 B2
Maywood Avenue	23 B2	Merchant's Quay	35 C2	Milltown Park	43 B2	Montpelier Gardens	35 B2 [5]
Maywood Close	23 B2	Merchant's Road	37 A1	Milltown Path	43 B2	Montpelier Gardens	35 B2
Maywood Crescent	23 B3	Merchant's Square	36 F2 [15]	Milltown Road	43 B1	Montpelier Hill	35 B2
Maywood Drive	23 B2	Meretimo Villas	58 D3 [2]	Milltown Terrace (Dundrum)	43 B3 [4]	Montpelier Manor	45 B4 [2]
Maywood Grove	23 B2	Merlyn Drive	44 D1	Millview	40 E1 [7]	Montpelier Parade	45 B4
Maywood Lawn	23 B3	Merlyn Park	44 D1	Millview Close	3 A3	Montpelier Park	35 B2
Maywood Park	23 B2	Merlyn Road	44 D1	Millview Court	3 A2	Montpelier Place	45 B4 [2]
Maywood Road	23 B2	Merrion	44 E1	Millview Lawns	3 A3	Montrose Avenue	22 D2
McAuley Avenue	22 F2	Merrion Close	36 E3 [26]	Millview Road	3 A3	Montrose Close	22 D2
McAuley Drive	22 F2	Merrion Court	44 E1 [1]	Millwood Court	23 A1	Montrose Court	22 D2
McAuley Park	22 F2	Merrion Crescent	44 E2 [3]	Millwood Park	23 A1	Montrose Crescent	22 D1
McAuley Road	22 F2	Merrion Gates	44 E1 [2]	Millwood Villas	23 A1	Montrose Drive	22 D1
McCabe Villas	44 E3	Merrion Grove	44 E3	Milton Terrace	57 C2 [13]	Montrose Grove	22 D2
McCarthy Terrace	35 B3 [25]	Merrion Park	44 E3	Milward Terrace	58 D2 [13]	Montrose Park	22 D2
McCreadies Lane	3 A3	Merrion Place	36 E3 [8]	Mine Hill Lane	55 B3	Moore Lane	36 D2 [15]
McDowell Avenue	35 B3 [8]	Merrion Road	37 A4	*Minstrel Court	52 F2	Moore Street	36 D2
McGrane Court	51 C1 [5]	Merrion Row	36 E3	(Charles Sheil's Houses)		Moorefield	54 E4
McKee Avenue	20 E1	Merrion Square East	36 E3	Misery Hill	36 F2	Moore's Cottages	53 A1 [3]
McKee Park	35 B1	Merrion Square North	36 E3	Moatfield Avenue	22 F1	Mooretown	1 B1
McKee Road	20 E1	Merrion Square South	36 E3	Moatfield Park	22 F1	Mooretown Avenue	1 C1
McKelvey Avenue	9 A4	Merrion Square West	36 E3	Moatfield Road	22 F1	Mooretown Grove	1 C1
McKelvey Road	9 A4	Merrion Strand	44 E1	Moatview Avenue	11 B4	Mooretown Park	1 C1
McMahon Street	36 D4 [27]	Merrion Street Lower	36 E3 [27]	Moatview Court	11 B4	Mooretown Road	1 C1
McMorrough Road	42 F2 [14]	Merrion Street Upper	36 E3	Moatview Drive	11 B4	Moorfield Avenue	33 A4
Meade's Terrace	36 E3 [6]	Merrion View Avenue	44 D1 [1]	Moatview Gardens	11 B4	Moorfield Close	33 A4 [2]
Meadow Avenue	51 B1 [1]	Merrion Village	44 E1	Mobhi Court	21 A3 [16]	Moorfield Drive	33 A4
Meadow Close (Dundrum)	51 A1	Merton Avenue	35 C4 [25]	Mobhi Road	21 A3	Moorfield Green	33 A4
Meadow Close	53 A1	Merton Drive	43 B1	Moeran Road	41 C1	Moorfield Lawns	33 A4
(Newtown Park Ave)		Merton Park	35 C4 [27]	*Moira Road	35 B1	Moracrete Cottages	35 B4 [4]
Meadow Copse	17 C1	Merton Road	43 B2	(off Oxmanstown Road)		Moran's Cottages	43 B1 [12]
Meadow Court	54 D4 [2]	Merville Avenue (Fairview)	21 C4	Moland Place	36 E2 [21]	Moreen Avenue	52 D2 [8]
Meadow Dale	17 C1 [1]	Merville Avenue (Stillorgan)	52 F1	Molesworth Place	36 E3 [24]	Moreen Avenue	52 D2
Meadow Downs	17 C1	Merville Road	52 F1	Molesworth Street	36 E3	Moreen Close	52 D2
Meadow Drive	17 C1	Mespil Road	36 E4	Molyneux Yard	35 C3 [19]	Moreen Lawn	52 D2 [2]
Meadow Green	17 C1	Michael Collins Park	40 D1	Monalea Grove	49 C1	Moreen Park	52 D2
Meadow Grove	51 B1	Middle Third	22 E3	Monalea Park	49 C1	Moreen Road	52 D2
Meadow Mount	51 A1	Milesian Avenue	2 E2	Monalea Wood	49 C1	Moreen Walk	52 D2
Meadow Park	51 A1	Milesian Court	2 E2	Monaloe Avenue	53 C3	Morehampton Lane	36 F4
Meadow Park Avenue	43 A4	Milesian Grove	2 E2	Monaloe Court	53 B3 [6]	Morehampton Mews	36 F4 [12]
Meadow Vale	53 B2	Milesian Lawn	2 E2	Monaloe Crescent	53 B3 [4]	Morehampton Road	36 F4
Meadow View	5 B2	Milestown	15 C1	Monaloe Drive	53 C3	Morehampton Square	36 F4 [11]
Meadow View	51 A1	Milford	3 A2	Monaloe Park	53 C3	Morehampton Terrace	43 B1
Meadow Villas	51 A1 [2]	Military Road	35 B3	Monaloe Park Road	53 C3	Morgan Place	35 C2 [14]
Meadow Way	17 C1	Military Road (Killiney)	54 E4	Monaloe Way	53 C3	Morgans Place	19 A3
Meadowbank	42 F3	Military Road (Phoenix Park)	34 F2	Monasterboice Road	42 E1	Morning Star Avenue	35 C2 [14]
Meadowbrook Avenue	24 D1	Military Road (Rathmines)	36 D4	Monastery Crescent	40 E1	Morning Star Road	35 B3 [19]
Meadowbrook Lawn	24 D1	Military Road (Woodtown)	50 D3	Monastery Drive	40 E1	Mornington Avenue	46 E4 [1]
Meadowbrook Park	24 D1	Mill Lane	31 A1	Monastery Gate	40 F1	Mornington Grove	22 E2
Meadowview Grove	31 C2	Mill Lane (Ashtown)	19 B3 [1]	Monastery Gate Avenue	40 F1	Mornington Park	22 E2
Meakstown Cottages	9 B3	Mill Lane (Loughlinstown)	56 E2	Monastery Gate Close	40 F1	Mornington Road	43 B1
Meath Market	35 C3 [16]	Mill Lane (Newmarket)	35 C3 [26]	Monastery Gate Copse	40 F1	Morrogh Terrace	21 C3 [2]
Meath Place	35 C3	*Mill Lane (off Castle St Bray)	57 C2	Monastery Gate Green	40 F1	Moss Street	36 E2
Meath Place	57 C2	Mill Lane (Palmerston)	33 C1	Monastery Gate Lawn	40 F1	Mount Albany	53 A1
Meath Road	58 D2	Mill Road (Blanchardstown)	18 F2	Monastery Gate Villas	40 F1	Mount Albion Road	51 B1 [3]
Meath Square	35 C3 [42]	Mill Road (Saggart)	47 A2	Monastery Heights	40 E1 [2]	Mount Albion Road	51 B1
Meath Street	35 C3	Mill Street	35 C3	Monastery Park	40 E1	Mount Alton	49 C1
*Meath Terrace (on Meath Place)	35 C3	Mill Street (Dun Laoghaire)	46 D4 [19]	Monastery Rise	40 E1	Mount Alton Court	50 D1
*Meathville Terrace	36 D3	Millbourne Avenue	21 A4	Monastery Road	40 E1	Mount Andrew	32 F2
(on Long Lane)		Millbrook Avenue	23 A1	Monastery Walk	40 E1	Mount Andrew Avenue	32 F2
Meetinghouse Lane	36 D2 [33]	Millbrook Court	35 B3 [35]	Monck Place	35 C1	Mount Andrew Close	32 F2
Mellifont Avenue	46 D4	Millbrook Drive	23 A1	Monks Meadow	4 D4	Mount Andrew Dale	32 F2

STREET NAME	PAGE/GRID REFERENCE	STREET NAME	PAGE/GRID REFERENCE	STREET NAME	PAGE/GRID REFERENCE	STREET NAME	PAGE/GRID REFERENCE
Mount Andrew Grove	32 F1	Mountdown Park	41 C3	Murphystown Road	52 E3	Newcastle Road	32 D2
Mount Annville Road	44 D4	Mountdown Road	41 C3	Murray's Cottages	34 F3 [4]	Newcomen Avenue	36 E1
Mount Annville Wood	44 D4	Mountjoy Parade	36 E1 [36]	Murtagh Road	35 C2 [30]	Newcomen Court	36 E1 [29]
Mount Anville Lawn	44 D4	Mountjoy Place	36 E1 [22]	Muskerry Road	34 E3	Newcourt	2 D1
Mount Anville Park	44 D4	Mountjoy Square	36 E1	Mutton Lane	50 E4	Newcourt	58 D4
Mount Argus Avenue	42 F1	Mountjoy Square Apts	36 E1 [65]	Myra Cottages	35 A3 [21]	Newcourt Avenue	58 D3
Mount Argus Close	42 F1	Mountjoy Square East	36 E1	Myrtle Avenue	54 D1 [3]	Newcourt Road	58 D3
Mount Argus Court	42 F1	Mountjoy Square North	36 E1	Myrtle Grove	52 F1	Newcourt Villas	57 C3 [8]
Mount Argus Crescent	42 F1	Mountjoy Square South	36 E1	Myrtle Grove	57 B1 [3]	Newgrange Road (Cabra)	20 F4
Mount Argus Green	42 F1	Mountjoy Square West	36 D1	Myrtle Park	54 D1	Newgrove Avenue	37 B4
Mount Argus Grove	42 F1	Mountjoy Street	36 D1	Myrtle Street	36 D1 [23]	Newhall Court	48 D2
Mount Argus Park	42 F1	Mountjoy Street Middle	36 D1 [9]			Newlands Avenue	40 E2
Mount Argus Road	42 F1	Mountpleasant Avenue Lower	36 D4	**N**		Newlands Drive	40 E2
Mount Argus Terrace	42 F1	Mountpleasant Avenue Upper	36 D4	Naas Road	41 A1	Newlands Park	40 E2
Mount Argus View	42 F1	Mountpleasant Parade	36 D4 [39]	Naas Road (Saggart)	47 B1	Newlands Road	40 E2
Mount Argus Way	42 F1	Mountpleasant Place	36 E4 [22]	Nangor Crescent	39 C1 [2]	Newmarket	35 C3
Mount Auburn	54 E3 [2]	Mountpleasant Square	36 D4	Nangor Crescent	40 D1 [5]	Newmarket Street	35 C3 [25]
Mount Brown	35 B3	Mountpleasant Terrace	36 D4 [40]	Nangor Road (Clondalkin)	40 D1	Newport Street	35 C3
Mount Carmel Avenue	43 C4	**Mountpleasant Terrace Upper	36 E4	Nangor Road (Fox & Geese)	40 F1	Newtown	5 A3
Mount Carmel Park	49 C1	(off Mountpleasant Place)		Nanikin Avenue	23 A3	Newtown	50 E3
Mount Carmel Park	49 C1	Mountpleasant Villas	57 B2 [13]	Nash Street	34 F3	Newtown Avenue	22 F1
Mount Carmel Road	43 C4	*Mountpleasant Villas	36 E4	Nashville Park	26 E2	Newtown Avenue	45 A3
Mount Dillon Court	22 E2	(off Mountpleasant Place)		Nashville Road	26 D2	Newtown Cottages	9 A1
Mount Drinan Avenue	2 E3	Mountsandel	53 B4	Nassau Street	36 E3	Newtown Cottages	22 F1
Mount Drinan Crescent	2 E3	Mountshannon Road	35 B3	Naul Road	1 C4	Newtown Court	11 C4
Mount Drinan Grove	2 E3	Mounttown Cottages	45 C4 [26]	Navan Road	6 F4	Newtown Court	43 A3 [5]
Mount Drinan Lawn	2 E3	Mounttown Lower	53 C1	Navan Road (Blanchardstown)	18 E1	Newtown Drive	22 F1
Mount Drinan Park	2 E3	Mounttown Park	53 C1 [3]	Navan Road (Cabra)	20 D4	Newtown Glendale	16 D4
Mount Drinan Walk	2 E3	Mounttown Upper	45 C4	Navan Road (Clonee)	6 E3	Newtown House	43 A3 [12]
Mount Drummond Avenue	35 C4	Mourne Road	35 A4	Navan Road (Dunboyne)	5 B2	Newtown Park	16 D4
Mount Drummond Court	35 C4 [30]	Moy Elta Road	36 F1	Neagh Road	42 E2	Newtown Park	22 F1
Mount Drummond Square	36 D4	Moy Glas Avenue	32 E3	Neillstown Avenue	33 A3	Newtown Park (Blackrock)	53 A1
Mount Eagle Court	52 E3	Moy Glas Chase	32 E3	Neillstown Crescent	33 A3	Newtown Park (Tallaght)	49 B1
Mount Eagle Drive	52 E3	Moy Glas Close	32 E3	Neillstown Drive	33 A3	Newtown Park Avenue	45 A4
Mount Eagle Green	52 E3	Moy Glas Court	32 E3	Neillstown Gardens	33 A3	Newtown Park Court	53 A1 [1]
Mount Eagle Grove	52 E3	Moy Glas Dale	32 E3	Neillstown Park	33 A3	Newtown Road	11 C4
Mount Eagle Lawn	52 E3	Moy Glas Dene	32 E3	Neilstown Cottages	33 A4 [3]	Newtown Road	30 D4
Mount Eagle Park	52 E3	Moy Glas Drive	32 E3	Neilstown Road	33 A3	Newtown Villas	43 A3 [4]
Mount Eagle Rise	52 D3	Moy Glas Glen	32 E3	Nelson Street	36 D1	Newtown Villas	45 A3 [1]
Mount Eagle View	52 E3	Moy Glas Grove	32 E3	Nephin Road	20 D4	Newtownsmith	46 E4
Mount Eagle Way	52 E3	Moy Glas Lawn	32 E3	Neptune Terrace	54 E1 [17]	Niall Street	35 B2 [11]
Mount Eden Road	43 C1	Moy Glas Park	32 E3	Nerano Road	54 F2	Nicholas Avenue	35 C2 [7]
Mount Gandon	32 D1 [9]	Moy Glas Road	32 E3	Nerney's Court	36 D1 [44]	Nicholas Street	36 D3
Mount Harold Terrace	42 F1 [1]	Moy Glas Vale	32 E3	Neville Road	43 A2	Ninth Lock Road	40 D1
Mount Merrion	44 E4	Moy Glas View	32 E3	Nevinstown Lane	1 C3	Nore Road	20 E3
Mount Merrion Avenue	44 F3	Moy Glas Way	32 E3	New Bawn Drive	49 A2	Norfolk Road	20 F4
Mount Norris Villas	58 D2 [19]	Moy Glas Wood	32 E3	New Bawn Park	49 A2	Norseman Place	35 C2
Mount Olive Grove	23 B1	Moyclare Avenue	24 D1	New Brighton Terrace	57 C2 [47]	North Avenue	44 E4
Mount Olive Park	23 B1	Moyclare Close	24 D1	New Grange Park	58 D2 [22]	North Bull Island	23 B4
Mount Olive Road	23 B1	Moyclare Drive	24 D1	New Grange Rd (Deans Grange)	53 A1	North Circular Road	35 C1
Mount Prospect Avenue	22 F4	Moyclare Gardens	24 D1 [2]	New Grove Estate	12 E4	(Phibsborough)	
Mount Prospect Drive	22 F4	Moyclare Park	24 D1	New Hall Court	48 D1	North Circular Road	35 B1
Mount Prospect Grove	22 F4	Moyclare Road	24 D1	New Ireland Road	35 B3	(Phoenix Park)	
Mount Prospect Lawn	22 F4	Moycullen Road	33 C3	New Park Lodge	53 A2 [3]	North Clarence St Flats	36 E1 [66]
Mount Prospect Park	22 F4	Moyle Crescent	40 E1	New Park Road	53 A1	North Great George's St	36 D1
Mount Salus Road	54 F2	Moyle Road	20 E3	New Rathmore Terrace	57 B2 [23]	North Quay Extension	37 A2
Mount Sandford	43 C1 [14]	Moyne Court	43 B1 [22]	New Ravenswell Row	57 B2 [20]	North Road	9 A4
Mount Street Crescent	36 F3 [32]	Moyne Road	43 B1	New River Road	19 A2	North Road (Phoenix Park)	35 A1
Mount Street Lower	36 E3	Moynihan Court	49 B1 [6]	New Road (Clondalkin)	40 E2	North Strand Road	36 F1
Mount Street Upper	36 E3	Moyville	50 E2	New Road (Howth)	26 E3	North Street	2 D1
Mount Tallant Avenue	42 F2	Moyville Lawns	50 E1	New Road (Inchicore)	34 F3	North Wall	36 F2
Mount Temple Road	35 C2	Muckross Avenue	42 D2	New Row	34 E2 [12]	North Wall Quay	36 F2
Mount Venus Road	50 D4	Muckross Crescent	42 D2	New Row South	35 C3	Northbrook Avenue (Ranelagh)	36 E4
Mount View Road	18 D2	Muckross Drive	42 D2 [1]	New Row Square	35 C3 [32]	Northbrook Avenue Lower	36 F1
Mount Wood	53 C1	Muckross Green	42 D2	New Street	3 B2	Northbrook Avenue Upper	36 F1
Mountain Park	49 A1	Muckross Grove	42 D2	New Street	36 D3	Northbrook Lane	36 E4 [20]
Mountain View	48 D2	Muckross Parade	36 D1 [32]	*New Street Garden's	36 D3	Northbrook Road	36 E4
Mountain View Apartments	57 C3 [11]	Muckross Park	42 D2	(off New Street)		Northbrook Terrace	36 F1 [1]
Mountain View Avenue	42 F1 [3]	Muirfield Drive	34 F4 [1]	*New Street North	35 C2	*Northbrook Villas	36 E4
Mountain View Cottages	18 D4	Mulberry Crescent	18 F4	(off Church Street)		(on Northbrook Road Ranelagh)	
(Castleknock)		Mulberry Drive	18 E4	New Vale	56 E3	Northcote Avenue	45 C4
Mountain View Cottages	43 B1 [13]	Mulberry Park	18 E4	New Vale Cottages	56 D3	Northcote Place	45 C4 [23]
(Ranelagh)		Muldowney Court	3 C3	New Vale Crescent	56 E3	Northcote Terrace	45 C4 [20]
*Mountain View Court	36 E1	Mulgrave Street	46 D4	New Wapping Street	36 F2	Northland Drive	20 F3 [2]
(off Summerhill Place)		Mulgrave Terrace	46 D4	Newbridge Avenue	37 A3	Northland Grove	20 F3 [1]
Mountain View Drive	51 A1	Mulhuddart	7 A4	Newbridge Drive	37 A3	Northumberland Avenue	46 D4
Mountain View Park	43 A4	Mulhuddart Wood	7 A4	Newbrook Avenue	23 B1	Northumberland Park	46 D4 [11]
Mountain View Road	43 B1	Mullinastill Road	56 D2	Newbrook Road	23 B1	Northumberland Place	36 F3 [42]
Mountain View Road	54 E4 [5]	Mullingar Terrace	34 E2 [10]	Newbury Avenue	11 A4	Northumberland Place	46 D4 [10]
Mountain Villa	54 E4 [3]	Mulroy Road	20 E4	Newbury Drive	11 A4	Northumberland Road	36 F3
Mountainview Drive	57 C4	Mulvey Park	43 C3	Newbury Grove	11 A4	Northumberland Square	36 E2 [5]
Mountbrook	44 E3 [2]	Munster Street	20 F4	Newbury Lawns	11 B4	Northway Estate	9 A4
Mountdown Avenue	41 C3	Munster Terrace	54 E1 [16]	Newbury Park	11 A4	Norton's Avenue	35 C1 [11]
Mountdown Drive	41 C3	Murphy's Lane	55 B4	Newbury Terrace	11 A4 [1]	Norwood	56 E1

STREET NAME	PAGE/GRID REFERENCE
Norwood Park	43 C1 [7]
Nottingham Street	36 F1
Novara Avenue	57 C2
Novara Park	57 C2 [7]
Novara Terrace	57 C2 [27]
Nowlan Avenue	51 B1
Nugent Road	43 A4
Nunciature Road	19 C4
Nurney Lawn	12 D4
Nutgrove Avenue	43 A4
Nutgrove Avenue	43 B4 [14]
Nutgrove Court	43 A4 [2]
Nutgrove Park (Clonskeagh)	43 C2
Nutgrove Way	51 A1
Nutley Avenue	44 D1
Nutley Lane	44 D2
Nutley Park	44 D2
Nutley Road	44 D1
Nutley Square	44 D2 [1]

O

STREET NAME	PAGE/GRID REFERENCE
O'Hogan Road	34 E3
Oak Apple Green	43 A2
Oak Avenue	10 F4
Oak Court	10 F4
Oak Crescent	10 F4
Oak Dene	54 E3
Oak Downs	40 D2
Oak Drive	10 F4
Oak Glen Close	57 C4
Oak Glen Park	57 C4
Oak Glen View	57 C4
Oak Green	10 F4
Oak Grove	10 F4
Oak Lawn	10 F4
Oak Lawn (Castleknock)	18 F3
Oak Lodge	19 A4
Oak Rise	10 F4
Oak Rise	40 D2
Oak Road (Donnycarney)	22 D3
Oak Road (Fox & Geese)	40 F1
Oak View	10 E4
Oak Way	40 D2
Oakcourt Avenue	33 C2
Oakcourt Close	33 C2
Oakcourt Drive	33 C2
Oakcourt Grove	33 C2
Oakcourt Lawn	33 C2
Oakcourt Park	33 C2
Oakdale Close	49 B3
Oakdale Crescent	49 B3
Oakdale Drive	49 B3
Oakdale Drive	53 C2
Oakdale Grove	49 B3
Oakdale Road	49 B3
Oakdale View	49 B3
Oakdown Road	43 A4
Oakfield Place	36 D4 [50]
Oaklands Avenue	2 D2
Oaklands Crescent	43 A2
Oaklands Drive (Rathgar)	43 A2
Oaklands Drive (Sandymount)	37 A4
Oaklands Park	2 D2
Oaklands Park	37 A4
Oaklands Terrace	42 F2
Oaklawn	15 C4
Oaklawn Close	15 C4
Oaklawn West	15 C4
Oakleigh	29 C4
Oakley Court (Flats)	43 B1 [10]
Oakley Grove	45 A4
Oakley Park (Blackrock)	45 A4
Oakley Park (Clontarf)	22 F4
Oakley Park (Ranelagh)	43 B1 [23]
Oakley Road	43 B1
Oakpark Avenue	21 C1
Oakpark Close	21 C1
Oakpark Drive	21 C1
Oakpark Grove	21 C1
Oakton Court	54 E4 [1]
Oakton Drive	54 D4
Oakton Green	54 D4 [3]
Oakton Park	54 D4
Oaktree Avenue	18 E3

STREET NAME	PAGE/GRID REFERENCE
Oaktree Drive	18 E3
Oaktree Green	18 E3
Oaktree Grove	18 E3
Oaktree Lawn	18 E3
Oaktree Road	52 F1
Oakview Avenue	17 C1
Oakview Close	17 C1
Oakview Court	17 C1
Oakview Drive	17 C1
Oakview Grove	17 C1 [2]
Oakview Lawn	17 C1
Oakview Park	17 C1
Oakview Rise	17 C1
Oakview Walk	17 C1
Oakview Way	17 C1
Oakwood	23 A4
Oakwood	45 C4 [7]
Oakwood Avenue	1 C2
Oakwood Avenue	20 E1
Oakwood Close	20 E1
Oakwood Grove Estate	33 A4
Oakwood Park	20 E1
Oakwood Road	20 E1
Oatfield Avenue	33 B3
Oatfield Close	33 B3
*Oatfield Crescent (off Oatfield Drive)	33 B2
Oatfield Drive	33 B3
Oatfield Grove	33 B3
Oatfield Lawn	33 B3
Oatfield Park	33 B3
Obelisk Court	53 A1
Obelisk Rise	53 A1
Obelisk View	53 A1
Oblate Drive	34 F3 [14]
O'Brien Road	41 C1
O'Brien's Place North	21 A3 [13]
O'Brien's Terrace	21 A4 [15]
Observatory Lane	43 A1 [14]
O'Byrne Road	57 C3
O'Byrne Villas	57 C3 [9]
O'Carolan Road	35 C3 [29]
O'Connell Avenue	36 D1 [6]
O'Connell Gardens	37 A3
O'Connell Street	36 D2
*O'Curry Avenue (off O'Curry Road)	35 C3
O'Curry Road	35 C3
O'Daly Road	21 A3
Odd Lamp Road	34 F1
O'Devaney Gardens	35 B2
O'Donnell Gardens	54 D1 [1]
O'Donoghue Street	34 F3
O'Donovan Road	35 C4
O'Dwyer Road	41 C1 [4]
Offaly Road	20 F4
Offington Avenue	25 B2
Offington Court	25 B2
Offington Drive	25 B2
Offington Lawn	25 B2
Offington Manor	25 B1
Offington Manor	25 B1
Offington Park	25 B1
O'Hanlon's Lane	3 B2
O'Hara Avenue	36 D4 [56]
O'Hogan Road	34 E3 [1]
O'Hogan Road	34 E3
Olaf Road	35 C2 [33]
Old Bawn Avenue	49 A2
Old Bawn Close	49 A2
Old Bawn Drive	49 A2
Old Bawn Park	49 A2
Old Bawn Road	49 A2
Old Bawn Terrace	49 A2
Old Bawn Way	49 A2
Old Belgard Road	40 F4
Old Bridge Road	42 D4
Old Brighton Terrace	57 C2 [46]
Old Cabra Road	35 B1
Old Carrickbrack Road	26 D4
Old Conna Wood	57 B1
Old Connaught	57 A1
Old Connaught Avenue	57 B1
Old Connaught Grove	57 B2

STREET NAME	PAGE/GRID REFERENCE
Old Connaught View	57 B2
Old Corduff Road	18 E1
Old Cornmill Road	31 C2
Old County Glen	35 B4
Old County Road	35 A4
Old Dunleary	45 C4
Old Fairgreen	5 B2
Old Hill	16 D4
Old Kilmainham	35 B3
Old Kilmainham Village	35 B3 [2]
Old Mill Court	35 C3 [52]
Old Mountpleasant	36 E4 [9]
Old Naas Road	34 E4
Old Naas Road Cottages	34 E4 [1]
Old Quarry	54 F2
Old Rathmore Terrace	57 B2 [22]
Old Ravenswell Row	57 B2 [19]
Old Rectory	32 D1 [11]
Old Rectory Park	43 C4
Old Road (Portmarnock)	12 E2
Old Street	3 B2
Old Yellow Walls Road	2 F2
Oldbawn	49 A2
Oldbridge	32 E3
Oldcastle Avenue	25 B2
Oldcastle Drive	39 B1
Oldchurch Avenue	39 C1
Oldchurch Close	39 C1
Oldchurch Court	39 C1
Oldchurch Crescent	39 C1
Oldchurch Drive	39 C1
Oldchurch Grove	39 C1
Oldchurch Grove	39 C1
Oldchurch Lawn	39 C1
Oldchurch Park	39 C1
Oldchurch Way	39 C1
Oldcourt	57 B3
Oldcourt Avenue	49 B2
Oldcourt Avenue	57 B3
Oldcourt Close	49 B2
Oldcourt Cottages	49 B3
Oldcourt Drive	57 B3
Oldcourt Grove	57 B4
Oldcourt Lawn	49 B2 [1]
Oldcourt Manor	49 B3
Oldcourt Park	57 B3
Oldcourt Road	49 B3
Oldcourt Terrace	57 C3 [15]
Oldcourt View	49 B2
Oldtower Crescent	33 A2
Oldtown Avenue	21 A1
Oldtown Cottages	29 C3
Oldtown Park	21 A1 [3]
Oldtown Road	21 A1
O'Leary Road	35 A3
Olivemount Grove	43 C3 [2]
Olivemount Road	43 C3
Olivemount Terrace	43 C3 [6]
Oliver Bond Street	35 C2
Oliver Plunkett Avenue (Dun Laoghaire)	53 C1
Oliver Plunkett Avenue (Ringsend)	37 A3
Oliver Plunkett Road	53 C1
Oliver Plunkett Square	53 C1 [1]
Oliver Plunkett Terrace	53 C1 [5]
Oliver Plunkett Villas	53 B1 [3]
Olney Crescent	42 F2
Olney Grove	42 F2 [17]
Omni Park	21 B1
O'Moore Road	34 E3
O'Neachtain Road	21 A3 [14]
O'Neill's Buildings	36 D3 [14]
Ontario Terrace	36 D4 [11]
Onward Close	3 C4
Onward Walk	3 C4
Ophaly Court	43 C4 [1]
*O'Quinn Avenue (off Mount Brown)	35 B3
O'Quinns Avenue	35 B3 [40]
O'Rahilly House Flats	37 A3 [28]
O'Rahilly Parade	36 D2 [26]
Oranmore Road	33 C3
Oratory Mews Court	46 D4 [24]

STREET NAME	PAGE/GRID REFERENCE
Orby Avenue	52 E3
Orby Close	52 F3
Orby Court	52 F3
Orby Park	52 F3
Orby View	52 E3
Orchard Avenue	17 C2
Orchard Close	18 D2
Orchard Close	18 D2
Orchard Cottages	53 A1 [1]
Orchard Court	18 E2
Orchard Green	18 D2
Orchard Grove	18 E2
Orchard Lane	36 E4 [24]
Orchard Lane (Blackrock)	53 A1
Orchard Lane (Clondalkin)	40 E1
Orchard Lawns	33 C3
Orchard Road (Ballybough)	21 B4
Orchard Road (Raheny)	23 B2
Orchard Road South	43 B2
Orchard Square	43 B3
Orchard Terrace	57 C3 [19]
*Orchard Terrace (Grangegorman Upper)	35 C1
*Orchard View (Grangegorman Upper)	35 C1
Orchardstown Avenue	42 E4
Orchardstown Drive	42 E4
Orchardstown Park	42 E4
Orchardstown Villas	42 E4
Orchardstown Villas	50 E1
Orchardton	50 E1 [1]
Ordnance Survey Road	34 E1
O'Reilly Avenue	35 B3 [9]
Oriel Street Lower	36 F1
Oriel Street Upper	36 E2
Orlagh Avenue	50 D2
Orlagh Close	50 D2
Orlagh Court	50 D2
Orlagh Crescent	50 D2
Orlagh Downs	50 D2
Orlagh Grange	50 D2
Orlagh Green	50 D2
Orlagh Grove	50 D2
Orlagh Grove	50 D2
Orlagh Lawn	50 D2
Orlagh Lodge	50 D2
Orlagh Meadows	50 D2
Orlagh Park	50 D2
Orlagh Pines	50 D2
Orlagh Rise	50 D2
Orlagh View	50 D2
Orlagh Way	50 D2
Orlagh Wood	50 D2
Ormeau Drive	54 F1 [2]
Ormeau Street	36 F3 [7]
Ormond Avenue	1 B1
Ormond Close	1 B1
Ormond Crescent	1 B1
Ormond Drive	1 B1
Ormond Grove	1 B1
Ormond Lawn	1 B1
*Ormond Market (off Ormond Quay Upper)	36 D2
*Ormond Place (off Ormond Quay Upper)	36 D2
Ormond Quay Lower	36 D2
Ormond Quay Upper	36 D2
Ormond Road	21 B4
Ormond Road South (Rathmines)	43 B1
Ormond Square	36 D2 [37]
Ormond Street	35 C3
*Ormond Terrace (off Sorrento Road)	54 F2
Ormond View	1 B1
Ormond Way	1 B1
O'Rourke Park (Sallynoggin)	53 C2
Orpen	52 F1
Orpen Close	44 F4
Orpen Dale	44 F4 [2]
Orpen Green	44 F4 [6]
Orpen Green	52 F1
Orpen Hill	52 F1
Orpen Rise	52 F1
Orwell Bank	43 A3 [7]

STREET NAME	PAGE/GRID REFERENCE
Orwell Court	43 A3 [3]
Orwell Gardens	43 A3
Orwell Mews	43 A2 [8]
Orwell Park	41 C4
Orwell Park	43 A3
Orwell Park Avenue	42 D3
Orwell Park Close	42 D3
Orwell Park Crescent	42 D3
Orwell Park Dale	41 C4
Orwell Park Drive	42 D3
Orwell Park Glade	41 C3
Orwell Park Glen	42 D3
Orwell Park Green	42 D3
Orwell Park Grove	41 C3
Orwell Park Heights	41 C4
Orwell Park Lawns	41 C3
Orwell Park Rise	41 C4
Orwell Park View	41 C4
Orwell Park Way	42 D3
Orwell Road	43 A2
Orwell Walk	43 A3 [13]
Orwell Woods	43 A2
*Osborne Terrace (Northbrook Road)	36 E4
Oscar Square	35 C3 [23]
Oscar Traynor Road	22 E1
O'Shea's Cottages	53 C3 [3]
Osprey Avenue	41 C3
Osprey Drive	41 C3
Osprey Lawn	41 C3
Osprey Park	41 C3
Osprey Road	41 C3
Ossory Road	36 F1
Ostman Place	35 C2 [1]
O'Sullivan Avenue	36 E1 [1]
Oswald Road	37 A3
Otranto Place	54 E1
Oulart	1 C3
Oulton Road	22 E4
*Our Lady's Close (off Our Lady's Road)	35 C3
Our Lady's Road	35 C3
Outlands	1 C1
Ovoca Road	36 D4
Owendoher Lodge	50 E1
Owendore Avenue	42 F4
Owendore Crescent	42 F4
Owen's Avenue	35 B3 [39]
*Owen's Avenue (off Mount Brown)	35 B3
Owenstown Park	44 D3
Oxford Road	36 E4
*Oxford Terrace (on Hawthorn Terrace)	36 F1
*Oxford Terrace (off Church Road)	36 F1
Oxmantown Lane	35 C2 [21]
Oxmantown Road	35 B1

P

STREET NAME	PAGE/GRID REFERENCE
Pace Avenue	6 E4
Pace Crescent	6 E4
Pace Road	6 E4
Pace View	6 E4
Pacelli Avenue	23 C1
Pairc Gleann Trasna	49 A3
Pairc Mhuire	47 A2
Pakenham	45 C4 [28]
Pakenham Road	45 C4
*Palace Street (off Dame Street)	36 D2
Palatine Square	35 B2
Palmer Park	50 E2
Palmer Park	50 F2
Palmers Avenue	33 B2
Palmers Close	33 B2
Palmers Copse	33 B2
Palmers Court	33 B2
Palmers Crescent	33 B2
Palmers Drive	33 B2
Palmers Glade	33 B2
Palmers Grove	33 B2
Palmers Lawn	33 B2
Palmers Park	33 B2
Palmers Road	33 B2

STREET NAME	PAGE/GRID REFERENCE
Palmers Walk	33 B2
Palmerston	33 C1
Palmerston Close	43 B1 [21]
*Palmerston Close (rere of Palmerston Road)	43 B1
Palmerston Gardens	43 B2
Palmerston Grove	43 C2 [5]
Palmerston Lane	43 B2
Palmerston Park	33 B2
Palmerston Park	43 B2
Palmerston Place	36 D1 [8]
Palmerston Road	43 B1
Palmerston Villas	43 A2
Palmerstown Avenue	33 C2
Palmerstown Close	33 B2
Palmerstown Court	33 C2
Palmerstown Drive	33 C2
Palmerstown Green	33 B2
Palmerstown Heights	33 B2
Palmerstown Lawn	33 B2
Palmerstown Manor	33 B2
Palmerstown Woods	33 B4
Paradise Place	36 D1
Park Avenue	1 B2
Park Avenue	18 F3
Park Avenue (Deans Grange)	53 A1
Park Avenue (Sandymount)	37 B4
Park Avenue (Willbrook)	50 F1
Park Avenue West	35 B2 [13]
Park Close (Sallynoggin)	54 D2
Park Court (Sandymount)	37 A4 [16]
Park Court Apts	19 A3 [4]
Park Crescent	35 A1
Park Crescent (Kimmage)	42 D2
Park Crescent House	20 D4 [6]
Park Drive (Cabinteely)	53 B3
Park Drive (Ranelagh)	43 B1
Park Drive Avenue	18 F3
Park Drive Close	18 F3
Park Drive Court	18 F3
Park Drive Crescent	18 F3
Park Drive Green	18 F3
Park Drive Grove	18 F3
Park Drive Lawn	18 F3
Park Lane	46 D4 [21]
Park Lane (Chapelizod)	34 E2 [1]
Park Lane (Sandymount)	37 A4
Park Lawn	23 A4
Park Lodge	18 F3
Park Place	35 A2 [4]
Park Road (Dun Laoghaire)	46 D4
Park Road (off Navan Road)	19 C3
Park Road (Sallynoggin)	54 D2
Park Spring's	20 D4 [5]
Park Street	34 F3 [1]
*Park Street (off Hanover St West)	35 C3
Park Terrace (Coombe)	35 C3 [6]
*Park Terrace (on Lower Dargle Road)	57 B2
Park View	22 F4 [1]
Park View	43 A3 [10]
Park View (Cabra)	35 B1
Park View (Castleknock)	19 B4
Park View (Clonsilla)	18 D2
Park View (Portmarnock)	13 A1
Park View Lawns	40 D2
Park Villas	19 A3
Park Villas	44 F4 [3]
Park West Avenue	33 C4
Park West Road	33 C4
Parker Hill	43 A1 [12]
Parkgate Street	35 B2
Parkhill Avenue	40 F3
Parkhill Close	41 A3
Parkhill Court	40 F3
Parkhill Drive	40 F3
Parkhill Green	40 F3
Parkhill Heights	41 A3 [1]
Parkhill Lawn	40 F3
Parkhill Rise	40 F3
Parkhill Road	40 F3
Parkhill Way	41 A3
Parkhill West	40 F4

STREET NAME	PAGE/GRID REFERENCE
Parklands Road	49 B2
Parkmore	19 A3
Parkmore Drive	42 E2
Parknasilla Avenue	56 D2
Parknasilla Close	56 D2
Parknasilla Lane	56 D2
Parknasilla Rise	56 D2
Parkvale	24 D1
Parkvale	51 C1
Parkview	1 B2
Parkview	41 A3 [2]
Parkview Avenue (Harold's Cross)	42 F1
Parkview Court	35 A1 [1]
Parkview Court	42 F1 [8]
*Parkview Court (on Blackhorse Avenue)	35 A1
Parkview Place	37 A3 [14]
Parkview Terrace	57 B2 [16]
Parkwood Avenue	49 A2
Parkwood Grove	49 A2
Parkwood Lawn	49 A2
Parkwood Road	49 A2
Parliament Street	36 D2
Parlickstown Court	7 A4
Parlickstown Gardens	7 A3
Parlickstown Green	7 A4
Parnell Avenue	35 C4
Parnell Cottages	3 B3
Parnell Court	35 C4 [13]
Parnell Place	36 D1 [16]
Parnell Road	35 C4
Parnell Road	57 C2
Parnell Square East	36 D1
Parnell Square North	36 D1
Parnell Square West	36 D1
Parnell Street	36 D2
Parnell Street (Sallynoggin)	54 D1
Parochial Avenue	13 A4 [2]
Parslickstown Avenue	7 A4
Parslickstown Close	7 A4
Parslickstown Drive	7 A4
Partridge Terrace	34 F3 [5]
Patrician Park	53 C1 [2]
Patrician Villas	44 F4
Patrick Doyle Road	43 B2
Patrick Street	36 D3
Patrick Street (Dun Laoghaire)	46 D4
Patrick's Row	45 A3 [14]
Patrickswell Place	20 D2
Paul Street	35 C2 [36]
Pea Field	44 F3
Pear Tree Field	52 F1 [5]
Pearse Avenue	54 D2
Pearse Brothers Park	50 F1
Pearse Close	54 D2 [3]
Pearse Drive	54 D2
Pearse Gardens	53 C2
Pearse Green	54 D2
Pearse Grove	36 F3 [38]
Pearse House	36 E2 [1]
Pearse Park	54 D2
Pearse Road	54 D2
Pearse Road	57 B2 [12]
Pearse Square (Bray)	57 B2
Pearse Street	36 E2
Pearse Street (Sallynoggin)	54 D2
Pearse Villas	54 D2
Peck's Lane	19 A3
Pembroke Cottages (Booterstown)	44 F3 [2]
Pembroke Cottages (Donnybrook)	43 C1 [2]
Pembroke Cottages (Dundrum)	43 C4 [5]
Pembroke Cottages (Ringsend)	37 A2
Pembroke Gardens	36 F4
Pembroke Lane (Lr Baggot Stt)	36 E3
Pembroke Lane (Pembroke Rd)	36 F4
Pembroke Park	36 F4
Pembroke Place (Ballsbridge)	36 F4 [15]
Pembroke Place (Pembroke St Upr)	36 E4 [32]
Pembroke Road	36 F4
Pembroke Row	36 E3
Pembroke Street	37 A3
Pembroke Street Lower	36 E3
Pembroke Street Upper	36 E3

STREET NAME	PAGE/GRID REFERENCE
Pembroke Terrace	43 C4 [6]
Penrose Street	36 F3 [6]
Percy French Road	41 C1 [3]
Percy Lane	36 F3
Percy Place	36 F3
Peter Place	36 D4 [19]
Peter Row	36 D3
Peter Street	36 D3
Peter's Court	36 D1 [38]
Peterson's Court	36 E2 [16]
Petrie Road	35 C4
Pheasant Run	6 F4
Pheasant Run The Drive	6 F4
Pheasant Run The Green	6 F4
Pheasant Run The Grove	6 F4
Pheasant Run The Park	6 F4
Phibsboro	35 C1 [22]
Phibsborough	35 C1 [24]
Phibsborough	36 D1
Phibsborough Avenue	35 C1 [6]
Phibsborough Place	36 D1 [1]
Phibsborough Road	36 D1
Philipsburgh Avenue	21 C4
Philipsburgh Terrace	21 C4
*Philomena Terrace (off Oliver Plunket Ave)	37 A3
Phoenix Avenue	19 A3
Phoenix Court	19 A3
Phoenix Court	35 B1 [15]
Phoenix Court	35 B2 [17]
Phoenix Drive	19 A3
Phoenix Gardens	19 A3
Phoenix Manor	35 B1
Phoenix Place	19 A3
Phoenix Street	34 F3 [1]
Phoenix Street West	35 C2 [15]
Phoenix Terrace	44 F3
Phoenix View	35 B3 [43]
Pickford's Terrace	36 F2 [13]
Pig Lane	36 E1
*Pig Lane (off Summer Place)	36 E1
Pigeon House Road	37 B3
Pigeon House Road (Ringsend)	37 A3
*Pile's Tce (Sandwith St Upper)	36 E3
Pilot View	54 F1 [1]
Pim Street	35 C3
Pimlico	35 C3
Pimlico Cottages	35 C3 [12]
Pine Avenue	53 A2
Pine Copse Road	51 B1
Pine Court	13 A1
Pine Court	53 A1
Pine Grove	50 D1 [1]
Pine Grove Park	1 C1
Pine Grove Road	1 C1
Pine Haven	44 F3
Pine Hurst	20 E4
Pine Lawn (Deans Grange)	53 A1
Pine Lawn (Tallaght)	49 A2
Pine Road	37 A3
Pine Valley Avenue	51 B2
Pine Valley Drive	51 B3
Pine Valley Grove	51 B3
Pine Valley Park	51 B3
Pine Valley Way	51 B3
Pinebrook Avenue	22 D2
Pinebrook Close	17 C1
Pinebrook Crescent	22 D2
Pinebrook Downs	17 C1
Pinebrook Drive	22 E2
Pinebrook Glen	17 C1
Pinebrook Grove	22 E2
Pinebrook Heights	17 C1
Pinebrook Lawn	17 C1
Pinebrook Rise	22 D2
Pinebrook Road	22 D2
Pinebrook Vale	17 C1
Pinebrook View	17 C1
Pinebrook Way	17 C1
Pinetree Crescent	40 F4 [1]
Pinetree Grove	40 F3 [1]
Pineview Avenue	49 A2
Pineview Drive	49 A2
Pineview Grove	49 A2

STREET NAME	PAGE/GRID REFERENCE
Pineview Lawn	49 A2
Pineview Park	49 A2
Pineview Rise	49 A2
Pineview Road	49 A2
Pinewood	54 D4
Pinewood Avenue	20 F1
Pinewood Close	57 C4
Pinewood Court	6 F4
Pinewood Crescent	20 F1
Pinewood Drive	20 F1
Pinewood Green	20 F1
Pinewood Grove	21 A1 [1]
Pinewood Park	50 E1
Pinewood Villas	20 F1
Pinewoods	40 D2
Pleasants Lane	36 D3 [15]
Pleasants Place	36 D3 [21]
Pleasants Street	36 D3
Plums Road	52 D1
Plunkett Avenue (Finglas)	20 D1
Plunkett Avenue (Foxrock)	53 A3
Plunkett Crescent	9 A4
Plunkett Drive	20 D1
Plunkett Green	20 D1
Plunkett Grove	20 D1
Plunkett Road	20 D1
Poddle Close	42 E1
Poddle Green	42 E1 [6]
Poddle Park	42 E2
Polo Road	35 A1
Poolbeg Street	36 E2
Poole Street	35 C3 [38]
Poplar Row	36 F1
Poppintree	9 C4
Porters Avenue	18 D2
Porters Gate	17 C2
Porters Gate Avenue	17 C2
Porters Gate Close	17 B2
Porters Gate Court	17 B2
Porters Gate Crescent	17 B2
Porters Gate Drive	17 B2
Porters Gate Green	17 B2
Porters Gate Grove	17 B2
Porters Gate Heights	17 C2
Porters Gate Rise	17 C2
Porters Gate View	17 B2
Porters Gate Way	17 B2
Porters Road	18 D2
Porterstown Road	18 D2
Portland Close	36 E1 [50]
*Portland Court	36 D1
(off Portland Place)	
Portland Place	36 D1
Portland Row	36 E1
Portland Square	36 E1 [70]
*Portland Square	36 E1
(off Portland St North)	
Portland Street North	36 E1
Portland Street West	35 C3
Portmahon Drive	35 B3
Portmarnock	13 A1
Portmarnock Avenue	13 A1
Portmarnock Crescent	13 A1
Portmarnock Drive	4 D4
Portmarnock Grove	4 D4
Portmarnock Park	4 D4
Portmarnock Rise	13 A1
Portmarnock Walk	4 D4
Portobello Harbour	36 D4 [6]
Portobello Place	36 D4 [36]
Portobello Road	36 D4
Portside Court	36 F1 [22]
Pottery Road	53 C2
Pound Street	31 A1
Power's Court	36 F3
*Power's Square	36 D3
(off John Dillon Street)	
Prebend Street	35 C2
Preston Street	36 E1 [14]
*Price's Lane (Aston Quay)	36 D2
Price's Place (Ranelagh)	36 D4
Priestfield Cottages	35 C4 [4]
Priestfield Drive	35 C4 [28]
Primrose Avenue	36 D1

STREET NAME	PAGE/GRID REFERENCE
Primrose Grove	11 C4
Primrose Hill	30 D3
Primrose Hill	45 C4 [25]
Primrose Lane	32 D1
*Primrose Street	36 D1
(off Wellington Street Upper)	
Prince Arthur Terrace	43 A1 [3]
Prince Edward Terrace Lower	45 A4 [2]
Prince Edward Terrace Upper	45 A4 [3]
Prince of Wales Terrace	37 A4 [7]
Prince of Wales Terrace	57 C2 [26]
Prince's Street North	36 D2 [20]
Prince's Street South	36 E2 [12]
Princeton	44 D3
Prior Hall	35 B3 [36]
Priorswood Road	11 C4
Priory Avenue	44 F4
Priory Chase	29 C4
Priory Close	29 C4
Priory Court	51 A2 [1]
Priory Court (Celbridge)	29 C4
Priory Crescent	29 C4
Priory Drive	44 F4
Priory Drive (Celbridge)	29 C4
Priory East	20 D4
Priory Green	29 C4
Priory Grove	44 F4
Priory Grove (Celbridge)	29 C4
Priory Hall	42 D2
Priory Hall	44 E4
Priory North	20 D3
Priory Road	42 F1
Priory Square	29 C3
Priory View	29 C3
Priory Walk	29 C4
Priory Walk	42 D2
Priory Way	29 C3
Priory Way	42 D2
Priory West	20 D4
Proby Garden	45 A4
Proby Hall	54 E2
Proby Park	54 E2
Proby Square	45 A4
Proby's Lane	36 D2 [28]
Promenade Road	37 A1
Prospect	50 E2
Prospect Avenue	21 A4
Prospect Avenue	50 E2
Prospect Court	50 E3
Prospect Drive	50 E2
Prospect Glen	50 E2
Prospect Grove	50 E2
Prospect Heath	50 E2
Prospect Heights	50 E2
Prospect Lane	43 C2 [1]
Prospect Lawn	53 B3
Prospect Meadows	50 E2
Prospect Road	21 A4
Prospect Square	21 A4 [5]
Prospect Terrace (Kilmainham)	35 A3 [14]
Prospect Terrace (Sandymount)	37 B3 [1]
Prospect View	50 E2
Prospect Way	21 A4
Protestant Row	36 D3 [12]
Proud's Lane	36 D3 [24]
Provost Row	35 C2 [46]
Prussia Street	35 C1
Pucks Castle Lane	55 C3
*Purcell Lane	57 C2
(off Main Street Bray)	
Purley Park	3 C4
Purser Gardens	43 A1 [10]
Putland Road	57 C3
Putland Villas	57 C3 [14]
Pyro Villas	35 C3 [60]

Q

STREET NAME	PAGE/GRID REFERENCE
Quarry Cottages	22 E3 [3]
Quarry Drive	41 C2
Quarry Road	20 E4
Quarry Road	56 D4
Queen's Park	45 B4
Queen's Road	46 D4
Queen's Street	35 C2

STREET NAME	PAGE/GRID REFERENCE
Quinn's Lane	36 E3
Quinn's Road	56 E3
Quinsborough Road	57 C2

R

STREET NAME	PAGE/GRID REFERENCE
Radcliffe	25 A1 [3]
Radlett Grove	4 D4
*Rafter's Ave (off Rafter's Rd)	35 A4
Rafter's Lane	35 A4
Rafter's Road	35 A4
Raglan Lane	36 F4
Raglan Road	36 F4
Raheen Avenue	48 E1
Raheen Close	48 E1
Raheen Court	48 E1
Raheen Crescent	48 E1
Raheen Drive (Ballyfermot)	34 D3
Raheen Drive (Tallaght)	48 E1
Raheen Green	48 E1
Raheen Park (Ballyfermot)	34 D3
Raheen Park (Bray)	58 D3
Raheen Park (Tallaght)	48 E1
Raheen Road	48 E1
Raheny	23 A2
Raheny Park	23 A3
Raheny Park	23 A1
Railway Avenue	3 B2
Railway Avenue (Baldoyle)	24 D1
Railway Avenue (Inchicore)	34 F3
Railway Cottages	37 A4 [8]
Railway Court	3 B2 [3]
Railway Road	54 F2 [2]
Railway Street	36 E1
*Railway Tce (off Macken St)	36 F3
Rainsford Avenue	35 C3 [3]
Rainsford Lane	54 E4 [6]
Rainsford Street	35 C3
Ralahine	54 D4
Raleigh Square	42 D1
Ralph Square	31 A1 [1]
Ramillies Road	34 E3
Ramleh Close	43 C2
Ramleh Park	43 C2
Ramor Park	18 E2
Ranelagh	36 E4
Ranelagh Avenue	36 E4
Ranelagh Road	36 E4
Raphoe Road	42 D1
Rathbeal Court	1 C1 [2]
Rathbeale Court	1 C1
Rathbeale Crescent	1 C1
Rathbeale Rise	1 C2
Rathbeale Road	1 C1
Rathclaren	57 B3 [2]
Rathdown Avenue	42 F3
Rathdown Court	42 F2 [10]
(off Templeogue Road)	
Rathdown Crescent	42 F3
Rathdown Drive	42 E3
Rathdown Grove	52 D2 [9]
Rathdown Park	42 F3
Rathdown Road	35 C1
Rathdown Square	35 C1 [20]
Rathdown Terrace (Sandyford)	52 D2 [5]
Rathdown Villas	42 F3
Rathdrum Road	35 B4
Rathfarnham	42 F3
Rathfarnham Park	42 F3
Rathfarnham Road	42 F3
Rathfarnham Wood	42 F4
Rathgar	43 A2
Rathgar Avenue	42 F2
Rathgar Park	42 F2 [16]
Rathgar Park	43 A2 [7]
Rathgar Place	43 A1
Rathgar Road	43 A1
Rathgar Villas	42 F2 [11]
Rathingle Road	1 B3
Rathland Drive	42 E2 [4]
Rathland Road	42 E2
Rathlin Road	21 A3
Rathlyon	49 C2
Rathlyon Estate	49 C2
Rathlyon Park	49 C2

STREET NAME	PAGE/GRID REFERENCE
Rathmichael	55 C3
Rathmichael Dales	56 D3
Rathmichael Hill	55 C2
Rathmichael Lane	55 C2
Rathmichael Manor	56 D2
Rathmichael Road	55 C2
Rathmichael Woods	56 E2
Rathmines	43 A1
Rathmines Avenue	43 A1
Rathmines Avenue Court	43 A1 [25]
Rathmines Close	43 A1
Rathmines Park	43 A1 [1]
Rathmines Road Lower	43 A1
Rathmines Road Upper	43 A1
Rathmintan Close	48 D2
Rathmintan Court	48 D2
Rathmintan Crescent	48 D2
Rathmintan Drive	48 D2
Rathmore Avenue	52 D1
Rathmore Park	23 A2
Rathmore Villas	42 F2
Rathsallagh Avenue	56 E2
Rathsallagh Drive	56 E2
Rathsallagh Grove	56 E2
Rathsallagh Park	56 E2
Rathvale Avenue	22 F1
Rathvale Drive	22 F1
Rathvale Grove	22 F1
Rathvale Park	22 F1
Rathvilly Drive	20 D2
Rathvilly Park	20 D2
Ratoath Avenue	20 D2
Ratoath Drive	19 C1
Ratoath Estate	20 D3
Ratoath Road	20 E4
Ratoath Road (Hollystown)	7 B1
Ratra Park	19 C4
Ratra Road	19 C4
Ravens Court	20 D2 [5]
Ravens Rock Road	52 E2
Ravensdale Drive	42 E2
(off Ravensdale Park)	
Ravensdale Park	42 E2
Ravensdale Road	36 F1
Ravenswell Road	57 C2
Raverty Villas	57 B1 [1]
Raymond Street	35 C4
Rectory Slopes	57 B3
Red Brick Terrace	53 A1 [2]
Red Cow Cottages	33 C1 [1]
Red Cow Lane	35 C2
Redberry	32 D3
Redesdale Crescent	44 D4
Redesdale Road	44 D4
Redfern Avenue	3 C4
Redmond's Court	23 B1 [1]
Redmond's Hill	36 D3 [11]
Redwood Avenue	41 A4
Redwood Close	41 A4
Redwood Court (Churchtown)	43 A3
Redwood Court (Tallaght)	40 F4
Redwood Drive	40 F4
Redwood Grove	44 F3
Redwood Heights	41 A4
Redwood Lawn	40 F4
Redwood Park	41 A4
Redwood Rise	41 A4
Redwood View	41 A4
Redwood Walk	40 F4
Reginald Square	35 C3 [43]
Reginald Street	35 C3
Rehoboth Avenue	35 C4 [3]
Rehoboth Place	35 B4
Reilly's Avenue	35 B4 [6]
Reuben Avenue	35 B3
Reuben Street	35 B3
*Rhodaville	36 D4
(off Mountpleasant Ave)	
Rialto Buildings	35 B3 [14]
Rialto Cottages	35 B3
*Rialto Cottages (off Rialto St)	35 B3
Rialto Drive	35 B4 [3]
*Rialto Park(off Echlin Street)	35 B3
Rialto Street	35 B3

STREET NAME	PAGE/GRID REFERENCE
Ribh Avenue	22 F2
Ribh Road	22 F2
Richelieu Park	44 E1
Richmond	53 A1
Richmond Avenue (Fairview)	21 B4
Richmond Avenue (Monkstown)	45 C4
Richmond Avenue South	43 B2
Richmond Cottages (Summerhill)	36 E1 [9]
Richmond Cottages North	36 E1 [37]
Richmond Court	43 B2
Richmond Crescent	36 E1 [8]
Richmond Estate	21 C4
Richmond Green	45 C4 [12]
Richmond Grove	45 C4
Richmond Hill (Monkstown)	45 C4
Richmond Hill (Rathmines)	36 D4
Richmond Lane	36 E1 [20]
Richmond Manor	36 D2
Richmond Mews	36 D4 [43]
Richmond Parade	36 E1 [10]
Richmond Park	45 B4
Richmond Park	57 A4
Richmond Place (Rathmines)	36 D4 [10]
Richmond Place South (Sth Richmond St)	36 D4 [44]
Richmond Road	21 B4
Richmond Row	36 D4 [7]
Richmond Street North	36 E1
Richmond Street South	36 D4
Richmond Terrace	58 D2 [12]
Richmond Villas	36 D4 [22]
Richview	43 C2
Richview Park	43 B2
*Richview Villas (off Clonskeagh Road)	43 C2
Riddlesford	57 C4
Ridge Hill	56 E1
Ridgewood Avenue	1 B3
Ridgewood Close	1 B3
Ridgewood Green	1 B3
Ridgewood Park	1 B3
Ridgewood Square	1 B3
Rinawade Avenue	30 E1
Rinawade Close	30 E1
Rinawade Crescent	30 E1
Rinawade Downs	30 E1
Rinawade Glade	30 E1
Rinawade Grove	30 E1
Rinawade Lawns	30 E1
Rinawade Park	30 F1
Rinawade Rise	30 E1
Rinawade View	30 E1
Ring Street	34 F3 [12]
Ring Terrace	34 F3
Ringsend	37 A3
Ringsend Park	37 A2
Ringsend Road	36 F3
Ripley Court	57 B3
Ripley Hills	57 B3
River Court	5 B3 [2]
River Forest	16 D3
River Forest View	15 C3
River Gardens	21 A3 [15]
River Lane (Bray)	57 B2
River Lane (Loughlinstown)	56 E2 [1]
River Lawns	29 C4
River Road	18 F2
River Road	19 C3
River Road Cottages	19 A2
River Valley Avenue	1 C2
River Valley Close	1 B2
River Valley Court	1 B2
River Valley Drive	1 C2
River Valley Grove	1 C3
River Valley Heights	1 C2
River Valley Lawn	1 C2
River Valley Park	1 C2
River Valley Rise	1 C3
River Valley Road	1 C2
River Valley View	1 B2
River Valley Way	1 B2
River View	29 C4
Riverbank	43 A3 [6]
Riverdale	16 D4

STREET NAME	PAGE/GRID REFERENCE
Riversdale	33 C1
Riversdale Avenue	42 F3
Riversdale Avenue (Clondalkin)	40 E1
Riversdale Avenue (Palmerston)	33 C1
Riversdale Court	33 C1
Riversdale Crescent	40 E1
Riversdale Drive	40 E1
Riversdale Green	33 B4
Riversdale Grove	33 B1
Riversdale Grove	42 E2 [1]
Riversdale Park	33 C1
Riversdale Park	40 E1
Riversdale Road	40 E1
Riverside	40 E1 [6]
Riverside Avenue	11 A4
Riverside Cottages	42 E4
Riverside Crescent	11 A4
Riverside Drive (Coolock)	11 B4
Riverside Drive (Palmerston)	33 C1
Riverside Drive (Rathfarnham)	43 A3
Riverside Grove	11 A4
Riverside Park	11 A4
Riverside Road	11 A4
Riverston Abbey	20 D4
Riverview	33 C1
Riverview	49 A2
Riverview Court	34 E2 [11]
Riverwood Chase	18 D3
Riverwood Close	18 D3
Riverwood Copse	18 D3
Riverwood Court	18 D3
Riverwood Crescent	18 D3
Riverwood Dale	18 D3
Riverwood Dene	18 D3
Riverwood Drive	18 D3
Riverwood Gardens	18 D3
Riverwood Glebe	18 D3
Riverwood Glen	18 D3
Riverwood Green	18 D3
Riverwood Grove	18 D3
Riverwood Heath	18 D3
Riverwood Lawn	18 D3
Riverwood Park	18 D3
Riverwood Place	18 D3
Riverwood Terrace	18 D3
Riverwood Vale	18 D3
Riverwood View	18 D3
Riverwood Way	18 D3
Robert Place	21 B4 [7]
Robert Street (James's Street)	35 C3
Robert Street (Jones's Road)	21 B4 [6]
Robin Villas	33 C1
Robinhood Park	41 B1
Robinhood Road	41 A1
Roby Place	46 D4 [17]
Rochestown Avenue	53 C2
Rochestown Park	54 D2
Rochfort Avenue	32 F2
Rochfort Close	32 F2
Rochfort Crescent	32 F3
Rochfort Downs	32 F2
Rochfort Green	32 F2
Rochfort Park	32 E1
Rochfort Way	32 F3
Rock Field Drive (Clondalkin)	40 D2
Rock Hill	45 A3
*Rock Lane (Baggot St Lower)	36 E3
Rock Lodge	54 E4
Rock Road	45 A3
Rockbrook	50 E4
Rockfield	32 D3
Rockfield Avenue	42 D2
Rockfield Close	18 D3
Rockfield Drive (Coolmine)	18 D3
Rockfield Drive (Kimmage)	42 D2
Rockfield Park	18 D2
Rockford Park	53 B1
Rockford Terrace	45 B4 [14]
Rockfort Avenue	54 F2
Rockingham Avenue	15 C4
Rockingham Green	15 C4
Rockingham Grove	15 C4
Rockingham Park	15 C4
Rockingham Terrace	2 D2

STREET NAME	PAGE/GRID REFERENCE
Rocklands	54 F1 [6]
Rockville Crescent	45 B4
Rockville Drive	45 B4
Rockville Drive	55 A1
Rockville Estate	45 A4 [9]
Rockville Park	45 B4
Rockville Road	45 A4
Rockwell Cove	45 A3 [9]
Rockwood	32 D3
Rocwood	52 F2
Roebuck Avenue	44 E3
Roebuck Castle	44 D3
Roebuck Crescent	43 C3
Roebuck Downs	43 C3
Roebuck Drive	42 D2
Roebuck Road	44 D3
Roger Casement Park	57 B2
Roger's Lane	36 E3 [15]
Roland Court	43 A1 [20]
Rollins Court	54 D1 [12]
Rollins Villas	53 C1 [15]
Rollins Villas	54 D1
Ronanstown	33 A4
Roncalli Road	23 C1
Roosevelt Cottages	20 D4 [1]
Rooske Road	5 B3
Rope Walk Place	37 A3
Ropewalk Pace	37 A3 [30]
Rory O'Connor Park	53 B1
Rosary Gardens East	46 D4 [2]
Rosary Gardens West	45 C4 [1]
Rosary Road	35 B3
Rosary Terrace (Ringsend)	37 A3
*Rosary Terrace (off Library Rd)	46 D4
Rosbeg Court	23 C2
Rose Park	53 C1
Rosebank	49 A2
*Rosedale Terrace (Lower Clanbrassil St)	35 C4
Roseglen Avenue	23 B2
Roseglen Road	23 B2
Rosehill	53 A1 [5]
Roselawn	32 E1
Roselawn Avenue	18 E2
Roselawn Close	18 F2
Roselawn Court	18 F2
Roselawn Crescent	18 E2
Roselawn Drive	57 C3
Roselawn Drive (Castleknock)	18 E2
Roselawn Glade	18 E2
Roselawn Grove	18 E2
Roselawn Park	57 C3 [2]
Roselawn Road	18 E2
Roselawn Road	18 F2
Roselawn View	18 E2
Roselawn Walk	18 E2
Roselawn Way	18 F2
Rosemount	22 D3
Rosemount (Churchtown)	43 C4
Rosemount Avenue	22 E2
Rosemount Court	43 C4
Rosemount Court	44 E3
Rosemount Court (Inchicore Rd)	35 A3 [19]
Rosemount Crescent (Roebuck Road)	43 C3
Rosemount Park	43 C4
Rosemount Road	35 C1 [4]
Rosemount Tce (Arbour Hill)	35 C2 [29]
Rosemount Tce (Booterstown)	44 F3
Rosemount Tce (Dundrum)	43 B4 [11]
Rosevale Court	22 F3
Rosevale Mansions	22 F3
Roseville Terrace	43 C4 [4]
Rosewood Grove	32 F3
Rosmeen Gardens	46 D4
Rosmeen Park	54 D1
Ross Road	36 D3
Ross Street	35 B1
Ross View	33 C1
Rossfield Avenue	48 D1
Rossfield Crescent	48 D1
Rossfield Drive	48 D1
Rossfield Gardens	48 D1
Rossfield Grove	48 D1

STREET NAME	PAGE/GRID REFERENCE
Rossfield Park	48 D1
Rossfield Way	48 D1
Rosslyn	57 C2 [37]
Rosslyn Court	57 C2
Rosslyn Grove	57 C2 [4]
Rossmore Avenue	41 C4
Rossmore Avenue (Ballyfermot)	34 D3
Rossmore Avenue (Templeogue)	41 C4
Rossmore Close	42 D4
Rossmore Crescent	42 D4
Rossmore Drive (Ballyfermot)	34 D2
Rossmore Drive (Templeogue)	41 C4
Rossmore Grove	41 C4
Rossmore Grove	41 C4
Rossmore Grove	42 D4
Rossmore Lawns	42 D4
Rossmore Park	42 D4
Rossmore Road (Ballyfermot)	34 D2
Rossmore Road (Templeogue)	42 D4
Rostrevor Road	43 A3
Rostrevor Terrace (Lr Grand Canal St)	36 F3 [25]
Rostrevor Terrace (Orwell Road)	43 A2
Rothe Abbey	35 A3
Rowan Avenue	52 D2
Rowan Close	30 D3
Rowan Grove	57 B2
Rowan Hall	43 C1 [15]
Rowan Park Avenue	45 B4
Rowanbyrn	45 B4
Rowanbyrn	53 B1
Rowans Road	52 D2
Rowlagh Avenue	33 A3
Rowlagh Crescent	33 A3
Rowlagh Gardens	33 A3
Rowlagh Green	33 A3
Rowlagh Park	33 A3
Rowserstown Lane	35 A3 [20]
Royal Canal Bank	21 A4
Royal Canal Bank	36 D1
Royal Canal Terrace	35 C1 [12]
Royal Canal Way	21 A4
Royal Canal Way	36 E1
Royal Hibernian Way	36 E3 [10]
Royal Marine Terrace	57 C2 [12]
Royal Oak	10 F4
Royal Terrace East	54 D1
Royal Terrace Lane	54 D1 [10]
Royal Terrace North	54 D1 [2]
Royal Terrace West	54 D1
Royse Road	21 A4
Royston	42 D2
Ruby Hall	53 C2
Rugby Road	43 B1
Rugby Villas	43 B1 [6]
Rus in Urbe Terrace (on Glenageary Road Lr)	54 D1
Rushbrook	18 E2
Rushbrook Avenue	41 C3
Rushbrook Court	41 C4
Rushbrook Crescent	41 C3
Rushbrook Drive	41 C3
Rushbrook Grove	41 C3
Rushbrook Park	41 C3
Rushbrook Road	41 C3
Rushbrook View	41 C3
Rushbrook Way	41 C3
Rusheeney	17 B1
Rusheeney Avenue	17 B1
Rusheeney Close	17 B1
Rusheeney Court	17 B1
Rusheeney Crescent	6 F4
Rusheeney Green	17 B1
Rusheeney Grove	17 B1
Rusheeney Manor	17 B1
Rusheeney Park	17 B1
Rusheeney View	17 B1
Rusheeney Way	17 B1
*Rus-in-Urbe Terrace	54 D1 [19]
Russell Avenue	36 E1
Russell Avenue East	36 F1 [14]
Russell Street	36 E1
Rutland Avenue	35 B4
Rutland Avenue	42 E1

STREET NAME	PAGE/GRID REFERENCE
Rutland Cottages	36 E1 [55]
Rutland Grove	42 F1
Rutland Place North	36 E1 [48]
Rutland Place West	36 D1
Rutland Street Lower	36 E1
Rutledge Terrace	35 C4 [26]
Ryan's Cottages (Harold's Cross)	42 F1 [7]
Ryder's Row	36 D2 [9]
Rye River Avenue	16 D4
Rye River Close	16 D4
Rye River Court	16 D4
Rye River Crescent	16 D4
Rye River Gardens	16 D4
Rye River Grove	16 D4
Rye River Mall	16 D4
Rye River Park	16 D4
Ryecroft	57 C3
Ryemont Abbey	16 D4
Ryevale Lawns	16 D4
Rynville Manor	57 B3

S

STREET NAME	PAGE/GRID REFERENCE
Sackville Avenue	36 E1
Sackville Gardens	36 E1 [2]
Sackville Place	36 D2 [24]
Saddlers Avenue	7 A4
Saddlers Close	7 A4
Saddlers Court	36 D4 [55]
Saddlers Crescent	7 A4
Saddlers Drive	7 A4
Saddlers Glade	7 A4
Saddlers Grove	7 A4
Saddlers Lawn	7 A4
Sadleir Hall	5 A2
Saggart	47 B2
Saintsbury Avenue	54 E4
Salamanca	44 D4
Salem Court	43 A1 [17]
Sally Park	49 C1
Sally Park Close	49 C1
Sallymount Avenue	43 B1
Sallymount Gardens	43 B1 [1]
Sallymount Terrace	43 B1 [14]
Sallynoggin	54 D2
Sallynoggin Park	53 C2
Sallynoggin Road	53 C2
Salthill	45 C4
*Salthill Place (off Crofton Rd)	46 D4
Saltzburg	44 D4
Sampson's Lane	36 D2 [14]
Sandford Avenue (Donnybrook)	43 C1
Sandford Avenue (Donore Ave)	35 C4
Sandford Close	43 B1
Sandford Gardens	35 C4 [33]
Sandford Gardens (Donnybrook)	43 C1 [10]
*Sandford Gdns (off Donore Ave)	35 C4
Sandford Park	35 C4 [32]
*Sandford Pk (off O'Donovan Rd)	35 C4
Sandford Road	43 B1
Sandford Terrace	43 B1
Sandford Wood	1 C1
Sandon Cove	22 E4
Sandwith Street Lower	36 E2
Sandwith Street Upper	36 E3
Sandycove Avenue East	54 E1
Sandycove Avenue North	46 E4
Sandycove Avenue West	54 E1
Sandycove Point	46 E4
Sandycove Road	54 E1
Sandyford	52 D2
Sandyford Downs	52 D3
Sandyford Hall	52 E3
Sandyford Hall Avenue	52 E3
Sandyford Hall Close	52 E4
Sandyford Hall Court	52 E3
Sandyford Hall Crescent	52 E3
Sandyford Hall Drive	52 E4
Sandyford Hall Green	52 E3
Sandyford Hall Grove	52 E4
Sandyford Hall Lawn	52 E3
Sandyford Hall Place	52 E3
Sandyford Hall Rise	52 E3
Sandyford Hall View	52 E3
Sandyford Hall Walk	52 E3

STREET NAME	PAGE/GRID REFERENCE
Sandyford Park	52 D2
Sandyford Road	51 C1
Sandyford Village	52 D3
Sandyhill Avenue	20 F1
Sandyhill Gardens	20 F1
Sandymount	37 A4
Sandymount Avenue	37 A4
Sandymount Castle	37 A4 [5]
Sandymount Castle Drive	37 A4 [3]
Sandymount Castle Park	37 B4 [2]
Sandymount Castle Road	37 A4 [2]
Sandymount Court	37 A3 [26]
Sandymount Green	37 A4 [1]
Sandymount Road	37 A3
Sans Souci Park	44 F3
Santa Sabina Manor	25 B2
Santry Avenue	10 E4
Santry Close	10 F4
Santry Court	10 F4
Santry Villas	10 E4
Sarah Curran Avenue	50 F1
Sarah Curran Road	50 F1 [1]
Sarah Place	35 A2 [3]
Sarsfield Court	32 D1 [4]
Sarsfield Park	32 D1
Sarsfield Quay	35 C2 [8]
Sarsfield Road	34 F3
Sarsfield Street (Phibsborough)	36 D1 [5]
Sarsfield Street (Sallynoggin)	54 D1
Sarsfield Terrace	32 D1 [1]
Sarto Lawn	23 C1
Sarto Park	23 C1
Sarto Rise	23 C1
Sarto Road	23 C2
Saul Road	42 E1
Saval Grove	54 E2
Saval Park Crescent	54 E2
Saval Park Gardens	54 E2
Saval Park Road	54 E2
Scholarstown Park	50 D2
Scholarstown Road	50 D2
School Avenue	22 E2
School Street	35 C3
Schoolhouse Lane	21 B1
Schoolhouse Lane	36 E3 [12]
*Schoolhouse Lane West (off High Street)	36 D3
Schools Road	57 B4
Scott Park	57 C3
Scribblestown Road	19 B3
Sea Road	3 A2
Seabank Court	54 E1 [21]
Seabury	44 E1
Seabury Avenue	2 F2
Seabury Close	2 F2
Seabury Court	2 F2
Seabury Crescent	2 F2
Seabury Dale	2 F2
Seabury Downs	2 F2
Seabury Drive	3 A2
Seabury Gardens	2 F2
Seabury Glen	2 F2
Seabury Green	2 F2
Seabury Grove	2 F2
Seabury Heights	2 F2
Seabury Lane	2 F2
Seabury Lawns	2 F2
Seabury Meadows	2 F2
Seabury Orchard	2 F2
Seabury Parade	2 F2
Seabury Park	2 F2
Seabury Place	2 F2
Seabury Vale	2 F2
Seabury View	2 F2
Seabury Walk	2 F2
Seabury Wood	2 F2
Seacliff Avenue	23 C1
Seacliff Drive	23 C1
Seacliff Road	23 C1
Seacourt	22 F4
Seacrest	57 C3
Seafield (Shankill)	56 F2
Seafield Avenue (Clontarf)	22 F4

STREET NAME	PAGE/GRID REFERENCE
Seafield Avenue (Monkstown)	45 B4
Seafield Close	44 E2
Seafield Court	24 D1 [2]
Seafield Court	56 E1
Seafield Court (Malahide)	3 B2
Seafield Crescent	44 E2
Seafield Downs (off Kincora Road Clontarf)	22 F4
Seafield Drive	44 E2
Seafield Grove	23 A4 [1]
Seafield Park	44 E2 [1]
Seafield Road (Ballybrack)	56 E1
Seafield Road (Booterstown)	44 E2
Seafield Road (Killiney)	54 E4
Seafield Road East	22 F4
Seafield Road West	22 E4
Seafield Terrace	54 F2 [15]
Seafort Avenue	37 A4
Seafort Cottages	37 A4 [18]
Seafort Gardens	37 A3 [10]
Seafort Parade	44 F3
Seafort Terrace	37 A4 [19]
Seafort Villas	37 A4 [20]
Seagrange Avenue	12 F4
Seagrange Drive	23 C1
Seagrange Road	23 C1
Seamount Drive	3 C3
Seamount Heights	3 C3
Seamount Road	3 C3
Seamount View	2 E2
Seamus Ennis Road	20 E1
Sean MacDermott Street Lower	36 E1
Sean MacDermott Street Upper	36 D2
Sean Moore Road	37 A3
Sean O'Casey Avenue	36 E1 [47]
Sean Tracey House	36 E1 [12]
Sean Walsh Memorial Park	48 F1
Seapark	3 C3
Seapark (Dollymount)	22 F4
Seapark Drive	22 F4
Seapark Hill	3 C3
Seapark Road	22 F4
Seapoint Avenue	45 B3
Seapoint Avenue (Baldoyle)	13 A4 [1]
Seapoint Court	13 A4 [7]
Seapoint Court	57 C1
Seapoint Road	57 C2
Seapoint Terrace	37 A3 [4]
Seapoint Terrace	57 C2 [24]
Seapoint Terrace (Blackrock)	45 B3 [4]
Seapoint Villas	57 C2 [20]
Seatown Road	2 D1
Seatown Terrace	2 D2
Seatown Walk	2 D2
Seatown West	2 E1
Seaview Avenue East	36 F1
Seaview Avenue North	22 D4
Seaview Cottages	55 C4
Seaview Lawn	56 E2
Seaview Park	56 E2
Seaview Terrace (Donnybrook)	44 D1
Seaview Terrace (Dun Laoghaire)	45 C4 [15]
Seaview Terrace (Howth)	26 D2 [2]
Seaview Wood	56 E2
Second Avenue	40 F4
Second Avenue (Seville Place)	36 F2 [6]
Sefton	53 C2
Sefton Green	53 C2
Selskar Terrace	36 E4 [21]
Serpentine Avenue	37 A4
Serpentine Park	37 A4
Serpentine Road	37 A4
Serpentine Terrace	37 A4
Seskin View Avenue	49 A2
Seskin View Drive	49 A2
Seskin View Park	49 A2
Seskin View Road	49 A2
Setanta Place	36 E3 [11]
Seven Houses	54 D1 [13]
Seven Oaks	21 B3
Seville Place	36 E1
Seville Terrace	36 E1 [59]
Seymour Road	57 C2

STREET NAME	PAGE/GRID REFERENCE
Shamrock Cottages	36 E1 [31]
Shamrock Place	36 E1 [15]
Shamrock Street	36 D1 [69]
*Shamrock Street (off Royal Canal Bank)	36 D1
Shamrock Terrace	36 E1 [16]
Shamrock Villas	42 F1
Shanagarry	43 B2 [9]
Shanard Avenue	21 A1
Shanard Road	21 A1
Shanboley Road	21 C1
Shancastle Avenue	33 A2
Shancastle Close	33 A2
Shancastle Crescent	33 A2
Shancastle Drive	33 A2
Shancastle Lawns	33 A2
Shancastle Park	33 A2
Shandon Crescent	20 F4
Shandon Drive	20 F4
Shandon Gardens	20 F4
Shandon Green	20 F4 [8]
Shandon Mill	20 F4 [9]
Shandon Park (Monkstown)	45 B4
Shandon Park (Phibsborough)	20 F4
Shandon Road	20 F4
Shangan Avenue	21 B1
Shangan Gardens	21 B1
Shangan Green	21 B1
Shangan Park	21 B1
Shangan Road	21 A1
Shanganagh Cliffs	56 E2
Shanganagh Grove	56 E3
Shanganagh Road	21 A4
Shanganagh Road	56 E1
Shanganagh Terrace	54 E4
Shanganagh Vale	54 D4
Shanglas Road	21 C1
Shanid Road	42 F1
Shankill	56 E3
Shankill View	57 C2 [38]
*Shankill View (on Seapoint Rd)	57 C2
Shanliss Avenue	21 B1
Shanliss Drive	21 B1
Shanliss Gardens	21 A1 [2]
Shanliss Grove	21 B1
Shanliss Park	21 B1
Shanliss Road	21 A1
Shanliss Walk	21 B1
Shanliss Way	21 B1
Shannon Terrace	35 B3 [3]
Shanowen Avenue	21 A1
Shanowen Crescent	21 B1
Shanowen Drive	21 B1
Shanowen Grove	21 A1
Shanowen Park	21 A1
Shanowen Road	21 B1
Shanrath Road	21 B1
Shantalla Avenue	21 C1
Shantalla Drive	21 C2
Shantalla Park	21 C2
Shantalla Road	21 C2
Shanvarna Road	21 B1
Sharavogue	54 E2
Shaw Street	36 E2 [10]
Shaw's Lane	36 F3 [13]
Shea's Court	35 C1 [23]
Sheelan Drive	56 E1
Sheelin Avenue	56 E1
Sheelin Drive	56 E1 [15]
Sheelin Grove	56 E1 [7]
Sheelin Hill	56 E1 [13]
Sheelin Walk	56 E1 [14]
Sheephill Avenue	7 C4
Sheephill Green	7 C4
Sheephill Park	7 C4
Sheepmoor Avenue	18 D1
Sheepmoor Close	18 D1
Sheepmoor Crescent	18 D1
Sheepmoor Gardens	18 D1
Sheepmoor Green	18 D1
Sheepmoor Grove	18 D1
Sheepmoor Lawn	18 D1
Sheepmoor Way	18 D1
Shelbourne Avenue	36 F4 [5]

STREET INDEX

STREET NAME	PAGE/GRID REFERENCE
Shelbourne Lane	36 F4 [3]
Shelbourne Road	36 F3
Shelerin Road	17 C2
Shellys Banks Road	37 B3
Shelmalier Road	36 F1
Shelmartin Avenue	21 C4
Shelmartin Terrace	21 C4 [2]
Shelton Drive	42 D2
Shelton Gardens	42 D2
Shelton Grove	42 D2
Shelton Park	42 D2
Sheriff Street Lower	36 E2
Sheriff Street Upper	36 F2
Sherkin Gardens	21 B3
Sherrard Avenue	36 D1 [28]
*Sherrard Court	36 D1
(off Portland Place)	
Sherrard Street Lower	36 D1
Sherrard Street Upper	36 D1
Sherrards Court	36 D1 [65]
Shielmartin Drive	25 B3
Shielmartin Park	25 B3 [1]
Shielmartin Road	25 B3
Ship Street Great	36 D3
Ship Street Little	36 D3
Shrewsbury	37 A4
Shrewsbury Hall	56 E3
Shrewsbury Lawn	53 C4
Shrewsbury Park	44 D1
Shrewsbury Road	44 D1
Shrewsbury Road	56 E3
Shrewsbury Woods	53 C4
Sibthorpe Lane	36 E4 [28]
Sidbury Court	58 D2 [5]
Sidmonton Avenue	57 C2
Sidmonton Court	57 C2
Sidmonton Court	58 D3 [5]
Sidmonton Gardens	57 C2 [36]
Sidmonton Park	58 D2
Sidmonton Place	57 C2 [6]
Sidmonton Road	57 C2
Sidmonton Square	57 C2 [1]
Sigurd Road	35 C2 [31]
Silchester Court	54 D1
Silchester Crescent	54 D1
Silchester Park	54 D1
Silchester Road	54 D1
Silchester Wood	54 D1 [16]
Silleachain Lane	16 D4
Silloge Avenue	21 A1
Silloge Gardens	21 A1
Silloge Road	21 A1
Silver Birches	5 B2
Silver Birches	43 C4
Silver Birches Close	5 B2
Silver Birches Crescent	5 B2
Silver Pines	52 F2 [3]
Silverberry	32 D3
Silverdale	32 D3
Silverpine	57 B3
Silverwood	32 D3
Silverwood Drive	42 E4
Silverwood Road	42 E4
Simmon's Court	44 D1 [3]
*Simmon's Place	36 E1
(off Thompson's Cottages)	
Simmonscourt Avenue	44 D1 [2]
Simmonscourt Castle	44 D1
Simmonscourt Road	37 A4
Simmonscourt Terrace	43 C1 [18]
Simmonstown Park	30 D4
Simpsons Lane	37 A3 [32]
Sion Hill Avenue	42 F1
Sion Hill Court	21 C3 [5]
Sion Hill Road	21 C3
Sion Road	54 D2
Sir Ivor Mall	52 F2 [7]
Sir John Rogerson's Quay	36 F2
*Sitric Place (off Sitric Road)	35 C2
Sitric Road	35 C2
Skelly's Lane	22 D2
Skreen Road	35 A1
Slade Row	35 C2 [35]
Slademore Avenue	22 F1
Slademore Close	22 F1
Slademore Court	11 C4
Slademore Court	22 F1
Slademore Drive	22 F1
Slane Road	35 B4
Slaney Close	20 E3
Slaney Road	20 E3
Slate Cabin Lane	51 C3
Slemish Road	35 A1
Slemish Road	35 D1
Slieve Rua Drive	52 D1
Slievebloom Park	41 C1
Slievebloom Road	41 C1
Slievemore Road	35 A4
Slievenamon Road	35 A4
Sloan Terrace	58 D2 [8]
*Sloan Terrace (on Meath Road)	57 C2
Sloperton	45 C4
Smithfield	35 C2
Smithfield Terrace	35 C2 [37]
Smith's Cottages (Donnybrook)	43 B1 [18]
Smith's Lane	42 F1 [13]
Smith's Villas	45 C4 [3]
Snowdrop Walk	11 C4
Snugborough Road	18 F1
Snugborough Road (Extention)	18 D2
Somerset Street	36 F3 [8]
Somerton Mews Est	53 C2
Somerville Avenue	41 C1
Somerville Drive	42 D1
Somerville Park	41 C1
Somerville Park	41 C1 [7]
Sommerton Road	18 E4 [28]
Sommerton Road	18 E4
Sommerville	43 C4
Sonesta	3 A2
Sophie Baret Residence	44 D4 [2]
Sorbonne	44 D4
Sorrento Close	54 F2 [25]
Sorrento Court	54 F2 [29]
Sorrento Drive	54 F2 [12]
Sorrento Heights	54 F2 [30]
Sorrento Lawn	54 F2 [13]
Sorrento Mews	54 F2 [28]
*Sorrento Park (on Sorrento Rd)	54 F2
Sorrento Road	54 F2
Sorrento Terrace	54 F2
South Avenue	44 F4
South Bank Road	37 B3
South Circular Rd (Dolphin's Barn)	35 B3
South Circular Rd (Islandbridge)	35 A2
South Circular Rd (Kilmainham)	35 B3
South Circular Rd (Portobello)	35 C4
*South City Market	36 D3
(on South Great Georges St)	
South Dock Place	36 F3 [35]
South Dock Road	36 F3 [24]
South Dock Street	36 F3
South Esplanade	58 D2
South Great George's St	36 D3
South Hill	25 C3
South Hill	43 B2
South Hill Avenue	44 F3
South Hill Park	44 F3
South Lotts Road	36 F3
South Park	1 C1
South Park	53 B2
South Park Drive	53 B2
South Winds	54 F1 [4]
South Wood Park	44 F3
Southdene	45 B4 [18]
Southern Cross Avenue	35 A3
Southview Terrace	35 B3 [38]
Spa Road	34 F3
Spa Road (Phoenix Park)	35 A1
Spafield Terrace	37 A4 [13]
Spencer Dock	36 F2 [12]
Spencer Dock (Guild Street)	36 F2
*Spencer Place (off Spencer St N)	36 F1
Spencer Street North	36 F1
Spencer Street South	36 D4 [48]
*Spencer Terrace (off Cork St)	35 B3
Spencer Villas	54 E1
Sperrin Road	35 A4
Spiddal Park	33 C3
Spiddal Road	33 C3
Spire View	20 D4
Spire View Lane	43 A1
Spitalfields	35 C3 [46]
Spittal Hill	2 D1
Spring Garden Lane	36 E2 [14]
Spring Garden Street	36 E1
Springbank Cottages	47 A2
Springdale Road	22 F2
Springfield (Cabra)	35 A1
Springfield (Tallaght)	48 F1
Springfield Avenue	42 E4
Springfield Crescent	42 E4
Springfield Drive	42 E4
Springfield Park (Deans Grange)	53 A2
Springfield Park (Templeogue)	42 E4
Springfield Road	42 E3
Springhill Avenue	53 A1
Springhill Cottages	53 B1 [5]
Springhill Park (Dalkey)	54 E2
Springhill Park (Deans Grange)	53 B1
Springlawn	18 E2
Springlawn Close	18 E2
Springlawn Court	18 E2
Springlawn Drive	18 E2
Springlawn Heights	18 E2
Springlawn Road	18 E2
Springvale	50 E2
Spruce Avenue	52 D2
*St Agnes Tce (on St Agnes Rd)	42 D1
*St Agatha Court	36 E1
(off William St N)	
St Agnes Park	42 D1
St Agnes Road	42 D1
St Agnes Terrace (Rathfarnham)	42 F3 [2]
St Aidan's Drive	44 D4
St Aidan's Park	21 C4 [6]
St Aidan's Park Avenue	21 C4
St Aidan's Park Road	21 C4
St Aidan's Terrace	57 C2 [23]
St Alban's Park	44 E1
St Alban's Road	35 C4
St Alphonsus Avenue	21 A4 [11]
St Alphonsus Rd	21 A4
St Andrew Street	36 D3
St Andrew's Grove	3 B3
*St Andrew's Lane	36 D3
(off Exchequer Street)	
St Andrews Park	1 C1
St Annes	42 E2
St Anne's Avenue	23 A3
St Anne's Drive	23 A3
St Anne's Park	56 E3
St Anne's Road North	21 A4
St Anne's Road South	35 C4 [5]
St Anne's Square (Blackrock)	45 A3 [7]
St Anne's Square (Portmarnock)	12 F2
St Anne's Terrace (Cabra)	20 F4
St Anne's Terrace (Raheny)	23 A3
St Ann's Square	12 F2 [6]
St Ann's Square Lower	12 F2 [5]
St Anthony's Avenue	40 E2
St Anthony's Crescent	41 C2
*St Anthony's Place	36 D1
(off Temple Street North)	
St Anthony's Road	35 B3
St Aongus Court	41 B4
St Aongus Crescent	41 B4
St Aongus Green	41 B4
St Aongus Grove	41 B4
St Aongus Lawn	41 B4
St Aongus Road	41 B4
St Assam's Avenue	23 A2
St Assam's Drive	23 A2
St Assam's Park	23 A2
St Assam's Road East	23 B2
St Assam's Road West	23 A2
St Attracta Road	20 F4
St Aubyn's Court	56 E1 [5]
*St Audoen's Tce (off High St)	36 D3
St Augustine Street	35 C2
St Augustine's Park (Estate)	53 A1
St Barnabas Gardens	36 F1 [12]
St Begnet's Villas	54 E1
St Benedicts Gardens	36 D1 [35]
St Brendan's Avenue	22 E2
St Brendan's Cottages	37 A3 [6]
St Brendan's Crescent	41 B2
St Brendan's Drive	22 E2
St Brendan's Park	22 F2
St Brendan's Road	21 A4 [12]
St Brendan's Tce (Coolock)	22 E1
St Brendan's Tce (Dun Laoghaire)	45 C4 [19]
St Brendan's Tce (Rockbrook)	50 E4
St Bricin's Park	35 B2
St Bridget's Ave (North Strand)	36 F1
St Bridget's Drive (Greenhills)	41 B2
St Bridget's Flats	43 C2 [8]
St Brigid's Avenue	12 F2 [4]
St Brigid's Church Road	52 F1
St Brigid's Cottages	18 F2
(Blanchardstown)	
St Brigid's Cottages (Clondalkin)	40 F2
St Brigid's Cottages (North Strand)	36 F1 [24]
St Brigid's Court	22 E3 [2]
St Brigid's Crescent	22 E2
St Brigid's Drive (Clondalkin)	40 E2
St Brigid's Drive (Killester)	22 E3 [1]
St Brigid's Lawn	22 E2
St Brigid's Park (Clondalkin)	40 E2 [1]
St Brigid's Park (Cornelscourt)	53 B3
St Brigid's Pk (Blanchardstown)	18 F2
St Brigid's Road (Artane)	22 E2
St Brigid's Road (Clondalkin)	40 E2
St Brigid's Road Lower	21 A4
St Brigid's Road Upper	21 A4
St Broc's Cottages	43 C1 [1]
St Canice's Park	20 F2
St Canice's Road	21 A2
St Catherine's Avenue	35 C4
St Catherine's Lane West	35 C3 [14]
St Catherine's Park	54 E1
St Catherine's Road	54 E1
St Catherine's Terrace	25 A1 [2]
St Catherine's View	16 E4
St Clair's Lawn	57 B3
St Clair's Terrace	57 B3 [3]
St Clare's Avenue	35 C4 [20]
St Clare's Terrace	36 D4
(on Mount Drummond Avenue)	
St Clement's Road	21 A4 [13]
St Colmcilles Court	2 D2 [3]
St Columbanus Avenue	43 B3
St Columbanus Place	43 B3 [1]
St Columbanus Road	43 B3
St Columbas Heights	1 C2
St Columbas Rise	1 C2
St Columba's Road	41 B2
St Columba's Road Lower	21 A4
St Columba's Road Upper	21 A4
St Columcille's Crescent	2 D2 [1]
St Columcille's Drive	2 D2
St Columcille's Terrace	57 C2 [18]
St Columcills Park	2 D2
St Conleth's Road	41 C2
St Cronan's Avenue	1 B2
St Cronan's Close	1 B2
St Cronan's Court	1 B1
St Cronan's Grove	1 C1
St Cronan's Lawn	1 B1
St Cronan's Road	57 C2 [8]
St Cronan's View	1 B2
St Cronan's Way	1 C2
St David's	22 D2
St David's Court	22 E4
St David's Terrace (Blackhorse Ave)	35 B1 [7]
St David's Terrace (Glasnevin)	21 A3 [7]
St Davids Wood	22 D2
St Declan's Road	21 C4
St Declan's Terrace	21 C4 [5]
St Dominic's Avenue	49 A1
St Dominic's Road	49 A1
St Dominic's Terrace	49 A1
St Donagh's Crescent	23 B1
St Donagh's Park	23 B1

STREET NAME	PAGE/GRID REFERENCE
St Donagh's Road	23 B1
St Edmundsbury Hospital	32 E1
St Eithne Road	20 F4
St Elizabeth's Court	35 C1 [14]
St Enda's Drive	50 F1
St Enda's Park	50 F1
St Enda's Road	42 F2
St Finbarr's Close	41 B3
St Finbarr's Road	20 E4
St Finnians Avenue	32 D2
St Finnians Close	32 D2
St Finnians Crescent	32 D2
St Fintan Road (Cabra)	20 F4
St Fintan Terrace (Cabra)	20 F4
St Fintan's Crescent	25 B3
St Fintan's Grove	25 B3
St Fintan's Park (Dean's Grange)	53 B1
St Fintan's Park (Sutton)	25 B2
St Fintan's Road (Sutton)	25 B3
St Fintan's Terrace	33 C1 [5]
St Fintan's Villas	53 B1
St Francis Square	36 D3 [48]
St Gabriel's Court	23 A4 [2]
St Gabriel's Road	22 F4
St Gall Gardens North	43 B3 [2]
St Gall Gardens South	43 B3 [3]
St Gatien Road	50 F1 [2]
St George's Ave (Clonliffe Road)	21 B4
St George's Ave (Killiney)	54 E3
St George's Villas (Inchicore)	34 F3 [18]
St Gerard's Road	41 C2
St Helena's Court	20 E2 [3]
St Helena's Drive	20 E2
St Helena's Road	20 E2
St Helen's	54 E1 [22]
St Helen's Road	44 E2
St Helen's Villas	44 F2 [1]
St Helen's Wood	44 E3
St Helier's Copse	44 F4 [1]
St Ignatius Avenue	36 D1 [17]
St Ignatius Road	21 A4
St Ita's Road	21 A3 [6]
St Ives	3 B2
St James Avenue (Clonliffe Rd)	36 E1
*St James Place	37 A3
(Sandymount Road)	
St James Terrace (Sandymount)	37 A3 [23]
St James's Avenue (James's St)	35 B3 [21]
St James's Place (Inchicore)	34 F3 [17]
St James's Road	41 B2
St James's Tce (Dolphin's Barn)	35 B4 [2]
St James's Walk	35 B3
St Jarlath Road	20 F4
St John Street	35 C3 [58]
St John's	44 E1
St John's Avenue	35 C3 [39]
St John's Avenue	40 D2
St John's Close	40 D2
St John's Cottages	35 B3 [28]
St John's Court	40 D2
St John's Court (Beaumont)	22 D1
St John's Crescent	40 D2
St John's Drive	40 D2
St John's Green	40 D2
*St John's Lane (off Strand Road)	44 E1
St John's Lawn	40 D2
St John's Park (Dun Laoghaire)	45 C4
St John's Park East	40 D2
St John's Road	40 D2
St John's Road East	44 E1
St John's Road West	35 B2
St John's Road West	35 B2
St John's Terrace (Mount Brown)	35 B3 [33]
St John's Wood	22 E4 [2]
St John's Wood	40 D2
St John's Wood West	40 D2
St Joseph Street	36 D1 [27]
St Joseph's Ave (Ballybough)	21 B4 [2]
St Joseph's Ave (Drumcondra)	21 A4
St Joseph's Cottages	19 C4 [3]
St Joseph's Court	35 C1 [16]
St Joseph's Grove	43 C4 [9]
St Joseph's Mansions	36 E1 [60]
St Joseph's Parade	36 D1

STREET NAME	PAGE/GRID REFERENCE
St Joseph's Place	35 C1 [15]
St Joseph's Place	36 D1 [59]
St Joseph's Road (Aughrim St)	35 C1
St Joseph's Road (Walkinstown)	41 C2
St Joseph's Square	37 C1 [2]
*St Joseph's Street (off Leo St)	36 D1
St Joseph's Terrace	36 E1 [35]
St Joseph's Terrace (Fairview)	21 C4 [4]
*St Joseph's Terrace	35 B4
(off Dolphin's Barn)	
*St Joseph's Terrace	37 A3
(off Pembroke Street)	
*St Joseph's Terrace	46 D4
(on Tivoli Road)	
St Joseph's Villas (Summerhill)	36 E1 [38]
*St Kevin's Ave (off Blackpitts)	35 C3
St Kevin's Cottages	36 D4 [29]
St Kevin's Court	43 A2
St Kevin's Gardens	43 A2
St Kevin's Parade	36 D4 [52]
St Kevin's Park (Rathgar)	43 A2
St Kevin's Park (Stillorgan)	52 D1
St Kevin's Road	36 D4 [3]
St Kevin's Square	57 C2
St Kevin's Terrace	57 C2 [14]
*St Kevin's Tce (New Bride St)	36 D3
St Kevin's Villas	54 D1
St Killian's Avenue	41 B2
St Killians Crescent	57 B4
St Killian's Park	40 E1 [1]
St Laurence Grove	34 E2 [4]
St Laurence O'Toole Avenue	12 F2 [1]
St Laurence Park	44 F4
St Laurence Place	36 D1 [66]
St Laurence Place (Fontenoy St)	36 D1
*St Laurence Place	36 F2
(Lr Sheriff Street)	
St Laurence Road	34 E2
St Laurence Terrace (Chapelizod)	34 E2 [9]
St Laurences Glen	34 E3 [4]
St Laurence's Terrace	57 C2 [17]
St Lawrence Road (Clontarf)	22 D4
St Lawrence Road (Howth)	26 D1
St Lawrence's Court	22 D4
St Lawrence's Terrace (Howth)	26 D2 [1]
St Lukes Court	22 D1 [3]
St Luke's Crescent	43 B2 [3]
St Maelruans Park	49 A1
St Maignenn's Terrace	35 B3 [6]
St Malachy's Drive	41 C2
St Malachy's Road	21 A3 [7]
St Margaret's	9 B1
St Margaret's Avenue	3 B3
*St Margaret's Ave (off Pimlico)	35 C3
St Margaret's Avenue North	36 E1 [34]
St Margaret's Court	9 A4 [1]
St Margaret's Halting Site	9 C4
St Margaret's Park	3 B3
St Margaret's Road	3 B3
St Margaret's Road (Ballymun)	10 D4
St Margaret's Road (Finglas)	9 A4
St Margaret's Terrace	35 C3 [7]
St Mark's Avenue	33 A2
St Mark's Crescent	33 A3
St Mark's Drive	33 A3
St Mark's Gardens	33 A3
St Mark's Green	33 A3
St Mark's Grove	33 A3
St Marnock's Avenue	12 F2
St Martin's Drive	42 E2
St Martin's Park	42 E1
St Mary's Ave Nth (Mountjoy St)	36 D1 [7]
St Mary's Ave (Rathfarnham)	42 F4
St Mary's Avenue West	34 F3
St Mary's Crescent	41 C1
St Mary's Drive	41 C1
St Mary's Lane	36 F3 [17]
St Mary's Mansions	36 E1 [62]
St Mary's Park	16 D4
St Mary's Park	19 C2
St Mary's Park	41 C1
St Mary's Place (Howth)	26 D2 [4]
St Mary's Place North	36 D1 [48]
St Mary's Road (Crumlin)	42 D1

STREET NAME	PAGE/GRID REFERENCE
St Mary's Road (Howth)	26 D2 [3]
St Mary's Road Nth (East Wall)	36 F1
St Mary's Road Sth (Ballsbridge)	36 F4
St Mary's Street	45 C4 [5]
St Marys Terrace	58 D2 [20]
St Mary's Terrace	5 B2 [1]
St Mary's Terrace	57 C4 [6]
St Mary's Terrace (Arbour Hill)	35 C2 [34]
*St Mary's Terrace (Bath Street)	37 A3
St Mary's Terrace (Chapelizod)	34 E2 [5]
St Mary's Terrace (Mountjoy St)	36 D1 [10]
St Mary's Terrace (Rathfarnham)	42 F4 [5]
St Mel's Avenue	41 B3
*St Michael's Close	36 D3
(off High Street)	
St Michael's Estate	35 A3 [8]
*St Michael's Hill (off High St)	36 D3
St Michael's Place	36 D1 [51]
St Michael's Road	21 A3 [8]
St Michael's Tce (Blackpitts)	35 C3 [57]
St Michael's Tce (Dun Laoghaire)	45 C4 [18]
*St Michan's Place	36 D2
(off Chancery Street)	
St Michan's Street	36 D2 [44]
St Mobhi Avenue	21 A3
St Mobhi Boithirin	21 A3
St Mobhi Drive	21 A3
St Mobhi Grove	21 A3 [10]
St Mobhi Road	21 A3
St Mochtas Avenue	18 D3
St Mochtas Drive	18 D3
St Mochtas Lawn	18 D2
St Mochtas Road	18 D3
St Mochtas Vale	18 D3
St Mura's Terrace	36 F1 [17]
St Nathy's House	43 B4 [5]
St Nathy's Villas	43 B4 [17]
St Nessan's Close	26 D2 [9]
St Nessans Court	26 D2 [12]
St Nessan's Terrace	26 D2 [5]
St Nicholas Place	36 D3 [2]
St Oliver's Park	33 B3
St Pappin's Green	20 F2
St Pappin's Road	21 A2
St Patrick's Avenue (Clondalkin)	40 D1 [1]
St Patrick's Avenue (Dalkey)	54 F2 [1]
St Patrick's Avenue (Fairview)	36 F1 [16]
St Patrick's Close	36 D3
St Patrick's Close	53 C1 [9]
St Patrick's Cottages	42 F4
St Patrick's Crescent	53 C1
St Patrick's Parade	21 A4
St Patrick's Park	5 B2
St Patrick's Park	30 D3
St Patrick's Park (Blanchardstown)	18 E2
St Patrick's Park (Clondalkin)	40 A1
*St Patrick's Place	21 A4
(off Royal Canal Bank)	
St Patrick's Road (Clondalkin)	33 A4
St Patrick's Road (Dalkey)	54 F2 [8]
St Patrick's Road (Drumcondra)	21 A4
St Patrick's Road (Walkinstown)	41 C2
St Patrick's Square	54 F2 [4]
St Patrick's Square	57 C1 [1]
St Patrick's Terrace (Inchicore)	34 F3 [9]
St Patrick's Terrace	53 C1 [7]
(Kill O' the Grange)	
*St Patrick's Terrace	35 C2
(Nth Brunswick St)	
St Patrick's Terrace	21 B4
(off Fitzroy Avenue)	
St Patrick's Terrace (Russell St)	36 E1
St Patrick's Villas	37 A3 [3]
St Paul's Street	54 E1 [5]
(Off Blackhall Place)	
St Paul's Terrace	54 E1 [5]
St Peter's Close	36 D1 [62]
*St Peter's Close	36 D1
(off Royal Canal Bank)	
St Peter's Crescent	41 C2
St Peter's Drive	41 C2
St Peter's Park	5 B2
St Peter's Road (Bray)	57 B1
St Peter's Road (Phibsborough)	35 C1

STREET NAME	PAGE/GRID REFERENCE
St Peter's Road (Walkinstown)	41 C2
St Peter's Square	36 D1 [37]
St Peter's Tce	57 B1 [2]
St Peter's Tce (Dun Laoghaire)	54 E1 [6]
St Peter's Tce (Howth)	26 D2
St Peter's Tce Walkinstown	41 C2 [1]
(off Peters Road)	
St Philomena's Road	20 F4 [1]
St Ronan's Avenue	33 A3
St Ronan's Close	33 A3
St Ronan's Crescent	33 A3
St Ronan's Drive	33 A3
St Ronan's Gardens	33 A3
St Ronan's Green	33 A3
St Ronan's Grove	33 A3
St Ronan's Park	33 A3
St Ronan's Way	33 A3
St Stephen's Green East	36 E3
St Stephen's Green North	36 E3
St Stephen's Green South	36 D3
St Stephen's Green West	36 D3
St Sylvester Villas	3 B3
St Teresa's Gardens	35 C3
St Teresa's Place	21 A4 [9]
St Teresa's Road (Crumlin)	42 D2
St Teresa's Road (Glasnevin)	21 A4 [8]
St Thomas Mead	44 E3
St Thomas Road (Ardee Street)	35 C3
St Thomas's Road (Mt. Merrion)	44 E3
St Ultan's Flats	36 D4 [21]
St Vincent Street North	36 D1 [1]
St Vincent Street South	36 D4
St Vincent Street West	35 A3
St Vincent's Cottages	19 C4 [2]
St Vincent's Court	21 C3 [7]
St Vincent's Park	45 A4
St. Aiden's Halting Site	48 D1
St. Andrews	32 F2
St. Andrews Drive	32 F2
St. Andrews Fairway	32 F2
St. Andrews Green	32 F2
St. Andrews Wood	32 F2
St. Anne's Court	23 A3 [2]
St. Augustine's Park	53 A1 [1]
St. Brigid's Green	22 E2
St. Finbarrs Court	20 E4 [2]
St. John's Court (Donnycarney)	22 D3
St. Johns Park West	40 D1
St. Lawrence Way	26 D1 [8]
St. Maelruans Park (Estate)	49 A1
St. Margaret's Close	54 E1 [30]
St. Patricks Avenue	12 F2
St. Patricks Park	40 D1
St. Patricks Park	52 E3
St. Peter's Avenue	35 C1
St. Raphaels Avenue	29 C4
St.Brigid's Grove	22 E2
St.Finian's Grove	32 D2
St.Werburghs	2 E2
Stable Lane (Harcourt Street)	36 D3 [19]
Stable Lane (Leeson St Lr)	36 E3 [37]
Stable Lane (Smithfield)	35 C2 [16]
Stamer Street	36 D4
Stanford Green	41 C1
Stanhope Street	35 C2 [2]
Stanley Street	35 C2 [39]
Stanley Street	35 C2
(off Brunswick Street North)	
Stannaway Avenue	42 D1
Stannaway Court	42 D2 [3]
Stannaway Drive	42 E1
Stannaway Road	42 E1
Stapolin Lawns	12 F4
Station Road	5 B3
Station Road	15 C4
Station Road (Glenageary)	54 E1
Station Road (Killiney)	54 E4
Station Road	33 A4
(off Clover Hill Road)	
Station Road (Portmarnock)	12 E2
Station Road (Raheny)	23 A2
Station Road (Sutton)	25 A1
Steeven's Lane	35 B2
Stella Avenue	21 A3

STREET NAME	PAGE/GRID REFERENCE
Stella Gardens	37 A3
Stepaside	52 E4
Stepaside Park	52 E3
Stephen Street Lower	36 D3
Stephen Street Upper	36 D3
Stephen's Lane	36 E3
Stephen's Place	36 E3 [36]
Stephen's Road	35 A3
Stillorgan	52 E1
Stillorgan Court	52 E1 [2]
Stillorgan Grove	44 F4
Stillorgan Heath	52 E1 [3]
Stillorgan Heath	52 E1
Stillorgan Park	44 F4
Stillorgan Park Avenue	52 F1
Stillorgan Road (Donnybrook)	44 D1
Stillorgan Road (Foxrock)	53 A2
Stillorgan Road (Mount Merrion)	44 E3
Stillorgan Road (Stillorgan)	44 E4
Stillorgan Wood	52 E1
Stirling Park	43 A3 [2]
*Stirrup Lane (off Church Street)	35 C2
Stockhole Lane	10 F1
Stocking Lane	50 D3
Stockton Court	19 A3
Stockton Drive	19 A3
Stockton Green	19 A3
Stockton Grove	19 A3
Stockton Lawn	19 A3
Stockton Park	19 A3
Stokes Place	36 D3 [27]
Stone Mews	43 A1 [8]
Stonebridge	17 B2
Stonebridge Avenue	17 B2
Stonebridge Close	56 E3 [2]
Stonebridge Drive	17 B2
Stonebridge Road	17 B2
Stonebridge Road	56 D2
Stonemasons Way	51 A2
Stonepark Abbey	42 F4
Stoneview Place	46 D4 [13]
Stoney Road (Dundrum)	43 C4
Stoney Road (East Wall)	36 F1 [2]
Stoneybatter	35 C2
Stoneylea Terrace	57 C3 [10]
Store Street	36 E2
Stormanstown Road	21 A2
Stradbrook Close	53 B1
Stradbrook Gardens	45 B4 [8]
Stradbrook Grove	45 B4
Stradbrook Hall	45 B4 [20]
Stradbrook Hill	53 B1 [4]
Stradbrook Lawn	45 B4
Stradbrook Park	45 B4
Stradbrook Road	45 B4
Strand Lane	44 E1 [3]
Strand Road (Baldoyle)	13 A4
Strand Road (Bray)	57 C2
Strand Road (Merrion)	44 E1
Strand Road (Portmarnock)	4 D4
Strand Road (Portmarnock)	12 F2
Strand Road (Portmarnock)	13 A1
Strand Road (Sandymount)	37 B4
Strand Road (Sutton)	25 B2
Strand Street	3 B2
Strand Street	37 A3
Strand Street Great	36 D2
Strand Street Little	36 D2 [36]
Strand Terrace	43 B2 [2]
Strandmill Avenue	12 F2
Strandmill Park	13 A2
Strandmill Road	13 A2
Strandville Ave (North Strand)	36 F1 [4]
Strandville Ave East (Clontarf)	22 D4
Strandville House	22 D4 [4]
Strandville Place	36 F1 [19]
Strangford Gardens	36 F1
Strangford Road	36 F1
Strasburg Terrace	37 A3 [21]
Stratford	43 A2 [9]
Strathmore Road	54 E4
Streamville Court	56 E1 [10]
Streamville Road	23 A1
Strong's Court	36 D1 [67]
*Strong's Court (off Findlater Place)	36 D2
Suffolk Street	36 D2
Sugarloaf Crescent	57 C3
Sugarloaf Terrace	57 C3 [21]
Suir Road	35 A3
Sullivan Street	35 B2 [3]
*Summer Arch (off Summer St N)	36 E1
Summer Place	36 E1 [46]
*Summer Row (off Summer Street North)	36 E1
Summer Street North	36 E1
Summer Street South	35 C3
Summerfield	49 A2 [1]
Summerfield Avenue	18 E2
Summerfield Close	18 E2
Summerfield Close	54 F2 [10]
Summerfield Green	18 E2
Summerfield Grove	18 E2
Summerfield Lawns	18 E2
Summerfield Meadows	18 E2
Summerfield Park	18 E2
Summerfield Rise	18 E2
Summerhill	36 E1
Summerhill Court	46 E4 [3]
Summerhill Parade (Dun Laoghaire)	46 D4 [6]
Summerhill Parade (Summerhill)	36 E1
Summerhill Place	36 E1 [26]
Summerhill Road	5 A2
Summerhill Road	46 D4
Summerville	37 B1
Summerville Park	43 A1
*Summerville Terrace (on Dalkey Ave)	54 F2
Sunbury Gardens	43 A2
Suncroft Avenue	12 F2 [3]
Suncroft Drive	48 D2
Suncroft Park	48 D2
Sundale Avenue	48 D2
Sundale Close	48 D2
Sundale Crescent	48 D1
Sundale Green	48 D1
Sundale Grove	48 D2
Sundale Heights	48 D1
Sundale Lawn	48 D1
Sundale Meadows	48 D1
Sundale Parade	48 D1
Sundale Park	48 D2
Sundale Road	48 D2
Sundale Villas	48 D1
Sundale Walk	48 D1
Sundrive Park	42 E1
Sundrive Road	42 E1
Sunville Green	42 D1 [1]
Susan Terrace	35 C3
Susanville Road	21 B4
Sussex Road	36 E4
Sussex Street	46 D4 [16]
Sussex Terrace	36 E4 [11]
Sutton	25 A1
Sutton Court	24 D1 [1]
Sutton Downs	24 D1
Sutton Grove	24 D1
Sutton Lane	55 A3
Sutton Lawns	24 D1
Sutton Park	24 D1
Sutton Road	57 B2 [9]
Sutton Villas	57 B2 [17]
Swallowbrook	6 F4
Swallowbrook Crescent	6 F4
Swallowbrook Park	6 F4
Swallowbrook View	6 F4
Swan Alley	35 C3 [51]
Swan Grove	36 E4 [23]
Swan Place	36 E4 [31]
*Swan Yard (off Harry Street)	36 D3
Swanbrook	57 C4
Swan's Nest Avenue	23 B1
Swan's Nest Court	23 B1 [2]
Swan's Nest Road	23 B1
Swanville Place	43 A1 [4]
Swanward Court	35 C4 [39]
Sweeney's Terrace	35 C3 [36]
Sweetbriar Lane	52 D1
Sweetman's Avenue	45 A3 [21]
Sweetman's Avenue	45 A3
Sweetmount Avenue	43 B4 [15]
Sweetmount Drive	51 B1
Sweetmount Park	43 B4
Sweetmount Park	51 B1
Swiftbrook	48 D1
Swiftbrook Avenue	48 D1
Swiftbrook Close	48 D1
Swiftbrook Drive	48 D1
Swiftbrook Park	48 D1
Swift's Alley	35 C3
Swift's Grove	11 A3
*Swift's Row (off Ormond Quay)	36 D2
Swilly Road	20 E4
Swords	2 D1
Swords Manor Avenue	1 B2
Swords Manor Court	1 B1
Swords Manor Crescent	1 B1
Swords Manor Drive	1 B1
Swords Manor Grove	1 B2
Swords Manor View	1 B1
Swords Manor Way	1 B1
Swords Road	21 B1
Swords Road (Collinstown)	10 F2
Swords Road (Malahide)	3 A3
Swords Street	35 B2 [8]
Sybil Hill Avenue	22 F3
Sybil Hill Road	22 F3
Sycamore Avenue (Cabinteely)	53 B3
Sycamore Avenue (Castleknock)	18 E3
Sycamore Avenue (Mt Merrion)	44 E4
Sycamore Avenue (Tallaght)	41 A3
Sycamore Close	40 F3
Sycamore Close	53 B3
Sycamore Court	53 C2 [3]
Sycamore Crescent	44 E4 [4]
Sycamore Crescent (Cabinteely)	53 B3
Sycamore Drive (Cabinteely)	53 B4
Sycamore Drive (Castleknock)	18 E3
Sycamore Drive (Dundrum)	51 B1 [4]
Sycamore Drive (Tallaght)	41 A3
Sycamore Green (Cabinteely)	53 B3
Sycamore Grove	53 A2 [7]
Sycamore Grove	53 B3
Sycamore Lawn (Cabinteely)	53 B3
Sycamore Lawn (Castleknock)	18 E3
Sycamore Park (Castleknock)	18 E3
Sycamore Park (Finglas)	20 E1
Sycamore Park (Tallaght)	41 A3
Sycamore Road (Dundrum)	51 B1
Sycamore Road (Finglas)	20 E1
Sycamore Road (Fox & Geese)	41 A1
Sycamore Road (Mount Merrion)	44 E4
Sycamore Street	36 D2 [21]
Sycamore View	18 E3
Sycamore Walk	53 B4
Sydenham	46 D4 [23]
Sydenham Mews	58 D3
*Sydenham Place (on Kilmacud Rd Upr)	43 C4
Sydenham Road (Ballsbridge)	37 A4 [4]
Sydenham Road (Dundrum)	43 C4
Sydenham Villas	51 C1
Sydenham Villas	58 D3 [6]
Sydney Avenue	45 A3
Sydney Parade Avenue	44 E1
Sydney Terrace	45 A3
Sykes Lane	42 F2
Sylvan Avenue	41 A3
Sylvan Close	40 F3
Sylvan Drive	40 F3
Sylvester Villas	3 B3
Synge Lane	36 D4 [25]
Synge Place	36 D4 [24]
Synge Street	36 D4
Synnott Place	36 D1
Synnott Row	36 D1 [26]
Synnott Terrace	45 C4 [16]

T

STREET NAME	PAGE/GRID REFERENCE
Taaffe's Place	36 F1 [15]
Talbot	2 F3
Talbot Avenue	2 F3
Talbot Court	3 A2
Talbot Court	18 F2
Talbot Downs	18 F2
Talbot Lane	36 E2 [6]
Talbot Lodge	44 F4
Talbot Park	2 F3
Talbot Place	36 E2
Talbot Road	2 F3
Talbot Road	54 E3 [3]
Talbot Street	36 E2
Tallaght	49 A1
Tallaght Bypass	48 F1
Tallaght Road	41 C4
Tallaght Road	49 B1
Tamarisk Avenue	41 A3
Tamarisk Close	41 A3
Tamarisk Court	41 A3
Tamarisk Dale	41 A3
Tamarisk Drive	41 A3
Tamarisk Grove	41 A3
Tamarisk Heights	41 A3
Tamarisk Lawn	41 A3
Tamarisk Park	41 A3
Tamarisk View	41 A3
Tamarisk Walk	41 A3
Tamarisk Way	41 A3
Tandys Lane	31 C3
Taney Avenue	43 C4
Taney Court	43 C4
Taney Crescent	43 C4
Taney Drive	43 C4
Taney Grove	43 C4
Taney Lawn	43 C4
Taney Manor	43 C4
Taney Park	43 C4
Taney Rise	43 C4
Taney Road	43 C4
*Tangier Lane (off Grafton Street)	36 D3
Tara Hill Crescent	42 F4
Tara Hill Grove	42 F4 [2]
Tara Hill Road	42 F4
Tara Lawn	23 A1
Tara Street	36 E2
Taylor's Lane (Ballyboden)	50 E1
Taylor's Lane (Pimlico)	35 C3 [13]
Temple Bar	36 D2
Temple Buildings	36 D1 [60]
Temple Cottages	36 D1
Temple Court	35 B2 [16]
Temple Court (Off Hogan Place)	36 F3 [40]
Temple Crescent	45 B4
Temple Gardens	43 B2
Temple Hill	45 B4
Temple Hill (on Terenure Rd West)	42 E2
Temple Lane North	36 D1 [41]
Temple Lane South	36 D2 [4]
*Temple Lane South (off Temple Bar)	36 D2
Temple Lawns	30 D3
Temple Manor	5 B2
Temple Manor	29 C4
Temple Manor	41 C3
Temple Manor Avenue	41 C3
Temple Manor Close	41 C3
Temple Manor Court	41 C3
Temple Manor Drive	41 C3
Temple Manor Grove	41 C3
Temple Manor Way	41 C3
Temple Park	43 B2
Temple Park Avenue	45 B3
Temple Place	36 E4 [26]
Temple Road (Blackrock)	45 A3
Temple Road (Rathgar)	43 B2
Temple Square	43 B2 [5]
Temple Street North	36 D1
Temple Street West	35 B2 [7]
Temple Terrace	54 F2 [16]
*Temple Villas (Arbour Hill)	35 C2
Temple Villas (on Palmerston Road)	43 B1
Templemore Avenue	43 A2
Templeogue	42 D4
Templeogue Road	42 E3

STREET NAME	PAGE/GRID REFERENCE	STREET NAME	PAGE/GRID REFERENCE	STREET NAME	PAGE/GRID REFERENCE	STREET NAME	PAGE/GRID REFERENCE
Templeogue Wood	42 D4	The Close (Ballyboden)	50 E2	The Glade	40 F4	The New Road	19 B1
Templeroan	50 D1	The Close (Grange Manor)	32 D3	The Glade (Ballinteer)	51 B2	The Nurseries	7 A4
Templeroan Avenue	50 D1	The Close (Kinsaley)	2 E3	The Glade (Palmerston)	33 B2	The Nurseries	54 E4 [4]
Templeroan Close	50 E1	The Close (Manorfields)	17 B1	The Glebe	32 D2	The Nurseries	57 B3
Templeroan Court	50 D1	The Close (Mount Merrion)	44 E3	The Glebe	32 E2	The Nurseries (Swords)	1 C3
Templeroan Crescent	50 D1	The Close (Tallaght)	40 F3	The Glen	54 D1 [14]	The Nursery	7 A4
Templeroan Downs	50 E1	The Close (Tallaght)	49 A2 [2]	The Glen (Ballinteer)	51 B2	The Oaks	7 C1
Templeroan Drive	50 D1	The Close (Temple Manor)	29 C4	The Glen (Ballyboden)	50 E1	The Oaks	30 D3
Templeroan Green	50 D2	The Close (Templeogue)	42 D3	The Glen (Raheny)	23 B3	The Oaks	40 E4
Templeroan Grove	50 D1	The Coombe	35 C3	The Grange	53 B1	The Oaks	43 B4
Templeroan Lodge	50 D2	The Coppice	33 C1	The Green	21 C1	The Oaks	56 D1 [1]
Templeroan Meadows	50 E1	The Coppice	33 C2	The Green	29 C3	The Oaks (Ballinteer)	51 B2
Templeroan Mews	50 D1	The Coppins	30 D3	The Green (Ballinteer)	51 B2	The Old Forge	32 D3
Templeroan Park	50 D1	The Coppins (Foxrock)	53 A3	The Green (Ballyboden)	50 E1	The Old Golf Links	3 C3
Templeroan View	50 D1	The Court	5 A2	The Green (Bray)	57 C1	The Old Hill	32 D1
Templeroan Way	50 D1	The Court	5 B2	The Green (Kinsaley)	2 E3	The Orchard	53 A1
Templeview Avenue	12 D4	The Court	21 C2	The Green (Malahide)	3 B2	The Orchard (Killester)	22 E3
Templeview Close	12 D4	The Court	23 B3 [2]	The Green (Manorfields)	17 B1	The Orchard (Kimmage)	42 E2
Templeview Copse	12 D4	The Court	29 C3	The Green (Mulhuddart)	7 A4	The Orchard (Palmerston)	33 B1
Templeview Court	12 D4	The Court (Ballinteer)	51 B2	The Green (Swords)	2 D1	The Oval	33 C2
Templeview Crescent	12 D4	The Court (Clontarf)	22 D4	The Green (Tallaght)	40 F3	The Paddock	19 C4
Templeview Downs	12 D4	The Court (Donnybrook)	43 C2	The Green (Templeogue)	42 D3	The Paddocks	5 B2
Templeview Drive	12 D4	The Court (Mulhuddart)	7 A4	The Green Road	54 F2	The Paddocks	54 F1 [3]
Templeview Green	12 D4	The Court (Sutton)	25 A1	The Greenlands	42 F4	The Paddock's (Clontarf)	22 E4 [6]
Templeview Grove	12 D4	The Court (Swords)	2 D1	The Grove	5 A2	The Palms	44 D3
Templeview Lawn	12 D4	The Court (Tallaght)	40 F3	The Grove	23 B3 [1]	The Park	5 A2
Templeview Park	12 D4	The Court (Tallaght)	40 F4	The·Grove (Abbeyfarm)	29 C4	The Park	21 C1
Templeview Place	12 D4	The Court (Temple Manor)	29 C4	The Grove (Ballinteer)	51 B2	The Park	29 C3
Templeview Rise	12 D4	The Court (Templeogue)	42 D3	The Grove (Bray)	57 C1	The Park (Abbeyfarm)	29 C4
Templeview Row	12 D4	The Courtyard	18 D3	The Grove (Celbridge)	30 D4	The Park (Grange Manor)	32 D3
Templeview Square	12 D4	The Courtyard	42 F4	The Grove (Grange Manor)	32 D3	The Park (Kinsaley)	2 E3
Templeview Vale	12 D4 [1]	The Courtyard	57 B2	The Grove (Kinsaley)	2 E3	The Park (Tallaght)	40 F3
Templeview Walk	12 D4	The Coutryard	53 A2 [10]	The Grove (Swords)·	2 D1 [3]	The Park (Tallaght)	49 A2
Templeview Way	12 D4	The Cove	3 A2	The Grove (Tallaght)	40 E4	The Park (Templeogue)	42 D3
Templeville Avenue	42 D3	The Covert	33 C1 [1]	The Grove (Tallaght)	40 F3	The Park Lands	42 F4 [7]
Templeville Drive	42 D3	The Crescent	5 A2	The Grove (Tallaght)	49 A1	The Pines	19 A3
Templeville Park	42 E3 [1]	The Crescent	31 C2	The Grove (Whitehall)	21 B3	The Pines	22 E3
Templeville Road	42 D3	The Crescent (Abbeyfarm)	29 C4	The Haggard (Howth)	26 D2 [6]	The Pines	52 D1 [3]
Terenure	42 F2	The Crescent (Ballinteer)	51 B2 [1]	The Haven	3 B2	The Pines	57 B3
Terenure Park	42 F2	The Crescent (Ballyboden)	50 E2	The Haven	21 A3 [17]	The Poplars	45 B4 [7]
Terenure Place	42 F2 [3]	The Crescent (Castleknock)	18 F3 [1]	The Heath (Tallaght)	40 F4	The Priory	3 B2 [4]
Terenure Road East	42 F2	The Crescent (Donnybrook)	43 C1 [1]	The Heath (Templeogue)	42 D3	The Priory	20 D4
Terenure Road North	42 F2	The Crescent (Grange Manor)	32 D3	The Hedgerows	53 A3	The Priory	50 F1
Terenure Road West	42 E2	The Crescent (Kinsaley)	2 E3	The Heights (Ballinteer)	51 B2	The Rise	3 B3
Terminal Road North	37 C2	The Crescent (Sutton)	25 A1	The Heights (Kinsaley)	2 E3	The Rise (Ballinteer)	51 B2
Terminal Road South	37 C2	The Crescent (Swords)	2 D1	The Hill	3 B3	The Rise (Ballyboden)	50 E2
Termon Court	9 C4 [1]	The Crescent (Tallaght)	40 E4	The Hill (Ballinteer)	51 C2	The Rise (Dalkey)	54 E2
*Terrace Place (off Bella St)	36 E1	The Crescent (Tallaght)	40 F3	The Hill (Monkstown)	45 C4	The Rise (Glasnevin)	21 A2
Tetrarch Grove	5 C1	The Crescent (Tallaght)	49 A1	The Hill (Mulhuddart)	7 A4	The Rise (Kinsaley)	2 E3
Texas Lane	3 A2	The Crescent (Temple Manor)	29 C4	The Hill (Stillorgan)	52 F1	The Rise (Manorfields)	17 B1
The Alders	45 B4 [6]	The Crescent (Whitehall)	21 B3	The Hole in the Wall Rd	12 E4	The Rise (Mount Merrion)	44 E4
The Appian Way	36 E4	The Croft	30 D2	The Lakelands	42 F4 [8]	The Rise (Tallaght)	40 E4
The Avenue	5 A2	The Dale	29 C3	The Laurels	34 E4 [3]	The Rise (Tallaght)	40 F3
The Avenue (Ballinteer)	51 C2	The Dale	40 F3	The Laurels	42 F4 [13]	The Road (Manorfields)	17 B1
The Avenue (Ballyboden)	50 E2	The Dale	40 F4	The Laurels (Dundrum)	43 B4	The Rookery	50 D2
The Avenue (Celbridge)	30 D3	The Dale	57 B2	The Laurels (Terenure)	42 F2	The Sand Holes	18 F4 [1]
The Avenue (Grange Manor)	32 D3	The Dale (Manorfields)	17 B1	The Lawn	57 C1	The Scalp	55 A4
The Avenue (Kinsaley)	2 E3	The Deanery	29 C3 [1]	The Lawn (Ballinteer)	51 B2	The Slopes	45 C4
The Avenue (Manorfields)	17 B1	The Dell	51 A2	The Lawn (Ballyboden)	50 E2	The Square (Irishtown)	37 A3 [5]
The Avenue (Mulhuddart)	7 A4	The Dingle	33 B2	The Lawn (Finglas)	20 E2	The Square (Lucan)	32 D1 [5]
The Avenue (Swords)	2 D1	The Drive	5 A2	The Lawn (Kinsaley)	2 E3	The Stables	44 E3 [1]
The Avenue (Tallaght)	40 F3	The Drive	5 B2	The Lawn (Tallaght)	40 E4	The Stiles Road	22 E4
The Avenue (Templeogue)	42 D3	The Drive	57 C1	The Lawns (Abbeyfarm)	29 C4	The Summit (Howth)	26 E3
The Bawn	3 B3	The Drive (Abbeyfarm)	29 C4	The Lawns (Temple Manor)	29 C4	The Sweepstakes	37 A4 [22]
The Bawn Grove	3 B3	The Drive (Ballinteer)	51 B2	The Little Grove	30 D4	The Sycamores	56 E1 [3]
The Beeches	23 A1	The Drive (Ballyboden)	50 E1	The Lodge	54 D1	The Thatch Road	21 C2
The Beeches	45 B4 [21]	The Drive (Grange Manor)	32 D3	The Mall	3 B2	The Thicket	53 A3
The Belfry	35 A3 [17]	The Drive (Kinsaley)	2 E3	The Mall	31 A1	The Turrets	37 A4
The Birches	53 A3	The Drive (Manorfields)	17 B1	The Mall (Baldoyle)	13 A4 [4]	The Vale	33 C1
The Black Avenue	31 B1	The Drive (Mulhuddart)	7 A4	The Mall (Lucan)	32 D1	The View	29 C3
The Bramblings	22 E3	The Drive (Swords)	2 D1	The Maltings	57 C2	The View (Ballinteer)	51 B2
The Briars	33 C1	The Drive (Tallaght)	49 A1	The Manor	42 D4	The View (Manorfields)	17 B1
The Burgage	54 F2	The Drive (Temple Manor)	29 C4	The Maples	43 C3	The View (Tallaght)	40 F3
The Castlelands	42 F4 [11]	The Dunes	13 A1	The Maples	45 B4 [4]	The View (Tallaght)	49 B1
The Cedars	45 B4 [5]	The Elms	5 B2	The Mayne	6 E2	The Villa (Kinsaley)	2 E3
The Chase	52 F2	The Elms	44 E2	The Meadow	51 B2	The Village	21 B3 [2]
The Chase (Charles Sheil's Houses)	52 F2	The Elms	56 E1 [4]	The Meadows	22 F3	The Village	23 B3
The Cherries	51 A2 [2]	The Elms (Celbridge)	30 D2	The Meadows East	40 E4	The Village	54 F2
The Cloisters	21 B3 [5]	The Fairways	57 C1	The Meadows West	40 E4	The Village (Clonsilla)	17 C3
The Cloisters	42 F2	The Falls	42 F3 [5]	The Mews	43 A1 [19]	The Village Centre	32 D1 [12]
The Close	5 A2	The Fosters	44 E3	The Mews (Clontarf)	22 E4	The Village Court	32 D1 [13]
The Close	21 C1	The Gallops	52 E3	The Mews (Killester)	22 E3	The Village Gate	54 F2
The Close	29 C3	The Garth	40 E4	The Mill Pond Apts	40 D1 [4]	The Walk (Ballinteer)	51 B2
The Close (Ballinteer)	51 C2	The Garth	40 F3	The Moorings	3 C3	The Walk (Kinsaley)	2 E3

STREET NAME	PAGE/GRID REFERENCE
The Walk (Manorfields)	17 B1
The Walk (Tallaght)	49 A1
The Walk (Templeógue)	42 D3
The Walled Gardens	30 D2
The Warren	2 F2
The Willows	30 D3
The Willows	43 A3 [1]
The Willows (Glasnevin)	20 F3
The Willows (Monkstown)	45 B4 [3]
The Wood	49 A2
The Woodlands	30 D3
The Woodlands	42 F4 [9]
Third Avenue	40 F4
Third Avenue (Seville Place)	36 F2 [7]
Thirlestane Terrace	35 C3 [64]
Thomas Court	35 C3
Thomas Davis Street (South)	35 C3 [49]
Thomas Davis Street (West)	34 F3
Thomas Lane	36 D2 [17]
Thomas Moore Road	41 C1
Thomas Street	35 C3
Thomas Street West	35 C3 [65]
Thomastown Crescent	54 D2 [2]
Thomastown Road	54 D3
Thomond Road	34 E3
Thompson's Cottages	36 E1 [49]
Thor Place	35 B2 [1]
Thormanby Grove	26 D2 [10]
Thormanby Lawns	26 D2
Thormanby Lodge	26 E2
Thormanby Road	26 E2
Thormanby Woods	26 E2
Thornberry Apts.	6 F4
Thorncastle Street	37 A2
Thorncliff	43 B2 [8]
Thorncliffe Park	43 B3
Thorndale Avenue	22 D2
Thorndale Court	21 C2 [3]
Thorndale Crescent	22 D2
Thorndale Drive	22 D3
Thorndale Grove	22 D3
Thorndale Lawns	22 D2
Thorndale Park	22 D2
Thornhill Gardens	29 C2
Thornhill Heights	29 C2
Thornhill Meadows	29 C2
Thornhill Road	44 E4
Thornhill Road	57 A2
Thornhill View	57 B1 [5]
Thornville Avenue	23 B1
Thornville Drive	23 B2
Thornville Park	23 C1
Thornville Road	23 B1
Thornville Terrace	23 B2 [1]
Three Rock Close	41 B3 [1]
Three Rock Road	52 E2
Tibradden Close	41 B2 [1]
Tibradden Drive	41 B2
Tibradden Grove	41 B3
Tibradden Lane	50 F4
Tibradden Road	50 F3
Ticknock Road	51 B4
Tinkers Hill	17 A4
Tinkler's Path	34 E1
Tivoli Avenue	42 F1
Tivoli Close	53 C1
Tivoli Road	46 D4
Tivoli Terrace East	46 D4
Tivoli Terrace North	45 C4
Tivoli Terrace South	45 C4
Tobernea Terrace	45 B3 [2]
Tolka Cottages	20 F3
Tolka Estate Road	20 F3
Tolka Quay	37 A2
Tolka Quay Road	37 A2
Tolka Road	21 B4
Tolka Valley Road	20 D3
Tom Clarke House	21 B4 [1]
Tom Kelly Road	36 D4 [16]
Tonduff Close	41 B3
Tonguefield Road	42 E1 [1]
Tonlegee Avenue	22 F1
Tonlegee Drive	22 F1
Tonlegee Road	23 A1
Torca Road	54 F2
Torca View	54 F2 [33]
Torlogh Gardens	21 C4 [8]
Torlogh Parade	21 C3 [1]
Torquay Road	52 F2
Torquay Wood	52 F2
Tourmakeady Road	21 B2 [1]
Tourville Lodge	42 F3 [6]
Tower Avenue	42 F2
Tower Road	40 D1
Tower Road (Castleknock)	18 F4
*Tower Terrace (off Kilmainham Lane)	35 B3
Tower View Cottages	20 F4 [2]
Townsend Street	36 E2
Townyard Lane	3 B2
Traders Wharf	45 C3
Trafalgar Lane	45 B4
Trafalgar Terrace	45 B3
Trafalgar Terrace	57 C2 [31]
Tramway Court	25 A1
Tranquility Grove	22 D1
Traynor Place	35 B3 [41]
*Traynor Place (off Mount Brown)	35 B3
Treepark Avenue	41 A3
Treepark Close	41 A3
Treepark Drive	41 A3
Treepark Road	41 A3
Trees Avenue	44 E4
Trees Road Lower	44 E4
Trees Road Upper	44 E4
Treesdale	44 F4
Tresilian	53 A3
Trim Road	22 D1
Trimleston Avenue	44 E2
Trimleston Drive	44 E2
Trimleston Gardens	44 E2
Trimleston Park	44 E2
Trimleston Road	44 E2
Trinity Street	36 D2
Trinity Terrace	36 E1 [44]
Tritonville Avenue	37 A3 [8]
Tritonville Close	37 A3 [22]
Tritonville Court	37 A4
Tritonville Crescent	37 A3 [9]
Tritonville Road	37 A3
Trosyrafon Terrace	58 D2 [1]
Tubber Lane Road	31 B2
Tubbermore Avenue	54 F2
Tubbermore Road	54 F2
Tuckett's Lane	26 D2
Tudor Court	2 F2
Tudor Lawns	52 F2
Tudor Road	43 B1
Tulip Court	11 C4
Turnapin Cottages	10 F3
Turnapin Green	10 F3
Turnapin Grove	10 F3
Turnapin Lane	10 F3
Turnberry	24 D1
Turnpike Road	41 A2
Turret Road	33 C2
Turrets Flats	43 A1 [9]
Turvey Avenue	35 A3 [2]
Tuscany Downs	23 A2
Tuscany Park	24 D1
Twin Cottages	45 A4 [5]
Tymon Close	49 A2
Tymon Crescent	48 F2
Tymon Grove	49 A2
Tymon Heights	49 B2
Tymon Lane	41 B4
Tymon Lawn	49 A2
Tymon North	41 B4
Tymon North Avenue	41 B4
Tymon North Court	41 B4 [1]
Tymon North Gardens	41 B4
Tymon North Green	41 B4
Tymon North Grove	41 B4
Tymon North Lawn	41 B4
Tymon North Park	41 B4
Tymon North Place	41 B4 [2]
Tymon North Road	41 B4
Tymonville Avenue	41 B4
Tymonville Court	41 A4
Tymonville Crescent	41 A4
Tymonville Drive	41 A3
Tymonville Grove	41 B3
Tymonville Lawn	41 B4
Tymonville Park	41 B4
Tymonville Road	41 A4
Tynan Hall	40 F3
Tynan Hall Avenue	40 F3
Tynan Hall Grove	40 F3
Tynan Hall Park	40 F3
Tyrconnell Park	34 F3
Tyrconnell Road	34 F3
Tyrconnell Street	34 F3 [6]
Tyrconnell Villas	34 F3 [7]
Tyrone Place	35 A3 [12]
Tyrrell Place	36 E1 [45]
*Tyrrel's Lane (off Fitzwilliam St Ringsend)	37 A3

U

STREET NAME	PAGE/GRID REFERENCE
Ullardmor	54 F2 [27]
Ulster Street	20 F4
Ulster Terrace (North Strand)	36 E1 [58]
Ulster Terrace (Stillorgan Grove)	52 F1 [4]
Ulverton Close	54 F1 [5]
Ulverton Court	54 F1 [13]
Ulverton Road	54 F1
Upper Cliff Road	26 E2 [2]
Upper Dargle Road	57 A2
Upper Glen Road	34 E1
Uppercross	32 F1
Uppercross Road	35 B3
Urney Grove	54 E2 [7]
Usher Street	35 C2
Usher's Island	35 C2
Ushers Lane	1 A2
Usher's Quay	35 C2

V

STREET NAME	PAGE/GRID REFERENCE
*Vale Terrace (on lower Dargle Road)	57 B2 [21]
Vale view	57 B2
Vale View Avenue	53 B3
Vale View Close	53 B3
Vale View Grove	53 B3
Vale View Lawn	53 B3
Valentia Parade	36 D1 [34]
Valentia Road	21 B3
Valeview Crescent	20 D2 [6]
Valeview Drive	20 D2
Valeview Gardens	20 D2 [2]
Valley Park Avenue	20 D2 [1]
Valley Park Drive	19 C2
Valley Park Road	19 C2
Valley View	1 B2
Vanessa Close	29 C3
Vanessa Lawns	29 C3
Vauxhall Avenue	35 B3 [30]
Vavasour Square	36 F3
Venetian Hall	22 E3
Ventry Drive	20 D4
Ventry Park	20 E4
Ventry Road	20 E4
Verbena Avenue	23 C1
Verbena Avenue	53 A3
Verbena Grove	23 C1
Verbena Lawn	23 C1
Verbena Park	23 C1
Vergemount	43 C1 [12]
Vergemount Hall	43 C1 [9]
Vergemount Park	43 C1 [6]
Vernon Avenue	22 F4
Vernon Court	22 F4
Vernon Court	37 C1 [3]
Vernon Drive	22 F3
Vernon Gardens	22 F4
Vernon Grove (Clontarf)	22 F4
Vernon Grove (Rathgar)	43 A2
Vernon Heath	22 F4
Vernon Park	22 F4
Vernon Rise	22 F3
Vernon Street	36 D3
Vernon Wood	37 C1 [4]
*Veronica Terrace (off Oliver Plunket Ave)	37 A3
Verschoy Avenue	47 C2
Verschoy Close	47 C2
Verschoy Crescent	47 C2
Verschoy Heights	47 C2
Verschoy Park	47 C2
Verschoy Rise	47 C2
Verschoyle Court	36 F3
Verschoyle Place (off Lr Mount St)	36 E3
Vesey Mews	45 C4
Vesey Park (Lucan)	32 D2
Vesey Place	45 C4
Vesey Terrace (Lucan)	32 D1 [2]
*Vevay Arcade (on Vevay Road)	57 C3
Vevay Road	57 C3
Vevay Villas	57 C3 [18]
Vicar Street	35 C3 [20]
Vico Road	54 F3
*Vico Terrace (Vico Road)	54 F3
Victoria Avenue	43 C1
Victoria Avenue	58 D2
*Victoria Cottages (off Irishtown Rd)	37 A3
Victoria Lane	21 B4 [9]
*Victoria Lane (South Zion Rd)	43 A2
Victoria Quay	35 C2
Victoria Road (Clontarf)	22 E4
Victoria Road (Dalkey)	54 F2
Victoria Road (Killiney)	54 E3
Victoria Road (Terenure)	43 A2
Victoria Street	36 D4
Victoria Terrace (Dalkey)	54 F2 [11]
Victoria Terrace (Dun Laoghaire)	46 D4 [8]
Victoria Terrace (Dundrum)	43 C4
Victoria Village	42 F2 [7]
Victoria Villas (Clontarf)	22 D4
Victoria Villas (Rathgar)	42 F2 [5]
Viking Place	35 C2 [47]
*Viking Place (off Sitric Road)	35 C2
Viking Road	35 C2 [32]
*Villa Bank (Royal Canal Bank)	36 D1
Villa Blanchard	18 F2
Villa Park Avenue	20 D4
Villa Park Drive	20 D4
Villa Park Gardens	20 D4
Villa Park Road	20 D4
*Village Gate Arcade (on Main Street Bray)	57 C2
Village Green (Rathfarnham)	42 F3 [3]
Village Green (Tallagh)	49 A1
Village Heights	7 A4
Village Square (Tallagh)	49 A1
Village Weir	32 D2
Villarea Park	54 E1
Villiers Road	43 A2
Violet Hill Drive	20 F3
Violet Hill Park	20 F3
Violet Hill Road	20 F3
Virginia Drive	20 D2
Virginia Heights	48 F1
Virginia Park	20 D2
Viscount Avenue	10 F4

W

STREET NAME	PAGE/GRID REFERENCE
Wadelai Green	21 A2
Wadelai Road	21 A2
Wade's Avenue	23 A3
Wainsfort Avenue	42 D3
Wainsfort Crescent	42 D3
Wainsfort Drive	42 D2
Wainsfort Gardens	42 D3
Wainsfort Grove	42 E3
Wainsfort Manor	42 D3
Wainsfort Park	42 E3
Wainsfort Road	42 D3
Waldemar Terrace	43 B4 [12]
Walker's Cottages	36 D4 [37]
Walker's Court	36 D4 [38]
Walkinstown	41 B1
Walkinstown Avenue	41 B1
Walkinstown Crescent	41 B1

STREET NAME	PAGE/GRID REFERENCE
Walkinstown Cross	41 C2
Walkinstown Drive	41 B1
Walkinstown Green	41 B1
Walkinstown Parade	41 B1
Walkinstown Park	41 B1
Walkinstown Road	41 C1
Wallace Road	41 C1 [2]
Walnut Avenue (Clondalkin)	40 F3
Walnut Avenue (Whitehall)	21 B3
Walnut Close	40 F3
Walnut Close	40 F3
Walnut Court	21 B2
Walnut Drive	40 F3
Walnut Lawn	21 B3
Walnut Park	21 B3
Walnut Rise	21 B3
Walnut View	50 E2 [5]
Walsh Road	21 A3
Waltersland Road	52 F1
Waltham Terrace	44 F3
Walworth Road	36 D4 [33]
Warburton Terrace	58 D2 [7]
Ward's Hill	35 C3
Warner's Lane	36 E4 [18]
Warren Avenue	18 E3
Warren Close	18 E3
Warren Crescent	18 E4
Warren Green	18 E3
Warren Green	24 D1
Warren Park	18 E3
Warren Street	36 D4 [35]
Warrenhouse Road	24 D1
Warrenmount	35 C3 [27]
Warrenmount Place	35 C3 [28]
Warrenpoint	22 E4 [1]
Warrenstown	7 B4
Warrenstown Close	7 B4
Warrenstown Court	7 B4
Warrenstown Drive	7 B4
Warrenstown Garth	7 B4
Warrenstown Green	7 B4
Warrenstown Grove	7 B4
Warrenstown Lawn	7 B4
Warrenstown Park	7 B4
Warrenstown Place	7 B4
Warrenstown Rise	7 B4
Warrenstown Row	7 B4
Warrenstown Vale	7 B4
Warrenstown View	7 B4
Warrenstown Walk	7 B4
Warrenstown Way	7 B4
Warrington Lane	36 F3 [45]
*Warrington Lane	36 F3
(off Warrington Place)	
Warrington Place	36 F3
Warwick Terrace	36 E4 [27]
Wasdale Grove	42 F2
Wasdale Park	42 F3
Washington Lane	42 E4
Washington Park	42 E4
Washington Street	35 C4
Waterfall Avenue	21 B4
Waterfall Road	22 F3
Watergate Estate	49 A1
Waterloo Avenue	36 F1
Waterloo Lane	36 E4
Waterloo Road	36 E4
Watermeadow Drive	48 F2
Watermeadow Park	49 A2
Watermill Avenue	23 A3
Watermill Close	49 A2
Watermill Drive	23 A3
Watermill Grove	49 A2
Watermill Lawn	23 A3 [1]
Watermill Lawn	49 A2
Watermill Park	23 A3
Watermill Road	23 A3
Waterside Apartments	36 F3 [49]
Waterside Crescent	3 C4
Waterstown Avenue	33 C1
Watery Lane	1 C1
Watery Lane	40 E1
Watkins Buildings	35 C3 [64]
*Watkin's Buildings	35 C3
(off Ardee Street)	
Watling Street	35 C2
Watson Avenue	54 D4
Watson Drive	54 D4
Watson Park	54 D4
Watson Road	54 D3
Watson's Estate	54 D3
Waverley Avenue	21 C4
Waverley Terrace (Bray)	57 C2 [28]
Waverley Terrace	42 F1 [12]
(off Harolds Cross Road)	
Weaver Lane	36 D1 [39]
Weaver's Close	35 C3 [33]
Weaver's Row	17 C2
Weaver's Square	35 C3 [37]
Weaver's Street	35 C3
Webster's Cottages	45 A4 [8]
Wedgewood Estate	52 D2
Weirview	32 D1
Weirview Drive	52 F1
Weldon's Lane	13 A4
Well Road	2 D2 [2]
Wellesley Place	36 E1 [32]
Wellfield	12 D4
Wellington Cottages	41 C3 [3]
Wellington Court	42 D2 [5]
(on Whitehall Road West)	
*Wellington Gardens	43 B1
(off Oakley Road)	
Wellington Lane (Tallaght Rd)	41 C3
Wellington Lane (Wellington Rd)	36 F4
Wellington Park	42 D3
Wellington Place (Leeson Street)	36 F4
Wellington Place North	36 D1 [50]
Wellington Quay	36 D3
Wellington Road	36 F4
Wellington Road (Phoenix Park)	35 A2
Wellington Road (Templeogue)	42 D3 [1]
Wellington Street (Dun Laoghaire)	46 D4 [1]
Wellington Street Lower	36 D1
Wellington Street Upper	36 D1
Wellmount Avenue	20 D2
Wellmount Court	20 D2
Wellmount Crescent	20 D2
Wellmount Drive	20 D2
Wellmount Green	20 D2
Wellmount Parade	20 D2
Wellmount Park	20 D2
Wellmount Road	20 D2
Wellpark Avenue	21 B3
Wellview Avenue	7 A3
Wellview Crescent	7 A3
Wellview Green	7 A3
Wellview Grove	7 A3
Wellview Park	7 A3
Wendell Avenue	4 D4
Werburgh Street	36 D3
Wesbury	52 E1
Wesley Heights	51 C1
Wesley Lawns	51 C2
Wesley Place	35 C4 [7]
Wesley Road	43 A2
West Park Drive	20 F2
West Pier (Dun Laoghaire)	45 C3
West Pier (Howth)	26 D1
West Road	36 F1
West Terrace	34 F3
Westbourne Avenue	39 C1
Westbourne Avenue	39 C1
Westbourne Castle	39 C1
Westbourne Close	39 C1
Westbourne Close	39 C1
Westbourne Court	39 C1
Westbourne Drive	39 C1
Westbourne Drive	39 C1
Westbourne Grove	39 C1
Westbourne Grove	39 C1
Westbourne Lodge	50 D1
Westbourne Manor	39 C1
Westbourne Rise	39 C1
Westbourne Road	42 F3
Westbourne Terrace	57 C2 [52]
*Westbourne Terrace	57 C2
(on Quinnsborough Road)	
Westbourne View	39 C1
Westbrook	42 D2
Westbrook Glen	47 B2
Westbrook Lawns	47 C2
Westbrook Park	31 C2
Westbrook Road (Windy Arbour)	43 B3
Westbury	32 D3
Westbury Avenue	32 D3
Westbury Close	32 D3
Westbury Drive	32 D2
Westbury Park	32 D3
Western Parkway Motorway	18 E4
Western Road	35 C4 [29]
Western Way	36 D1
Westerton Rise	51 C1 [1]
Westfield Avenue	31 B1
Westfield Park	58 D3
Westfield Road	42 F1
Westfield Terrace	45 A3 [10]
Westhampton Place	42 F2 [2]
Westhaven	6 F4
Westland Row	36 E3
Westminister Lawns	52 F2
Westminister Road	53 A3
Westminster Park	53 A2
Westmoreland Park	43 B1 [4]
Westmoreland Street	36 D2
Weston Avenue	43 B4
Weston Close	31 B1
Weston Close	43 B4
Weston Court	31 B2
Weston Crescent	31 B1
Weston Drive	31 B1
Weston Green	31 B1
Weston Grove	43 B4
Weston Heights	31 B2
Weston Lawn	31 B1
Weston Meadow	31 B2
Weston Park	31 B1
Weston Park	43 B4
Weston Road	43 B4
Weston Terrace	43 B4 [9]
Weston Way	31 B2
Westpark (Coolock)	22 F2
Westpark (Tallaght)	49 A1
Westview Terrace	57 C2 [29]
Westway Close	7 C4
Westway Grove	7 C4
Westway Lawns	18 F1
Westway Park	7 C4
Westway Rise	7 C4
Westway View	7 C4
Westwood Avenue	19 C2
Westwood Road	19 C2
Wexford Street	36 D3
Wheatfield	57 C3
Wheatfield Grove	4 D4
Wheatfield Road	4 D4
Wheatfield Road	33 C2
Wheatfields Avenue	33 B3
Wheatfields Close	33 B3
Wheatfields Court	33 B3
Wheatfields Crescent	33 B3
Wheatfields Drive	33 B3
Wheatfields Grove	33 B3
Wheatfields Park	33 B3
Wheaton Court	34 F3 [20]
Whelan House Flats	37 A3 [29]
Whelan's Terrace	45 A3 [19]
Whitchurch Drive	50 F2
Whitchurch Road	50 F2
White Hall (Ballymount Road)	40 F3
White Oak	43 C3
White Oaks	57 B4
Whitebank Road	37 B3
Whitebarn Road	43 A4
Whitebeam Avenue	43 C2
Whitebeam Road	43 C2
Whitebeams Road	52 D2
Whitebrook Park	48 E1
Whitechapel Avenue	18 D2
Whitechapel Court	18 D2
Whitechapel Crescent	18 D2
Whitechapel Green	18 D2
Whitechapel Grove	18 D2
Whitechapel Lawn	18 D2
Whitechapel Park	18 D2
Whitechapel Road	18 D2
Whitechurch Abbey	50 F1 [4]
Whitechurch Avenue	50 F2
Whitechurch Close	50 F2
Whitechurch Court	50 F2
Whitechurch Crescent	50 F2
Whitechurch Green	50 F2
Whitechurch Grove	50 F2
Whitechurch Hill	50 F2
Whitechurch Lawn	50 F2
Whitechurch Park	50 F2
Whitechurch Pines	50 F1
Whitechurch Place	50 F2
Whitechurch View	50 F2
Whitechurch Walk	50 F2
Whitechurch Way	50 F2
Whitecliff	50 F1
*Whitefriar Gardens	36 D3
(off Whitefriar St)	
Whitefriar Place	36 D3 [42]
Whitefriar Street	36 D3 [41]
Whitehall	21 B2
Whitehall Close	42 D3
Whitehall Gardens	42 D2
Whitehall Mews	53 A2
Whitehall Park	42 D3
Whitehall Road (Churchtown)	43 A4
Whitehall Road (Kimmage)	42 D2
Whitehall Road West	42 D2
White's Lane North	36 D1 [3]
White's Road	19 A4
White's Villas	54 F1 [10]
Whitestown	18 D1
Whitestown Avenue	18 D1
Whitestown Crescent	18 D1
Whitestown Drive	18 D1
Whitestown Drive	48 E2
Whitestown Gardens	18 D1
Whitestown Green	18 D1
Whitestown Park	18 D1
Whitestown Road	48 F2
Whitethorn	33 B3
Whitethorn Avenue	22 D2
Whitethorn Close	22 D2
Whitethorn Crescent	22 D2
Whitethorn Crescent	33 B3
Whitethorn Drive	33 B3
Whitethorn Gardens	33 B3
Whitethorn Grove	22 D2
Whitethorn Park	22 D2
Whitethorn Park	33 B3
Whitethorn Rise	22 D2
Whitethorn Road (Artane)	22 D2
Whitethorn Road (Milltown)	43 C2
Whitethorn Walk	53 A2 [8]
Whitethorn Walk	53 C2 [2]
Whitethorn Way	33 B2
Whitton Road	42 F2
Whitworth Avenue	36 E1 [40]
(off Whitworth Place)	
*Whitworth Parade	21 A4
(off Saint Patrick's Road)	
Whitworth Place	21 A4 [16]
Whitworth Road	21 A4
*Whitworth Terrace	36 E1
(off Russell Ave)	
Whyteleaf Grove	12 D4
*Wicklow Lane	36 D3
(off Wicklow Street)	
Wicklow Street	36 D3
Wigan Road	21 A4
Wilderwood Grove	41 C4
Wilfield	37 A4 [15]
Wilfield Park	37 A4
Wilfield Road	37 A4
Wilfrid Road	42 F1
Wilfrid Terrace	42 F1 [5]
Willbrook	42 F4
Willbrook (Estate)	50 F1
Willbrook Downs	50 F1
Willbrook Grove	42 F4 [1]

STREET NAME	PAGE/GRID REFERENCE
Willbrook Lawn	42 F4
Willbrook Lawn	42 F4
Willbrook Park	42 F4
Willbrook Road	42 F4
Willbrook Street	42 F4
William Street North	36 E1
William Street South	36 D3
William's Lane	36 D2 [27]
William's Park	43 A1
*William's Place Lower (off Portland Place)	36 D1
William's Place South	36 D3 [6]
William's Place Upper	36 D1 [29]
Willie Bermingham Place	35 B3 [31]
Willie Nolan Road	13 A4
Willington Avenue	41 C3
Willington Court	41 C3
Willington Crescent	41 C3
Willington Drive	41 C3
Willington Green	41 C3
Willington Grove	41 C3
Willington Lawn	41 C3 [1]
Willington Park	41 C3
Willow Avenue	40 D2
Willow Bank	45 C4
Willow Bank Drive	50 E1
Willow Bank Park	50 E1
Willow Court	40 D2
Willow Drive	40 D2
Willow Gate	51 B1
Willow Grove	40 D2
Willow Grove	53 B3
Willow Grove	53 C1 [13]
Willow Mews	44 E1
Willow Park	53 A2 [6]
Willow Park (Dunboyne)	5 B2
Willow Park (Dunboyne)	5 C2
Willow Park Avenue	20 F1
Willow Park Close	20 F1
Willow Park Crescent	20 F1
Willow Park Drive	21 A1
Willow Park Grove	20 F1
Willow Park Lawn	20 F1
Willow Park Road	20 F1
Willow Place	44 F3
Willow Road (Dundrum)	51 B1
Willow Road (Fox & Geese)	41 A1
Willow Terrace	44 F2
Willow Vale	54 D4
Willow Wood Close	17 C2
Willow Wood Downs	17 C2 [1]
Willow Wood Green	17 C2
Willow Wood Grove	17 C2
Willow Wood Lawn	17 C2
Willow Wood Park	17 C2
Willow Wood Rise	17 C2
Willow Wood View	17 C2
Willow Wood Walk	17 C1
Willowbank	51 C1
Willowbrook Grove	29 C3
Willowbrook Lawns	29 C3
Willowbrook Lodge	29 C3
Willowbrook Park	29 C3
Willowfield	37 B4
Willowfield Avenue	43 C4
Willowfield Park	43 C4
Willowmount	44 F3 [3]
Willows Court	17 C2
Willows Drive	17 C2
Willows Green	17 C2
Willows Road	17 C2
Willsbrook Avenue	32 E2
Willsbrook Crescent	32 F1
Willsbrook Drive	32 E1
Willsbrook Gardens	32 E1
Willsbrook Green	32 E2
Willsbrook Grove	32 E1
Willsbrook Park	32 E2
Willsbrook Place	32 F2
Willsbrook View	32 E2
Willsbrook Way	32 E1
Wilmont Avenue	54 E1 [1]
Wilson Crescent	44 D4
Wilson Road	44 E4
Wilson Terrace	35 C3 [44]
Wilson's Place	36 E3 [35]
Wilton Place	36 E4
Wilton Terrace	36 E4
Windele Road	21 A3 [12]
Windermere	17 B2
Windgate Rise	26 D3
Windgate Road	26 D3
Windmill Avenue	1 C1
Windmill Avenue	42 D1
Windmill Crescent	42 D1 [2]
Windmill Lands	1 C2
Windmill Lane	36 E2
Windmill Park	42 D1
Windmill Rise	1 C2
Windmill Road	42 D1
Windsor Avenue	21 C4
Windsor Court (Dun Laoghaire)	53 B1 [1]
Windsor Drive	53 B1
Windsor Mews	3 B2 [5]
Windsor Park	53 B1
Windsor Park	53 B1
Windsor Place	36 E3 [32]
Windsor Road	43 B1
Windsor Terrace	3 B3
Windsor Terrace	36 D4
Windsor Terrace (Dun Laoghaire)	46 D4
Windsor Villas	21 C4 [3]
Windy Arbour	43 C3
Winetavern Street	36 D2
Winton Avenue	43 A2
Winton Grove	42 F2 [19]
Winton Road	36 E4
Wogans Field	31 A1
Wolfe Tone Avenue	46 D4 [4]
Wolfe Tone Quay	35 B2
Wolfe Tone Square East	57 C3
Wolfe Tone Square Middle	57 C3
Wolfe Tone Square North	57 C3
Wolfe Tone Square South	57 C3
Wolfe Tone Square West	57 C3
Wolfe Tone Street	36 D2 [12]
Wolseley Street	35 C4 [24]
Wolstan Haven Avenue	29 C3
Wolverton Glen	54 E2
Wood Avens	33 A3
Wood Dale Close	49 B2
Wood Dale Crescent	49 B2
Wood Dale Drive	49 B2
Wood Dale Green	49 B2
Wood Dale Green	49 C2
Wood Dale Grove	49 C2
Wood Dale Oak	49 C2 [1]
Wood Dale View	49 C2
Wood Lane	35 C2 [40]
*Wood Lane (off Benburb Street)	35 C2
Wood Quay	36 D2
Wood Street	36 D3
Woodbank Avenue	19 C2
Woodbank Drive	19 C2
Woodberry	18 E3
Woodberry	32 D3
Woodbine Avenue	44 E2
Woodbine Close	23 A1
Woodbine Drive	23 A1
Woodbine Park (Booterstown)	44 E2
Woodbine Park (Raheny)	23 A1
Woodbine Road (Booterstown)	44 E2
Woodbine Road (Raheny)	23 A1
Woodbine Terrace (Dundrum)	43 C4 [2]
Woodbrook Downs	56 E4
Woodbrook Glen	57 C1
Woodbrook Lawn	57 C3
Woodbrook Park	42 D4
Woodcliff Heights	26 E2
Woodfarm Avenue	33 C2
Woodfarm Drive	33 C2
Woodfield	50 D2
Woodfield Cottages	34 F3 [8]
Woodfield Place	34 F3 [15]
Woodford	52 E2
Woodford Avenue	40 F1
Woodford Close	40 F1
Woodford Court	40 F1
Woodford Court	42 F1 [10]
Woodford Crescent	40 F1
Woodford Downs	40 F1
Woodford Drive	40 F1
Woodford Garth	40 E1
Woodford Green	40 F1
Woodford Grove	40 F1
Woodford Heights	40 F1
Woodford Hill	40 F1
Woodford Lawn	40 F1
Woodford Meadow	40 F1
Woodford Parade	40 E1
Woodford Park	40 F1
Woodford Park Road	40 F1
Woodford Rise	40 F1
Woodford Road	40 E1
Woodford Terrace	40 F1
Woodford View	40 F1
Woodford Villas	40 E1
Woodford Walk	40 F1
Woodford Way	40 F1
Woodhaven	43 C2 [10]
Woodlands	12 F1 [1]
Woodlands	12 F1
Woodlands	18 D1 [3]
Woodlands	43 A2 [1]
Woodlands Ave (Cornelscourt)	53 C3
Woodlands Avenue (Stillorgan)	44 E4
Woodlands Court	13 A1
Woodlands Drive (Johnstown Rd)	53 C3
Woodlands Drive (Stillorgan)	44 E4
Woodlands Park (Johnstown Rd)	53 C3
Woodlands Pk (Mount Merrion)	44 F4
Woodlands Road	53 C3
Woodlawn	10 F4
Woodlawn Avenue	10 F4
Woodlawn Close	10 F4
Woodlawn Court	10 F4
Woodlawn Crescent	10 F4
Woodlawn Crescent	43 B4
Woodlawn Drive	10 F4
Woodlawn Green	10 F4
Woodlawn Grove	10 F4
Woodlawn Grove	43 B4 [7]
Woodlawn Park	10 F4
Woodlawn Park	43 B4
Woodlawn Park	49 C2
Woodlawn Park (Dun Laoghaire)	53 C1 [4]
Woodlawn Park Avenue	49 B1
Woodlawn Park Drive (Firhouse)	49 C1
Woodlawn Park Grove	49 C2
Woodlawn Rise	10 F4
Woodlawn Terrace	43 B4 [2]
Woodlawn View	10 F4
Woodlawn Walk	10 F4
Woodlawn Way	10 F4
Woodleigh	43 A2 [2]
Woodley Park	52 D1
Woodley Road	54 D3
Woodpark (Ballinteer)	51 B2
Woodpark (Blanchardstown)	18 F2
Woodside	15 C4
Woodside	22 F4
Woodside	26 D2
Woodside	43 A3
Woodside Drive	43 A3
Woodside Grove	43 A3
Woodside Road	51 C3
Woodstock Gardens	43 B1 [24]
Woodstock Park	50 D1
Woodstown	49 C2
Woodstown Abbey	49 C2 [9]
Woodstown Avenue	49 C2
Woodstown Close	49 C2 [4]
Woodstown Court	49 C2 [2]
Woodstown Dale	49 C2 [5]
Woodstown Heath	49 C2
Woodstown Height	49 C2 [6]
Woodstown Meadow	49 C2
Woodstown Park	49 C2 [3]
Woodstown Place	49 C2 [7]
Woodstown Rise	49 C2
Woodstown Vale	49 C2 [8]
Woodthorpe	52 E1 [5]
Woodtown	50 D3
Woodvale Avenue	17 C1
Woodvale Crescent	17 C1
Woodvale Drive	17 C1
Woodvale Garth	17 C1
Woodvale Green	17 C1
Woodvale Grove	17 C1
Woodvale Park	17 C1
Woodvale Way	17 C1
Woodview	31 C2
Woodview (Celbridge)	30 D2
Woodview (Dunboyne)	5 B3
Woodview Close	23 A1
Woodview Cottages	42 F3 [1]
Woodview Court	52 F1 [1]
Woodview Drive	57 C3 [4]
Woodview Grove	18 E2
Woodview Heights	31 C2
Woodview Heights (Dunboyne)	5 B3
Woodview Park	19 A3
Woodview Park	23 A1
Woodville Avenue	32 E1
Woodville Close	32 E1
Woodville Court	22 E1
Woodville Green	32 E1
Woodville Grove	32 E1
Woodville House	22 D1 [1]
Woodville Lawn	32 E1
Woodville Road	21 A4 [7]
Woodville Walk	32 E1
Woostock Court	43 B1 [1]
*Wormwood Gate (off Bridge Street Lower)	35 C2
Wyattville Close	56 D1
Wyattville Hill	56 D1
Wyattville Park	56 D1
Wyattville Road	56 D1
Wyckham Park Road	51 B1
Wynberg Park	45 B4
Wyndham Park	57 C2
Wynnefield Park	43 A1 [21]
Wynnefield Road	43 A1
Wynnsward Drive	43 C2
Wynnsward Park	43 C2
Wyvern Estate	54 E3

XYZ

STREET NAME	PAGE/GRID REFERENCE
Xavier Avenue	36 F1 [3]
Yale	44 D3
Yankee Terrace	45 A4
Yarnhall Street	36 D2 [45]
*Yarnhall Street (off Bolton St)	36 D2
Yeates Way	33 C4
Yellow Meadows Ave	40 F1
Yellow Meadows Drive	40 E1
Yellow Meadows Estate	40 F1
Yellow Meadows Grove	40 E1
Yellow Meadows Lawn	40 E1
Yellow Meadows Park	40 E1
Yellow Meadows Road	40 E1
Yellow Meadows Vale	40 E1
Yellow Road	21 C2
Yellow Walls	3 A2
Yellow Walls Road	3 A2
Yewlands Terrace	42 F2
York Avenue	43 A1
York Road (Dun Laoghaire)	45 C4
York Road (Rathmines)	43 A1
York Road (Ringsend)	37 A2
York Street	36 D3
York Terrace	45 C4 [4]
Zion Road	43 A2
Zoo Road	35 A2
*Zuma Terrace (Mount Drummond Ave)	35 C4

LIST OF STREETS NOT NAMED ON MAP BUT SHOWN AS SMALL NUMBERS

PAGE / GRID REF — STREET NAME

1 A2
1 Grove Court

1 C1
1 Elmwood Court
2 Rathbeale Court

2 D1
2 Mantua Park
3 The Grove (Swords)

2 D2
1 St Columcille's Crescent
2 Well Road
3 St Colmcilles Court

3 B2
1 Fair Haven
2 Haven View
3 Railway Court
4 The Priory
5 Windsor Mews

4 D4
1 Alder Court

5 B2
1 St Mary's Terrace

5 B3
2 River Court
3 Hamilton Court (Dunboyne)

9 A4
1 St Margaret's Court

9 C4
1 Termon Court

11 A4
1 Newbury Terrace

11 B4
1 Greenlawns
2 Clonshaugh Rise
3 Ferrycarrig Green

12 D4
1 Templeview Vale
3 Clonmellon Grove
4 Beechbrook Grove
5 Curraghcloe Drive

12 F1
1 Woodlands

12 F2
1 St Laurence O'Toole Avenue
2 Church Avenue
3 Suncroft Avenue
4 St Brigid's Avenue
5 St Ann's Square Lower
6 St Ann's Square
7 Hazel Court

13 A4
1 Seapoint Avenue (Baldoyle)
2 Parochial Avenue
3 Back Lane (Baldoyle)
4 The Mall (Baldoyle)
5 Breffni Gardens
6 Brookstone Lane
7 Seapoint Court
8 College Street

17 C1
1 Meadow Dale
2 Oakview Grove

17 C2
1 Willow Wood Downs
2 Cedar Grove

18 D1
1 Huntstown Lawn
2 Briarwood Park
3 Woodlands
4 Briarwood Road

18 D2
1 Coolmine Mews
2 Kirkfield

18 F2
1 Herbert Crescent

18 F3
1 The Crescent (Castleknock)
2 Castleknock Court

18 F4
1 The Sand Holes

19 A3
1 Beech Park Crescent
2 Hadleigh Green
3 Beechpark Close
4 Park Court Apts
5 Castleknock Manor

19 B3
1 Mill Lane (Ashtown)

19 B4
1 Castleknock Gate

19 C2
1 Eastwood

19 C4
1 Baggot Terrace
2 St Vincent's Cottages
3 St Joseph's Cottages
4 Ashgrove Lodge

20 D1
1 Cardiffsbridge Grove

20 D2
1 Valley Park Avenue
2 Valeview Gardens
3 Mellowes Court
4 Mellowes Crescent
5 Ravens Court
6 Valeview Crescent
7 Church View (Finglas)

20 D4
1 Roosevelt Cottages
2 Convent View Cottages
3 Convent View Crescent
4 Lyndon Gate
5 Park Spring's
6 Park Crescent House

20 E1
1 Georges Road
2 Gofton Hall

20 E2
1 Ballygall Place
2 Glenhill Villas
3 St Helena's Court
5 Johnstown Gardens
6 Collins Row
7 Glebe View

20 E4
1 Kilkieran Court
2 St. Finbarrís Court

20 F2
1 Drapier Green
2 Glasnamana Place
3 Johnstown House

20 F3
1 Northland Grove
2 Northland Drive
3 Glasnevin Oaks
4 Bellevue Cottages
5 Cremore Villas

20 F4
1 St Philomena's Road
2 Tower View Cottages
3 Delvin Road
4 Bengal Terrace
5 Fertullagh Road
6 Connaught Parade
7 Clareville Court
8 Shandon Green
9 Shandon Mill

21 A1
1 Pinewood Grove
2 Shanliss Gardens
3 Oldtown Park

21 A3
1 Claremont Avenue
2 Church Avenue (Glasnevin)
3 St David's Tce (Glasnevin)
4 Barron Place
5 Comyn Place
6 St Ita's Road
7 St Malachy's Road
8 St Michael's Road
9 Addison Place
10 St Mobhi Grove
11 Clonmore Court
12 Windele Road
13 O'Brien's Place North
14 O'Neachtain Road
15 River Gardens
16 Mobhi Court
17 The Haven

21 A4
1 Millmount Villas
2 De Courcy Square
3 Enniskerry Rd (Phibsborough)
4 Devery's Lane
5 Prospect Square
6 Glendalough Road
7 Woodville Road
8 St Teresa's Road (Glasnevin)
9 St Teresa's Place
10 Botanic Villas
11 St Alphonsus Avenue
12 St Brendan's Road
13 St Clement's Road
14 Botanic Park
15 O'Brien's Terrace
16 Whitworth Place

21 B1
1 Ailesbury

21 B2
1 Tourmakeady Road

21 B3
1 Clonturk Avenue
2 The Village
3 Clare Park Villas
4 Beaucourt
5 The Cloisters
6 Clonturk Court

21 B4
1 Tom Clarke House
2 St Joseph's Ave (Ballybough)
3 Clonturk Gardens
4 Kingston Lodge
5 Holycross Avenue
6 Robert Street (Jones's Road)
7 Robert Place
8 College Manor
9 Victoria Lane
10 Edgewood
11 College Mews

21 C1
1 Chestnut Court

21 C2
1 Dromnanane Road
2 Dromnanane Park
3 Thorndale Court
4 Laragh (Flats)
7 Beaumount Hall

21 C3
1 Torlogh Parade
2 Morrogh Terrace
3 Calderwood Grove
4 Croydon Terrace
5 Sion Hill Court
6 Collins Court
7 St Vincent's Court

21 C4
**
1 Annadale Avenue
2 Shelmartin Terrace
3 Windsor Villas
4 St Joseph's Terrace (Fairview)
5 St Declan's Terrace
6 St Aidan's Park
7 Fairview Green
8 Torlogh Gardens
9 Marino Mart
10 Fairview Passage
11 Fairview Terrace
12 Caragh Court
13 Marino Court
14 Fairview Court
15 Bushfield Square

22 D1
1 Kilbarron Court
2 Cromcastle Close
3 St Lukes Court
4 Woodville House
5 Kilmore Court
6 Cromcastle Court

22 D3
1 Cherrymount Crescent
2 Cherrymount Grove

22 D4
1 Brighton Avenue (Clontarf)
2 Hollybrook Court Drive
3 Hollybrook Court
4 Strandville House
5 Haddon Park
6 Crescent House
7 Kilronan Court

22 E1
1 Lismeen Grove
2 Brookville Crescent

22 E2
1 Maryfield Avenue
2 Artane Cottages Lower
3 Artane Cottages Upper

22 E3
1 St Brigid's Drive (Killester)
2 St Brigid's Court
3 Quarry Cottages
4 Killester Court
5 Killester Park

22 E4
1 Warrenpoint
2 St John's Wood
3 Lambourne Village
4 Knights Bridge
5 St David's Court
6 The Paddock's (Clontarf)

22 F1
1 Elton Court
2 Ayrefield Park

22 F2
1 Gorsefield Court

22 F4
1 Park View

23 A1
1 Elton Walk
2 Glentworth Park
3 Invermore Grove
4 Curracloe Drive
5 Laracor Gardens
6 Gables

23 A3
1 Watermill Lawn
2 St. Anneís Court

23 A4
1 Seafield Grove
2 St Gabriel's Court

23 B1
1 Howth Junction Cottages
2 Swan's Nest Court
3 Redmond's Court
4 Briarsfield Walk

23 B2
1 Thornville Terrace
2 Greendale Court

23 B3
1 The Grove
2 The Court

23 C1
1 Bayside Crescent

23 C2
1 Mariners Court
2 Del Val Court

24 D1
1 Sutton Court

PAGE / GRID REF	STREET NAME
	2 Moyclare Gardens
	2 Seafield Court
	3 Domhnach's Well
25 A1	1 James McCormack Gardens
	2 St Catherine's Terrace
	3 Radcliffe
25 B1	1 Corrbridge Terrac
	(off Claremont Road)
	2 Avalon Apts.
25 B3	1 Shielmartin Park
	2 Martello Terrace
26 D1	1 Dunbo Terrace
	2 Evora Terrace
	4 Dunbo Hill
	5 Howth Terrace
	6 Harbour View
	7 Marine Villas
	8 St. Lawrence Way
	9 Island View Apts.
	10 Cuan na Mara
	11 Abbey Terrace
26 D2	1 St Lawrence's Tce (Howth)
	2 Seaview Tce (Howth)
	3 St Mary's Road (Howth)
	4 St Mary's Place (Howth)
	5 St Nessan's Terrace
	6 The Haggard (Howth)
	7 Hillside Terrace
	8 Dungriffan Villas
	9 St Nessan's Close
	10 Thormanby Grove
	12 St Nessans Court
	13 Crosstrees Court
26 E2	1 Cannon Rock View
	2 Upper Cliff Road
29 C2	1 Crodaun Court
29 C3	1 The Deanery
30 D4	1 Balfe Gardens
31 A1	1 Ralph Square
	2 Liffey View Apts
32 D1	1 Sarsfield Terrace
	2 Vesey Terrace (Lucan)
	3 Hanbury Lane (Lucan)
	4 Sarsfield Court
	5 The Square (Lucan)
	6 Dispensary Lane (Lucan)
	7 Village Weir
	8 Brookvale
	9 Mount Gandon
	10 Gandon Mews
	11 Old Rectory
	12 The Village Centre
	13 The Village Court
32 E1	1 Edmondsbury Court
32 F3	1 Foxborough Hall
33 A3	1 Collinstown Crescent
33 A4	1 Ballymanagin Lane
	2 Moorfield Close
	3 Neilstown Cottages
33 C1	1 The Covert
	2 Glenside Villas
	3 Clarkeville Terrace
	4 Red Cow Cottages
	5 St Fintan's Terrace
33 C2	1 Culmore Park
	2 Glenaulin Green

PAGE / GRID REF	STREET NAME
33 C4	1 Gallanstown Way
34 D3	1 Le Fanu Drive
34 E2	1 Park Lane (Chapelizod)
	2 Maidens Row
	3 Hibernian Terrace
	4 St Laurence Grove
	5 St Mary's Tce (Chapelizod)
	6 Isolde Gardens
	7 Liffey Terrace
	8 Clayton Terrace
	9 St Laurence Tce (Chapelizod)
	10 Mullingar Terrace
	11 Riverview Court
	12 New Row
34 E3	1 O'Hogan Road
	2 Lynch's Lane
	4 St Laurences Glen
34 E4	1 Old Naas Road Cottages
	2 Millrose Estate
	3 The Laurels
	4 Hollybrooke
34 F3	1 Park Street
	2 Phoenix Street
	3 Inchicore Terrace North
	4 Murray's Cottages
	5 Partridge Terrace
	6 Tyrconnell Street
	7 Tyrconnell Villas
	8 Woodfield Cottages
	9 St Patrick's Tce (Inchicore)
	10 Abercorn Terrace
	11 Granite Terrace
	12 Ring Street
	13 Inchicore Square
	14 Oblate Drive
	15 Woodfield Place
	16 Hampton Court
	17 St James's Place (Inchicore)
	18 St George's Villas (Inchicore)
	19 Abercorn Square
	20 Wheaton Court
34 F4	1 Muirfield Drive
	2 Bernard Curtis House
	3 La Touche Court
	4 Grove Court
	5 Landsdowne Valley Park
35 A1	1 Parkview Court
35 A2	1 Islandbridge Court
	2 Hospital Lane
	3 Sarah Place
	4 Park Place
35 A3	1 Hybreasal
	2 Turvey Avenue
	3 Connolly Gardens
	4 Goldenbridge Gardens
	5 Goldenbridge Terrace
	6 Camac Close
	7 Kearn's Place
	8 St Michael's Estate
	9 Memorial Road
	10 Camac Court
	11 Heuston Square
	12 Tyrone Place
	13 Lady's Lane
	14 Prospect Tce (Kilmainham)
	15 Carrickfoyle Terrace
	16 Goldenbridge Walk
	17 The Belfry
	18 Beaconsfield Court
	19 Rosemount Court (Inchicore Rd)

PAGE / GRID REF	STREET NAME
	20 Rowserstown Lane
	21 Myra Cottages
	22 Harcourt Lodge
	23 Ashmount Court
	24 Millbrook Terrace
35 A4	1 Iveagh Gardens
35 B1	1 Glenmore Road
	2 Glencar Road
	3 Everton Avenue
	4 Ardmore Avenue
	5 Glenard Avenue
	6 Doon Avenue
	7 St David's Terrace (Blackhorse Avenue)
	8 Aughrim Place
	9 Carnew Street
	10 Ashford Street
	11 Dunard Road
	12 Aughrim Villas
	13 Arklow Street
	14 Drumalee Court
	15 Phoenix Court
	16 Ashford Place
	17 Ashford Cottages
	18 Auburn Walk
35 B2	1 Thor Place
	2 Halliday Square
	3 Sullivan Street
	4 Kinahan Street
	5 Montpelier Gardens
	6 Arbour Terrace
	7 Temple Street West
	8 Swords Street
	9 Black Street
	10 Findlater Street (Nth Circular Rd)
	11 Niall Street
	12 Finn Street
	13 Park Avenue West
	14 De Burgh Road
	15 Brodin Row
	16 Temple Court
	17 Phoenix Court
35 B3	1 Irwin Street
	2 Kennedy's Villas
	3 Old Kilmainham Village
	4 Shannon Terrace
	5 Cameron Square
	6 St Maignenn's Terrace
	7 Donnellan Avenue
	8 McDowell Avenue
	9 O'Reilly Avenue
	10 Madison Road
	11 Mayfield Road (Kilmainham)
	12 Ewington Lane
	13 Glenmalure Park
	14 Rialto Buildings
	15 Herberton Park
	16 Clarke Terrace
	17 Mallin Avenue
	18 Ave Maria Road
	19 Morning Star Road
	20 Emerald Square
	21 St James's Ave (James's St)
	22 Church Avenue South (Dolphin's Barn)
	23 Fatima Mansions (off James's Walk)
	24 Irwin Court
	25 McCarthy Terrace
	26 Almeida Avenue
	27 Almeida Terrace
	28 St John's Cottages
	29 Carrick Terrace
	30 Vauxhall Avenue
	31 Willie Bermingham Place
	32 Brandon Terrace
	33 St John's Terrace

PAGE / GRID REF	STREET NAME
	(Mount Brown)
	34 Knocknarrow Terrace
	35 Millbrook Court
	36 Prior Hall
	38 Southview Terrace
	39 Owen's Avenue
	40 O'Quinns Avenue
	41 Traynor Place
	42 Burke Place
	43 Phoenix View
35 B4	1 Dolphin House
	2 St James's Terrace (Dolphin's Barn)
	3 Rialto Drive
	4 Moracrete Cottages
	5 Dolphin Park
	6 Reilly's Avenue
	7 Dolphin Court
35 C1	1 Aughrim Lane
	2 Annamoe Parade
	3 Cherrymount Park
	4 Rosemount Road
	5 Fingal Place
	6 Phibsborough Avenue
	7 Leslie's Buildings
	8 Great Western Square
	9 Great Western Villas
	10 Kirwan Street Cottages
	11 Norton's Avenue
	12 Royal Canal Terrace
	13 Marne Villas
	14 St Elizabeth's Court
	15 St Joseph's Place
	16 St Joseph's Court
	17 Castle Terrace (Phibsborough Ave)
	18 Great Western Avenue
	19 King's Court
	20 Rathdown Square
	21 Aughrim Court
	22 Phibsboro
	23 Shea's Court
	24 Phibsborough
35 C2	1 Ostman Place
	2 Stanhope Street
	3 George's Lane
	4 Blackhall Parade
	5 Brown Street North
	6 Friary Avenue
	7 Nicholas Avenue
	8 Sarsfield Quay
	9 Hendrick Place
	10 Arran Quay Terrace
	11 Church Street New
	12 Marshalsea Lane
	13 Blackhall Street
	14 Morgan Place
	15 Phoenix Street West
	16 Stable Lane (Smithfield)
	17 Arran Street West
	18 Burgess Lane
	19 Liffey Street West
	21 Oxmantown Lane
	23 Fitzwilliam Place North (Grangegorman)
	24 Morning Star Avenue
	25 Church Avenue West (Church Street)
	26 Father Mathew Square
	27 Ard Right Place
	28 Houghton Terrace
	29 Rosemount Terrace (Arbour Hill)
	30 Murtagh Road
	31 Sigurd Road
	32 Viking Road
	33 Olaf Road
	34 St Mary's Terrace (Arbour Hill)
	35 Slade Row

PAGE / GRID REF	STREET NAME
	36 Paul Street
	37 Smithfield Terrace
	38 Ellis Street
	39 Stanley Street
	40 Wood Lane
	41 Friary Grove
	42 Coke Lane
	43 Lincoln Lane
	44 Ellis Court
	45 Malachi Road
	46 Provost Row
	47 Viking Place
35 C3	1 Marshal Lane
	2 Grand Canal Place
	3 Rainsford Avenue
	4 Market Street South
	5 Long's Place
	6 Park Terrace (Coombe)
	7 St Margaret's Terrace
	8 Huxley Crescent
	9 Darley's Terrace
	10 Maxwell Street
	11 Fingal Street
	12 Pimlico Cottages
	13 Taylor's Lane (Pimlico)
	14 St Catherine's Lane West
	15 Allingham Street
	16 Meath Market
	17 Brabazon Street
	18 Brabazon Row
	19 Molyneux Yard
	20 Vicar Street
	21 Garden Lane
	22 Catherine Lane
	22 Mark's Alley West
	23 Oscar Square
	24 Cow Parlour
	25 Newmarket Street
	26 Mill Lane (Newmarket)
	27 Warrenmount
	28 Warrenmount Place
	29 O'Carolan Road
	30 Geoffrey Keating Road
	31 Madden Road
	32 New Row Square
	33 Weaver's Close
	34 Ardee Row
	35 Brabazon Place
	36 Sweeney's Terrace
	37 Weaver's Square
	38 Poole Street
	39 St John's Avenue
	40 Brabazon Square
	41 Gray Square
	42 Meath Square
	43 Reginald Square
	44 Wilson Terrace
	45 Catherine Street (Swift's Alley)
	46 Spitalfields
	47 Hanover Street West
	48 Brickfield Lane
	49 Thomas Davis Street (South)
	50 John's Lane West
	51 Swan Alley
	52 Old Mill Court
	53 Ebenezer Terrace
	54 Harman Street
	55 Donore Terrace
	56 Hammond Street
	57 St Michael's Tce (Blackpitts)
	58 St John Street
	59 Marion Villas
	60 Pyro Villas
	61 Ivy Terrace
	62 Coombe Court
	63 Emerald Terrace
	64 Thirlestane Terrace
	64 Watkins Buildings
	65 Thomas Street West
	66 Marrowbone Lane

PAGE / GRID REF	STREET NAME
35 C4	1 Hamilton Street
	2 Ingram Road
	3 Rehoboth Avenue
	4 Priestfield Cottages
	5 St Anne's Road South
	6 Lyllymore Terrace
	7 Wesley Place
	8 Arbutus Avenue
	9 Greenmount Avenue
	10 Emmet St (Harold's Cross)
	11 Greenville Avenue
	12 Gilbert Road
	13 Parnell Court
	14 Greenmount Square
	15 Hatter's Lane
	16 Limekiln Lane (Harold's Cross)
	17 Clanbrassil Close
	18 Harold's Cross Cottages
	19 Greenmount Court
	20 St Clare's Avenue
	21 Donovan Lane
	22 Griffith Square
	23 Briansboro Terrace
	24 Wolseley Street
	25 Merton Avenue
	26 Rutledge Terrace
	27 Merton Park
	28 Priestfield Drive
	29 Western Road
	30 Mount Drummond Court
	31 Boyne Court
	32 Sandford Park
	33 Sandford Gardens
	34 Leonard's Court
	35 Greenville Place
	36 Harold Bridge Court
	37 Armstrong Street
	38 Le Vere Terrace
	39 Swanward Court
	40 Darley Street
36 D1	1 Phibsborough Place
	2 Lynch's Place
	3 White's Lane North
	4 St Vincent Street North
	5 Sarsfield St (Phibsborough)
	6 O'Connell Avenue
	7 St Mary's Ave North (Mountjoy Street)
	8 Palmerston Place
	9 Mountjoy Street Middle
	10 St Mary's Terrace (Mountjoy Street)
	11 Belvidere Court
	12 Hardwicke Place
	13 Graham Court
	14 Frederick Lane North
	15 Grenville Lane
	16 Parnell Place
	17 St Ignatius Avenue
	18 Glengarriff Crescent
	19 De Velara Place
	20 Eccles Court
	21 Cavendish Row
	22 Kelly's Lane
	23 Myrtle Street
	24 Leo Avenue
	25 Josephine Avenue
	26 Synnott Row
	27 St Joseph Street
	28 Sherrard Avenue
	29 William's Place Upper
	30 Killarney Parade
	31 Kenmare Parade
	32 Muckross Parade
	33 Derrynane Parade
	34 Valentia Parade
	35 St Benedicts Gardens
	36 Arranmore Avenue
	37 St Peter's Square
	38 Peter's Court
	39 Weaver Lane

PAGE / GRID REF	STREET NAME
	40 Gardiner Row
	41 Temple Lane North
	42 Bath Lane
	43 George's Place
	44 Nerney's Court
	45 Hardwicke Lane
	46 Frederick Court
	47 Britain Place
	48 St Mary's Place North
	49 Long Lane (New Street)
	50 Wellington Place North
	51 St Michael's Place
	52 Maunsell Place
	53 Blessington Lane
	54 Graham's Row
	55 Berkeley Avenue
	56 Blessington Court
	57 Berkeley Place
	58 Bethesda Place
	59 St Joseph's Place
	60 Temple Buildings
	61 Library View Villas
	62 St Peter's Close
	64 Glengariff Parade
	65 Sherrards Court
	66 St Laurence Place
	67 Strong's Court
	68 Broadstone Avenue
	69 Shamrock Street
36 D2	1 Linenhall Terrace
	2 Lisburn Street
	3 Lurgan Street
	4 Linenhall Parade
	5 Anne Street North
	6 George's Hill
	7 Anglesea Row
	8 Green Street Little
	9 Ryder's Row
	10 Jervis Lane Upper
	11 Jervis Lane Lower
	12 Wolfe Tone Street
	13 Chapel Lane (Parnell Street)
	14 Sampson's Lane
	15 Moore Lane
	16 Henry Place
	17 Thomas Lane
	18 Litton Lane
	19 Earl Place
	20 Prince's Street North
	21 Sycamore Street
	22 Cope Street
	23 Ball's Lane
	24 Sackville Place
	25 Findlater Place
	26 O'Rahilly Parade
	27 William's Lane
	28 Proby's Lane
	29 Hotel Yard
	30 Bachelors Way
	31 Byrne's Lane (Jervis St)
	32 Mary Street Little
	33 Meetinghouse Lane
	34 Campbell's Court
	35 Dominick Lane
	36 Strand Street Little
	37 Ormond Square
	38 Foster Place South (College Grn)
	39 Aston Place
	40 Crampton Quay
	41 Church Lane (College Green)
	42 Dame Lane
	43 Abbey Cottages
	44 St Michan's Street
	45 Yarnhall Street
	46 Temple Lane South
	47 Fownes Street Upper
36 D3	1 Hanover Lane
	2 St Nicholas Place
	3 Castle Street (Cork Hill)

PAGE / GRID REF	STREET NAME
	4 Iveagh Buildings
	5 Cathedral Lane
	6 William's Place South
	7 Dame Lane
	8 Longford Street Great
	9 Longford Street Little
	10 Aungier Place
	11 Redmond's Hill
	12 Protestant Row
	13 Montague Lane
	14 O'Neill's Buildings
	15 Pleasants Lane
	16 Dame Court
	17 Harry Street
	18 Clonmel Street
	19 Stable Lane (Harcourt Street)
	20 Liberty Lane
	21 Pleasants Place
	22 Camden Villas
	23 Aungier Lane
	24 Proud's Lane
	25 Montague Court
	26 Montague Place
	27 Stokes Place
	28 Glovers Alley
	29 Balfe Street
	30 Johnson's Court
	31 Lemon Street
	32 Duke Lane Upper
	33 Anne's Lane
	34 Coppinger Row
	35 Chatham Row
	36 Johnson Place
	37 Bow Lane East
	38 Digges Lane
	39 Fade Street
	40 John Field Road
	41 Whitefriar Street
	42 Whitefriar Place
	43 Cathedral View Court
	44 Cathedral View Walk
	45 Longford Lane
	46 Malpas Terrace
	47 Hanover Square
	48 St Francis Square
	49 Coolevin Road
	50 Malpas Court
	51 Christchurch Square
	52 John's Lane East
	53 Church Lane South
	54 Camden Buildings
	55 Bride Close
36 D4	1 Fitzgerald Street
	2 Desmond Street
	3 St Kevin's Road
	4 Kingsland Park Avenue
	5 Kingsland Parade
	6 Portobello Harbour
	7 Richmond Row
	8 Blackberry Lane
	9 Bessborough Parade
	10 Richmond Place (Rathmines)
	11 Ontario Terrace
	12 Atlumney Villas
	13 Cheltenham Place
	14 Harcourt Lane
	15 Albert Place West
	16 Tom Kelly Road
	17 Florence Street
	18 Albert Terrace
	19 Peter Place
	20 Charlemont Gardens
	21 St Ultan's Flats
	22 Richmond Villas
	23 Gordon Place
	24 Synge Place
	25 Synge Lane
	26 Avenue Road
	27 McMahon Street
	28 Camden Market
	29 St Kevin's Cottages
	30 Camden Court

PAGE / GRID REF **STREET NAME**

31 Lennox Terrace
32 Charlotte Way
33 Walworth Road
34 Martin Street
35 Warren Street
36 Portobello Place
37 Walker's Cottages
38 Walker's Court
39 Mountpleasant Parade
40 Mountpleasant Terrace
41 Bannaville
42 Garden View
43 Richmond Mews
44 Richmond Place South
   (Sth Richmond St)
45 Alexandra Tce (Portobello)
46 Bloomfield Park
47 Grove Ave (Harold's Cross)
48 Spencer Street South
49 Bloomfield Cottages
50 Oakfield Place
51 Arbutus Place
52 St Kevin's Parade
53 Lissenfield
54 Harold's Cross Cottages
55 Saddlers Court
56 O'Hara Avenue
57 Adelaide Court

36 E1
1 O'Sullivan Avenue
2 Sackville Gardens
3 Ardilaun Road
4 Ballybough Lane
5 Charlemont Parade
6 Clonmore Terrace
7 Clinch's Court
8 Richmond Crescent
9 Richmond Cottages
   (Summerhill)
10 Richmond Parade
11 Bailey's Row
12 Sean Tracey House
13 Killarney Avenue
14 Preston Street
15 Shamrock Place
16 Shamrock Terrace
17 Aldborough Parade
18 Drumcondra Park
19 Belvidere Avenue
20 Richmond Lane
21 Fitzgibbon Lane
22 Mountjoy Place
23 Langrishe Place
24 Gloucester Place Upper
25 Gloucester Place
26 Summerhill Place
27 Bella Street
28 Matt Talbot Court
29 Newcomen Court
30 Gilford Place
31 Shamrock Cottages
32 Wellesley Place
33 Brendan Behan Court
34 St Margaret's Avenue North
35 St Joseph's Terrace
36 Mountjoy Parade
37 Richmond Cottages North
38 St Joseph's Villas
   (Summerhill)
39 Clonmore Villas
40 Whitworth Avenue
   (off Whitworth Place)
41 Foster Place North
42 Ballybough Avenue
43 Ballybough Court
44 Trinity Terrace
45 Tyrrell Place
46 Summer Place
47 Sean O'Casey Avenue
48 Rutland Place North
49 Thompson's Cottages
50 Portland Close
51 Beaver Close

52 Gloucester Diamond
53 Gloucester Place Lower
54 Gloucester Place Lower
55 Rutland Cottages
56 Buckingham Village
57 Duke Row
58 Ulster Terrace (North Strand)
59 Seville Terrace
60 St Joseph's Mansions
61 Lourdes House
62 St Mary's Mansions
63 Avondale House
64 Liberty House
65 Mountjoy Square Apts
66 North Clarence St Flats
67 Clarence St Great North
68 Croke Villas
69 Campbell's Row
   (off Portland Street N)
70 Portland Square
71 Campbell's Lane
   (off Belvidere Ave)

36 E2
1 Pearse House
2 Erne Place Lower
3 Magennis Place
4 Mark's Lane
5 Deverell Place
6 Talbot Lane
7 Marlborough Place
8 Northumberland Square
9 Beresford Lane
10 Shaw Street
11 Leinster Market
12 Prince's Street South
13 Card's Lane (Pearse St)
14 Spring Garden Lane
15 Dowling's Court
16 Peterson's Court
17 Mabbot Lane
18 Harbour Court
19 Abbey Street Old
20 Frenchman's Lane
21 Moland Place
22 Spencer Row
23 Emerald Place
24 Corn Exchange Place
25 Luke Street
26 Mark Street
27 Custom House Harbour
28 Bracken's Lane
29 Magennis Square
30 Brunswick Villas
   (Pearse Street)
31 Crinan Strand
32 Champions Avenue
33 Lombard Court
34 Harbour Master Place
35 Marlborough Court

36 E3
1 Cumberland Street South
2 Boyne Lane
3 Bass Place
4 Erne Place Little
5 Grant's Row
6 Meade's Terrace
7 Holles Row
8 Merrion Place
9 Baggot Court
10 Royal Hibernian Way
11 Setanta Place
12 Schoolhouse Lane
13 Leinster Lane
14 Clare Lane
15 Roger's Lane
16 Leeson Lane
17 Duke Lane Lower
18 Dawson Lane
19 College Lane
20 Erne Terrace Front
21 Erne Terrace Rere
22 Devlin's Place
23 Harmony Row

24 Molesworth Place
25 Kildare Place
26 Merrion Close
27 Merrion Street Lower
28 Baggotrath Place
29 Little Fitzwilliam Place
30 Bell's Lane
31 Ely Place Upper
32 Windsor Place
33 Mackies Place
34 Holles Place
35 Wilson's Place
36 Stephen's Place
37 Stable Lane (Leeson St Lr)
38 Fitzwilliam Court
39 Hagan's Court
40 Convent Close
41 Herbert Lane

36 E4
1 Leeson Close
2 Hatch Lane
3 Leeson Place
4 Dartmouth Place
5 Dartmouth Terrace
6 Dartmouth Lane
7 Cambridge Terrace (Ranelagh)
8 Chelmsford Avenue
9 Old Mountpleasant
10 Mander's Terrace
11 Sussex Terrace
12 Convent Place
13 Hatch Place
14 Dartmouth Square North
15 Dartmouth Square South
16 Dartmouth Square East
17 Dartmouth Square West
18 Warner's Lane
19 Leeson Walk
20 Northbrook Lane
21 Selskar Terrace
22 Mountpleasant Place
23 Swan Grove
24 Orchard Lane
25 Berystede
26 Temple Place
27 Warwick Terrace
28 Sibthorpe Lane
29 Dexter Terrace
30 Leeson Village
31 Swan Place
32 Pembroke Place
   (Pembroke St Upr)
33 Burlington Gardens
34 Burleigh Court

36 F1
1 Northbrook Terrace
2 Stoney Road (East Wall)
3 Xavier Avenue
4 Strandville Avenue
   (North Strand)
5 Hibernian Avenue
6 Gaelic Street
7 Hyacinth Street
8 Courtney Place
9 Annesley Avenue
10 Enaville Road
11 Crescent Gardens
12 St Barnabas Gardens
13 Boolavogue Road
14 Russell Avenue East
15 Taaffe's Place
16 St Patrick's Ave (Fairview)
17 St Mura's Terrace
18 Malachi Place
19 Strandville Place
20 James's Street North
21 Leinster Street East
22 Portside Court
23 Austin's Cottages
24 St Brigid's Cottages
   (North Strand)
25 Caledon Court

36 F2
1 Emerald Street
2 Bellman's Walk
3 First Avenue (Seville Place)
4 Blythe Avenue
5 Laurence Place East
6 Second Avenue (Seville Place)
7 Third Avenue (Seville Place)
8 Fourth Avenue (Seville Place)
9 Carbury Terrace
10 Irvine Cottages
11 Alexander Tce (North Wall)
12 Spencer Dock
13 Pickford's Terrace
14 Ferryman's Crossing
15 Merchant's Square
16 Mariner's Port

36 F3
1 Clarence Place Great
2 Eblana Villas
   (Lr Grand Canal St)
3 Island Vill
4 Carlingford Parade
5 Hastings Street
6 Penrose Street
7 Ormeau Street
8 Somerset Street
9 Gerald Street
10 Bath Avenue Place
11 Margaret Place
12 Malone Gardens
13 Shaw's Lane
14 Albert Place East
15 Love Lane East
16 Estate Cottages
   (Northumberland Rd)
17 St Mary's Lane
18 Haddington Place
19 Cranmer Lane
20 Lansdowne Lane
21 Erne Place
22 Brunswick Place
23 Conway Court
24 South Dock Road
25 Rostrevor Terrace
   (Lr Grand Canal St)
26 Greenore Terrace
27 Hogan Avenue
28 Grattan Court East
29 Grattan Place
30 Albert Court
31 Macken Villa
32 Mount Street Crescent
33 Leitrim Place
34 Emerald Cottages
35 South Dock Place
36 Berkeley Terrace
37 Lansdowne Terrace
38 Pearse Grove
39 Camden Lock
40 Clanwilliam Terrace
41 Clanwilliam Square
42 Northumberland Place
43 Lansdowne Crescent
44 Lansdowne Villas
45 Warrington Lane
46 Temple Court
   (Off Hogan Place)
47 Cannon Mews East
48 Beggars Bush Court
49 Waterside Apartments

36 F4
1 Eastmoreland Place
2 Eastmoreland Lane
3 Shelbourne Lane
4 Herbert Lane
5 Shelbourne Avenue
6 Carlton Villas
7 Lansdowne Gardens
8 Beatty's Avenue
9 Dodder View Cottages
10 Granite Place
11 Morehampton Square
12 Morehampton Mews

PAGE / GRID REF	STREET NAME
	13 Estate Cottages (Shelbourne Rd)
	14 Ballsbridge Terrace
	15 Pembroke Place (Ballsbridge)
	16 Crampton Avenue
	17 Iveragh Court
37 A2	1 Fishermans Wharf
	2 Alexandra Quay
37 A3	1 Cambridge Street
	2 Fitzwilliam Street (Ringsend)
	3 St Patrick's Villas
	4 Seapoint Terrace
	5 The Square (Irishtown)
	6 St Brendan's Cottages
	7 Cambridge Avenue
	8 Tritonville Avenue
	9 Tritonville Crescent
	10 Seafort Gardens
	11 Leukos Road
	12 Clonlara Road
	13 Kyle-Clare Road
	14 Parkview Place
	15 Canon Mooney Gardens
	16 Caroline Row
	17 Havelock Terrace
	18 Dodder Terrace
	19 Ennis Grove
	20 Londonbridge Drive
	21 Strasburg Terrace
	22 Tritonville Close
	23 St James Tce (Sandymount)
	24 Cambridge Court
	25 Lansdowne Hall
	26 Sandymount Court
	27 Cambridge Park
	28 O'Rahilly House Flats
	29 Whelan House Flats
	30 Ropewalk Pace
	31 Kennedy Court
	32 Simpsons Lane
37 A4	1 Sandymount Green
	2 Sandymount Castle Road
	3 Sandymount Castle Drive
	4 Sydenham Road (Ballsbridge)
	5 Sandymount Castle
	6 Churchill Terrace
	7 Prince of Wales Terrace
	8 Railway Cottages
	9 Martin White Chalets
	10 Gilford Court
	11 Homelee
	12 Lynton Court
	13 Spafield Terrace
	14 Adair
	15 Wilfield
	16 Park Court (Sandymount)
	17 Dromard Terrace
	18 Seafort Cottages
	19 Seafort Terrace
	20 Seafort Villas
	21 Claremont Court
	22 The Sweepstakes
	23 Ballsbridge Park
	24 Lansdowne Square
	25 Ballsbridge Gardens
	26 Ballsbridge Avenue
37 B1	1 Alverno
	2 Haddon Court
37 B3	1 Prospect Tce (Sandymount)
37 B4	1 Gilford Terrace
	2 Sandymount Castle Park
	3 Martello View
	4 Bethany House
	5 Hempenstal Terrace
	6 Martello Wood
	7 Dromard Terrace

PAGE / GRID REF	STREET NAME
37 C1	1 Churchgate Avenue
	2 St Joseph's Square
	3 Vernon Court
	4 Vernon Wood
39 C1	1 Bawnogue Cottages
	2 Nangor Crescent
40 D1	1 St Patrick's Ave (Clondalkin)
	2 Leinster Terrace
	3 Beech Row
	4 The Mill Pond Apts
	5 Nangor Crescent
	6 Cherrywood Villas
40 D2	1 Church View (Clondalkin)
	2 Green Isle Court
40 E1	1 St Killian's Park
	2 Monastery Heights
	3 Bettysford
	4 Castle Crescent
	5 Friar's Walk
	6 Riverside
	7 Millview
40 E2	1 St Brigid's Park (Clondalkin)
40 F1	1 Knockmitten Close
	2 Knockmitten Lane North
40 F3	1 Pinetree Grove
	2 Belgard Close
40 F4	1 Pinetree Crescent
41 A3	1 Parkhill Heights
	2 Parkview
41 B2	1 Tibradden Close
41 B3	1 Three Rock Close
41 B4	1 Tymon North Court
	2 Tymon North Place
41 C1	1 Field Avenue
	2 Wallace Road
	3 Percy French Road
	4 O'Dwyer Road
	5 Esposito Road
	6 Landsowne Valley
	7 Somerville Park
	8 Harty Court
41 C2	1 St Peter's Terrace Walkinstown (off Peters Road)
41 C3	1 Willington Lawn
	2 Glenmurry Park
	3 Wellington Cottages
42 D1	1 Sunville Green
	2 Windmill Crescent
	3 Fr Kit Court
42 D2	1 Muckross Drive
	2 Lorcan O'Toole Court
	3 Stannaway Court
	4 Beechfield Mews
	5 Wellington Court (on Whitehall Road West)
42 D3	1 Wellington Rd (Templeogue)
42 D4	1 Hillcrest (Templeogue)
	2 Hillcrest Manor
42 E1	1 Tonguefield Road
	2 Cloyne Road
	3 Faughart Road
	4 Clonmacnoise Grove

PAGE / GRID REF	STREET NAME
	5 Bedford Court
	6 Poddle Green
42 E2	1 Riversdale Grove
	2 Hazel Park
	3 Kimmage Court
	4 Rathland Drive
	5 Brookfield Green
	6 Brookfield Court
	7 Hazlebrook Apartments
42 E3	1 Templeville Park
	2 Fortfield Court
42 F1	1 Mount Harold Terrace
	2 Le Bas Terrace
	3 Mountain View Avenue
	4 Manor Villas
	5 Wilfrid Terrace
	6 Fitzpatrick's Cottages
	7 Ryan's Cottages (Harold's Cross)
	8 Parkview Court
	9 Gandon Close
	10 Woodford Court
	11 Kenilworth Manor
	12 Waverley Terrace (off Harolds Cross Road)
	13 Smith's Lane
	14 Kengar Mews
42 F2	1 Ashdale Park
	2 Westhampton Place
	3 Terenure Place
	4 Eagle Hill Avenue
	5 Victoria Villas (Rathgar)
	6 Maple Drive
	7 Victoria Village
	8 Frankfort Court
	9 Frankfort Flats
	10 Rathdown Court (off Templeogue Road)
	11 Rathgar Villas
	12 Greenlea Place
	13 Brighton Green
	14 McMorrough Road
	14 McMorrough Road
	15 Earls Court
	16 Rathgar Park
	17 Olney Grove
	18 Eaton Hall
	19 Winton Grove
	20 Beechlawn Manor
	21 Beechlawn Mews
	22 Eaton Court
42 F3	1 Woodview Cottages
	2 St Agnes Tce (Rathfarnham)
	3 Dodder Park Drive
	4 Village Green (Rathfarnham)
	5 The Falls
	6 Tourville Lodge
	7 Le Brett Terrace
42 F4	1 Willbrook Grove
	2 Tara Hill Grove
	3 Beaufort Villas
	4 Glenann
	5 St Mary's Tce (Rathfarnham)
	7 The Park Lands
	8 The Lakelands
	9 The Woodlands
	10 Beaufort Court
	11 The Castlelands
	13 The Laurels
	14 Loftus Square
	15 Blackburn Square
43 A1	1 Rathmines Park
	2 Leinster Square
	3 Prince Arthur Terrace
	4 Swanville Place
	5 Castlewood Terrace

PAGE / GRID REF	STREET NAME
	6 Castlewood Place
	7 Grosvenor Park
	8 Stone Mews
	9 Turrets Flats
	10 Purser Gardens
	11 Esker Villas
	12 Parker Hill
	13 Alma Terrace
	14 Observatory Lane
	15 Belgrave Place (Rathmines)
	16 Cambridge Villas
	17 Salem Court
	18 Maxwell Court
	19 The Mews
	20 Roland Court
	21 Wynnefield Park
	23 Louis Lane
	24 Castlewood Close
	25 Rathmines Avenue Court
43 A2	1 Woodlands
	2 Woodleigh
	3 Highfield Court
	4 Cowper Mews
	5 Garville Place
	6 Garville Drive
	7 Rathgar Park
	8 Orwell Mews
	9 Stratford
	10 Garville Court
43 A3	1 The Willows
	2 Stirling Park
	3 Orwell Court
	4 Newtown Villas
	5 Newtown Court
	6 Riverbank
	7 Orwell Bank
	8 Crannagh Way
	9 Landore
	10 Park View
	11 Ard Na Greine
	12 Newtown House
	13 Orwell Walk
43 A4	1 Castle Court
	2 Nutgrove Court
43 B1	1 Sallymount Gardens
	2 Woostock Court
	3 Collier's Avenue
	4 Westmoreland Park
	5 Field's Terrace
	6 Rugby Villas
	7 Beechwood Park (Rathmines)
	8 Bushfield Avenue
	9 Charleston Court Flats
	10 Oakley Court (Flats)
	11 Cullenswood Road
	12 Moran's Cottages
	13 Mountain View Cottages (Ranelagh)
	14 Sallymount Terrace
	15 Chelmsford Lane
	16 Belgrave Villas (Rathmines)
	17 Bushfield Place
	18 Smith's Cottages (Donnybrook)
	19 Beechdale Mews
	21 Palmerston Close
	22 Moyne Court
	23 Oakley Park (Ranelagh)
	24 Woodstock Gardens
43 B2	1 Dartry Cottages
	2 Strand Terrace
	3 St Luke's Crescent
	4 Balnagowan
	5 Temple Square
	6 Milltown Grove
	7 Milltown Hill
	8 Thorncliff
	9 Shanagarry

PAGE / GRID REF — STREET NAME

43 B3
1 St Columbanus Place
2 St Gall Gardens North
3 St Gall Gardens South
4 Milltown Terrace (Dundrum)
7 Glenard Hall
8 Belfield Close

43 B4
1 Glenbower Park
2 Woodlawn Terrace
3 Beaumont Close
4 Briarly Court
5 St Nathy's House
6 Ardtona Avenue
7 Woodlawn Grove
8 Henley Court
9 Weston Terrace
10 Frankfort
11 Rosemount Tce (Dundrum)
12 Waldemar Terrace
13 Airfield Drive
14 Nutgrove Avenue
15 Sweetmount Avenue
16 Annadale
17 St Nathy's Villas

43 C1
1 St Broc's Cottages
2 Pembroke Cottages (Donnybrook)
3 Belmont Park
4 The Crescent (Donnybrook)
5 Harmony Avenue
6 Vergemount Park
7 Norwood Park
8 Brookvale Road (Donnybrook)
8 Floraville Road
9 Vergemount Hall
10 Sandford Gardens (Donnybrook)
11 Auburn Road (Donnybrook)
12 Vergemount
13 Eglinton Square
14 Mount Sandford
15 Rowan Hall
16 Cedar Hall
17 Millbrook Village
18 Simmonscourt Terrace
19 Brookfield
22 Eglinton Wood

43 C2
1 Prospect Lane
2 Beech Hill Villas
3 Beech Hill Crescent
4 Beech Hill Terrace
5 Palmerston Grove
6 Clonskeagh Drive
7 Clonskeagh Square
8 St Bridget's Flats
9 Crannagh
10 Woodhaven

43 C3
1 Annaville Grove
2 Olivemount Grove
3 Friarsland Avenue
4 Harlech Villas
5 Gledswood Drive
6 Olivemount Terrace

43 C4
1 Ophaly Court
2 Woodbine Terrace (Dundrum)
3 Alexandra Villas
4 Roseville Terrace
5 Pembroke Cottages (Dundrum)
6 Pembroke Terrace
7 Claremont Terrace
8 Glenville Terrace
9 St Joseph's Grove

44 D1
1 Merrion View Avenue
2 Simmonscourt Avenue
3 Simmon's Court

44 D2
1 Nutley Square
3 Donnybrook Green
4 Greenfield Manor

44 D4
1 Edenwood
2 Sophie Baret Residence

44 E1
1 Merrion Court
2 Merrion Gates
3 Strand Lane

44 E2
1 Seafield Park
2 Bellevue Court
3 Merrion Crescent

44 E3
1 The Stables
2 Mountbrook

44 E4
1 Greygates
2 Beaufield Mews
3 Ashurst
4 Sycamore Crescent

44 F2
1 St Helen's Villas

44 F3
1 Martello Tce (Booterstown)
2 Pembroke Cottages (Booterstown)
3 Willowmount
4 Cherbury Mews

44 F4
1 St Helier's Copse
2 Orpen Dale
3 Park Villas
4 Cedar Square
5 Grove House Gardens
6 Orpen Green

45 A3
1 Newtown Villas
2 Maretimo Road
3 Ben Inagh Park
4 Maretimo Gardens West
5 Craigmore Gardens
6 George's Place (Blackrock)
7 St Anne's Square (Blackrock)
8 Bath Place
9 Rockwell Cove
10 Westfield Terrace
11 Idrone Mews
12 Brusna Cottages
13 Collins Court
14 Patrick's Row
15 Eagle Hill
16 Maretimo Terrace
17 Maretimo Place
18 Maretimo Villas
19 Whelan's Terrace
20 Carbury Place
21 Sweetman's Avenue

45 A4
1 Avondale Park (Dun Laoghaire)
2 Prince Edward Terrace Lower
3 Prince Edward Terrace Upper
4 Lindenvale
5 Twin Cottages
6 Fieldview Cottages
7 Cullen's Cottages
8 Webster's Cottages
9 Rockville Estate
10 Avoca Hall

45 B3
1 Ardenza Terrace
2 Tobernea Terrace
3 Ardenza Park
4 Seapoint Terrace (Blackrock)

45 B4
1 Montpelier Place
2 Montpelier Manor
3 The Willows (Monkstown)
4 The Maples
5 The Cedars
6 The Alders
7 The Poplars
8 Stradbrook Gardens
9 Brighton Terrace
10 Belgrave Place (Monkstown)
11 Belgrave Terrace (Monkstown)
12 Brooklawn Avenue
13 Brooklawn Wood
14 Rockford Terrace
15 Beaupark Downs
16 Drayton Close
17 Heathfield
18 Southdene
19 Arundel
20 Stradbrook Hall
21 The Beeches
22 Brighton Lane

45 C4
1 Rosary Gardens West
2 Barrett Street
3 Smith's Villas
4 York Terrace
5 St Mary's Street
6 Crofton Terrace
7 Oakwood
8 Harbour Terrace
9 Grosvenor Terrace (Dun Laoghaire)
10 Clifton Lane
11 Clifton Avenue
12 Richmond Green
13 Clifton Terrace
14 Alma Place
15 Seaview Terrace (Dun Laoghaire)
16 Synnott Terrace
17 Bentley Villas
18 St Michael's Terrace (Dun Laoghaire)
19 St Brendan's Terrace (Dun Laoghaire)
20 Northcote Terrace
21 Knapton Court
22 Knapton Lawn
23 Northcote Place
24 Cambridge Terrace (Dun Laoghaire)
25 Primrose Hill
26 Mounttown Cottages
27 Knapton Terrace
28 Pakenham
29 Monkstown Gate
30 Alma Park

46 D4
1 Wellington Street (Dun Laoghaire)
2 Rosary Gardens East
3 Desmond Avenue
4 Wolfe Tone Avenue
5 Charlemont Avenue
6 Summerhill Parade (Dun Laoghaire)
7 Haddington Terrace
8 Victoria Terrace (Dun Laoghaire)
9 Marine Terrace
10 Northumberland Place
11 Northumberland Park
12 Dungar Terrace
13 Stoneview Place
14 Martello Avenue
15 Crosthwaite Terrace
16 Sussex Street
17 Roby Place
18 Charlemont Terrace
19 Mill Street (Dun Laoghaire)
20 Anglesea Lane
21 Park Lane
22 Clarinda Manor
23 Sydenham
24 Oratory Mews Court
25 Crofton Terrace
26 Connaught Place
27 Albert Terrace

46 E4
1 Mornington Avenue
2 Martello Terrace (Dun Laoghaire)
3 Summerhill Court

49 A1
1 Allenton Road
2 High Street

49 A2
1 Summerfield
2 The Close (Tallaght)
3 Allenton Crescent

49 B1
1 Bolbrook Drive
2 Glenview Drive
3 Bolbrook Avenue
4 Bolbrook Close
5 Avonmore Avenue
6 Moynihan Court

49 B2
1 Oldcourt Lawn

49 B3
1 Ely Crescent
2 Ely Grove
3 Ely Green
4 Ferncourt Drive
5 Ferncourt Crescent

49 C1
1 Brookmount Lawns
2 Knocklyon Mews
3 Homeville Court
4 Homeville

49 C2
1 Wood Dale Oak
2 Woodstown Court
3 Woodstown Park
4 Woodstown Close
5 Woodstown Dale
6 Woodstown Height
7 Woodstown Place
8 Woodstown Vale
9 Woodstown Abbey

50 D1
1 Coolamber Court
2 Pine Grove
3 Ballyroan Court

50 E1
1 Orchardton

50 E2
1 Beechview Court
2 Cypress Avenue
3 Larch Drive
4 Beech Walk
5 Walnut View

50 F1
1 Sarah Curran Road
2 St Gatien Road
3 Fonthill Abbey
4 Whitechurch Abbey
5 Edenbrook Court
6 Forthill Court

51 A1
1 Marley Villas
2 Meadow Villas
3 Barton Court

51 A2
1 Priory Court
2 The Cherries
3 Elm Way

51 B1
1 Meadow Avenue
2 Hawthorn Drive
3 Mount Albion Road
4 Sycamore Drive (Dundrum)
5 Hillview Glade
6 Hillview Grove

51 B2
1 The Crescent (Ballinteer)
2 Ballinteer Court
3 Ballinteer Park

PAGE / GRID REF — STREET NAME

51 C1
1 Westerton Rise
2 Ashgrove Terrace
3 Eagle Terrace
4 Castle Court Dundrum
5 McGrane Court
6 Ballyolaf Manor
7 Castleview
8 Ashgrove Court

51 C2
1 Clonlea Wood
2 College Park Court
3 College Park Drive
4 College Park Drive
4 Delbrook Manor
5 Delbrook Manor

52 D1
1 Drummartin Crescent
2 Carrick Lawn
3 The Pines

52 D2
1 Balally Terrace
2 Moreen Lawn
3 Blackthorn Grove
4 Blackthorn Court
5 Rathdown Terrace
(Sandyford)
6 Blackthorn Green
7 Blackthorn Close
8 Moreen Avenue
9 Rathdown Grove

52 D3
1 Lamb's Brook

52 E1
1 Dale Close
2 Stillorgan Court
3 Stillorgan Heath
4 Convent Court
5 Woodthorpe

52 E3
1 Glencairn Garth
2 Glencairn Heath

52 F1
1 Woodview Court
2 Ard Lorcain Villas
4 Ulster Terrace
(Stillorgan Grove)
5 Pear Tree Field

52 F2
1 Leopardstown Court
2 Leopardstown Lawn
3 Silver Pines
4 Ellesmere
5 Ballymoss Parade
6 Arkle Square
7 Sir Ivor Mall
8 Fey Yerra

52 F4
1 Ballyogan Park
1 Ballyogan Road

53 A1
1 Orchard Cottages
2 Red Brick Terrace
3 Moore's Cottages
4 Hawthorn Manor
5 Rosehill
6 Ardagh Close
7 St. Augustine's Park
8 Newtown Park Court
9 Galloping Green

53 A2
1 Knocksinna Grove
2 Knocksinna Court
3 New Park Lodge
4 Foxrock Mount
5 Chestnut Park
6 Willow Park
7 Sycamore Grove
8 Whitethorn Walk
9 Birch Dale
10 The Coutryard

53 A3
1 Brighton Cottages

2 Kilteragh Pines
3 Avalon
4 Brighton Lodge

53 B1
1 Windsor Court
(Dun Laoghaire)
2 Grange Grove
3 Oliver Plunkett Villas
4 Stradbrook Hill
5 Springhill Cottages
6 Grange Cottages
7 Abbey Court (Monkstown)
8 Abbey Road
9 Faber Grove
10 Deans Court
11 Devon Close

53 B3
1 Kerrymount Close
2 Hainault Grove
3 Hainault Lawn
4 Monaloe Crescent
5 Clonkeen Lawn
6 Monaloe Court

53 C1
1 Oliver Plunkett Square
2 Patrician Park
3 Mounttown Park
4 Woodlawn Park
(Dun Laoghaire)
5 Oliver Plunkett Terrace
6 Fitzgerald Park
7 St Patrick's Terrace
(Kill O' the Grange)
8 Dunedin Drive
9 St Patrick's Close
10 Highthorn Woods
11 Aspen Park
12 Birch Dale
13 Willow Grove
14 Carricklea Court
15 Rollins Villas

53 C2
1 Hillview Cottages
2 Whitethorn Walk
3 Sycamore Court
4 Hazel Lawn

53 C3
1 Little Meadow
2 Cabinteely Park
3 O'Shea's Cottages
4 Cabinteely Court
5 Cabinteely Court

53 C4
1 Kilbogget Villas

54 D1
1 O'Donnell Gardens
2 Royal Terrace North
3 Myrtle Avenue
4 Emmet Street (Sallynoggin)
5 Eden Villas
6 Laurel Hill
7 Granite Hall
8 Magenta Place
9 Marlborough Park
10 Royal Terrace Lane
11 Beechwood Grove
12 Rollins Court
13 Seven Houses
14 The Glen
15 Glengara Close
16 Silchester Wood
17 Carlisle Terrace
18 Durham Place
19 Rus-in-Urbe Terrace

54 D2
1 Honey Park
2 Thomastown Crescent
3 Pearse Close

54 D3
1 Auburn Road (Cabinteely)
2 Granville Crescent

54 D4
1 Annabeg

2 Meadow Court
3 Oakton Green

54 E1
1 Wilmont Avenue
2 Congress Gardens
3 Albert Park
4 Claremont Villas
5 St Paul's Street
(Off Blackhall Place)
5 St Paul's Terrace
6 St Peter's Terrace
(Dun Laoghaire)
7 Findlater Street
(Dun Laoghaire)
8 Devitt Villas
9 Dixon Villas
10 Glen Terrace
11 Glasthule Buildings
12 Hastings Terrace
13 Brighton Terrace
(Dun Laoghaire)
14 Lawson Terrace
15 Killiney Terrace
16 Munster Terrace
17 Neptune Terrace
18 Cliff Terrace
19 Beaufort
20 Ballygihen Villas
21 Seabank Court
22 St Helen's
23 Chester Square
24 Dundela Haven
25 Arkendale Woods
26 Arkendale Court
27 Adelaide Villas
28 Adelaide Terrace
(Dun Laoghaire)
29 Atmospheric Road
30 St. Margaretís Close

54 E2
1 Barnhill Lawn
2 Killiney Towers
3 Barnhill Park
4 Kilcolman Court
5 Edwin Court
6 Fairlawns
7 Urney Grove
8 Malborough Court

54 E3
1 Hill Cottages
2 Mount Auburn
3 Talbot Road

54 E4
1 Oakton Court
2 Dale View Park
3 Mountain Villa
4 The Nurseries
5 Mountain View Road
6 Rainsford Lane
7 Killiney Avenue
8 Firgrove

54 F1
1 Carysfort Drive
2 Ormeau Drive
3 The Paddocks
4 South Winds
5 Ulverton Close
6 Rocklands
7 Bayswater Terrace
8 Bullock Steps
9 Liscanor
10 White's Villas
11 Mayville Terrace
12 Castlelands Grove
13 Ulverton Court
14 Pilot View
15 Bailey View
16 Castlelands
17 Churchill Mews
18 Bartra Rock (Apts.)

54 F2
1 St Patrick's Avenue (Dalkey)
2 Railway Road

3 Anastasia Lane
4 St Patrick's Square
5 Cats Ladder
6 Dalkey Grove
7 Barnhill Grove
8 St Patrick's Road (Dalkey)
9 Monte Vella
10 Summerfield Close
11 Victoria Terrace (Dalkey)
12 Sorrento Drive
13 Sorrento Lawn
14 Coliemore Villas
15 Seafield Terrace
16 Temple Terrace
17 Grosvenor Terrace (Dalkey)
18 Charlotte Terrace
19 Heany Avenue
20 Desmond Cottages
21 Ardbrugh Villas
22 Burmah Close
23 Dalkey Court
24 Kilbegnet Close
25 Sorrento Close
26 Craiglands
27 Ullardmor
28 Sorrento Mews
29 Sorrento Court
30 Sorrento Heights
31 Ardbrugh Close
32 Castle Cove
33 Torca View

56 D1
1 The Oaks
2 Cherry Court
3 Cois Coillte
4 Holly Court

56 E1
1 Killiney Court
2 Killiney Oaks
3 The Sycamores
4 The Elms
5 Maryland
5 St Aubyn's Court
6 Ennel Court
7 Sheelin Grove
8 Glencarr Court
9 Domville Grove
10 Streamville Court
11 Glen Druid
12 Bayview Glade
13 Sheelin Hill
14 Sheelin Walk
15 Sheelin Drive

56 E2
1 River Lane (Loughlinstown)
2 Clonasleigh
3 Beechfield Haven
4 Athgoe Drive

56 E3
1 Guilford Terrace
2 Stonebridge Close

56 E4
1 Kiltuck Park

57 B1
1 Raverty Villas
2 St Peter's Terrace
3 Myrtle Grove
4 Arbutus Grove
5 Thornhill View

57 B2
1 Auburn Villas
2 Glenburgh Terrace
3 Ashley Heights
4 Dargle Crescent
5 Copper Beech Grove
6 Sutton Road
9 Sutton Road
10 Dargan Street
11 Fairgreen Road
12 Pearse Road
13 Mountpleasant Villas
15 Diamond Terrace
16 Parkview Terrace
17 Sutton Villas

PAGE / GRID REF	STREET NAME
	18 Esmonde Terrace
	19 Old Ravenswell Row
	20 New Ravenswell Row
	21 Vale view
	22 Old Rathmore Terrace
	23 New Rathmore Terrace
	25 Gertrude Terrace
	26 Herbert View
57 B3	1 Ballynoe Court
	2 Rathclaren
	3 St Clair's Terrace
57 B4	1 Ballywaltrim Cottages
57 C1	1 St Patrick's Square
	2 Martello Terrace
57 C2	1 Sidmonton Square
	3 Eglington Road
	4 Rosslyn Grove
	5 James Connolly Square
	6 Sidmonton Place
	7 Novara Park
	8 St Cronan's Road
	9 Cill Manntan Park
	10 Kilmantain Place
	11 Father Colohan Terrace
	12 Royal Marine Terrace
	13 Milton Terrace
	14 St Kevin's Terrace
	15 Darley Cottages
	16 Brabazon Cottages
	17 St Laurence's Terrace
	18 St Columcille's Terrace
	20 Seapoint Villas
	21 Dunbur Terrace
	22 Elmgrove Terrace
	23 St Aidan's Terrace
	24 Seapoint Terrace
	25 Goldsmith Terrace
	26 Prince of Wales Terrace
	27 Novara Terrace
	28 Waverley Terrace (Bray)
	29 Westview Terrace
	30 Augustine Villas
	31 Trafalgar Terrace
	32 Fairgreen Terrace
	33 St Brigid's Terrace
	34 Loretto Avenue
	35 Loretto Terrace
	36 Sidmonton Gardens
	37 Rosslyn
	38 Shankill View
	39 Florence Terrace
	40 Florence Villas
	41 Carlton Terrace
	42 Carlton Villas
	43 Alexander Terrace
	44 Belton Terrace
	45 Church Terrace
	46 Old Brighton Terrace
	47 New Brighton Terrace
	48 Killarney Villas
	49 Market Square
	50 Fairgreen Court
	51 Bayview
	52 Westbourne Terrace
	53 King Edward Court
	54 Loretto Villas
	55 Marie Villas
57 C3	1 Cherry Tree Drive
	2 Roselawn Park
	4 Woodview Drive
	5 Kennedy Park
	8 Newcourt Villas
	9 O'Byrne Villas
	10 Stoneylea Terrace
	11 Mountain View Apartments
	14 Putland Villas
	15 Oldcourt Terrace
	16 Lauderdale Terrace

PAGE / GRID REF	STREET NAME
	17 Mayfield Terrace
	18 Vevay Villas
	19 Orchard Terrace
	20 Bray Head Terrace
	21 Sugarloaf Terrace
57 C4	3 Bentley Avenue
	6 St Mary's Terrace
58 D2	1 Trosyrafon Terrace
	2 Montebello Terrace
	3 Esplanade Terrace
	4 Brennans Terrace
	5 Sidbury Court
	6 Dargan Court
	7 Warburton Terrace
	8 Sloan Terrace
	9 Belgrave Villas
	10 Belgrave Terrace
	11 Claremount Terrace
	12 Richmond Terrace
	13 Milward Terrace
	14 Brennans Parade
	15 Claddagh Terrace
	16 Marlborough Terrace
	17 Marine Terrace
	18 Jones Terrace
	19 Mount Norris Villas
	20 St Marys Terrace
	21 Fitzwilliam Terrace
	22 New Grange Park
58 D3	1 Eaton Court
	2 Meretimo Villas
	3 Grosvenor Avenue
	4 Brookfield Avenue
	5 Sidmonton Court
	6 Sydenham Villas